# Building Global Democracy

GU00734322

The scale, effectiveness and legitimacy of global governance lag far behind the world's needs. This ground-breaking book examines how far civil society involvement provides an answer to these problems. Does civil society make global governance more democratic? Have citizen action groups raised the accountability of global bodies that deal with challenges such as climate change, financial crises, conflict, disease and inequality? What circumstances have promoted (or blocked) civil society efforts to make global governance institutions more democratically accountable? What could improve these outcomes in the future? The authors base their arguments on studies of thirteen global institutions, including the UN, G8, WTO, ICANN and IMF. Specialists from around the world critically assess what has and has not worked in efforts to make global bodies answer to publics as well as states. Combining intellectual depth and political relevance, *Building Global Democracy?* will appeal to students, researchers, activists and policymakers.

JAN AART SCHOLTE is Professorial Research Fellow in the Centre for the Study of Globalisation and Regionalisation at the University of Warwick.

# Building Global Democracy?

*Civil Society and Accountable*
*Global Governance*

*Edited by*

Jan Aart Scholte

CAMBRIDGE
UNIVERSITY PRESS

CAMBRIDGE UNIVERSITY PRESS
Cambridge, New York, Melbourne, Madrid, Cape Town,
Singapore, São Paulo, Delhi, Tokyo, Mexico City

Cambridge University Press
The Edinburgh Building, Cambridge CB2 8RU, UK

Published in the United States of America by Cambridge University Press, New York

www.cambridge.org
Information on this title: www.cambridge.org/9780521140553

© Cambridge University Press 2011

First published 2011

Printed in the United Kingdom at the University Press, Cambridge

*A catalogue record for this publication is available from the British Library*

*Library of Congress Cataloguing in Publication data*
Building global democracy? : civil society and accountable global governance /
[edited by] Jan Aart Scholte.
    p.   cm.
  ISBN 978-0-521-14055-3 (pbk.)
  1. Democratization.   2. Civil society.   3. International organization.
  I. Scholte, Jan Aart.
  JC423.B8646   2011
  321.8–dc22
            2010052188

ISBN 978-0-521-19219-4 Hardback
ISBN 978-0-521-14055-3 Paperback

# Contents

# Figures

# Participants in the Gothenburg Workshop

**Affiliations as at June 2007**

*Note*: practitioners contributed in a personal capacity, not as institutional spokespersons

Hans Abrahamsson, School of Global Studies, Gothenburg University

Saied Reza Ameli, University of Tehran

Erik Andersson, School of Global Studies, Gothenburg University

Srilatha Batliwala, Hauser Center for Nonprofit Organizations, Harvard University

Thomas Bernes, Independent Evaluation Office of the International Monetary Fund

Renate Bloem, Conference of NGOs in Consultative Relationship with the United Nations

Leonardo Burlamaqui, Ford Foundation

Mawaki Chango, GNSO Council, Internet Corporation for Assigned Names and Numbers

Daisy Cooper, Commonwealth Secretariat

Karin Dalborg, Globalverkstan

Meggan Dissly, Organisation for Economic Cooperation and Development

Edmé Dominguez, School of Global Studies, Gothenburg University

Nata Duvvury, International Center for Research on Women

Alnoor Ebrahim, Harvard University

Tina Ebro, Institute for Popular Democracy

Ingrid Ekenberg, School of Global Studies, Gothenburg University

John Evans, Trade Union Advisory Committee

Sylva Frisk, School of Global Studies, Gothenburg University

Julie Gilson, University of Birmingham

Andréas Godsäter, School of Global Studies, Gothenburg University

Marcia Grimes, Quality of Government Institute, Gothenburg University

Malin Hasselskog, School of Global Studies, Gothenburg University

Dhammika Herath, School of Global Studies, Gothenburg University
Björn Hettne, School of Global Studies, Gothenburg University
Rosalba Icaza Garza, School of Global Studies, Gothenburg University
Jo Marie Griesgraber, New Rules for Global Finance
Yuriy Isakov, Russian Federation Civil Society Liaison for the 2006 G8
   Summit
Lisa Jordan, Ford Foundation
Johny Joseph, Creative Handicrafts
Alice Urusaro Karekezi, School of Global Studies, Gothenburg
   University
Milly Katana, Health Rights Action Group
Bernard Kuiten, World Trade Organization
Tatsuro Kunugi, International Christian University (ex-United
   Nations)
Helena Lindholm Schulz, School of Global Studies, Gothenburg
   University
Jan Lindström, School of Global Studies, Gothenburg University
Robert Lloyd, One World Trust
Carolyn Long, International Center for Research on Women
Mikael Löfgren, Swedish Committee of Civil Society Research
Kerstin Martens, University of Bremen
Pamela Mbabazi, Mbarara University of Science and Technology
Ricardo Meléndez-Ortiz, International Centre for Trade and
   Sustainable Development
Andrea Morf, School of Global Studies, Gothenburg University
Mike Muchilwa, International Fair Trade Association
Milissao Nuvunga, School of Global Studies, Gothenburg University
Morten Ougaard, Copenhagen Business School
Valentina Pellizzer, Association for Progressive Communication
Ziad Abdel Samad, Arab NGO Network for Development
Bassirou Sarr, International Monetary Fund
Jan Aart Scholte, School of Global Studies and University of Warwick
Michael Schulz, School of Global Studies, Gothenburg University
Timothy Shaw, Royal Roads University
Rajesh Tandon, Participatory Research in Asia
Ramesh Thakur, Centre for International Governance Innovation
   (ex-United Nations)
Marie Thynell, School of Global Studies, Gothenburg University
Håkan Thörn, Department of Sociology, Gothenburg University
Heidi Ullrich, International Centre for Trade and Sustainable
   Development
Olav Unsgaard, Globalverkstan

Stellan Vinthagen, School of Global Studies, Gothenburg University
Shanta Wanninayake, School of Global Studies, Gothenburg University
Muthoni Wanyeki, ex-FEMNET
Marc Williams, University of New South Wales
Rachel Winter Jones, World Bank
David Winters, Secretariat of the Global Fund to Fight AIDS,
    Tuberculosis and Malaria

# Contributors

SAIED REZA AMELI, author of the OIC study, is Professor of Media Studies, Dean of the Faculty of World Studies and Policy Vice President at the University of Tehran, Iran. He is also an honorary Research Fellow at the University of Birmingham. His publications cover various aspects of globalisation, global media, cyberspace, virtual cities, e-public relations, e-government, m-government, religion and interculturality.

MAWAKI CHANGO, author of the ICANN study, is a doctoral candidate in the School of Information Studies at Syracuse University. His research interests include digital identity systems, Internet governance and public policy. Prior to PhD studies he worked on various projects in the area of information and communication technologies for development. He also worked with the Secretariat of the Working Group on Internet Governance and held a two-year term as member of the ICANN-GNSO Council.

NATA DUVVURY, co-author of the Global Fund study, is Co-Director of the Global Women's Studies Programme at the National University of Ireland, Galway. Previously she was Director of the Gender, Violence and Rights Team at the International Center for Research on Women in Washington, DC. In addition to work on the Global Fund, her areas of publication include gender issues and human rights.

ALNOOR EBRAHIM, co-author of the World Bank study, is Associate Professor at Harvard Business School. His publications include the award-winning *NGOs and Organizational Change: Discourse, Reporting and Learning* (2005: Cambridge University Press) and a co-edited book *Global Accountabilities: Participation, Pluralism and Public Ethics* (2007: Cambridge University Press). He has prepared several reports on civil society relations with multilateral development banks and has testified before a US Congressional committee hearing on the World Bank (2009).

JULIE GILSON, author of the ASEM study, is Senior Lecturer in the Department of Political Science and International Studies at the University of Birmingham. Her publications include *Asia Meets Europe* (of which she is the author) and *The European Union and East Asia: Inter-Regional Linkages in a Changing Global System* (which she co-edited). She has also written articles and chapters on the ASEM process, including civil society engagement with it.

PETER I. HAJNAL, author of the G8 study, is Research Fellow at the Munk Centre for International Studies, University of Toronto. He has authored and (co-)edited several books on civil society and global governance, including: *Civil Society in the Information Age*; *Sustainability, Civil Society and International Governance: Local, North American and Global Perspectives*; and *The G8 System and the G20: Evolution, Role and Documentation*. He has attended twelve G7/G8 summits and conducted several consultancies on civil society relations with the body.

STEVEN HERZ, co-author of the World Bank study, is Founder and President of Lotus Global Advocacy, a legal and policy consultancy based in Oakland, California. He advises global civil society organisations on international environmental and human rights law, and sustainable development policy. A focus of his practice has been the public participation and accountability requirements and environmental and social standards of the World Bank and other international financial institutions. He is the author of a number of articles and reports on these issues.

CAROLYN LONG, co-author of the Global Fund study, is an international development consultant. Her research for this chapter was done on assignment with the Gender, Violence and Rights Team at the International Center for Research on Women in Washington, DC. Her areas of publication include gender issues, participatory development, and NGO advocacy. She has worked for over twenty years with NGOs, especially in strengthening their capacity to carry out policy advocacy.

KERSTIN MARTENS, author of the UN study, is Associate Professor of International Relations at the University of Bremen. She holds a PhD from the European University Institute, Florence. Her areas of publication include NGOs, the United Nations, global governance more generally, and education policy.

PAMELA MBABAZI, co-author of the Commonwealth study, is Associate Professor and Dean of the Faculty of Development Studies at Mbarara

University of Science and Technology. Her areas of publication include globalisation, rural development, governance and peace-building. She actively engages with civil society in Uganda and participated in civil society activities around the 2007 Commonwealth Heads of Government Meeting in Kampala.

PETER NEWELL, author of the climate change study, is Professor of International Development Studies at the University of East Anglia. He previously held appointments at the University of Oxford, the University of Warwick and the Institute of Development Studies. His areas of publication include the political economy of environment and development, global environmental governance, and corporate accountability. He has worked for and with many environmental organisations, governments and international institutions including the United Nations Development Programme and the Global Environment Facility.

MORTEN OUGAARD, author of the OECD study, is Professor of International Political Economy and Program Director, International Business and Politics at the Copenhagen Business School. His areas of publication include globalisation, global governance, and global business. He has written on the OECD for *The Encyclopedia of Globalization* and the Seminar on Globalisation, Statehood and World Order (Florence, 1999).

JAN AART SCHOLTE, editor of this book and author of the IMF study, is Professorial Research Fellow in the Centre for the Study of Globalisation and Regionalisation at the University of Warwick. His areas of publication include globalisation, global governance, global civil society, global finance, and global democracy. He helped draft the IMF *Staff Guide for Relations with Civil Society Organizations* in 2003 and prepared an assessment of IMF-civil society relations for the Independent Evaluation Office in 2009.

TIMOTHY SHAW, co-author of the Commonwealth study, is Director of the Institute of International Relations at the University of the West Indies, St. Augustine. He is also Professor Emeritus at the University of London and Visiting Professor at Mbarara University of Science and Technology, Makerere University Business School, and Stellenbosch University. His areas of publication include globalisation, development, foreign policy and the Commonwealth. He has also been associated with the Commonwealth Foundation Civil Society Advisory Committee, the Commonwealth Scholarship Commission in London and the Commonwealth Summit Office in Trinidad.

HEIDI ULLRICH, author of the WFTO study, is Director of At-Large with the Internet Corporation for Assigned Names and Numbers. Previously she worked with the International Centre for Trade and Sustainable Development in Geneva and Consumers International in London. She has served as a lecturer at the London School of Economics, where she also obtained her PhD, and the University of Southampton. Currently she is a visiting fellow at the University of Birmingham. Her areas of publication include global trade, global accountability, and civil society interaction with the World Trade Organization.

MARC WILLIAMS, author of the WTO study, is Professor of International Relations at the University of New South Wales. His areas of publication include global political economy, global trade, global environmental issues, and civil society engagement of the World Trade Organization.

# Editor's acknowledgements

The Civil Society and Accountable Global Governance project was initiated in a year of productive calm as Olof Palme Guest Professor in the School of Global Studies (SGS) at Gothenburg University. SGS also hosted the workshop where draft chapters of this book were discussed in June 2007. I am particularly grateful to Helena Lindholm Schulz and Fredrik Söderbaum of SGS for encouraging the project from the outset and facilitating some of its funding. A score of other Gothenburg researchers (named above as workshop participants) also gave much appreciated inputs during early stages of the work. Annika Forssell and Andreas Godsäter at SGS provided impeccable logistical support to the workshop together with Louise Griffiths at my permanent base in the University of Warwick.

Huge thanks go also to my fifteen author colleagues. As readers will readily realise, the contributors did not quickly crank out loosely connected chapters that lightly revised their earlier writings. Instead, everyone endeavoured through several drafts to answer a common set of questions with a common framework of analysis. All authors were in addition graciously patient with a protracted editorial process.

The project gained a further major boost from two dozen practitioners in civil society groups and global governance agencies who contributed to the Gothenburg workshop as discussants (also listed above). This practitioner-researcher interchange greatly enriched the project and hopefully will allow the results presented in this book to enhance policy action as well as academic knowledge.

Between the Gothenburg workshop and the final text, most of the chapters were presented in one or the other panels at several venues. Thanks for feedback therefore also go to audiences at the Centre for the Study of Globalisation and Regionalisation Tenth Anniversary Conference (September 2007), the Globalization Studies Network Conference (August 2008), the United Nations Secretariat (November 2008), the International Monetary Fund (November 2008) and the

Academic Council on the United Nations System Annual Conference (June 2009).

Turning to book production, John Haslam at Cambridge University Press calmly allowed the project to mature in its own time and remained encouraging throughout. Laura Downey, administrator of the Building Global Democracy Programme (for which this project became a pilot), provided highly professional editorial assistance.

Gratitude is also due to funders who generously contributed the necessary resources. The Swedish Research Council financed my Palme Professorship, while the project itself received grants from CSGR at the University of Warwick, the Ford Foundation, the Swedish International Development Cooperation Agency (SIDA) and the Peace and Governance Program at the United Nations University (UNU). For their confidence in the project I am grateful to: Chris Hughes at CSGR; Leonardo Burlamaqui, Mike Edwards and Lisa Jordan at Ford; Tekaligne Godana at SIDA; and Ramesh Thakur at UNU.

As ever I close an Acknowledgements section with thanks to Masha and Polly, who more than anyone live with the consequences of my exuberant project plans.

# Abbreviations

| | |
|---|---|
| AAOIFI | Accounting and Auditing Organisation for Islamic Financial Institutions |
| ABC | Group Australia, Britain and Canada |
| ACU | Association of Commonwealth Universities |
| ACUNS | Academic Council on the United Nations System |
| AEBF | Asia-Europe Business Forum |
| AEPF | Asia-Europe People's Forum |
| AFTF | Asia Fair Trade Forum |
| AH | Anno Hegirae (of the Islamic calendar) |
| AIDS | Acquired Immune Deficiency Syndrome |
| ALAC | At-Large Advisory Committee |
| ANC | African National Congress |
| AOSIS | Alliance of Small Island States |
| APR | Africa Personal Representative |
| ARV | Antiretroviral (AIDS treatment) |
| ASEAN | Association of South East Asian Nations |
| ASEF | Asia-Europe Foundation |
| ASEM | Asia-Europe Meeting |
| ASEMUS | Asia-Europe Museum Network |
| ASO | Address Supporting Organisation |
| ATUC | ASEAN Trade Union Council |
| ATUF | ASEM Trade Union Forum |
| AU | African Union |
| BATU | Brotherhood of Asian Trade Unions |
| BCAS | Bangladesh Centre for Advanced Studies |
| BIAC | Business and Industry Advisory Committee |
| BIC | Bank Information Center |
| BIS | Bank for International Settlements |
| BWC | Bretton Woods Committee |
| CAIP | Commonwealth Association of Indigenous Peoples |
| CAN | Climate Action Network |

| | |
|---|---|
| CBC | Commonwealth Business Council |
| CBD/CDD | Community-Based and Community-Driven Development |
| CBOs | community-based organisations |
| CCMs | Country Coordinating Mechanisms |
| ccNSO | Country Code Names Supporting Organisation |
| CCS | Council of Commonwealth Societies |
| CDM | Clean Development Mechanism |
| CE | Common Era (year-numbering system) |
| CGD | Center for Global Development |
| CGF | Commonwealth Games Federation |
| CHOGM | Commonwealth Heads of Government Meeting |
| CHRI | Commonwealth Human Rights Initiative |
| CI | Consumers International |
| CIEL | Center for International Environmental Law |
| CIGI | Centre for International Governance Innovation |
| CIME | Committee on International Investment and Multinational Enterprises |
| CIRA | Canadian Internet Regulatory Authority |
| CJMA | Commonwealth Judges and Magistrates Association |
| CLGF | Commonwealth Local Government Forum |
| CMAG | Commonwealth Ministerial Action Group |
| CMJA | Commonwealth Magistrates and Judges Association |
| COFTA | Cooperation for Fair Trade in Africa |
| COG | Commonwealth Organisations Group |
| ComSec | Commonwealth Secretariat |
| COP | Conference of the Parties |
| COPOLCO | Consumer Policy Committee |
| COW | Committee of the Whole |
| CPA | Commonwealth Parliamentary Association |
| CPF | Commonwealth People's Forum |
| CPLP | Community of Portuguese Language Countries |
| CPSU | Commonwealth Policy Studies Unit |
| CPU | Commonwealth Press Union |
| CSAC | Civil Society Advisory Committee |
| CSD | Commission for Sustainable Development |
| CSER | Corporate Social and Environmental Responsibility |
| CSOs | civil society organisations |
| CSPR | Civil Society for Poverty Reduction |
| CTP | Centre for Tax Policy and Administration |
| CTUG | Commonwealth Trade Union Group |
| CWN | Commonwealth Women's Network |

| | |
|---|---|
| CYEC | Commonwealth Youth Exchange Council |
| DATA | Debt AIDS Trade Africa |
| DAW | Division for the Advancement of Women |
| DAWN | Development Alternatives with Women for a New Era |
| DENIVA | Development Network of Indigenous Voluntary Associations |
| DESA | Department of Economic and Social Affairs |
| DNS | Domain Name System |
| DOC | Department of Commerce |
| DOT | Digital Opportunities Task Force |
| DPI | Department of Public Information |
| DSM | Dispute Settlement Mechanism |
| EB | Executive Board |
| ECOSOC | Economic and Social Council |
| ED | Environmental Defence |
| ED | Executive Director |
| EEB | European Environmental Bureau |
| EFF | Electronic Frontier Foundation |
| EFTA | European Fair Trade Association |
| EMTA | Trade Association for the Emerging Markets |
| EPA | Environmental Protection Agency |
| EPOC | Environmental Policy Committee |
| ESAF | Enhanced Structural Adjustment Fund |
| ETUC | European Trade Union Confederation |
| EU | European Union |
| Eurodad | European Network on Debt and Development |
| EXR | External Relations Department |
| FAD | Fiscal Affairs Department |
| FATF | Financial Action Task Force |
| FCIC | Federation of Consultants from Islamic Countries |
| FDC | Freedom from Debt Coalition |
| FEALAC | Forum for East Asia-Latin America Cooperation |
| FFD | Financing for Development |
| FIEL | Foundation for Latin American Economic Investigations |
| FIELD | Foundation for International Environmental Law and Development |
| FIM | Forum international de Montréal |
| FLO | Fairtrade Labelling Organisations International |
| FOE | Friends of the Earth |
| FOEI | Friends of the Earth International |

| | |
|---|---|
| FSAP | Financial Sector Assessment Program |
| FSC | Forestry Stewardship Council |
| FTAO | Fair Trade Advocacy Office |
| G5 | Group of Five |
| G7 | Group of Seven |
| G77 | Group of Seventy-Seven |
| G8 | Group of Eight |
| GA | General Assembly |
| GAA | Global AIDS Alliance |
| GAC | Governmental Advisory Committee |
| GATS | General Agreement on Trade in Services |
| GATT | General Agreement on Tariffs and Trade |
| GCAP | Global Call to Action Against Poverty |
| GCC | Gulf Cooperation Council |
| GFATM | Global Fund to Fight AIDS, Tuberculosis and Malaria |
| GHCs | greenhouse gases |
| GigaNet | Global Internet Governance Academic Network |
| GLOBE | Global Legislators Organization for a Balanced Environment |
| GMOs | Genetically Modified Organisms |
| GNSO | Generic Name Supporting Organization |
| GOPIO | Global Organization of People of Indian Origin |
| GTI | Global Transparency Initiative |
| gTLD | Generic Top-Level Domain |
| HIPC | Highly Indebted Poor Countries |
| IACHR | Inter-American Commission on Human Rights |
| IASB | International Accounting Standards Board |
| IATP | Institute for Agriculture and Trade Policy |
| IBASE | Brazilian Institute for Social and Economic Analysis |
| IBRD | International Bank for Reconstruction and Development |
| ICANN | Internet Corporation for Assigned Names and Numbers |
| ICC | International Chamber of Commerce |
| ICC | Inuit Circumpolar Conference |
| ICCI | Islamic Chamber of Commerce and Industry |
| ICFTU | International Confederation of Free Trade Unions |
| ICFTU/APRO | ICFTU Asian and Pacific Regional Organisation |
| ICHRP | International Council on Human Rights Policy |
| ICJ | International Court of Justice |
| ICLEI | ICLEI – Local Governments for Sustainability |

| | |
|---|---|
| ICMA | International Capital Market Association |
| ICRW | International Center for Research on Women |
| ICS | Institute of Commonwealth Studies |
| ICSID | International Centre for the Settlement of Investment Disputes |
| ICTSD | International Centre for Trade and Sustainable Development |
| IDA | International Development Association |
| IDB | Islamic Development Bank |
| IDN | Internationalized Domain Name |
| IEA | International Energy Agency |
| IEG | Independent Evaluation Group |
| IEO | Independent Evaluation Office |
| IETA | International Emissions Trading Association |
| IETF | Internet Engineering Task Force |
| IFAT | International Fair Trade Association |
| IFAT-LA | International Fair Trade Association in Latin America |
| IFC | International Finance Corporation |
| IFIs | International Financial Institutions |
| IGC | Internet Governance Caucus |
| IGF | Internet Governance Forum |
| IGOs | intergovernmental organisations |
| IGP | Internet Governance Project |
| IHEM | Institute of Higher Studies in Management |
| IHRC | Islamic Human Rights Commission |
| IIE | Institute for International Economics |
| IIED | International Institute of Environment and Development |
| IIF | Institute of International Finance |
| IIFA | International Islamic Fiqh Academy |
| IINA | International Islamic News Agency |
| IISD | International Institute for Sustainable Development |
| ILO | International Labour Organisation |
| ILRF | International Labour Rights Forum |
| IMF | International Monetary Fund |
| INGO | international non-governmental organisation |
| IOC | International Organising Committee |
| IOE | International Organisation of Employers |
| IP | Internet Protocol |
| IPCC | Intergovernmental Panel on Climate Change |
| IPD | Institute for Popular Democracy |

| ISBO | Islamic States Broadcasting Organisation |
| ISEAL | International Social and Environmental Accreditation and Labelling Alliance |
| ISESCO | Islamic Educational, Scientific and Cultural Organisation |
| ISO | International Organisation for Standardisation |
| ISOC | Internet Society |
| ITGN | International Trade and Gender Network |
| ITO | International Trade Organisation |
| ITU | International Telecommunication Union |
| ITUC | International Trade Union Confederation |
| IUCN | International Union for the Conservation of Nature |
| J8 | Junior Eight |
| JCIF | Japan Centre for International Finance |
| JPA | Joint Project Agreement |
| JWPTE | Joint Working Party on Trade and Environment |
| L20 | Leaders' 20 |
| LFAs | Local Fund Agents |
| MAI | Multilateral Agreement on Investment |
| MAP | Multi-Country HIV/AIDS Program |
| MCM | Monetary and Capital Markets Department |
| MD | Managing Director |
| MDGs | Millennium Development Goals |
| MDRI | Multilateral Debt Relief Initiative |
| MEAs | multilateral environmental agreements |
| MEJN | Malawi Economic Justice Network |
| MERCOSUR | Southern Common Market |
| MIGA | Multilateral Investment Guarantee Agency |
| MNEs | multinational enterprises |
| MOU | Memoranda of Understanding |
| MSF | Médecins Sans Frontières |
| MSN | Monitoring Sustainability of Globalisation |
| NACP3 | National AIDS Control Plan |
| NCPs | National Contact Points |
| NCUC | Noncommercial Users Constituency |
| NEPAD | New Partnership for Africa's Development |
| NEWS! | Network of European Worldshops |
| NGLS | Non-Governmental Liaison Service |
| NGO | non-governmental organisation |
| NIEO | New International Economic Order |
| NRDC | Natural Resources Defence Council |

| NTIA | National Telecommunications and Information Administration |
| O5 | Outreach 5 |
| OAU | Organisation of African Unity |
| ODI | Overseas Development Institute |
| OECD | Organisation for Economic Cooperation and Development |
| OEEC | Organisation for European Economic Co-operation |
| OIC | Organisation of the Islamic Conference |
| OISA | Organisation of the Islamic Shipowners Association |
| P7 | Poor 7 |
| PANA | Pan-African News Agency |
| PDR | Policy Development and Review |
| PF | Partnership Forum |
| PIN | Public Information Notices |
| PNoWB | Parliamentary Network on the World Bank |
| PRGF | Poverty Reduction and Growth Facility |
| PRSP | Poverty Reduction Strategy Paper |
| PSI | Policy Support Instrument |
| PSI | Public Services International |
| QAG | Quality Assurance Group |
| RALOs | Regional At-Large Organisations |
| RCS | Royal Commonwealth Society |
| REBRIP | Brazilian Network for the Integration of Peoples |
| RSSAC | Root Server System Advisory Committee |
| SADC | Southern African Development Community |
| SAN-ROC | South African Non-Racial Olympic Committee |
| SAPA | Solidarity for Asian People's Advocacy |
| SAPRI | Structural Adjustment Participatory Review Initiative |
| SBI | Subsidiary Body on Implementation |
| SBSTA | Subsidiary Body on Science and Technological Advice |
| SC | Security Council |
| SCF | Save the Children Fund |
| SCIMF | Sub-Committee on IMF matters |
| SEATINI | Southern and Eastern African Trade Information and Negotiations Institute |
| SESRTCIC | Statistical, Economic and Social Research and Training Centre for Islamic Countries |
| SFTMS | Sustainable Fair Trade Management System |
| SIDS | Small Island Developing States |

SMEs            small and medium enterprises
SOMs            Senior Official Meetings
SOMTI           Senior Officials' Meeting on Trade and Investment
SOs             Supporting Organisations
SPR             Strategy, Policy and Review Department
SPS             Phytosanitary Measures
SRH             Sexual and Reproductive Health
SSAC            Security and Stability Advisory Committee
TDRI            Thailand Development Research Institute
TERI            The Energy and Resources Institute
TI              Transparency International
TLD             Top-Level Domain
TLG             Technical Liaison Group
TNCs            transnational companies
TNI             Transnational Institute
TOES            The Other Economic Summit
TRIPS           Trade-Related Aspects of Intellectual Property
                Rights
TRPM            Trade Policy Review Mechanism
TUAC            Trade Union Advisory Committee
TWG             Transitional Working Group
TWN             Third World Network
UCLG            United Cities and Local Governments
UDN             Uganda Debt Network
UN              United Nations
UNCTAD          United Nations Conference on Trade and
                Development
UNDP            United Nations Development Programme
UNEP            United Nations Environment Programme
UNF             United Nations Foundation
UNFCCC          United Nations Framework Convention on Climate
                Change
UNGASS          United Nations General Assembly Special Session on
                HIV/AIDS
UNHCR           United Nations High Commissioner for Refugees
UNICEF          United Nations Children's Fund
UNIW            Union of NGOs of the Islamic World
VCS             Voluntary Carbon Standard
VSO             Voluntary Service Overseas
W3C             World Wide Web Consortium
WBCSD           World Business Council for Sustainable
                Development

| WCL | World Confederation of Labour |
| WDM | World Development Movement |
| WEDO | Women's Environment and Development Organization |
| WEF | World Economic Forum |
| WFP | World Food Programme |
| WFTO | World Fair Trade Organization |
| WFUNA | World Federation of United Nations Associations |
| WGIG | Working Group on Internet Governance |
| WGSC | Working Group on the Security Council |
| WHO | World Health Organisation |
| WIDE | Women in Development Europe |
| WMD | weapons of mass destruction |
| WSF | World Social Forum |
| WSIS | World Summit on the Information Society |
| WTO | World Trade Organization |
| WWF | World Wide Fund for Nature |
| WWW | Women Won't Wait |

# Introduction

*Jan Aart Scholte*

Contemporary society is a more global society. Over the past half-century people have, alongside their local, national and regional spheres, also come to interact globally on an unprecedented scale. More than ever, persons are interconnected with one another wherever on the earth they happen to live. Many of the principal policy challenges of the present day, including climate change, crime, infectious disease, financial stability, employment, (dis)armament, identity politics, social inequality and human rights, have pronounced global dimensions.

Whenever a given arena becomes important in people's collective lives, rules and regulatory institutions emerge to bring a certain order and predictability to that realm. Governance arrangements are needed if the societal space in question is to have any measure of stability and longevity. Thus at various historical junctures, village councils have developed in respect of localities and nation-states in respect of countries. More recently, regional domains have begun to acquire formal regulatory apparatuses, such as the European Union (EU) and the Southern African Development Community (SADC). By the same logic, global-scale regimes could be expected to grow as global-scale social relations rise in prominence.

Such a trend has indeed occurred. The past half-century has witnessed an unprecedented expansion of governance instruments that apply to jurisdictions and constituencies of a planetary scope. The United Nations (UN), the Bretton Woods institutions and the World Trade Organization (WTO) are some of the best-known examples of global governance agencies. Many more planet-spanning regulatory bodies get less public attention, such as the Organisation of the Islamic Conference (OIC) and the Internet Corporation for Assigned Names and Numbers (ICANN). To be sure, these proliferating and growing global-scale regimes have not replaced nation-states and local authorities, which on the whole remain as vibrant as ever. However, global governance has become highly significant in contemporary history, even if the various institutional frameworks show no signs of coalescing to form a world government, in the sense of a sovereign state scaled up to planetary proportions.

To be effective and legitimate, governance needs to be accountable. With accountability the governors are answerable to the governed for their (the governors') actions and omissions. Regulatory processes that lack sufficient accountability generally fail to achieve their purposes adequately, i.e. they are not effective. In addition, poorly accountable regimes generally attract limited support from affected populations, i.e. they are not legitimate. On both counts – ineffectiveness and illegitimacy – weak accountability yields weak governance, and weak governance means that the public policy needs of a society are not adequately met.

Accountable global governance is therefore essential for today's more global world. As the chapters in this book demonstrate, shortfalls in accountability substantially hamper planet-spanning regulatory institutions in delivering on their respective goals and mandates. These shortcomings in global governance in turn undermine the realisation of core societal values such as material wellbeing, distributive justice, ecological sustainability, cultural vibrancy, moral decency, democracy, solidarity, liberty and peace. Seen in this light, the stakes in securing accountable global governance could not be higher.

How, then, can regulatory arrangements that apply over different continents and oceans across the earth be made suitably answerable to the people whose lives are affected by them, in many cases deeply so? Global governance institutions lack the kinds of formal accountability mechanisms that are generally found in national and local governments. Bodies such as the Commonwealth, the Global Fund to Fight AIDS, Tuberculosis and Malaria (GFATM), and the World Bank have neither a popularly elected executive, nor a directly elected parliamentary arm for oversight, nor their own (non-partisan) judiciary. Hence different kinds of accountability processes need to operate for global-scale regimes.

Fifty years ago the answer to the problem of global governance accountability was relatively straightforward. At that time a regulatory agency of planetary scope (or 'international organisation', as the prevailing vocabulary then described it) was accountable to affected people through the member states of the institution. Each state was meant to ensure that the actions of the global governance body concerned benefited the citizens of that state or, in the case of malfunctions and harms, that due compensation would be exacted. In addition, states collectively were meant to ensure that the global governance arrangement served the general interests of a putative 'international community'.

However, this 'statist' formula (where the accountability of global governance is obtained wholly and solely through national governments) is insufficient today on at least nine major counts. First, a number of planet-spanning regulatory agencies have over the past half-century become so large and influential that many of their (especially smaller) state members lack the power, by themselves, to hold the institution sufficiently to account for its impacts on their citizens. The government of Malawi in its relationship with the International Monetary Fund (IMF) is a case in point. Second, stronger as well as weaker states often demonstrate a lack of energy in exacting accountability from global governance bodies. National parliaments have generally been particularly remiss in this regard, while legal immunity has shielded many global authorities from national courts. Third, the officials who act for states in global governance institutions are usually unelected technocrats with little connection to the everyday lives of most of their fellow national citizens. Fourth, a number of important global governance arrangements such as the Group of Eight (G8) and the Organisation for Economic Cooperation and Development (OECD) have far-reaching impacts on countries spread across the globe whose governments are not members of the institution in question. Fifth, some emergent elements of global governance directly involve substate local governments or suprastate regional institutions rather than nation-states per se; for instance, organisations such as United Cities and Local Governments (UCLG) function largely outside the purview of states, while the EU maintains its own representation in over a hundred countries across the planet. Sixth, large parts of contemporary global governance operate through private regulatory bodies where states are not members at all. The many examples include the World Fair Trade Organization (WFTO), which groups producer and consumer organisations, and various schemes of corporate social and environmental responsibility (CSER), where the protagonists are firms. Seventh, turning traditional assumptions on their head, today some non-state actors directly engage global governance arrangements in order to call their national governments to account. Thus, for instance, a number of women's groups and other human rights campaigners have sought to counter the democratic failings of their state through the UN. Eighth, in contemporary global affairs many people embrace political identities and solidarities that are often not adequately represented through nation-states. In this vein various diasporas, faith groups and indigenous peoples do not look solely – and in some cases only barely, if at all – to the government of the country in which they reside to be their agent of global governance accountability. Finally, some people with cosmopolitan orientations feel that, as 'global citizens' in addition to, or perhaps even more than, national citizens, their relationship to global regulatory arrangements should be one of direct accountability, unmediated by states.

Thus many constituents and stakeholders in today's world cannot obtain sufficient accountability from global governance arrangements through their state alone. National governments remain very important channels for holding planet-spanning regulatory agencies answerable for their decisions and policies, but in many cases this check is not working well, or by itself is insufficient. Given the absence of official mechanisms of direct accountability and the inadequacy of indirect accountability through states, current global governance has large accountability deficits in respect of formal channels. Insufficient accountability compromises effectiveness and legitimacy, which in turn exacerbate many of the foremost problems of contemporary society (for example poverty, inequality, environmental degradation, disease and violence). Weakly accountable global governance is therefore not just a peripheral preoccupation for democratic purists, but a core challenge for anyone concerned with obtaining decent human lives for all in the twenty-first century.

How, then, can states be supported when (as in the first six circumstances identified above) they are unable by themselves to secure sufficiently accountable global governance for their citizens? Moreover, how can accountable global governance be achieved when (as in the last three situations indicated) states could not be adequate on their own even if they had the necessary capacities? In particular, how can this more accountable (and thus more effective and legitimate) global governance be attained when there is little prospect in the foreseeable future of directly elected global executives and legislatures or a fully-fledged global judiciary being introduced?

This book explores one possible avenue for the reduction of these accountability gaps in contemporary global governance, namely through civil society. The various studies in the book examine ways and extents that citizen action groups can further the answerability of global-scale regulatory organisations to the people whose lives and life chances are affected by them. Many academic theorists and policy practitioners alike have welcomed dynamic, value-driven, democratically mobilising civil society activities as a potential (at least partial) answer to accountability deficits in global governance. On the other hand, sceptics have worried that incompetent, co-opted, elite-centred and themselves poorly answerable civil society associations could actually exacerbate accountability problems in global governance. What do experiences to date suggest regarding this debate?

In order to investigate these matters, this book opens with a conceptually oriented chapter, elaborating on the issues introduced above surrounding 'global governance', 'accountability', 'civil society' and the relationships between them. Then thirteen more empirically oriented chapters explore how civil society activities have and/or have not promoted the democratic accountability of a diverse range of global governance institutions: UN,

World Bank, IMF, WTO, the Commonwealth, OIC, OECD, G8, the Asia-Europe Meeting (ASEM), the global climate change regime, GFATM, ICANN and WFTO. Each of these chapters sets out: (a) the mandate and activities of the regulatory apparatus concerned; (b) the accountability challenges that the global governance arrangement in question faces; (c) the range of civil society engagements of the institution; (d) the accountability effects of that civil society involvement; and (e) the main circumstances that have helped or hindered civil society contributions to global governance accountability in the case at hand. The concluding chapter synthesises these findings and reflects on their implications for future practices of civil society and democratically accountable global governance.

To enhance the quality of these findings and recommendations, the investigations for the book have developed through processes of practitioner-researcher exchange. Thus the project design and execution have emerged and evolved through consultations among academics, civil society actors and global governance officials, and most of the authors have extensively interviewed relevant practitioners in preparing their case studies. The draft chapters received detailed scrutiny by civil society and official actors in a workshop at Gothenburg University in June 2007. Also in order to engage practitioner circles, the project results have been presented orally at various civil society and global governance venues.

The resulting book gives a fuller version of the above analysis and aims thereby to enlarge an as-yet small corner of knowledge. Although the issue of accountable global governance is increasingly recognised as being highly important, research on the subject remains sparse. Only a handful of published academic studies have explored the general problem of accountability in global regulation (Keohane and Nye 2003; Held and Koenig-Archibugi 2005; Ebrahim and Weisband 2007). Among think tanks the Global Accountability Project of the One World Trust has conducted important research on the subject (Kovach *et al.* 2003; Blagescu and Lloyd 2006; Lloyd *et al.* 2007, 2008). A few other works have examined accountability in relation to particular global governance institutions, albeit without focusing on the role of civil society (Woods and Narlikar 2001; Carin and Wood 2005). Some notable research has considered civil society engagement of global regulatory agencies, but without systematic and explicit assessment of accountability issues (Weiss and Gordenker 1996; Willetts 1996; Charnovitz 1997; Foster and Anand 1999; Florini 2000; O'Brien *et al.* 2000; Edwards and Gaventa 2001; Scholte and Schnabel 2002; Clark 2003; Friedman *et al.* 2005; Martens 2005; Joachim 2007; Scholte 2007; Steffek *et al.* 2008; Walker and Thompson 2008; MacKenzie 2009; McKeon 2009; Gaventa and Tandon 2010; Jönsson and Tallberg (2010)). To date just one book regarding the World Bank, and two other general pieces, have focused on the civil society angle to accountable global governance (Fox and Brown 1998; Scholte 2004a; Van Rooy 2004). To that extent this book endeavours to map largely uncharted territory in contemporary global political analysis.

Regarding general themes that run through the text as a whole, the various chapters consistently show that the accountability equation between civil society and global governance is highly complex. For one thing, accountability in global governance is anything but straightforward: precisely who is accountable? For what? To whom? By what means? And when? Civil society is no less problematic: what sorts of citizen action groups make global regulatory agencies most accountable? To which constituencies? And using what kinds of strategies and tactics? Moreover, global regulatory arrangements are highly diverse, such that civil society interventions which advance democratic accountability in respect of one institution may not do so in respect of another. Civil society contributions to accountable global governance can also vary according to issue: for example, they have generally greater impact in regard to human rights than macroeconomic policy. Given these intricacies, the question of the role of civil society in democratically accountable global governance is not open to a single, precise and concise answer.

That said, the chapters do in general suggest that civil society activities can, when the circumstances are conducive, serve to reinforce, complement or in some cases even supplant states in exacting accountability from global governance institutions. Indeed, it is largely civil society interventions that have alerted policymakers, the mass media and the wider public to shortfalls of democracy in contemporary global governance. Moreover, efforts by citizen groups can – and, as the case studies show, often do – induce global authorities to be more answerable to various constituencies. In particular, civil society inputs can in some instances increase global governance accountability to disadvantaged and marginalised circles, including countries of the global south, impoverished people, women, and other social groups that experience silencing and exclusion. The chapters in this book contain many examples of positive civil society contributions that could inspire further initiatives in the future.

At the same time, however, the studies also give cause to temper enthusiasm for civil society activism as a means to attain more accountable global governance. For one thing, the scale of civil society relations with the various global regulatory bodies is generally rather small and/ or sporadic, thereby limiting the extent of accountability benefits that can be generated. In addition, many civil society actors have only limited awareness of the aims, institutional organisation and policy tools of the global governance agencies that they address. Moreover, when civil society associations engage a given global governance apparatus they often do not have an explicit focus on, or a clear strategy for, enhancing the accountability of that institution. Greater contacts and exchanges do not of themselves generate greater accountability. Thus future politics would benefit from more – and more deliberate – civil society efforts to make global authorities answerable for their actions and omissions.

On another sobering note, the investigations in this book indicate that civil society involvement does not inherently improve the *democratic* accountability of global governance. For instance, certain civil society interventions may mainly make global regulatory agencies more answerable to constituents like big business that are already disproportionately served through other channels. Indeed, civil society involvement may even detract from democratic accountability, for example if in consequence a global agency gives more attention to certain special interest groups than to popularly elected parliaments. In addition, ritualised global governance 'consultations' with civil society associations may produce little policy change and instead serve to defuse challenges to deeper structures of unaccountable power. The ability of civil society actors to exact global governance accountability can also be compromised to the degree that the citizen associations are insufficiently answerable to the constituencies that they purport to serve. Civil society, too, faces its own accountability challenges. Thus future democracy would benefit from more critical self-awareness on the part of civil society actors as they seek to make global governance more answerable to affected publics.

In sum, civil society most certainly can influence accountability in global governance; however, the impacts could be greater and more beneficial, and it is important for vitally needed effective and legitimate global governance that these results improve. This general conclusion, as well as suggested forward actions that follow from it, are elaborated further in the closing chapter of the book.

# 1 Global governance, accountability and civil society

*Jan Aart Scholte*

## Introduction

As an initial step in exploring the relationship between civil society and accountability in global governance it is important to clarify the core terms. Each of the principal elements in this equation is subject to multiple and often conflicting interpretations. The point of this opening chapter is not to resolve these theoretical and political disputes with definitive definitions. Such an aim is neither achievable nor – from the perspective of creative democratic debate – desirable. Hence the following discussion only sketches broad conceptions and concerns in order to provide a starting framework of analysis for the subsequent case studies. Individual authors will, in those chapters, elaborate their particular understandings of the general issues in relation to specific global governance arrangements.

The present chapter has three parts that successively address the three central concepts in this study. The first part identifies 'global governance' as *a complex of rules and regulatory institutions that apply to transplanetary jurisdictions and constituencies*. In line with globalisation as a major general trend of contemporary history, global governance has grown to unprecedented proportions and significance in recent decades. The second part of the chapter discusses 'accountability' in terms of *processes whereby an actor answers for its conduct to those whom it affects*. Shortfalls of accountability (especially democratic accountability) in respect of global governance agencies constitute a major challenge to the delivery of effective and legitimate public policy. The third part of the chapter introduces 'civil society' as *a political arena where associations of citizens seek, from outside political parties, to shape societal rules*. The present enquiry considers the ways and extents that civil society activities can contribute to greater accountability in global governance.

## Global governance

Globalisation is one of the most striking broad trends of contemporary history (Held *et al.* 1999; Scholte 2005b). Over the past half-century the collective lives of human beings have acquired much larger planet-spanning (or 'transplanetary') dimensions. All manner of flows connect people with one another wherever on earth they might be located: for example through communications, merchandise, microbes, migrants, money, organisations, pollutants and weapons. Although global-scale exchanges have been going on for many centuries, transplanetary social relations have today reached unprecedented and qualitatively larger amounts, ranges, frequencies, speeds, intensities and impacts. Concurrently, society is also marked by greater global consciousness: that is, people have acquired heightened awareness of planetary realms as a significant aspect of their social existence. Indeed, many individuals have oriented their cultural identities and political solidarities partly to global spheres, as witnessed with phenomena like so-called 'world music' and humanitarian relief programmes. Materially and ideationally, therefore, contemporary society operates substantially through global frames alongside (and in complex interrelations with) social spaces on other scales such as neighbourhood, province, country and region.

Like all realms of social relations, global social relations require governance: that is, an array of rules along with regulatory institutions to administer those norms and standards. As any arena of human collective life becomes significant – be it a locality, country or other social space – frameworks of governance develop to bring a certain order and predictability to that sphere. Rules are set, maintained, adjusted and enforced. The rules may be strict or loose, formal or informal, permanent or transitory, enabling or oppressive. But even if it is softly applied and barely perceptible, regulation of some kind will transpire if a given social space is to have any stability and longevity.

So it is with global domains also. The intense globalisation of recent history has entailed, as part of the process, increased governance of transplanetary affairs. Much of this regulation has developed through pre-existent institutions such as nation-states and local governments. In addition, however, growing needs to govern global matters have prompted the establishment and expansion of many suprastate regulatory arrangements. Some of these new apparatuses, like the European Union (EU), operate in respect of regional jurisdictions while others, like the United Nations (UN), govern in respect of transplanetary jurisdictions. The latter type of regulation – namely rules and administering agencies that apply to places and people spread across the earth – can be termed 'global governance'.

The phrase 'global governance' first surfaced in the late 1980s in connection with the Commission on Global Governance, which reported in 1995 on various challenges of regulating a more global world (Carlsson *et al.* 1995). Twenty years later the vocabulary figures in the titles of textbooks and countless other publications. A journal named *Global Governance* was launched in 1995 and quickly became a significant outlet in its field (Coate and Murphy 1995; Carin *et al.* 2006). More than a dozen universities across the world now house research centres specifically dedicated to the study of 'global governance'. Indeed, a number of recently created regulatory arrangements with a planetary scope have incorporated the adjective 'global' into their names, rather than the previously favoured term 'international'. Examples include the Global Environment Facility (launched in 1991), the Global Reporting Initiative (1998), the Global Compact (2000) and the Global Fund to Fight AIDS, Tuberculosis and Malaria (2002).

Like any key concept, the notion 'global governance' can be problematic if it is invoked loosely and uncritically (Hewson and Sinclair 1999; Sinclair 2004; Grugel and Piper 2006; Soederberg 2006). However, if used with precision and vigilance this idea can open important insights into contemporary politics. In particular, the newer term 'global governance' is arguably more exact and revealing than the older label 'international organisation', which dates from the early twentieth century. 'Global' specifically designates activities and conditions on a planetary scale, whereas 'international' covers any circumstance (bilateral, regional or global) that extends beyond the confines of a country-nation-state unit. Moreover, 'global' suitably highlights planetary realms as having become significant social domains in their own right, while 'inter-*national*' (as well as its cousin 'trans-*national*') still frame phenomena with primary reference to country arenas. Meanwhile, the word 'organisation' in 'international organisation' could encompass any association, whatever its activities, whereas 'governance' specifies the regulatory character of the circumstances in question. Furthermore, 'international organisation' has usually been understood in terms of relations among nation-states, while contemporary 'global governance' involves not only nation-states, but also other types of actors such as business enterprises, civil society associations, local governments and regional agencies. Finally, in contrast to the traditional conception of international organisations as being wholly and solely the servants of states, contemporary global governance institutions are to some extent also players in their own right: they influence states (and other actors) at the same time as being influenced by states (and other actors).

Global *governance* is not the same thing as global *government*. To speak of global governance is not to suggest the existence, emergence or goal of a world state. Global-scale regulation can operate in the absence of a centralised, sovereign, public entity that is elevated from a national to a planetary scale. After all, governance has historically taken many forms. Societal regulation has occurred not only through states, but also through empires (e.g. the Byzantine, Inca and Songay empires), corporations (e.g. the Dutch and English East India Companies), and diffuse networks (e.g. as in medieval Europe). Thus global governance need not, does not, and in all probability will not take shape as a nation-state writ large.

Instead, contemporary global governance operates through a complex array of numerous and diverse institutional mechanisms. Broadly speaking, six different types of global regulatory body can be distinguished in contemporary society: intergovernmental, transgovernmental, inter-regional, translocal, private, and public-private hybrids. The first of these categories, intergovernmental agencies, covers the conventional multilateral institutions that operate through state-based ministers and diplomats supported by a permanent suprastate secretariat (Diehl 2005). Examples include the International Monetary Fund (IMF), the Organisation of the Islamic Conference (OIC) and the World Trade Organization (WTO).

Transgovernmental networks lack the formal character of intergovernmental institutions. In these cases senior and middle-ranking civil servants from multiple states jointly pursue governance of common concerns through informal collaboration by, for example, conferences and memoranda of understanding (Raustiala 2002; Slaughter 2004). Examples of transgovernmental regulation include the Competition Policy Network, the Group of Eight (G8) and the Nuclear Suppliers Group. The Organisation for Economic Cooperation and Development (OECD) also operates largely through transgovernmental committees and working groups. Although transgovernmental networks lack a basis in conventional international law and have no distinct permanent institutional expression, they perform important regulatory tasks in areas such as crime prevention, disease control, environmental protection, financial supervision, human rights promotion and trade policy.

Less extensive to date, but potentially more important for the future, is global governance through interregional arrangements (Hänggi *et al.* 2005). In these cases, regulation of global issues is pursued among several macro-regional groupings of states. So far interregionalism has mainly occurred through EU relations with other regional institutions including the Southern Common Market (MERCOSUR) and the Association of South East Asian Nations (ASEAN). The Asia-Europe Meeting (ASEM) is the most developed interregional arrangement (Gilson 2002). This multilateralism of regions could well spread worldwide in years to come as regionalism consolidates in areas outside Europe.

The future may also bring increased global governance through translocalism. In such arrangements, substate municipal and provincial authorities from across the planet collaborate directly, without the mediation of nation states, in the regulation of common problems. Examples of translocal global governance include United Cities and Local Governments (UCLG), with several thousand members in 127 countries, and ICLEI – Local Governments for Sustainability, which links some 500 substate authorities across 67 countries to pursue improvements in global environmental conditions.

Still further expansion of global governance has transpired in recent decades through private mechanisms with a transplanetary reach (Cutler *et al.* 1999; Hall and Biersteker 2003). Contrary to widely held assumptions, societal regulation does not, per se, have to occur through public sector bodies. Instead, business consortia and/or civil society associations can construct and administer governance arrangements for various aspects of global affairs. The many examples of private global governance include the Forestry Stewardship Council (FSC, to promote ecologically sustainable logging), schemes for corporate social and environmental responsibility (CSER), the International Accounting Standards Board (IASB, to improve and harmonise modes of financial reporting) and the World Fair Trade Organization (WFTO, to advance the position of poor producers in global commerce).

A final category of growing global governance in contemporary history crosses the public-private divide with hybrid arrangements (Bull and McNeill 2007). These constructions, which have mainly arisen during the past decade, involve global regulation through institutions that combine public, business and/or civil society elements. Examples of these trans-sectoral hybrids include the Internet Corporation for Assigned Names and Numbers (ICANN) and the Global Fund to Fight AIDS, Tuberculosis and Malaria (GFATM).

Given this sixfold variety of forms, contemporary global governance could be described as comprising multiple multilateralisms. The old-style 'international organisation' involved just one kind of multilateralism, namely intergovernmental arrangements. Thus the architects of 1945 envisioned that global governance would entail the United Nations system plus several intergovernmental institutions for finance and trade. In contrast, sixty years later global regulation encompasses in addition transgovernmental, interregional, translocal, private and hybrid multilateralisms. Rather than being an institutional umbrella for the whole of world order, the UN has become one site among many for planet-spanning governance.

The studies in this book examine cases of each of these diverse types of global governance, with the exception of translocalism. The next six chapters concern more traditional intergovernmental apparatuses (UN,

World Bank, IMF, WTO, Commonwealth, OIC). Then two chapters examine cases with significant transgovernmental qualities (OECD, G8). The tenth chapter considers ASEM as an interregional arrangement. In the final four case studies, ICANN and the WFTO involve private global governance, while the climate change regime and the Global Fund illustrate the development of public-private combinations. Of course the question arises whether some institutional forms of global governance are more amenable to positive civil society influence than others, a matter which is addressed in the Conclusion to this book.

Appearing in these diverse manifestations, global governance is a growing reality of contemporary society. The number of regulatory agencies with planetary jurisdictions and constituencies has proliferated over the past hundred years and at a generally increasing rate, especially in recent decades. Moreover, most global governance bodies have expanded over time in terms of their mandates and resources. Today global governance arrangements figure significantly in every area of public policy, including in the most politically charged matters such as human rights, migration, money, policing and military affairs.

Not all governance in contemporary society takes place through regulatory agencies with a planetary reach, of course. Global governance for the most part complements rather than cancels out regulatory arrangements on regional, national and local scales. In particular, there is no sign that growing global governance entails a contraction, let alone demise, of the nation-state. On the contrary, territorial states generally remain as robust as ever in today's more global world, if not more so (Weiss 1998; Sørensen 2004). The major national governments in particular nearly always figure as highly influential players in respect of global public policy concerns. Thus it is not a question of contemporary societal regulation occurring through global regimes *or* regional institutions *or* national governments *or* local authorities. Rather, the operative conjunction is 'and'.

Thus governance of any public policy issue today involves a multi-faceted trans-scalar network of institutions. In regard to trade, for example, the WFTO and the WTO operate on a global scale, while close to 300 inter-state trade agreements concluded since 1945 relate to regional domains (Cosbey *et al.* 2004: 2). In addition, states continue to act on trade in respect of national realms, and municipal and provincial governments regulate trade as it impacts their respective jurisdictions. Similar trans-scalar complexes of governance apply to any other area of contemporary public policy, such as communications, education, employment, environment, finance, health and migration. In all of these cases, global regulatory agencies do not stand alone, but are encompassed within larger polycentric governance networks (Reinecke 1999–2000; Scholte 2005b: Ch 6; Scholte 2008a).

Yet, although global-scale rules and regulatory institutions form only a part of the whole, they are a vital and indispensable aspect of contemporary governance. A more global world of the kind that has emerged over the past half-century requires some significant measure of planet-spanning governance arrangements for the provision of global public goods (Kaul *et al.* 1999, 2003; ITFGPG 2006). For one thing, global regimes of technical standardisation are required to make possible, for example, transplanetary communications, disease control and production processes. In addition, significant elements of global-scale coordination are required for effective responses to matters such as global ecological changes, global financial crises, global criminal networks and global arms proliferation. To be sure, there are strong arguments to embrace a principle of subsidiarity, whereby regulation should be devolved to the smallest possible scale. For both technical effectiveness and democratic legitimacy, governance generally works best in the closest possible connection with the affected persons. Yet even if global rules and regulatory institutions were pared down to the minimally required proportions, planet-spanning arrangements would still remain an important feature of governance in the more global society that people now inhabit. The question is therefore not *whether* global governance will exist in the years to come, but what forms and proportions it will take, and what policies and outcomes it will promote.

Of course global governance arrangements rarely have total planetary coverage, in the sense of affecting – or affecting to equal extents – every person at every spot on the earth. 'Global' (spread across the planet) can therefore be distinguished from 'universal' (encompassing the whole planet). Indeed, some global governance instruments like the Commonwealth, la Francophonie and the OIC only aim at some rather than all people and countries across the globe. A global regulatory apparatus need not reach everywhere and evenly across the planet, just as a nation-state usually does not touch every inhabitant and locale in a country to the same degree.

Finally, as should be apparent from the tone of this discussion so far, the term 'global governance' is not invoked here in any particular normative sense. To speak of global governance is not to assume anything – either positive or negative – concerning the effectiveness and legitimacy of the arrangements in question. Global governance is not inherently functional or dysfunctional, equitable or inequitable, democratic or undemocratic, culturally homogenising or culturally pluralising, imperialist or emancipatory. Global governance is not intrinsically a good or a bad thing. This book neither applauds it nor decries it as such. The analysis merely recognises that global-scale regulation exists as a functional necessity of a more global world. Moreover, the phenomenon will in all likelihood continue to grow – and grow very substantially – as further globalisation unfolds.

Whether global governance has beneficial or harmful effects depends on how it is practised. The compelling need is therefore for global governance to be carried out well. Positive accountability processes can help to that end. Indeed, critical investigations of accountability – such as undertaken in this book – could contribute to the construction of alternative and better global governance in the future.

## Accountability

As noted in the Introduction to this book, accountability is crucial to the establishment and maintenance of the effective and legitimate global governance that the present-day world vitally needs. In the absence of suitably accountable global-scale regulation, humanity today suffers major deficits in the provision of global public goods such as communications infrastructure, ecological integrity, financial stability, disease control, peaceful dispute settlement and potable water. Thus accountability is not an optional extra in planet-spanning governance institutions, but goes to the heart of providing decent human lives for all in the more global society that has emerged over the past half-century and looks very likely to develop further in the decades to come.

Yet what, more precisely, is entailed by 'accountability'? And how does it relate more specifically to global governance agencies? For what are these institutions accountable? To whom are they accountable? Over what timeframe does their accountability extend? By what means do global governance organisations practise accountability, and how adequate are the existing instruments? These questions are examined in turn below.

Ahead of that more detailed discussion it should be stressed from the outset that this book approaches accountability with a critical democratic purpose. That is, accountability is understood here principally as a means to constrain power and make it responsive to the people that it affects, especially people who tend otherwise to be marginalised and silenced. This emphasis on *democratic* accountability contrasts in particular with a widespread contemporary discourse of so-called 'good governance', in which accountability often figures primarily as a means to promote financial responsibility and efficient performance. Of course these more technical aspects of accountability are also important for policy success, and when well integrated with other concerns can complement and further democratic ends. However, as many painful historical experiences have shown – including such extremes as the slave trade and concentration camps – a fixation on efficiency can sideline and undermine democratic values, with potentially dire consequences. Given that prevailing approaches to political economy have in recent times tended to overplay efficiency aspects of accountability, it is important that other analyses, such as those collected in this book, give due emphasis to democratic concerns.

### What is 'accountability'?

In spite of contrasting notions regarding the purpose of accountability, orthodox and alternative perspectives can concur on its broad nature. Across the diverse conceptions there is general agreement that accountability is a condition and process whereby an actor answers for its conduct to those whom it affects. In a word, if A takes an action that impacts upon B, then by the principle of accountability A must answer to B for that action and its consequences. In elaborating this starting point different notions of accountability have contrasting ideas about who 'B' is, what kinds of impacts must be answered for, and how 'A' should answer for them. However, all approaches to accountability embrace the broad principle that actors should be answerable for their actions (and sometimes also inactions).

Accountability can be understood to have four principal aspects: transparency; consultation; evaluation; and correction. These apply whether the accountable agent is a global governance institution or any other kind of actor, be it a state, a corporation, a political party, a civil society association, a media organ or an individual. Other analysts have developed other fourfold conceptions of accountability on broadly similar lines, albeit with some different emphases (Coleman and Porter 2000; Blagescu et al. 2005; Ebrahim and Weisband 2007).

With respect to *transparency*, accountability requires that A is visible to B. In other words, the affected constituents must always, from the start to the finish of a given action, be able to see what the affecting actor is doing and how. In a situation of accountability, impacted circles should be able to discover readily what decisions are taken, when, by whom, through what procedures, on the basis of what evidence, drawing on what resources for implementation and with what expected consequences. Without such information B is left ignorant and cannot effectively scrutinise A; thus transparency is a sine qua non of accountability (Holzner and Holzner 2006; Hood and Heald 2006). Of course there are situations (such as criminal investigations and advance notice of certain changes to macroeconomic policy) where public interest may require some temporary restrictions on the release of information. However, in accountable governance the default position is timely and full disclosure, and any exceptions to that rule require thorough justification.

With respect to *consultation*, accountability requires that A explains intended actions to B and adjusts plans in the light of information, analysis and preferences heard from B. In other words, decision-taking is accountable when affected people are incorporated into the deliberations and have opportunities to shape the outcomes. In thorough accountability this participation extends across the policy cycle, from the initial agenda formulation to the final report. The consultation may be direct (involving the affected persons themselves) or indirect (involving mediating parties such as parliaments and civil society associations). In the case of indirect participation the mediating agent should in its turn be accountable to those for whom it purports to speak.

With respect to *evaluation*, accountability requires that the impacts of A's actions on B are thoroughly and independently monitored and assessed. Such evaluations might take the form of academic studies, civil society reports, judiciary proceedings, journalistic investigations, officially commissioned enquiries, parliamentary reviews, or testimonies of the affected persons themselves. Accountability entails an obligation to determine how affected circles have been affected. Impacted persons have a right to know how well the impacting agent has complied with its decisions and achieved the promised results. Stakeholders furthermore have a right to receive tenable explanations when outcomes have fallen short of expectations.

With respect to *correction*, accountability requires that A provides B with redress in cases where A's actions have had harmful consequences for B. This compensation might take the form of apologies, policy changes, institutional reorganisations, staff reprimands, management resignations, reparations or even incarcerations. In a situation of accountability, affected circles must be assured that affecting actors take responsibility for their actions and learn from any mistakes.

Applying these four general points to the issue at hand, a global governance institution would be accountable to the extent that it is transparent to those affected, consults those affected, reports to those affected and provides redress to those who are adversely affected. Each of the case study chapters in this book assesses the performance of the global governance agency in question on these four lines, and considers in what ways and to what extents civil society activities advance these four facets of accountability.

As diverse experiences across the thirteen cases show, there are multiple ways to practise accountability in global governance. On the one hand, the different institutions adopt different instruments to enact transparency, consultation, evaluation and correction. On the other hand, different constituencies (e.g. academe, business, diasporas, faith groups, governments, women, and workers) have different needs and expectations as regards accountability processes that are meaningful to them. Thus accountability is anything but straightforward and on the contrary remains heavily contested. Moreover, while it is important to identify and learn from good practices of global governance accountability, it would be unhelpfully simplistic to hold up certain frameworks as a 'best practice' blueprint that should be followed by all institutions in all circumstances.

### Who is accountable?

Are global governance agencies subject to accountability requirements? Do they fit the category 'A' in the general definition above? After all, traditional (often dubbed 'Westphalian') doctrines of international law and international organisation would have it that states are the sole actors in world affairs, with the implication that only national governments would have obligations of accountability in global arenas. Indeed, many state leaders today still insist on old-style notions of 'sovereignty' in their dealings with global governance institutions. Likewise, councils, management and staff of global regulatory agencies – especially the intergovernmental bodies – are often only too ready to absolve themselves of responsibility by attributing all power and accountability in their operations to the member states.

Fifty years ago few issues of accountability arose in respect of global governance institutions themselves. At that time 'international organisations' were few in number, small in size, and limited in scope. Societal regulation was undertaken more or less wholly and solely by nation-states. Thus accountability for public policy both domestically and internationally could be attached more or less entirely to national governments and key decision-takers within those governments. In this Westphalian world the buck stopped somewhere, and everyone more or less agreed where that was: the sovereign state.

However, contemporary governance has a post-statist character, in the sense that, as seen above, societal regulation now involves multiple kinds of actors in addition to national governments. Governance has become post-sovereign, in the sense that policy processes are institutionally diffuse and lack a single locus of supreme, absolute and comprehensive authority. Today no regulatory body – including a state – constructs public policy on its own. Global institutions, regional agencies, state bodies and substate authorities are embedded together in a host of polycentric networks that operate in respect of different public policy issues. None of the parties involved holds a clear position of final arbiter.

The relative simplicity of Westphalian accountability equations therefore no longer applies in world politics. In today's polycentric governance apparatus it is well-nigh impossible to link accountability neatly and simply to a single decision point, or even to a single type of actor like the state. Public policy emanates from – and accountability correspondingly applies to – complex networks rather than one or the other player in isolation.

For example, who is accountable in the case of Internet governance? Is it ICANN? Is it parallel private regulatory mechanisms such as the World Wide Web Consortium (W3C) and the Internet Engineering Task Force (IETF)? Is it (and should it be more so) the International Telecommunication Union (ITU) as the most relevant public global agency? Is it the United States Department of Commerce as (until recently) underwriter of ICANN? Is it the State of California under whose laws ICANN is incorporated? Is it other nation-states who acquiesce to these largely privatised arrangements of Internet governance? Is it the software companies, civil society groups and individual programmers who share in the operation of ICANN, W3C and IETF? The obvious answer is that all of these participating actors have a case to answer, both individually and collectively. Yet this principle of multifaceted accountabilities is not easily translated into practice: which parts of public policy networks should be held to account, to what respective degrees, how, and to whom?

Indeed, there is considerable danger that governance agencies exploit these post-sovereign circumstances of diffuse polycentric decision-taking in order to avoid accepting due responsibility for their actions and omissions. In one recurrent scenario, for example, major states and the UN blame each other for policy failures regarding peace and security. Likewise, client states and the IMF habitually fault one another for flawed macroeconomic policies: the governments complain of imposed conditionalities, and the Fund protests that its role is only advisory. Similarly, protagonists in other policy areas regularly claim that some other agency is responsible for failures: e.g. to deliver essential medicines to AIDS sufferers; to ensure adequate food for all; to take measures against climate change; and to halt manipulations of global finance for tax evasion. In situations of polycentric governance where the buck does not stop it is all too easily passed.

It is vital to resist these temptations of finger-pointing and to insist on retaining accountability as a cornerstone of effective and legitimate governance of global affairs. However, to reaffirm accountability in respect of polycentric public policy networks requires a shift in assumptions away from a now obsolete 'sovereigntist' mindset that seeks to attach ultimate responsibility to a single highest authority. Instead, accountability needs to be understood and practised in contemporary governance in a dispersed and shared fashion. All nodes in a given public policy network – including the global regulatory institutions involved – must play their part in delivering transparency, consultation, evaluation and correction.

Thus global governance agencies, too, must answer for their actions and omissions, albeit usually as parts of larger regulatory arrangements rather than as players in isolation. The councils, managements and staffs of global governance institutions share in generating the impacts of public policy on contemporary society. The influence of these transplanetary agencies must not be exaggerated, but it must not be denied and ignored either. The corresponding responsibilities cannot justifiably be wholly transferred to states and other parts of the relevant public policy network. Some responsibility – and associated requirements of accountability – lie with the global governance mechanism itself.

### Accountability for what?

If global governance institutions need to be held accountable for their share in contemporary societal regulation, for what more specifically is each agency answerable? This question can be addressed in terms of the overall purpose of the governance body, as well as the various activities that the organisation undertakes in pursuit of that mandate.

As noted earlier, global governance mechanisms are indispensable to the delivery of many public goods in today's more global society. Each of these regulatory instruments is meant to advance one or several planet-spanning public goods, whether in respect of conflict management, cultural creativity, disease control, ecological sustainability, financial stability or technical standardisation. Often this mandate is expressed explicitly in the constitutional document that established the institution, like the Charter of the United Nations. Instances of informal global governance like the G8 and certain CSER schemes lack a founding legal convention of this kind, and their respective purposes must be deduced from other declarations and actions. In some cases, such as the OECD, the objectives and corresponding activities of a global governance apparatus may range quite widely.

Yet however its mandate is expressed, a global governance institution is first and foremost answerable for the ways and degrees that it does or does not further whatever public good(s) it exists to promote. This accountability can be more specifically assessed in line with the fourfold framework set out above. Thus, first, how transparently does the agency in question pursue its delivery of the given global public good? Second, how consultative are the institution's policy processes in respect of providing that global public good? Third, how well is the organisation's performance evaluated in regard to furthering that global public good? Fourth, how well does the global governance actor in question correct its shortcomings in promoting the particular global public good?

To answer this 'accountability for what?' question, each of the case studies in this book identifies the general rationale for the global governance institution in question and summarises the various activities that the agency undertakes in pursuit of that raison d'être. This specification of mandate is important for the formulation of suitable accountability demands in respect of the organisation. A lack of clarity regarding the objectives and activities of different global governance bodies can lead people to formulate inappropriate calls for accountability and/or to direct them to the wrong places. In this vein, for example, civil society activists have often confused the IMF and the World Bank, which although related have distinct purposes and programmes.

That said, in some instances stakeholders may have understandable grounds to wish that a given global governance body would be tasked with a different mandate to the one that the institution formally holds. For example, some advocates might urge that bodies like the WTO should pursue more ambitious objectives in respect of ecological sustainability or social justice than those set out in their charters. In such cases the resulting demands of accountability will exceed those for which the regulators themselves may feel responsible.

### Accountability to whom?

Having established that global governance institutions need to practise accountability, and for something, a further issue arises about the audience for that accountability. Who are the constituents of global regulatory agencies? Who are the stakeholders who have a right to claim accountability from these bodies?

By the general definition of accountability adopted earlier, an actor ('A') is answerable to those whom it affects ('B'). In line with this 'affected principle', a global governance institution is accountable to those whose lives and life chances it influences. These people collectively form that agency's constituency: its public. As the political philosopher John Dewey expressed it, 'the public' comprises those persons who are affected by a given set of transactions to such an extent that the consequences need to be cared for (Dewey 1927: 15–16). Thus to determine who has a right to claim accountability of a given global regulatory body (or certain of its actions) one must in each case identify the relevant public.

The contours of this public may vary according to the institution. For example, the WFTO addresses a global public comprised mainly of the producers and consumers of fair trade goods. For its part, the OIC in the first place addresses a transplanetary community of Muslims, or *Ummah*. The Global Fund has as its key stakeholders donors and persons living with the three diseases that it combats. More diffusely, the UN claims in the Preamble to its Charter to serve 'we, the peoples', an umbrella that now encompasses more or less the whole of humanity.

Certainly, the question of constituency in global governance can become complicated, since different stakeholders may have divergent and competing interests in respect of a given regulatory arrangement. For example, in handling matters of Third World debt the G8 has affected creditor institutions, debtor governments, investors in global financial markets, and residents (including many destitute people) in poor countries. How does and/or should the G8 prioritise its accountabilities among these, to some extent rival, audiences? Similarly, how do CSER schemes related to climate change negotiate the various and sometimes contending claims for accountability held by company shareholders, employees, customers and persons who bear the brunt of global warming, both now and in future generations?

Thus accountability *to whom* is often a highly charged political matter in global governance, as elsewhere. Depending on which stakeholders are favoured, accountability practices in global governance can either perpetuate or alter existing configurations of power. In some cases, accountability arrangements in global governance may mainly serve constituents who are already strong, such as major governments and large corporations. Alternatively, a global regulatory body may practise transparency, consultation, evaluation and correction in ways that expand political space for marginalised groups such as slum dwellers and indigenous peoples. To put the matter in terms of deeper social structures, global governance accountability can, depending on its design and operation, either reinforce or counter established hierarchies of, for example, age groups, castes, countries, classes, cultures, (dis)abilities, genders, races and sexualities.

Hence there is nothing inherently democratising in accountability. On the contrary, certain kinds of transparency, consultation, evaluation and redress can actually widen social inequalities and entrench authoritarian rule. To make global governance more accountable is not in itself a sign of greater democracy. It all depends on which stakeholders are addressed by, and benefit from, accountability processes, and to what relative extents. To ensure that accountability in global governance has democratising consequences it is vital that all constituencies are identified, recognised and answered. To this end, global governance transparency would, for instance, need to be practised in ways that reach all stakeholders, including those who may be illiterate, face disability, speak minority languages or lack access to the Internet and libraries. Hence posting technical jargon in English on a website would not constitute effective transparency for many constituents. In addition, accountability processes that are more deeply democratic would need to give particular attention and priority to disadvantaged stakeholders who tend otherwise to remain marginalised. In this vein, for example, case studies in this book show how certain accountability exercises in global governance have enhanced voice for poor producers, women and citizens of weak states.

A further important consideration when identifying 'the public' in respect of global governance relates to time. The temporal frame for accountability arguably extends for whatever period given global governance actions have significant impacts. Depending on how one measures 'significance', that period could extend from seconds to centuries. Indeed, contemporary demands for reparations in respect of the harms of colonialism imply that accountability can apply over quite a long term. Likewise, some commentators maintain that today's policymakers are accountable to as-yet unborn future generations for the ecological consequences of current practices. The present discussion is not the place to elaborate on complex ethical issues of responsibility over time; it suffices here to stress that the constituency of a global governance institution has historical as well as social and political parameters.

### Accountability by what means?

In order to determine who is and is not being served by global governance accountability it is important to identify and assess the institutional mechanisms that a given agency uses in order to enact transparency, consultation, evaluation and redress. One of those channels of accountability – relations with civil society groups – is the subject of special attention in this book. However, before exploring this particular angle in greater detail, it is helpful to contextualise civil society engagement within the wider array of means that are available for making global regulatory institutions answer to stakeholders.

Regrettably, the review that follows suggests that global governance arrangements in general do not at present operate adequate accountability mechanisms, especially when measured against democratic criteria. To begin with, contemporary global regulatory institutions themselves incorporate very few formal procedures for direct accountability to affected persons. In addition, global governance accountability pursued indirectly through organs of the nation-state tends to be weak as well. Indirect accountability through local, regional and other global regulatory agencies is usually even thinner. Meanwhile informal accountability mechanisms for global governance – for example, as enacted through companies, mass media operations and civil society activities – do not come close to filling the gaps left by formal procedures.

### Direct mechanisms

To begin with direct links between the governors and the governed, the constitutions of global regulatory agencies lack the principal instruments of democratic accountability that operate in the modern state. No popular elections are held for global executives or global legislatures, so affected publics do not have this basic means of direct consultation and control. In a singular exception to this rule, ICANN conducted an online general election in 2000 for five 'at large' directors on its board; however, this unique experiment in putative global representative democracy proved highly problematic and has not been repeated since (Klein 2001). World federalists have proposed various designs of global parliaments (Falk and Strauss 2001; Monbiot 2003), but there is at present no particular prospect that such speculations will bear concrete results in the foreseeable future.

Similarly, global governance bodies generally lack their own judicial processes through which affected constituents might seek evaluation and correction of flawed policies. Such global courts as do exist (e.g. the International Court of Justice in The Hague, the International Court of Arbitration of the International Chamber of Commerce in Paris, and the International Criminal Court in Rome) examine cases related to states, firms and individuals; they do not adjudicate on conduct of global regulatory agencies. Nor is it possible for citizens to take a global intergovernmental institution to regional, national or local courts for alleged policy mistakes, since the agency and its personnel generally enjoy immunity from prosecution in respect of the official mandate of the organisation. Meanwhile transgovernmental networks like the G8 do not even have legal personality and so cannot be a named party in court.

In a quasi-judicial construction several global governance institutions have recently established permanent external review bodies that invite testimony from affected stakeholders as part of their assessment exercises. In this vein the World Bank has operated an Inspection Panel since

1994, and the IMF has had an Independent Evaluation Office since 2001. Yet these units are small and can at most conduct two or three enquiries per year, each involving only a handful of public inputs. Moreover, the recommendations that result from these occasional investigations are not binding. Other global governance agencies lack even this modest scale of regularised formal assessment of their policies. At best, bodies like the Commonwealth, the Global Fund, the OECD and the UN commission an occasional ad hoc external review of certain of their activities.

In sum, then, the contemporary growth in influence of global governance processes has not been accompanied by a corresponding development of formal accountability mechanisms which link these agencies directly to the publics they affect. The principal emphasis in official accountability procedures for planet-spanning governance remains with indirect processes, where connections between the global agency and impacted circles are forged through the mediation of third parties such as national governments, the mass media and civil society organisations.

### Indirect mechanisms: the state

Today, as in the past, nation-states are generally expected to be the main intermediaries between global governance institutions and citizens. Indeed, state oversight is built into the heart of the constitutions of many global governance bodies. Global intergovernmental institutions normally have an overseeing organ composed of high-ranking delegates of member states. Examples include the General Assembly of the United Nations, the Board of Governors of the IMF and the World Bank, the WTO Ministerial Conference, the Commonwealth Heads of Government Meeting (CHOGM), the Islamic Conference of Foreign Ministers of the OIC, and the OECD Council. Likewise, certain informal global governance instruments such as the Asia-Europe Meeting and the G8 convene periodic summits of state leaders that confirm principal policy initiatives. Some global regulatory agencies also have organs for day-to-day oversight of their operations by representatives of national governments. In this vein the United Nations has its three Councils (Economic and Social, Human Rights, and Security), while the Bretton Woods institutions have their respective Executive Boards. All of this on-site involvement by high-level national ministers and officials keeps global governance agencies of the intergovernmental and transgovernmental kind closely in touch with the views and priorities of their member states.

However, a state-based approach to global governance accountability also has several significant limitations. For example, some global regulatory arrangements like the G8, the OECD and the Bank for International Settlements (BIS) have substantial impacts on countries whose governments are not members. Although some of these excluded states might be informally consulted from time to time, they have no official seats in the institutions concerned, from which they can speak for their populations. Meanwhile, state monitoring is not integrated at all into the procedures of private global governance instruments like CSER and the WFTO. State involvement is also marginal in the daily operations of hybrid arrangements like the Global Fund and ICANN.

Even where states are members which have delegates integrated into the institutional operations of a global governance agency, those representatives may, especially in the case of weaker states, exercise little effective voice. For instance, how effectively can the government of Bangladesh make WTO arrangements genuinely accountable to the population of that country? How far can the fragile state apparatus in Sierra Leone provide an adequate check and balance on behalf of the national population vis-à-vis the comparatively formidable World Bank?

To be sure, member states working collectively can today still counter the influence of even the strongest global governance institution; yet it is questionable whether the voices of weaker governments obtain much volume in the overall chorus. A handful of states currently dominate most intergovernmental and transgovernmental arrangements, for example, with permanent membership in the UN Security Council and the largest shareholdings in the Bretton Woods institutions. The same elite of states often also figures strongly behind the scenes in private and hybrid regulatory mechanisms (e.g. the US Department of Commerce in relation to ICANN). In contrast, the scores of other states whose jurisdictions together encompass the large majority of humanity may participate in little more than name. Collective actions by the Group of 77 at the UN, the Group of 24 at the IMF and the World Bank, and the Group of 90 at the WTO have on the whole accomplished little in altering hierarchies of state influence in those institutions.

Yet in any case accountability to states, whether they be powerful or weak, does not necessarily translate into accountability to (all) affected people. To be successful mediating agents of global governance accountability, states must in turn answer to those for whom they purport to speak. However, it is not clear that, for instance, government ministers at an OIC conference or technocrats in the World Bank Executive Board are particularly attuned to the needs and opinions of various non-state stakeholders in their home countries. On the whole, only extended and weak chains of accountability link state delegates in a global governance arena to the wider publics that those officials notionally represent.

In principle, tighter democratic accountability of global governance institutions through states could be forged with rigorous oversight by national parliaments. After all, parliamentarians have direct links to well-defined popular constituencies, and electoral exigencies compel these legislators to be responsive to their voters. Yet in practice national parliamentary scrutiny of a state's actions in global regulatory arenas has been patchy at best. Indeed, outside North America and Western Europe such oversight has to date barely transpired at all. Global governance issues rarely figure with prominence in national legislative elections anywhere in the world, North or South, and citizens hardly ever take concerns about global governance to their national legislators. National parliaments hold few hearings, let alone full-scale enquiries, into global governance matters. Parliamentary outreach by global regulatory agencies has generally not gone beyond preparing an occasional seminar for legislators. Even more rarely has the director of a global governance body given evidence before a national parliamentary committee.

Developments have been only marginally more promising in respect of actions on global governance taken by international groupings of national legislators. The Inter-Parliamentary Union (in existence since 1889) and the Commonwealth Parliamentary Association (created in 1911) have performed no noteworthy scrutiny of global governance institutions. A somewhat stronger record has come from Parliamentarians for Global Action, a grouping of over 1,300 members from 110 national legislatures that has addressed various United Nations activities since the late 1970s. A Parliamentary Network on the World Bank (PNoWB) has operated since 2000 with an explicit aim to enhance the accountability of that institution. However, efforts since 2003 to create a similar Parliamentary Conference on the WTO have made less progress, and initiatives of this kind have not arisen at all in respect of other global governance bodies.

Given these and other disappointments, many citizens today have limited faith that their national government (either the executive or the legislative branch) can deliver adequate democratic accountability of any kind, whether in respect of global governance or more generally. High, and in many cases rising, levels of voter absenteeism are one obvious indicator of this scepticism. Indeed, rather than turn to the state to make global governance more accountable, some citizens today conversely look to global regulatory mechanisms to make their state more accountable. Using this so-called 'boomerang' tactic (Keck and Sikkink 1998), a number of human rights campaigners have sought to counter the democratic failings of their state through UN bodies. Likewise, civil society groups in some countries have used the Bretton Woods institutions to press for greater fiscal accountability in their national governments.

Still another way that states are, by themselves, inadequate as agents of global governance accountability relates to insufficient representation of political identities. The modern state generally addresses 'the demos' in terms of a national community whose homeland corresponds to the terrain of the state's jurisdiction. However, people in contemporary global affairs hold more complex political identities than their national citizenship alone. For example, many diasporas, faith groups, indigenous communities, peasant circles, sexual minorities and women's movements do not feel that the government of the country in which they reside 'represents' them sufficiently. Likewise, disabled persons could justifiably complain that states took until 2006 to pass a convention through the UN regarding their specific rights. Various non-national publics therefore seek alternative mechanisms in addition to, or even instead of, the state in order to obtain fuller accountability from global governance institutions.

In sum, then, while states singly and together can be an important force for accountable global governance, they have proved to be far from sufficient on their own. Many states obtain limited voice in global regulatory organisations or are excluded from membership altogether. Weak states can be in highly dependent relationships to some global governance agencies. National parliaments, both individually and collectively, have comprehensively neglected their potentials for advancing accountable global governance. Many states themselves have poor democratic credentials vis-à-vis all or part of their resident populations, including significant circles of people who do not turn solely or even substantially to the state to advance their political destiny. Accountable global governance therefore needs more than oversight by national governments.

### Other indirect mechanisms

If global governance agencies provide barely any direct accountability to affected persons, and if states provide only limited indirect accountability, what other indirect mechanisms could be available to address the remaining substantial democratic deficits? Some of the potential additional channels are official, namely through governance agencies constructed on other than national scales (local governments, regional institutions and other global regulatory bodies). Further possible channels of indirect accountability are unofficial, including corporate, media and civil society activities.

Given that local and regional institutions operate in contemporary governance with some relative autonomy from national governments, these substate and suprastate agencies could in principle extract some supplementary accountability from global regulatory bodies. Indeed, certain global governance instruments like UCLG and ASEM are themselves built around, and direct their accountability in the first place to, local and regional bodies rather than nation-states. Overall, however, translocal and interregional organisations have so far occupied only a tangential place in global governance.

Nor have local authorities made significant arrangements to monitor global intergovernmental and transgovernmental agencies, in the way that municipal and provincial bodies maintain a substantial presence in Brussels to engage the European Union. A few associations of local authorities hold consultative status at the UN, but they play only the most marginal of roles in that institution. Substate agencies are absent altogether in most other global regulatory agencies. Thus while local government may be the scale of governance that generally operates with closest proximity to the everyday lives of most people, at present municipal and provincial authorities generally do little to connect their constituents to global regimes.

As for suprastate regional governance institutions, at present only the EU has the potential to extract much accountability from global regulatory bodies. This significance is particularly striking in the WTO, where the EU rather than any of its member states is the principal player. The future may also see an EU seat replace those of the relevant member states on the overseeing boards of the Bretton Woods institutions. For its part the EU Parliament (directly elected since 1979 and now numbering 785 deputies) has given some, albeit irregular, attention to global governance matters, particularly in respect of trade; however, this scrutiny has not on the whole had major accountability effects.

Among regional institutions the EU is an exception in pursuing even limited global governance accountability. Other bodies, such as the African Union (AU), ASEAN and MERCOSUR, have to date barely made an appearance in global regulatory arenas. They have therefore done nothing of note to advance transparency, consultation, evaluation and redress in global governance agencies. Likewise other regional parliaments, such as the Consultative Assembly of the Arab Maghreb Union (launched in 1989) and the Latin American Parliament (operating since 1987), have generally done even less than national legislatures when it comes to monitoring global regulatory institutions.

Another possible channel of accountability vis-à-vis global governance institutions is among the planet-spanning agencies themselves; yet these relationships, too, have contributed little to date. The United Nations has at times aspired to the status of *primus inter pares* among planet-spanning regulatory institutions, where for example all global economic institutions would report to the UN Economic and Social Council (ECOSOC). However, in practice this wider oversight by the UN is weak. Indeed, many recently created global governance arrangements (especially those of a transgovernmental and private character) ignore the UN altogether. Meanwhile, in the reverse direction other global agencies accomplish little by way of holding the UN itself to account.

Some degree of informal peer review does operate among global economic institutions. In this vein management and staff of agencies such as the BIS, G8, IMF, OECD, UN, World Bank and WTO critically monitor one another's work through regular contacts. However, this mutual surveillance has a mainly technocratic character, centred on the niceties of macroeconomics. It also operates within a narrow and fairly closed circle of global managerial elites. Such processes of professional peer review incorporate few inputs from the experiences and preferences of wider publics and hence do little to strengthen democratic accountability.

Turning to unofficial channels, global governance accountability can be indirectly pursued through corporations, whether as individual firms or as business associations like the International Organisation of Employers (IOE) and the World Economic Forum (WEF). Corporate lobbies have developed significant relationships with most global regulatory agencies, especially those institutions that work in the fields of finance and trade. Indeed, many private global governance mechanisms – for example the IASB, the International Capital Market Association (ICMA) and the large gamut of CSER schemes – are borne of business initiatives. In addition, corporate philanthropy has become a significant source of financing for much of the UN system as well as for a number of public-private hybrid instruments such as the Global Fund. In these different ways business-based pressures for accountable global governance can come with considerable clout.

Yet, as and when corporate actors do seek to make global governance institutions more accountable, the crucial issues remain to what end and for whose benefit that accountability operates. The capitalist enterprises that dominate contemporary production normally focus on a 'bottom line' of financial profitability and a corresponding principal concern to advance shareholder interests. Those priorities do not necessarily further public interests of efficiency and/or democracy; indeed, they can sometimes lead companies to undermine these interests, for example with cartel behaviour and the exercise of undue influence over political parties. Drives to maximise financial returns may also sit uneasily with other qualities of a good society such as cultural creativity, distributive justice, ecological integrity and peace. Increased accountability to the corporate sector could therefore in some ways actually contradict urgent contemporary needs for more effective and legitimate global governance.

Recognising these tensions, some business circles have in recent times adopted notions of 'corporate social and environmental responsibility' that aim to broaden the accountability concerns of companies beyond shareholder returns alone. However, this promotion of a 'triple bottom line' (financial, social and ecological) has chiefly emanated from larger firms in the Anglophone North. CSER remains a relatively minor trend in overall business circles worldwide. Even companies that have embraced the principle have thus far often done so more in rhetoric than in concrete action. Indeed, sceptics worry that CSER is a minimalist exercise whose main aim is to pre-empt a more constraining public sector regulation of business, including through new planet-spanning bodies like a Global Competition Office, a Global Environmental Organisation and a Global Tax Authority. In any case, even where promoters of CSER work with the general interest at heart, global governance accountability pursued through companies can at best supplement public mechanisms. No amount of CSER can adequately reconcile the inherent tensions in privately owned capitalist enterprise between shareholder concerns and the overall public good.

This general conclusion also holds with respect to the specific mass media sector of corporate business. Certainly print, broadcast and Internet communications can in principle do much to advance democratically accountable governance, including in regard to global regulatory institutions. For one thing, the mass media can provide important channels to enhance the public transparency of global governance agencies. After all, newspapers, radio, television and websites constitute the main sources of day-to-day political information for most citizens in contemporary society. In addition, mass media reporting of public views regarding a given global governance policy or programme can constitute a sort of indirect stakeholder consultation. Likewise, investigative journalism can serve as an important informal evaluation mechanism in respect of global governance. The mass media can also provide powerful channels through which adversely impacted publics can demand redress from global regulatory bodies. Sympathetic media coverage is now pretty well indispensable to the satisfaction of political grievances. Given this substantial influence of mass communications in contemporary politics, most major global governance agencies have in recent decades devoted considerable attention to media relations, for example by hiring relevant experts onto their secretariats and by instituting media training for their professional staff.

Yet in practice the mass media have not extracted nearly as much accountability from global governance agencies as might be attained. For one thing the main print, broadcast and Internet outlets have provided at best incidental coverage of global regulatory institutions. Moreover, many journalists are poorly educated on global governance, so that their accounts of these matters are steeped in superficiality and inaccuracy. If affected publics are largely unaware even of the existence of many global governance arrangements, let alone the modus operandi and policies of those organisations, this ignorance is in good part due to the failure of mainstream mass media to report this information. In most cases the high-circulation outlets tend, particularly with commercial interests in view, to present only those relatively few global governance stories that involve scandal or compelling visual footage. Indeed, the capitalist media conglomerates that dominate contemporary global mass communications arguably have little interest in cultivating large-scale critical public awareness of the prevailing regimes that sustain their power. Alternative non-profit outlets such as Indy Media and openDemocracy provide possibilities to pursue deeper accountability in global governance, but their operations and audiences are small. On the whole, therefore, the mass media do little to fill accountability gaps vis-à-vis planet-spanning regulation.

Mass media, corporate business and broad networks of governance agencies: both singly and collectively, the various direct and indirect means reviewed above for extracting accountability from global governance arrangements are highly unsatisfactory. The problem is both quantitative and qualitative. Regarding quantity, these diverse channels generate inadequate amounts of transparency, consultation, evaluation and redress from global regulatory bodies. Regarding quality, these channels generally bias the limited accountability that is obtained towards the advantaged and the powerful, in terms of social strata as well as geographical areas of the world.

### Civil society

What then of civil society, the particular concern of this book? In what ways and to what extents do civil society associations provide channels of accountability in respect of global governance institutions? How far do these citizen action groups make planet-spanning regulatory bodies answer for their conduct to affected people? In particular, can civil society activities bring the required: (a) quantitatively, major increases in overall levels of global governance accountability; and (b) qualitatively, substantial redistributions of global governance accountabilities towards less privileged countries and social circles? The next thirteen chapters explore these questions in relation to a range of global regulatory institutions.

As a preliminary step, however, the present conceptual framing chapter examines the general notion of civil society as it relates to global governance. To that end the discussion below first sets out contrasting definitions of civil society and elaborates on the approach adopted in this book. The discussion then reviews the highly diverse manifestations of civil society that exist in relation to global governance. Further remarks consider the sometimes limited 'civility' of civil society and the consequent need for thorough accountability of civil society associations as well as global governance agencies.

### General conceptions of civil society

Like 'global governance' and 'accountability', 'civil society' has multiple and deeply contested definitions. These conceptions have also varied widely over time since the Latin term *societas civilis* first appeared more than two millennia ago. Aristotle, Locke, Ferguson, Hegel, Gramsci and other political philosophers have meant very different things by the concept (Cohen and Arato 1992). Different generations and different theories have appropriated the phrase 'civil society' in diverse ways in accordance with different contexts and different political struggles.

Today as well, notions of civil society arguably require some reinvention in order that they generate maximal insight and maximal democratic gains in respect of emergent conditions of polycentric governance. Modern political theory has generally conceptualised civil society in relation to the state. However, as seen earlier, contemporary governance extends beyond nation-states. In this light it makes sense to think of civil society in relation to a governance apparatus more generically, rather than in connection with the state per se. At an earlier historical juncture, when the mode of governance was statist, civil society engaged the state alone. However, at the present time, when the mode of governance is shifting towards polycentrism, civil society engages complex regulatory networks that involve multiple types of actors, including global governance agencies. Civil society today also relates to transplanetary regulatory institutions directly and in their own right, and not merely as adjuncts of states.

But what, more precisely, is 'civil society'? Four main contemporary usages of the term might be distinguished. First, for some analysts civil society refers to a general quality of a given human collectivity. From this perspective a 'civil' society is one where people relate with each other on a basis of openness, tolerance, respect, trust and non-violence (Keane 2003). A second type of definition identifies civil society as a political space, an arena where citizens congregate to deliberate on the actual and prospective circumstances of their collective life. This conception overlaps considerably with notions of 'the public sphere' (Habermas 1962; Fraser

2007) and 'deliberative democracy' (Gutmann and Thompson 2004; Bohman 2007). A third general approach treats civil society as the sum total of associational life within a given human collectivity (Tocqueville 1835). In this case civil society encompasses every non-official and non-profit organisation outside the family, including bodies like recreational clubs that lack an overtly political character. This third perspective is also broadly reflected in notions of 'social capital' (Putnam 2000). A fourth formulation, invoked widely in policy circles today, sees civil society as the aggregate of so-called non-governmental organisations (NGOs). On these lines civil society involves a 'third sector' (alongside governance agencies and market actors) of formally organised, legally registered and professionally staffed non-profit bodies that undertake advocacy and/or service delivery activities in respect of some public policy issue (Salamon *et al.* 1999).

Needless to say, assessments of the extent and consequences of civil society activities in regard to global governance accountability will vary depending on which of these four conceptions one adopts. Analyses based on notions of 'civil' society, or the public sphere, or social capital, or NGOs will generate very different results. The choice of definition therefore cannot be taken lightly and requires careful justification both intellectually and politically.

The present book draws primarily on the second type of conception distinguished above, while giving it some of the emphasis on associational life found in the third and fourth approaches. Civil society is taken here to entail *a political space where associations of citizens seek, from outside political parties, to shape societal rules.* As understood in the analyses that follow, then, civil society activities are an enactment of *citizenship*, that is, they are practices through which people claim rights and fulfil obligations as members of a given polity. These initiatives are also *collective*, that is, they involve citizens assembling in groups that share concerns about, and mobilise around, a particular problem of public affairs. In engaging that problem civil society associations are especially interested to affect the *rules* (i.e. norms, standards, principles, laws and policies) that govern the issue at hand. As self-consciously *political* actions, civil society operations are steeped in struggles to impact the ways that power in society is acquired, distributed and exercised. However, civil society efforts to shape governance do not – in the way of political parties – aim to attain or retain public office.

This conception of civil society seems more helpful, both theoretically and practically, than other available alternatives when it comes to assessing the effectiveness and legitimacy of contemporary global governance. The first notion identified above, that of civil society as a quality of civility in society, is a broad descriptor that adds little analytical value in respect of contemporary global social relations. With this approach the concept merely confirms the obvious, namely that openness, tolerance, respect, trust and non-violence are today often lacking in transplanetary social spaces.

The third conception has, significantly, helped Alexis de Tocqueville and others to see that the collective life of human beings involves more than states and markets. This principle applies as well to global spheres, where many relationships (e.g. among a diaspora or sufferers of a common disease) are not reducible to governmental and commercial logics. However, beyond this important general insight the concept of civil society as the totality of associational life is too diffuse to offer much guidance in research and policy (Chandhoke 2003). From this perspective everything from sports tournaments and travel clubs to environmental campaigns and human rights advocacy falls under one roof. More exact parameters are wanted so as to obtain a more precise assessment of the activities and impacts of civil society.

Going too far in the other direction, the fourth conception – that of civil society as the sum total of NGOs – is overly restrictive. This definition tends to exclude collective actions, such as found in social movements, which are not formally institutionalised, legally certified and professionally administered. Yet much citizen engagement of governance occurs outside an NGO framework, particularly when it involves non-Western political cultures and/or more subversive resistance. Global governance institutions generally favour a concept of civil society as NGOs inasmuch as bureaucracies generally find it more convenient to deal with other bureaucracies. Moreover, NGOs often (though not always) present fewer challenges to deeper social and political structures than other less bureaucratic forms of civil society organisation (Fisher 1997). It is important that research and policy consider the full range of possible citizen initiatives in respect of global governance and that the starting definition of civil society does not, in advance, exclude substantial areas of potentially significant activities.

Indeed, various commentators have come to interrogate the very term 'civil society' as being politically suspect. In a Gramscian vein, some sceptics worry that hegemonic power has promoted 'civil society' (particularly in the sense of an aggregation of depoliticised NGOs) as a way to discipline dissent and promote a false legitimacy for an oppressive capitalist order. In a post-colonialist vein, radical critics also worry that 'civil society' is so steeped in Western theory and practice that, in an imperialist project, it invariably marginalises and silences other political cultures (Germain and Kenny 2005).

While recognising these dangers, the present book is not as ready to dispense with a concept that has, in many contexts over a number of centuries, deepened analytical insight and advanced democratic practice. Certainly, ideas of 'civil society' must be employed carefully and critically so that the activities in question are not captured for hegemonic and imperialist ends – and thereby detract from democratic accountability. However, with vigilance against such co-optation and a determined focus on democratic purpose, it would seem that the particular definition of civil society invoked here can in fact be politically opportune, helping various subordinated circles in today's more global society to gain recognition, voice, resources and influence.

### Manifestations of civil society

If civil society is understood to be a political space where citizen groups seek, from outside political parties, to shape societal rules, what kinds of activities fall within this arena? In particular, what sorts of civil society initiatives might seek to extract greater accountability from global governance agencies? Who in civil society pursues transparency, consultation, evaluation and correction in respect of global regulatory arrangements like the WTO, ASEM, the climate change regime and ICANN?

The answers to these questions all involve diversity. Civil society actions in respect of global governance vary enormously in size (small to large), duration (ephemeral to long term), geographical scope (local to global), cultural context (diverse modernities to non-modernities), resource levels (destitute to affluent), constituencies (broad general interests to narrow special interests), ideologies (conformist to transformist), strategies (cautious to reckless) and tactics (collaboration to confrontation). With such huge variations it is difficult to draw specific overall conclusions about civil society impacts on global governance accountability.

In terms of issues of concern, the wide spectrum of civil society associations involved in global affairs includes animal rights activists, anti-poverty movements, business forums, caste solidarity groups, clan and kinship mobilisations, consumer advocates, democracy promoters, development co-operation initiatives, disabled persons alliances, environmental campaigns, ethnic lobbies, faith-based associations, human rights advocates, labour unions, local community groups, peace drives, peasant movements, philanthropic foundations, professional bodies, relief organisations, research institutes, sexual minorities associations, women's networks, and youth groups. As this list again emphasises, civil society in the conception adopted here takes multiple cultural forms and extends beyond NGOs to other types of actors.

Regarding cultural diversity, the content and style of civil society engagement of global governance varies greatly between, for example, the actions of pygmy groups in respect of World Bank support of the Chad-Cameroon oil pipeline, and Japan-based peace associations advocating a ban on landmines. Religious and secular organisations often co-exist uneasily in civil society relations with the UN. Asia-based and Europe-based civil society initiatives bring diverse political cultures to the table at ASEM congregations. Anglophone civil society relating to the Commonwealth is one thing, while Muslim civil society relating to the OIC is quite another. Amazonian groups invoke a discourse of 'florestania' in preference to that of 'citizenship' to convey their alternative, more ecologically centred, understanding of rights and obligations within a polity (GTA 2005). In short, while notions of civil society were until the late twentieth century long rooted in Western political theory and action, contemporary understandings and practices of civil society are most emphatically multicultural (Hann and Dunn 1996).

Regarding the types of actors involved, the inclusion of business forums in civil society is controversial for some and is indeed rejected by several contributors to the present book. Usually this exclusion rests on the argument that the business sector aims to advance self-interests of profit maximisation, whereas civil society should promote general public interests on a non-profit basis. However, a distinction can arguably be drawn between, on the one hand, business forums as civil society associations and, on the other, individual companies as market players. As civil society actors, chambers of commerce, employer federations, and issue-based corporate initiatives like the World Business Council for Sustainable Development (WBCSD) are often concerned with more than immediate financial returns for their members. Thus, for example, the Bretton Woods Committee, which assembles 700 members mainly from large corporations, has lent its weight to campaigns for poor-country debt relief (Orr 2002). Meanwhile other business associations that seek to shape societal rules are quite detached from big capital, including alternatively minded groups that promote creative commons licences, fair trade schemes, micro-credits, open source computer programming, and collective action by street vendors. Indeed, other civil society groups such as ethnic lobbies and labour unions can focus on narrow sectoral interests no less than some industry associations. Moreover, many advocacy groups like Amnesty International and Oxfam obtain substantial income from retail sales. Given such considerations the exclusion of business forums from civil society lacks logical consistency. The move is also politically dubious. The heavy weight of big business in contemporary advocacy operations may pose a major challenge to democratic global governance, but this problem is not satisfactorily addressed by wishing business-based citizen associations out of the definition of civil society.

Likewise, analysts disagree on whether political parties should, as in this book, be excluded from the scope of civil society. After all, as members of political parties citizens also openly seek to shape the rules that govern various aspects of social life. However, the position adopted here maintains that an important qualitative difference exists between activities which have as their aim the attainment of public office and those which keep greater institutional distance. Of course every dividing line blurs in practice, for example as individuals move between positions in civil society and officialdom. Meanwhile some environmental organisations and trade unions have tight connections with green parties and labour parties, respectively. In addition, fringe political parties may have as little expectation of leading a governance administration as student movements and human rights associations. Nevertheless, the general distinction between political parties and civil society associations identifies a significant difference in emphasis between the logics of plebiscites and representative democracy on the one hand and the logics of deliberation and participatory democracy on the other. Electoral-legislative strategies and civil society operations involve very different (albeit potentially complementary) ways of exacting accountability from governance authorities.

### The civility of civil society

While the notion of civil society as developed above usefully highlights a distinctive and significant dimension of political life, the terminology unfortunately carries some potentially misleading normative connotations. In particular, the adjective 'civil' can understandably be read to imply that the actors and activities in question have intrinsically positive consequences for effective and legitimate governance. The term can suggest that 'civil society' is inherently a good thing, promoting openness, respect, tolerance, trust and peace.

Indeed, many civil society initiatives do have positive qualities of this kind. Peace movements have often furthered arms control, non-violent conflict resolution and intercultural understanding. Human rights advocates have countered arbitrary detention and torture, as well as advanced the dignity of disabled persons, indigenous populations, outcastes, people of colour, sexual minorities and women. Citizen campaigns for animal rights and ecological integrity have on various occasions raised moral standards in human treatment of the rest of nature. Trade unions have in many contexts promoted decent working conditions. Consumer activists have also 'civilised' market relations after the production phase. Development solidarity groups, religious as well as secular, have frequently put issues of global distributive justice on the political agenda. All of this is to the good.

However, civil society is not inherently civil. The kinds of beneficial outcomes just described do not flow automatically from collective citizen action outside political parties. On the contrary, these positive impacts result from, and require, deliberate choices and concerted efforts. In other cases civil society initiatives can have negative consequences. These 'uncivil' potentials are most blatant in activities with criminal, fundamentalist, militarist, racist and terrorist qualities. After all, Al-Qaeda, Aum Shinrikyo, Gush Emunim, the Interahamwe, the Ku Klux Klan and global paedophile networks are also 'associations of citizens that seek, from outside political parties, to shape societal rules'. Many other civil society organisations also operate through arrogance, fraud, greed, hatred, narcissism and violence. In such cases of harm rather than good, 'civil society' can seem something of a misnomer (Ahrne 1998; Chambers and Kopstein 2001; Kopecky and Mudde 2002; Kaldor and Muro 2003).

Civil society associations can also exhibit more subtle democratic failings. For example, many of these organisations are insufficiently transparent regarding their aims, structure, procedures, personnel and funding. In addition, the group culture of some civil society initiatives may inhibit open and critical internal debate. Some citizen action organisations are captive of a particular business enterprise, family network, governance institution, political party or philanthropist. In many cases a given civil society body can be difficult to access, even for people whose interests the association claims to promote. Often civil society organisations fail to undertake searching evaluations of their own conduct and offer few if any mechanisms for redress when they err and cause harm.

Given these potential flaws, it is vital that civil society groups diligently pursue their own accountabilities as part of their strivings to improve the accountabilities of other actors. The question of civil society and accountable global governance is therefore partly a question of the accountability of the civil society associations themselves. Some citizen action groups engaging in global affairs have developed laudable good practices in this regard. The International Non-Governmental Organisations Accountability Charter launched in 2006 offers one possible way forward (INGO 2007). However, much further work is needed to enhance transparency, consultation, evaluation and correction in the operations of civil society organisations as they engage globally

(Edwards 2000; Bendell 2006; Jordan and Van Tuijll 2006; Ronalds 2010).

In sum, then, this book takes no *a priori* position on the desirability or otherwise of civil society involvement in global governance. The starting point is that global governance suffers major shortfalls in accountability and that civil society could, in principle, help to close these gaps. However, the actual nature of civil society influences on global governance accountability, positive and/or negative, cannot be established in advance. These assessments require detailed empirical investigations of the sort that are undertaken in the case studies that follow.

## Conclusion

If nothing else, this opening chapter has demonstrated that the relationship between civil society and accountability in global governance is anything but straightforward. Each of the three pivotal concepts – 'global governance', 'accountability' and 'civil society' – is subject to multiple and deeply contested interpretations. As emphasised at the outset, the purpose of this chapter has not been to resolve these theoretical and political disputes, but to outline a broad framework of analysis that lends internal coherence to the present collective research endeavour.

This framework is anything but apolitical. The study is unabashedly motivated by deep concern to promote democratic accountability as a cornerstone for effective and legitimate global governance. This chapter has therefore placed explicit emphasis throughout on identifying power relations and ways to democratise them. At the same time the conceptual framework guiding the book is not ideological, in the sense of imposing a particular vision for the future of global governance and the place of civil society within it. Individual authors and readers can and should draw their own conclusions in that regard.

The ensuing more empirical chapters now proceed to assess civil society impacts on the accountabilities of a range of specific global governance institutions. To this end each of the case studies sets out:

(a) the mandate and activities of the global regulatory apparatus concerned, thereby establishing for what that institution is accountable;
(b) the accountability challenges that the global governance arrangement in question faces, including in particular the shortfalls that remain after considering channels other than civil society (such as governments, parliaments and mass media);
(c) the range of civil society engagements of the global governance institution under discussion, including diverse issue foci, organisational forms and ideological positions;

(d) the accountability effects on the global regulatory agency of that civil society involvement, in other words how the citizen group interventions have and have not advanced transparency, consultation, evaluation and redress in respect of the global regulatory agency concerned – and in particular how well civil society involvements have supplemented other accountability mechanisms and filled the gaps left by those other channels;

(e) the main circumstances that have helped or hindered civil society contributions to democratically accountable global governance in the case at hand.

The concluding chapter then synthesises these findings and reflects on their implications for future practices of civil society and accountable global governance.

# 2 Civil society and accountability of the United Nations

*Kerstin Martens*

## Introduction

Established in 1945, the United Nations Organisation (UN) is the world's largest global governance institution. It encompasses almost universal state membership and addresses a full spectrum of issue areas. As of 2009 the UN Secretariat had 40,000 staff stationed around the world (UN 2009a). Another 120,000 persons from 116 countries were serving in 15 UN peacekeeping operations (UN 2010: 3). The regular budget of the core UN bodies (i.e. excluding related agencies and peacekeeping operations) came to US$5.2 billion in 2010, a figure that far exceeds that for any other global governance organisation examined in this book (UN 2009b).

Core organs of the UN include the General Assembly (GA), the Security Council (SC), the Economic and Social Council (ECOSOC), the Trusteeship Council, the International Court of Justice (ICJ) and the Secretariat. The wider UN system also comprises fifteen specialised agencies and a host of other related bodies. Civil society contributions to UN accountability often involve interrelations between the central bodies and the specialised agencies. However, for reasons of space and manageability, the present chapter focuses its attention on the core organs of the UN, rather than covering the full spectrum of related institutions. Other book-length works have considered civil society involvement in the wider UN system, albeit without a focus on accountability issues (e.g. Gordenker and Weiss 1996; Willetts 1996; Foster and Anand 1999; Joachim 2007; McKeon 2009).

The following discussion explores how engagement of civil society organisations (CSOs) has (and has not) furthered the accountability of the UN. Considering the conceptual framework laid out in Chapter 1,

For comments on earlier versions of this chapter I thank Nora McKeon, Jens Martens, Renate Bloem, Tatsuro Kunugi and other participants in the project workshop in Gothenburg. For assistance in preparing the manuscript, I thank Celia Enders, Jan Kellerhoff, Till Ludwig and Gesa Schulze.

it is argued that CSOs can make the UN more *transparent*, because they strengthen public awareness of UN processes and policies. In addition, CSOs can make the UN more *consultative*, since they often contribute to policy formulation. CSOs can also *evaluate* the implementation of UN policies, as they monitor and assess the execution of agreed measures and make stakeholders aware of non-compliance. By criticising unsuccessful policies and programmes, CSOs may in addition help to *correct* the UN when its activities go awry and cause harm.

Overall the chapter suggests that, although many CSO activities have made the UN more answerable for its conduct, one must not overestimate the influence of CSOs within the UN apparatus or assume that they provide a total answer to the many problems of UN accountability. True, UN-CSO relations have intensified since the mid-1990s, when the UN opened up significantly for more interaction with civil society. Yet the increase in formal options for UN-civil society relations has not always raised UN accountability, particularly to non-professional and poorly resourced groups. Moreover, in the final analysis it is the UN which still decides whether, when, how and to what extent it interacts with CSOs.

To elaborate this argument the chapter first reviews the UN's role in global governance. It is noted here that the UN has an especially broad membership base and also spans a particularly broad range of policy fields. It is the most universal global governance apparatus at present and in this sense is accountable to the whole world. The second section reviews UN interactions with civil society, including relevant formal constitutional provisions and liaison operations. It is especially noted that, more than other global governance agencies, the UN has set up an elaborate accreditation system for CSOs. The third section of the chapter then more specifically assesses civil society activities to enhance UN accountability. It provides examples – and also shows limits – of CSO contributions to UN policy processes. The fourth part examines the resources that CSOs invest in their interactions with the UN. It is shown here that representation of CSOs at the UN has become increasingly professionalised over the years, but is only affordable for a small number of associations, a situation that raises problematic questions of accountability *to and for whom.*

## The UN in the orchestra of global governance

As successor to the defunct League of Nations, the UN was founded at the close of the Second World War with the hope of creating a more encompassing intergovernmental organisation that would prevent armed violence as a means of international politics. Over the following decades, the UN agenda broadened to include many policy fields in addition to the prevention of war. Today, this multifunctional global forum considers a full range of issues including culture, environment, economic development, human rights and nuclear power as well as military security. Thus, unlike most other global governance agencies, the UN might be held accountable in respect of a full spectrum of policy issues.

As well as witnessing an expanding agenda, the UN has experienced a widening membership. From the original 51 signatories of the Charter, the UN has grown to the present 192 member states. By that measure it is the largest intergovernmental organisation in the world. In addition, the UN recognises permanent observers including, for example, the International Federation of Red Cross and Red Crescent Societies, the Sovereign Military Order of Malta, the Holy See, and Palestine. Thus, rather uniquely among global governance bodies, the UN can be accountable to a full panoply of states, particularly through the General Assembly. The UN can therefore be described as an intergovernmental organisation with universal membership and comprehensive competence (Rittberger and Zangl 2006: 11).

That said, through the Security Council – perhaps the institution's most significant organ – UN accountability is focused on a much smaller group of fifteen states. Of these, five (China, France, Russia, the UK and the USA) hold permanent seats and have the so-called rule of 'great power unanimity', which boils down to a right of veto. The General Assembly elects another ten states to the Security Council for two-year terms. Reflecting the realities of 1945, this arrangement poorly represents today's global circumstances, particularly inasmuch as major states such as Brazil, India, Japan and South Africa lack a permanent presence on the Security Council. Progress on Security Council reform has been very slow (Idris and Bartolo 2000; Müller 2006).

The UN suffers from other accountability problems, too. It does not have a popularly elected parliament, but rather a General Assembly run by diplomats who are generally very detached from the ordinary citizens of their state. In the Security Council, fifteen states make decisions that affect the whole world. For these reasons and more, states alone cannot provide sufficient democratic accountability for the UN.

The question then arises whether interaction with civil society could be a way of overcoming the democratic deficits of the UN. Today, civil society associations have manifold ways of accessing the institution. CSOs assist UN bodies, provide them with information on issues of concern, advise UN commissions and committees, and collaborate with UN operational bodies, including on the implementation of joint projects. But does this involvement of civil society enhance UN accountability?

## Civil society engagement at the UN

Through most of its history the UN has spoken of civil society in terms of 'non-governmental organisations' (NGOs). In this vein, Article 71 of the 1945 Charter stipulated that 'the Economic and Social Council may make suitable arrangements for consultation with non-governmental organizations which are concerned with matters within its competence'. Over time the term 'NGO' also found widespread application outside the UN (Martens 2002; Kelly 2007).

Due to its negative connotation (i.e. identifying the object by what it is not), other expressions have increasingly been preferred to 'non-governmental organisations'. Amongst these alternatives the phrase 'civil society organisations' has also figured prominently in the UN context. Since the late 1990s the UN, like many other global governance bodies, has begun to invoke the 'CSO' vocabulary interchangeably with 'NGO'. Indeed, in 2002 the Secretary-General convened a Panel of Eminent Persons on United Nations-Civil Society Relations (also known as the Cardoso Panel) (UN 2004). The present chapter uses both terms and their abbreviations.

Civil society associations have been integrated into the activities of the UN since its inauguration. In fact, the US government invited 42 CSOs as consultants to its delegation during the founding United Nations Conference on International Organisation, April to June 1945. Another 160 US-based NGOs attended the San Francisco Conference as observers (Seary 1996: 25). The Conference of Non-Governmental Organisations in Consultative Relationship with the United Nations (CONGO) has actively facilitated the participation of civil society groups in UN debates and decision-making since 1948.

Although UN interactions with NGOs/CSOs date back to the origins of the institution, they have grown particularly since the 1990s and especially in the aftermath of the UN-sponsored world conferences of that decade (Friedman *et al.* 2005). To quote the UN from that time, the organisation sought 'to be open to and work closely with civil society organisations that are active in their respective sectors, and to facilitate increased consultation and co-operation between the United Nations and such organisations' (UN 1997). New studies like the Cardoso Report have been initiated to review existing practices that affect access and participation of CSOs in UN processes (Martens 2006; Willetts 2006).

As mentioned above, according to the UN Charter, CSOs which seek to interact with the UN have to work in fields that concern the Economic and Social Council. In practice, however, the ensemble of CSOs that engage with the UN is wide-ranging and not restricted to particular policy fields. In addition, CSOs from all regions of the world, of different sizes and various aims, are accredited. This includes, for example, big international NGOs such as CARE International, Human Rights Watch and Greenpeace; labour organisations such as the International Trade Union Confederation (ITUC); faith-based groups, for example the Bahá'í International Community; think tanks such as the Global Policy Forum; and business associations, including the International Chamber of Commerce (ICC). (For a database of all ECOSOC-accredited NGOs, see UNOG 2010.)

The list of accredited bodies also contains CSOs whose very raison d'être has been to address UN issues. These organisations include the World Federation of United Nations Associations (WFUNA), the United Nations Foundation (UNF) and the Academic Council on the United Nations System (ACUNS). As later chapters indicate, this phenomenon of certain CSOs specialising in engaging a particular global governance agency also surfaces in relation to the Bretton Woods institutions, the World Trade Organization (WTO), the Commonwealth and other bodies.

Civil society associations are today involved with the UN system in a variety of policy fields, across a broad range of levels, and in different procedural ways. Civil society groups in relations with the UN contribute to the formulation, execution and review of global public policy. They influence UN politics by providing information and analysis on policy concerns, by lobbying governmental representatives and UN staff, and by monitoring UN policies. CSOs can enhance the effectiveness of UN policies by providing expertise. CSOs can also promote the democratic legitimacy of UN activities by injecting public voices into the intergovernmental arena (Bichsel 1996; Willetts 2006). CSOs have sometimes become involved at the highest levels of UN policymaking, including the Security Council.

The role of NGOs/CSOs in the implementation of UN activities also bears particular mention. In the field of humanitarian aid, for example, CSOs and the UN frequently co-ordinate their activities and divide up the tasks, with CSOs often taking over duties such as the distribution of food or clothes. CSOs can also be subcontracted to implement specific parts of UN programmes (Gordenker and Weiss 1998). For instance, the United Nations High Commissioner for Refugees (UNHCR) disburses between a third and half of its operational budget through NGOs (Hill 2004: 3). Co-operation with CSOs supports the UN in fulfilling its mandate, because their advantages 'lie in the proximity to their members or clients, their flexibility and the high degree of people's involvement and participation in their activities, which leads to strong commitments, appropriateness of solutions and high acceptance of decisions implemented' (UN 1998a). Moreover, some large transnational NGOs have more resources at their disposal to address a particular issue than does the relevant UN programme.

The UN offers several institutional frameworks through which to associate CSOs with its work. One is consultative status with ECOSOC; a second is association with the Department of Public Information (DPI); a third is direct relations with certain operational departments; a fourth is through the UN Non-Governmental Liaison Service (NGLS). In addition, individual UN specialised agencies apply their own modes of associating CSOs. In many cases, there are temporary NGO accreditation schemes for specific UN conferences as well.

The currently operating ECOSOC regime for consultative status is laid down in Resolution 1996/31 (UN 1996). This measure was introduced after CSOs had participated with high numbers and intensity in a series of UN global issue conferences held during the first half of the 1990s: on, for example, environment and development in 1992; human rights in 1993; population and development in 1994; and social development in 1995. The ECOSOC arrangements provide for three different statuses for NGOs/CSOs at the UN: general consultative status, special consultative status, and roster status.

NGOs with general consultative status must represent major segments of society in a large number of countries across different regions of the world (UN 1996: §22). The rights and privileges pertaining to this status are the most far-reaching of the three categories. Organisations with this designation have the right to attend and speak at meetings of ECOSOC and its subsidiary bodies. They are also allowed to make proposals to the provisional agenda of ECOSOC or its exercising bodies and to circulate statements of up to 2,000 words to the Council (UN 1996: §28–31).

Special consultative status applies for CSOs with a smaller scope of activity. This category differs from general consultative status inasmuch as these organisations can neither submit proposals to the agenda nor speak at meetings of ECOSOC. Organisations with special consultative status may circulate written statements to the Council, but they are limited to 500 words (UN 1996: §23, 29–31).

CSOs that do not fulfil the criteria for either general or special status are put on a 'roster'. NGOs in this category can only attend meetings of ECOSOC and related bodies within their field of competence. Moreover, they need an invitation from the Secretary-General to make a written contribution to the official proceedings, and such a statement may not exceed 500 words (UN 1996: §24, 31).

Applications for all three classes of accreditation are considered by the Committee on Non-Governmental Organisations of ECOSOC. This body consists of nineteen government representatives chosen according to a geographic ratio that allows the various regions of the world to be covered. Some states have been particularly keen to sit on the committee in order to ensure that applications from CSOs which seek to undermine their authority will not succeed. For example, China and Cuba have sat on the NGO Committee for decades and have thereby blocked the applications of CSOs who are critical of their policies. The organisation, Human Rights in China, has tried for years to receive status, but has been turned down several times (Martens 2004). Hence NGO accreditation is not automatic for all applicants, even when they fulfil all of the formal criteria set by the UN. Moreover, accredited CSOs have to play by the rules of the game and can have their consultative status withdrawn by the Committee if they do not.

ECOSOC status opens important doors at the UN for CSOs. It facilitates access to the work of the regional and special committees and entitles CSOs to receive official documents. Accredited associations may also be invited to attend UN conferences and meetings or to make formal statements on a particular issue. Representatives of these organisations receive a pass and a badge which allow them to enter official UN buildings, thus increasing their opportunities of making direct contact with governmental delegates and UN staff.

The UN requires accredited NGOs to nominate at least one 'liaison person' from their organisation who can be contacted by the UN for all administrative purposes. A CSO may nominate up to fifteen different representatives, five in each of the three UN locations where NGO liaison offices are maintained (New York City, Geneva and Vienna). For special events such as international conferences, CSOs are allowed to nominate additional representatives, sometimes even without an upper limit. CSOs often use up their allotment of representatives so that different people can enter the UN without coming up against bureaucratic hurdles, even if those persons do not represent that CSO on a regular basis. One or two positions are often reserved for senior office-holders within the organisation (president, secretary-general or vice-president), although these officers may actually only rarely make use of the pass.

Many CSOs designate a particular staff member to conduct all the UN-related affairs of their organisation. Other CSOs divide up their representation at the UN so that different staff members take over the representation of the organisation when their subject of expertise is on the agenda of the UN. Some CSOs have even established permanent offices in major UN locations and devote professional full-time personnel to their representation. However, the total number of NGO representatives at the UN, the positions that they hold within their organisation and the intensity with which they make use of their representational status, are not statistically reported.

The number of CSOs maintaining official relations with the UN has risen tremendously since the establishment of the 1996 ECOSOC accreditation scheme. When consultative status was introduced in the 1940s, only 41 organisations were accredited. In the late 1960s this number grew to 377, and by the early 1990s it had increased to 744. The ranks of accredited CSOs then skyrocketed after the mid-1990s: from 1,226 in 1996 to almost double that figure by 2001, and 3,287 in 2009. Of the latter number, 138 maintained general consultative status, 2,166 had special consultative status, and 983 held roster status (UN 2009c). In terms of issue foci these CSOs described themselves as working especially on human rights (29 per cent), education (13 per cent) and social matters (12 per cent) (author's calculations).

There are two main reasons for this exponential growth of ECOSOC accreditations. First, following the UN conferences many CSOs that had before only maintained ad hoc relations with the UN sought to formalise their position. Unlike previous resolutions of 1952 and 1968 regarding NGO accreditation, the 1996 scheme allows for CSOs with only national reach to apply for status. Many national CSOs became aware of the benefits of working with the UN and therefore also applied for accreditation to ECOSOC. A second reason for the large expansion is that various UN bodies and agencies, some of which maintain their own mechanisms for accreditation, were asked in the late 1990s to provide lists of associated organisations which then automatically became enrolled in the consultative status scheme (Martens 2005: Ch. 5).

UN capacities for accreditation have now reached their limits. After the 1996 ECOSOC accreditation scheme, applications have risen to more than 400 per year, but the Committee on Non-Governmental Organisations of ECOSOC can only process around 100 applications at each of its annual sessions (UN 1998b). For this reason, CSOs now have to wait several years for their application to be processed.

As noted earlier, CSOs can also relate to the UN via the Department of Public Information (DPI). The NGO Section of the DPI provides a wide range of information services to associated CSOs. These include weekly briefings, various communication workshops, a yearly NGO conference and an annual orientation programme for newly associated NGOs. As of early 2010, 1,549 CSOs are associated with DPI. Of these, 728 are also associated with ECOSOC (UNDPI 2010).

Several other offices of the UN Secretariat also maintain bureaux for relations with CSOs (McKeon 2009: 227–31). Within the Department of Economic and Social Affairs (DESA), for example, civil society units are found in the Division for the Advancement of Women (DAW), the Financing for Development Office (FFD), and the Commission for Sustainable Development (CSD). Other civil society contact points are located at the Secretariat in the UN Human Settlements Programme (UN-Habitat), the UN Conference on Trade and Development (UNCTAD), the UN High Commissioner for Refugees (UNHCR), the UN Environment Programme (UNEP), the UN Development Programme (UNDP) and the World Food Programme (WFP). Some of these bodies of the Secretariat also have designated civil society liaison staff in the field, both in country offices and regional offices. That said, the UN core organs tend on the whole to have a weaker presence at country level than the specialised agencies such as the Food and Agriculture Organisation (FAO) and the World Health Organisation (WHO).

Many CSOs also link up with the United Nations through its Non-Governmental Liaison Service (NGLS). This body, with offices in Geneva and New York, was created in 1975 by several agencies of the UN system to serve as a bridge with civil society organisations. NGLS aims to provide for more civil society engagement in UN processes and deliberations. Similar to DPI, NGLS also organises and conducts briefings, orientation sessions and workshops for CSOs. NGLS has also co-hosted consultations with a number of UN agencies, programmes and funds to provide for exchange between UN institutions and CSOs.

All in all, then, there are multiple formal channels for relations between the core United Nations bodies and civil society. In addition, some CSOs – including a number of social movements – have concerns about the UN without pursuing direct interaction with the organisation. For example, many citizen groups have held public demonstrations around UN conferences without being accredited to attend those meetings.

## Civil society and UN accountability

Having now mapped the terrain of UN-CSO relations, what can be said about the accountability effects of these exchanges? In a recent report on NGO accountability, Jem Bendell notes (2006: 33):

the benefits of NGO engagement with [intergovernmental organisations] are generally seen in terms of participation and deliberation, pluralizing power beyond governments, and addressing the failure of intergovernmental representation … NGOs are seen to both reflect and facilitate the social engagement of people on issues of common concern, and thus even at local levels, stimulate political awareness and expression.

How far have these potential gains for accountability been realised in the case of civil society engagement of the United Nations? The following section examines this question in relation to civil society involvement in UN policy processes. The next section indicates that CSOs have tended to achieve greater accountability for some constituents (especially professional and well-resourced groups) than others.

Preliminarily it may be noted that many civil society activities have helped to raise the public transparency of the UN, thereby opening the institution more to scrutiny by people whose lives are affected by it. For example, across the world more than a hundred United Nations Associations have for decades raised public awareness of the UN and its work. Meanwhile, the United Nations Foundation (UNF) maintains a 'UN Wire' that as of 2010 distributed information regarding the UN to 70,000 subscribers; and the UNF website, rich in detail on the UN, attracted 54,000 visitors per month (Kimble 2010). Arguably the UN would have had a lower public visibility in the absence of such spotlights coming through civil society channels.

However, civil society groups have not mounted concerted campaigns to have the UN improve its own transparency. There has not been the equivalent vis-à-vis the UN of the kind of Global Transparency Initiative that CSOs have pursued vis-à-vis the Bretton Woods institutions (see Chapters 3 and 4). Thanks in part to this civil society omission, the UN today lags well behind many other global governance agencies in the field of disclosure policy.

Civil society activities have achieved much more at the UN in the second dimension of accountability, namely consultation. Contributions by CSOs are included at some stage in many UN mechanisms or modes of work, such as annual sessions, committees, meetings and conferences. CSO submissions to these proceedings have included research reports, short oral statements and written comments. Moreover, consultative status allows representatives of CSOs to enter UN buildings where they can lobby governmental representatives or UN personnel on issues of concern.

However, there are notable limits to the consultative role of CSOs at the UN. For example, they have no formal access to regular meetings of the General Assembly. On these occasions representatives of CSOs can sit at the visitors' stand, but they may not officially intervene in the proceedings. Such participation is more possible at special sessions of the General Assembly (such as the Copenhagen+5 meeting in 2000), where CSOs have had the right to give oral and written statements. There is also a formalised procedure of co-operation through a CSO Advisory Committee in relation to recently established General Assembly subsidiary bodies such as the Human Rights Council and the Peacebuilding Commission.

CSOs also lack formal access to the Security Council, although informal and semi-formal mechanisms for co-operation have evolved significantly since the mid-1990s. The Arria Formula, for example, allows the Security Council to be briefed informally by non-Council members on international peace and security issues. Today, Arria meetings usually take place at least once a month and sometimes include CSO participants. Between 1996 and 2005, at least thirty-four such meetings occurred where representatives of civil society briefed Security Council members (Global Policy Forum 2007).

So far, UN-CSO engagement on the basis of the Arria Formula has mainly addressed issues of humanitarian intervention and human rights (UN 2004: §V 97). For instance, CARE International, Médecins sans Frontières and Oxfam International were the first humanitarian CSOs to brief the Security Council on the Great Lakes Crisis (Willetts 2000: 200). Amnesty International has often been invited when human rights issues are discussed.

Although Arria meetings have become a recognised means of communication between CSOs and the Security Council, their status remains semi-formal (UN 2004: §V 97). The exchanges are typically held at a very high level, usually involving all Security Council members, often at the level of permanent representative or deputy. These meetings are in fact announced by the Security Council President at the beginning of each month as part of the regular schedule. No other Security Council meetings are scheduled at the time when Arria Formula meetings take place, and the UN Secretariat provides full language translations. However, no codified rules exist yet concerning the conduct of an Arria Formula briefing (Paul 2003).

Another example of semi-formal modes of consultation is the NGO Working Group on the Security Council (WGSC), founded in 1995. The WGSC assembles about thirty large CSOs which have special interests in issues of the Security Council. Prospective members must demonstrate 'their organization's special program concern with the Security Council' (Global Policy Forum 2000). The Working Group includes organisations from different issue areas, such as human rights, humanitarian relief, disarmament, faith, global governance, and development. Similarly to the Arria Formula, the WGSC allows CSOs to gain astonishingly close access to high-ranking UN officials and government delegates, even though the Working Group has no official status in the UN system.

CSOs have also often become involved in UN processes as policy advisors and policy formulators. UN officials sometimes invite CSO representatives to provide advice on a particular issue because they have the necessary legal expertise or the technical knowhow. In the human rights sector, for example, representatives of CSOs have participated in committees or working groups during the preparation of drafts (the so-called *travaux préparatoires*) which later become UN final documents. Since the 1993 UN Human Rights Conference in Vienna, CSOs in this field have become particularly valued for their expert assistance in the development of human rights standards. Here CSOs have been 'offered the prospect of becoming "insiders" working through and with the UN to achieve what had not been possible or desirable for them in the past – the delivery of legal services' (Gaer 1996: 60). While UN officials often lack the necessary knowledge – as their profession involves rotating between posts, locations and tasks – representatives of CSOs in this area are not changed on a routine basis (Clapham 2000: 188; Clark 2001: 35).

In addition to the above consultation inputs, CSOs have also entered into UN accountability processes with their work in monitoring and assessing the performance of the organisation and its policies. For example, United Nations Associations, ACUNS and multiple other NGOs and research bodies have produced a continual stream of studies that evaluate various UN activities. In addition, civil society initiatives such as Social Watch have tracked progress with the implementation of undertakings made at UN global issue conferences.

On the whole, however, CSOs have accomplished relatively little in respect of correction and redress for shortfalls in UN performance. Much like the Commonwealth (see Chapter 6), CSOs have done more to press the UN to correct transgressions by its member states than to correct the UN itself. In the human rights area, for example, CSOs have often contributed to UN debates by submitting reports on human rights violations in order to place a country with a particularly bad record on the agenda of the Commission on Human Rights. CSOs have also sought to advance new international human rights standards through the UN system and to promote corresponding institutional arrangements to push them. In this vein, Amnesty International's campaign in the 1970s in respect of a ban on torture has been repeatedly interpreted as 'one of the most successful initiatives ever undertaken by an NGO' (Korey 1998: 171; also Rodley 1986: 130–3; Cook 1996: 189; Clark 2001).

In sum, CSOs have various possibilities for interaction with the UN in order to enhance its accountability. They are part of the full policy cycle: they can initiate policies, contribute to the development of new policies, and participate in implementation and evaluation processes. Since the 1990s, new and additional opportunities have been established to bring CSOs into the UN system. As a result, CSOs can contribute to enhancing the UN's accountability.

### Who gets heard?

Yet *to whom* does the UN become more accountable through these civil society activities? As noted in Chapter 1, in analysing civil society and accountable global governance it is not enough simply to describe the various CSO contributions to transparency, consultation, evaluation and correction. It is equally important to ask which constituencies are (and are not) served by this accountability. In the case of the UN, it is evident that political considerations, organisational set-ups, professionalisation and resource levels can all strongly affect the possibility and degree of CSO access.

In terms of political considerations, it was noted earlier that some CSOs are refused access to the UN because pivotally placed states block their entry. Religious organisations, CSOs engaged in minority rights, and human rights advocates are the most likely groups to face such difficulties. Even Human Rights Watch was denied ECOSOC status when it first applied in the early 1990s. Other CSOs whose status has been under discussion include, for example, Freedom House, Christian Solidarity International, and the Transnational Radical Party (Aston 2001; UN 2001a; UN 2001b: §70–124). Consultative status can also be withdrawn, and country delegates sometimes search for reasons to expel particular CSOs who are disliked by their governments. Thus, committee decisions can be highly political.

A second mode of exclusion in CSO relations with the UN is more subtle and relates to the organisational form that civil society activity takes. The UN tends to interact only with those associations of civil society that are formally organised. Such bodies have an established headquarters, an official constitution, an executive organ and officer, an authority to speak for the members, and (usually) financial independence from governmental bodies. In contrast, the UN has interacted little with social movements that lack formal organisational provisions. In this vein, UN agencies have had minimal contact with counter-globalisation or 'global social justice' movements. UN bodies have had little engagement with the World Social Forum and were involved in only 1 of 266 sessions at the 2003 European Social Forum in Paris (Bendell 2006: 50). Moreover, associations that seek contact with the UN must be concerned with matters which fall under the competence of ECOSOC or its subsidiary bodies, and they need to represent large sections of the population. These stipulations may exclude community groups that are only concerned with local issues. In any case such groups can regard the global policy forums of the UN as far away and irrelevant to their day-to-day struggles (see McKeon and Kalafatic 2009).

A third type of hierarchy of civil society access to the UN has come with professionalisation. For a long time, CSO representation at the UN was predominantly conducted by volunteers. Early studies describe CSO representatives engaging with the UN as 'volunteers, retired, or representing their organisations in their spare time' (Archer 1983: 303). CSO representation then had little impact on the UN, because it 'seemed confined to collecting documents and attending meetings' (Chiang 1981: 235). Owing to this low calibre of representation, many secretariat and governmental delegates did not take CSO representation at the UN seriously at this time (Chiang 1981: 328). Few UN or government officials attended when CSO representatives gave oral presentations.

Yet over the years the character of CSO representation has shifted tremendously from volunteerism to professionalism. Many CSOs have increasingly invested in their international representation with highly skilled, full-time professional personnel. In fact, with growing professionalism there have been increasing job exchanges between CSOs and UN bodies. For example, when in the early 1990s the UN needed quickly to acquire a large number of properly prepared human rights staff, NGOs became the main source of experts (Weschler 1998: 154). Conversely, it has become increasingly acceptable for CSOs to recruit into their ranks former government or UN employees for positions similar to their past roles, for instance as researchers on a particular specialised topic. In the 1980s, CSOs feared that their integrity and independence would be questioned if they recruited former UN officials. However, in the 1990s it became commonly accepted to do so. The new prevailing perception was that CSOs needed specialists for complex issues with very specific skills that could sometimes only be found in official organisations.

The shift to professionalism is well illustrated by the example of Amnesty International. Its representation in New York was first led by local members from the city. They started the 'office' in a personal home in the early 1970s and represented the organisation at the UN in their spare time. However, Amnesty soon recognised that its interaction with UN bodies in charge of human rights required more work than could be handled by volunteer members or staff flying in from London. In 1977, its representation in New York became fully equipped with professional staff. Over time the number of professional representatives increased, and today three full-time staff members represent Amnesty International in New York. The organisation also maintains staff at its international headquarters in London who work almost entirely on relations with the UN. To fill these positions Amnesty recruits highly qualified people, most of whom have studied law and/or a subject with an international focus. An increasing number have even specialised in international human rights studies (Martens 2005: 104).

On the one hand, the shift towards professionalisation just described has opened more doors for CSOs at the UN. It has led to a greater recognition of CSO capacities, and they have become perceived as serious actors in global politics. Yet on the other hand, the demands of professionalism can also tend to marginalise less formally educated and skilled activists. Thus increased access for the high-powered professionals can come at the cost of entry for others who might actually have closer links with affected people on the ground.

The shift to professionalism has often been closely associated with a fourth force of inequality in CSO access to the UN, namely economic resources. Permanent professional representation at UN level is very costly, as the example of Amnesty International shows, and only affordable for a small number of CSOs. Thus CSOs from the global north are disproportionately represented at the UN relative to CSOs from the global south, and middle-class professionals are far more prevalent CSO actors in the UN corridors than activists from underclasses.

## Conclusion

CSO-UN relations have intensified progressively, particularly over the last decade and especially following the revision of the ECOSOC accreditation scheme in 1996. In many ways a new generation of relations has started to evolve, in which coalitions of like-minded governments and civil society groups co-operate together. As a former Director of NGLS puts it (Hill 2004: 3–4):

the UN has shifted from an organisation in which only governments spoke only to themselves, to one that now brings together the political power of governments, the economic power of the corporate sector, and the 'public opinion' power of civil society ... as participants in the global policy dialogue.

As seen in this chapter, these increased relations have given CSOs multiple possibilities to enhance the accountability of the UN regime. CSOs are involved in all stages of the policy process. They shape the policy agenda and the development of global standards at the UN, as the example of the Arria Formula has shown. CSOs participate as experts when UN resolutions are drafted, as seen in the field of human rights. They support the UN system in implementing policies at the country level, as observed in the case of humanitarian relief operations.

However, despite these developments, provisions for CSO participation in the UN system should not be overestimated. As indicated earlier,

CSOs so far have acquired neither direct access to the General Assembly nor any formal status with the Security Council. Moreover, states reacted reluctantly to the most significant initiative of recent years on UN-civil society relations, namely the so-called Cardoso Report (UN 2004), which has so far had no significant impact on further opening of the UN system for CSOs. In fact, many CSOs criticised the report as well and were disappointed with its vague suggestions regarding participation in the General Assembly (Willetts 2006; McKeon 2009). Constitutional provisions and liaison operations at the UN in respect of CSOs seem to have stalled. Indeed, the 'Millennium+5' meeting in 2005 saw CSOs face more restricted access, and one could even speak of a retreat in civil society access to the UN.

As seen above, many CSOs have invested in their representation at the UN level in order to take advantage of the opportunities for inter-action. However, these developments have also split the community of CSOs into privileged 'insiders' and others who are formally accredited, but unable owing to lack of resources to realise the opportunities for interaction with the UN in order to enhance its accountability. A huge number of CSOs – especially those from the developing world – have very limited means at their disposal and are consequently left with little influence. Thus, increased opportunities for activities with the UN and the correlating greater participation of CSOs has not necessarily led to a balanced representation of civil society in international affairs, but may rather reproduce the North-South divide of the governmental world (cf. O'Brien *et al.* 2000; Friedman *et al.* 2005).

However, some attempts to correct this imbalance have been made. For example, in reaction to the Cardoso Report, former Secretary-General Kofi Annan aimed to create a trust fund to support the participation of CSOs from the South at UN conferences, although the proposal did not get beyond a concept note. In addition, some Northern CSOs with the means of interacting with the UN have become more aware that they have a double constituency: both those supporting them at home and stakeholders in the South (Bichsel 1996: 239). More North-South collaboration among CSOs would be another way to achieve a more even UN accountability across the globe. More importantly, however, Southern stakeholders do not wish to be considered a constituency of Northern NGOs, and want direct voice for themselves.

# 3    The World Bank and democratic accountability: the role of civil society

*Alnoor Ebrahim and Steven Herz*

## Introduction

The World Bank is one of the most visible institutions of global governance, and one of the most frequently targeted by civil society organisations (CSOs). The critiques vary widely. Some see the Bank as an irredeemable instrument of a discredited neoliberal agenda that has increased poverty, indebtedness and environmental destruction. Others view the institution as a necessary actor in global development, but one that is much in need of reform. The tactics of these civil society critics have also varied greatly, ranging from highly visible protests and confrontations to more collaborative efforts with Bank management and staff to promote institutional reform.

What difference has this civil society activism made? More specifically, how and to what extent have civil society actors furthered the accountability of the World Bank to its constituents? This chapter argues that CSOs have been fairly successful in expanding Bank accountability at the project and policy levels, particularly through improved transparency and consultation requirements, the establishment and enforcement of social and environmental safeguards, and the creation of complaint and response mechanisms. However, these civil society impacts have been limited, particularly because accountability to affected peoples has not been well integrated into the incentive structure for Bank staff. Officials continue to be rewarded largely on the basis of considerations that tend to impede meaningful public participation and control (such as streamlining procedures and maximising loan disbursements). Moreover, civil

The authors are grateful to Srilatha Batliwala, particularly for crystallising the 'deep structure' element of our argument; and to Rachel Winter-Jones, John Garrison and Carolyn Reynolds-Mandel of the World Bank's Global Civil Society Team for very helpful and generous feedback. In addition to secondary literature as cited, the analysis draws upon interviews conducted in 2005 with twenty-three civil society actors engaged in influencing the Bank, twenty-five officials and consultants of the Bank staff, and five academics. Members of the World Bank-Civil Society Joint Facilitation Committee were also interviewed (see Herz and Ebrahim 2005).

society has not been successful in improving Bank accountability at the level of board governance, for example through greater transparency in decision-making, a more representative allocation of votes, or better parliamentary scrutiny. Thus, although civil society efforts have led to some gains in accountability with respect to Bank policies and projects, deeper structural features of the institution – the incentives staff face and how the institution is governed – remain largely unchanged.

This chapter begins with a brief introduction to the World Bank and offers a normative argument for expanding democratic accountability in all aspects of its decision-making. The discussion then considers civil society activities to improve the Bank's accountability, assessing these reform efforts first in relation to projects, then with regard to policies, and finally in respect of board governance.

### The World Bank and its accountability

The declared mission of the World Bank Group is 'to fight poverty with passion and professionalism for lasting results' (World Bank 2009a). The Group comprises five organisations: the International Bank for Reconstruction and Development (IBRD), the International Development Association (IDA), the International Finance Corporation (IFC), the Multilateral Investment Guarantee Agency (MIGA) and the International Center for the Settlement of Investment Disputes (ICSID). The IBRD provides loans to governments for development and poverty alleviation initiatives, charging interest to recover the cost of borrowing. IDA provides grants, as well as loans on highly concessional terms, to governments of the poorest countries. The IFC and MIGA seek to encourage private sector investment in middle- and low-income countries: the IFC by providing loans and equity finance and MIGA by providing political risk insurance. ICSID provides a forum for settling investment disputes between foreign investors and host countries (World Bank 2006d). This chapter focuses primarily on the IBRD and IDA.

The normative arguments for increasing World Bank accountability to citizens reflect its role both as a public body and as a development organisation. First, as a public institution, the Bank's legitimacy depends in part on decision-making processes that conform to basic norms about transparent, participatory and responsive governance. As citizens increasingly evaluate their national governments against these democratic standards, they are also insisting on the same attributes from regional and global governance institutions. This has created significant pressure on bodies such as the World Bank to democratise and pluralise their decision-making.

Second, as a development institution, the World Bank's effectiveness depends on a degree of inclusiveness and responsiveness to those who are affected by its work. The Bank has consistently found a high correlation between the extent and quality of public participation and overall project quality (World Bank 1996; 2000c; 2002a; 2006e). Equally important, development is now understood to require more than alleviating income poverty (Bradlow 2004: 207). It also includes improving the capacity of the poor to gain equitable access to resources and opportunities, and to defend their rights and interests in the political process (Narayan 1999: 7, 12). The World Bank has now recognised that empowering the poor to influence the decisions that will affect their lives is a critical dimension of development (McGee and Norton 2000: 68; World Bank 2002b: vi; World Bank 2004b: 79).

The present analysis focuses in particular on the role of civil society associations in advancing World Bank accountability to affected citizens and communities, especially the poor. These efforts have largely occurred in respect of three levels: *projects* that the Bank supports in developing countries; *policies* that guide the Bank's work; and *governance* in terms of the Bank's two boards of directors. Civil society attempts at Bank reform are assessed in three successive sections below. Again, the general argument is that CSOs have booked greatest accountability advances in respect of projects and policies, but with little success at the board level, or in influencing performance incentives for staff.

### Civil society and project level accountability

Since the 1980s, civil society organisations have mounted sustained advocacy campaigns to hold the Bank accountable for negative environmental and social impacts of its operations (Fox and Brown 1998; Keck and Sikkink 1998; Clark, Fox and Treakle 2003). The most important success of these campaigns has been to press the Bank to establish a variety of 'safeguard policies' on sensitive issues such as environmental impacts, involuntary resettlement, and effects on indigenous peoples (Fox and Brown 1998; Powell and Baker 2007; World Bank 2009d). Ten safeguard policies have become the touchstone of the Bank's accountability in respect of its projects. They set norms regarding planning processes and development outcomes that a project or programme must meet in order to be eligible for Bank support. They also establish minimum standards for the protection of the rights and interests of locally affected communities and provide some assurances that the costs of Bank-financed projects will not be disproportionately borne by the most vulnerable members of society or their natural environment. Some of the safeguard policies also provide minimum guarantees that local communities will have the opportunity to participate in Bank decisions that affect them.

In addition, civil society advocacy has led the World Bank to adopt and expand an information disclosure policy. The Bank conducted a series of external consultations with CSOs on these matters in 2001, and again for revisions in 2005 (World Bank 2009e). The policy requires that certain key planning, appraisal and oversight documents are placed in the public domain in a timely fashion. Such transparency facilitates public participation in decision-making on Bank projects. In 2009 the Bank undertook a further review of its information disclosure policy, with public consultations in thirty-three countries, adopting new practices in 2010.

Civil society pressure also encouraged the Bank to establish, in 1994, an Inspection Panel for its IBRD and IDA lending (Clark, Fox, and Treakle 2003). The Inspection Panel is a mechanism of quasi-judicial accountability that reviews complaints by persons (often supported by CSOs) who allege that they have been harmed (or are likely to be harmed) by Bank-supported projects. The Panel may only investigate claims that the Bank has violated its own operational policies and procedures (i.e. not different standards that outside parties might wish to demand). The Inspection Panel operates independently of Bank management and reports directly to the Board of Executive Directors.

In contrast, CSOs have played little role in the creation of other project evaluation processes at the World Bank. A small evaluation programme was begun in the budgeting department of the Bank in 1971 without any notable civil society urgings; external pressure for project evaluation came on this occasion from the United States Congress and its audit arm, the General Accounting Office (Grasso *et al.* 2003). Two years later the Bank established a fully-fledged evaluation department, and now the Independent Evaluation Group (IEG) conducts detailed analyses of project quality and performance. The IEG, too, was formed without notable civil society pressure, and it does not respond directly to concerns raised by affected populations. However, CSOs have often used IEG criticisms of Bank projects as evidence in their advocacy efforts. In another move to strengthen accountability through evaluation, in 1996 the Bank created a Quality Assurance Group (QAG) to improve the quality of projects and impacts, after internal evaluations showed that one-third of Bank projects were unlikely to achieve their objectives (World Bank 2009b, 2009c). While it is hard to ascertain the role of civil society in the creation of the QAG, it is plausible that some quality pressures emerged from concerns about compliance with social and environmental safeguards (Clark, Fox, and Treakle 2003: 236, 270).

Civil society advocacy has been more successful in helping to build internal Bank support for a 'participation' agenda and for greater inclusion of voices from the global south in shaping projects and policies. In 1981 Bank staff and NGO leaders (mostly from the South) formed the NGO-World Bank Committee. The NGO members of this committee also established an autonomous Working Group in 1984 to develop and co-ordinate their advocacy efforts. Successes of the Working Group during the 1990s included: the creation of a formal NGO unit within the strategic planning division of the Bank; two important World Bank workshops on participation; the formation of a World Bank 'Learning Group on Popular Participation'; and an ambitious effort to monitor participation in the Bank's policies and projects (Long 2001). More generally, the Working Group altered the technocratic culture of the Bank to build legitimacy for civil society and citizen participation. These efforts were backed up by resources developed within the Bank, including a *Participation Sourcebook* in 1996 and a guide on *Participation and Social Assessment: Tools and Techniques* in 1998 (World Bank 1996; Rietbergen-McCracken and Narayan 1998).

The World Bank now encourages its staff and borrowing governments to engage with civil society actors throughout the project cycle (World Bank 2000b). The Bank's own research shows that civil society participation in projects significantly improves design, quality of service, and public support (Rukuba-Ngaiza *et al.* 2002: 14). CSO involvement also increases transparency and accountability in contracting and procurement, while improving relationships between citizens and their public agencies (World Bank 2002c). The Bank itself finds that civil society participation leads to better outcomes, lower risks and increased development effectiveness (World Bank 2005b: 5–6, paras. 11, 13).

Indeed, since the early 1990s the Bank has made some notable progress in improving civil society involvement in its projects. According to the IEG, stakeholder participation rose from 32 per cent of new projects approved in 1990 to 72 per cent in 2006 (World Bank 2006e: 23). Similarly, CSO consultations in Environmental Assessments rose from about 50 per cent in 1992 to 87 per cent in 2001 (Rukuba-Ngaiza *et al.* 2002). Modest qualitative gains are also apparent. In 1992 Environmental Assessment consultations were often limited to surveying affected groups and making results publicly available. By 1997 the process included better use of public meetings, greater disclosure and increased interaction between the Bank and stakeholders. By 2006 Bank staff and partners were beginning to note the positive results of improved information disclosure and increased community participation at various stages of the project cycle (World Bank 1993, 1997, 2006b).

Despite these innovations, World Bank project lending rcmains a source of contention with civil society. Persistent problems of transparency continue to prompt widespread concern. The Bank's 2002 *Policy on Disclosure of Information* provided that 'timely dissemination of information to local groups affected by the projects and programs supported by the Bank, including nongovernmental organizations, is essential for the effective implementation and sustainability of projects' (World Bank 2002e). However, the policy did not require the release of some materials that are critical for informed participation, such as certain draft project documents that would provide citizens with information while decisions are still under consideration. Nor did the policy require the disclosure of supervision documents, which would enable CSOs to better monitor implementation. Even where the disclosure policy required that documents are made publicly available, there was no independent review mechanism to ensure that Bank staff respond appropriately to information requests (Saul 2003: 6–8).

A revised disclosure policy adopted in 2010, with considerable input from civil society, addressed some of these concerns. The new approach has expanded routine disclosure to documents created during project implementation. It also provides a clearer list of exceptions to disclosure and establishes an appeals process (World Bank 2010). The policy thus adopted a number of recommendations from a model policy put forward by a global network of CSOs (Global Transparency Initiative 2009). However, some serious civil society concerns remain. The revised policy gives veto power to governments and some third parties such as contractors on releasing information that they provide to the Bank. It also allows internal information to be withheld on the grounds of protecting the 'deliberative process' (Ekdawi 2010).

Another continuing concern relates to opportunities for civil society consultation throughout the project cycle. For example, the Bank still does not require that borrowers solicit public inputs during the early stages of needs assessments and project identification and design, when fundamental decisions about project type and risk are made, and when the full range of policy and project options can be considered. Rather, public consultations typically do not occur until the problem to be addressed has already been framed and the proposed response has been formulated. An IEG review found that only 12 per cent of sampled projects were participatory during project identification (World Bank 2000c: vi). Thus the scope for participation becomes limited to refining established project proposals.

Civil society participation has also been weak during monitoring and evaluation stages of the project cycle. The IEG found that only 9 per cent of sampled projects had participatory monitoring and evaluation (Rukuba-Ngaiza *et al.* 2002: 16). Not surprisingly then, the QAG has identified poor-quality monitoring and evaluation as one of four major 'persistent problems' that have shown little improvement over the years (World Bank 2000d: 25). A subsequent assessment found that, while the quality of project supervision had generally improved, monitoring and evaluation of results showed persistent weaknesses (World Bank 2007b). This neglect continues despite substantial evidence that participatory monitoring and evaluation can: (a) improve project sustainability, accountability and local ownership; (b) help implementing agencies to identify and respond to unanticipated problems; and (c) capture lessons and disseminate lessons learned from individual projects (Ashman 2002; IFC undated).

Moreover, CSOs have frequently complained that participatory processes in Bank-supported projects are ad hoc, arbitrary and poorly administered. These complaints include 'lack of clear and consistent parameters for consultation and feedback, arrogance or defensive posturing by Bank staff, lack of transparency about who is invited, late distribution of consultation documents, lack of translation, and lack of funds to cover CSO time and travel expenses', plus lack of attention to alternative project options (World Bank 2005b: 16–17, para. 32). As a result, so-called 'consultations' have often amounted to little more than information dissemination exercises, in which affected peoples are notified of decisions that have already been taken elsewhere (Herz and Ebrahim 2005: Appendix F, 24).

Overall, the Bank has lacked an effective organisational strategy for improving civil society consultation. Its efforts have been 'half-hearted at best, and have not come close to reaching the goal of fully incorporating participation into its operations' (Long 2001: 56). The Bank's own reviews have largely concurred with this assessment. For example, the IEG found that participation was 'often poorly planned and executed, rushed, superficial, failed to adequately include or protect the interests of marginalized groups, dominated by the more powerful and vocal, unrepresentative, or failed to make a difference' (World Bank 2000c: 11). Similarly, in its *Issues and Options* paper on Bank-civil society engagement, the Bank noted that 'consultation guidelines are not widely followed', and consultations 'often occur in an arbitrary fashion with very short notice and/or very late in the process'. In part, this is because task managers tend to '"tick the box" that CSOs have been involved, rather than take proactive steps to ensure engagement is viewed as satisfactory by all stakeholders' (World Bank 2005b: 16).

Civil society access at various stages of the project cycle is further complicated by insufficient capacity for effective participation by local CSOs.

These actors often lack: (a) abilities to understand and critique technical issues; (b) sufficient knowledge of their rights under national law and Bank policy; and (c) skills to negotiate with more powerful actors. Bank efforts to build CSO capacity, where they exist at all, have tended to focus on technical information and typically do not seek to enhance negotiation and conflict resolution skills (Rukuba-Ngaiza *et al.* 2002: 26; World Bank 2000c: 21).

Finally, civil society efforts to hold the Bank to account for its project work are severely constrained by two systemic factors. First, as various Bank reports have noted, satisfactory data to track, monitor and evaluate engagement with CSOs are not available; nor have appropriate indicators of impact and effectiveness of CSO participation been developed. Second, few if any meaningful avenues for redress are available to citizens who believe that participatory processes have been deficient and/or unresponsive to their concerns.

### Staff incentives at the project level

Civil society efforts to improve World Bank accountability at the project level thus present a paradox. On the positive side, CSOs have successfully pushed the Bank to develop policies on safeguards and information disclosure. Basic notions of citizen participation have also gained currency in the institution. But why does participation remain ad hoc? Why are improvements in the quantity of participation not necessarily accompanied by advances in its quality?

In large measure this disconnect may be ascribed to the Bank's failure to align accountability initiatives with corresponding adjustments to its staff incentive structure. Like most large and complex bureaucracies, the Bank has multiple and, at times, competing organisational cultures that influence how its procedures and stated priorities are actually implemented. Generally, World Bank task managers 'paint a sobering picture of the environment for participation within the Bank' (World Bank 2000c: 25). Impediments to engaging project-affected people have included insufficient funding, inadequate time for work in the field, pressure to process loans and disburse funds rapidly, and inadequate support from management (World Bank 2000c: 25–7; World Bank 2005b: 16, para. 30).

Lending pressures at the Bank reward quick appraisal and disbursement. Moving money is valued when it comes to promotion, while attention to participatory planning, monitoring and evaluation generally is not. The pressure to lend results in rigid and short project cycles that do not allow for time-consuming and labour-intensive participatory processes. A 2005 Bank evaluation of its projects in *Community-Based and*

*Community-Driven Development* (CBD/CDD) found that the pressures associated with short project cycles remain significant, despite a recognition that the one-year subproject cycle typical of most Bank activities is too short for participatory community projects (World Bank 2005c: 21, 46). This problem of reward structures has been recognised for some time, but the Bank has done little to correct it (World Bank 1992: 14, 16).

On the contrary, pressure to lend may be increasing as the World Bank responds to changes in its traditional markets. The Bank has in recent years returned to higher-risk large infrastructure projects, particularly in middle-income countries with better repayment rates. Project staff have worried that the transaction costs of the Bank's environmental and social safeguard policies are a substantial impediment to doing business (World Bank 2001a; World Bank 2005a: 5, 8). Moreover, in poorer countries China is increasingly making available loans that are not encumbered with environmental and social conditions. This competition may further reinforce lending pressures at the expense of civil society engagement and downward accountability (Wallis 2007).

Another incentive problem is that staff appraisals do not evaluate the quality and impact of participatory mechanisms employed by staff, who have neither positive nor negative encouragements to improve the quality of participation beyond compliance with the letter of consultation requirements. Guidance and training are optional, and incentives to improve participation skills are weak. Arguably, better project outcomes as a result of participation could provide a positive incentive; however, these are offset by stronger incentives to move money and perform on short budget cycles, rather than to achieve results on the longer time horizons of project impacts.

Furthermore, although the Bank has greatly expanded resources for civil society engagement, they are not systematically available for all projects. Considerable funds for consultations are available for conscientious task managers (or team leaders) who seek them. However, these monies are not earmarked across all projects. For example, the CBD/CDD evaluation found that 'the Bank's preparation and supervision costs for CBD/CDD projects are already higher than for [other] projects, and there are no additional incentives for country directors to provide the additional resources required to prepare and supervise these operations' (World Bank 2005c: 21, 46).

Finally, in staff recruitment and promotion the Bank places high value on technical expertise. This priority can discourage the consideration of alternative policy and project options that may draw on other sorts of knowledge. The emphasis on technical skills, combined with a dearth of incentives to undertake civil society consultation, serves to dissuade even well-meaning staff from spending scarce time and resources on developing means of downward accountability to citizen groups and affected communities.

As a result of these constraints, managers at the World Bank frequently view community participation and accountability as 'add-ons' and a drain on time and capacity. This approach reflects a broader climate at the Bank, in which participation is encouraged but not mandated. Nevertheless, those task managers who do pursue civil society consultation tend to believe strongly in its benefits. In these cases experience with public participation has motivated more participation (Rukuba-Ngaiza *et al.* 2002: 8, 25; World Bank 2005b: 21).

Two units within the World Bank – the Civil Society Team and the Participation and Civic Engagement Team – have consistently sought to support staff in engaging with CSOs and to raise the profile of such engagement within the institution. These teams have offered detailed recommendations for more systematically drawing on civil society experience and for improving the Bank's responsiveness to communities and civic groups. Their report, *Issues and Options for Improving Engagement between the World Bank and Civil Society*, laid out a ten-point action plan (World Bank 2005b). Proposals included a review of funding opportunities and procurement framework for civil society engagement, the development of new guidelines for collaboration with CSOs, holding regular meetings with senior management and the Board to review Bank-civil society relations, and better staff support through an institution-wide advisory service and learning programme. Progress on this action plan since 2005 has largely consisted of new training offerings and mechanisms for assistance with engagements.

In sum, while the World Bank has increased CSO consultations around its projects and improved social and environmental protections as a result, public accountability remains modest and uneven. Downward accountability is limited by a disclosure policy that makes some information available only after key decisions have been made, and by an absence of CSO participation throughout the project cycle. Although considerably increased resources for citizen engagement are available to task managers, performance incentives continue to reward the quantity and speed of fund disbursement rather than meaningful civil society participation for improved project quality.

## Civil society and policy level accountability

Civil society efforts to influence World Bank policies (as distinct from specific projects) can be traced back to the early 1980s and have booked a number of significant successes. Around 1983 a group of large membership-based advocacy NGOs with offices in Washington, DC began lobbying Congress and the US Treasury to reform the Bank's environmental practices. Their efforts, combined with those of other actors inside and outside the Bank, resulted in the creation of an Environment Department at the Bank in 1987 and the formalisation of an environmental assessment policy in 1989. These early successes helped build momentum on Bank policy advocacy and reform by a range of CSOs throughout the North and South (Fox and Brown 1998; Keck and Sikkink 1998; Long 2001; Clark, Fox and Treakle 2003).

During James D. Wolfensohn's tenure as President of the World Bank in 1995–2005, the institution revised several of its most important environmental and social safeguard policies, including those on resettlement, indigenous peoples, and forests. The Bank also conducted strategic reviews of some of its most controversial lending practices, including structural adjustment credits and its support for extractive industries and large dams. In contrast to earlier generations of policy reviews, each of these exercises included a significant component of civil society input. The Bank recognised that its review processes would not now be considered legitimate or methodologically rigorous unless they included the perspectives of affected stakeholders (Sherman 2001: 4).

However, because the Bank lacked clear and mandatory protocols for gathering civil society views on its general policies, mechanisms were created on an ad hoc basis. Since 1997 the Bank has employed three different approaches: unilateral; independent; and collaborative. These approaches differ in the extent to which the Bank controls the nature and timing of the public inputs. In all three approaches the Bank remains the final arbiter of how those consultations would influence policy outcomes.

In the unilateral approach, public inputs to policy reviews are almost entirely structured by the World Bank itself. In these cases, Bank staff devise the format and timing of public participation, convene the process and evaluate the evidence thereby obtained. The unilateral approach is by far the most common. It has been used in policy reviews on forestry, resettlement, indigenous peoples, and IFC safeguards, as well as in consultations around the Country Systems proposal, all carried out between 1998 and 2005.

In contrast, the independent approach relies upon outside parties to drive the policy review and formulate the resultant recommendations. In the World Commission on Dams (WCD), for example, the World Bank and the World Conservation Union (IUCN) established an independent panel comprised of experts from civil society, government and industry to conduct a review of the development effectiveness of large dams (WCD

2000). Similarly, in the Extractive Industries Review (EIR) the Bank commissioned an 'Eminent Person' to evaluate the development impacts of its activities in this sector (Extractive Industries Review 2003).

Meanwhile, under the collaborative approach, the Bank and its key stakeholders share responsibility for structuring the review and assessing its outcomes. The principal example of this review framework was the Structural Adjustment Participatory Review Initiative (SAPRI), launched in 1996. SAPRI was conceived as a collaborative exercise in which the World Bank, CSOs and government officials would agree upon methodology and jointly assess the impacts of structural adjustment (SAPRIN 2004).

Despite these improvements in access, civil society organisations have noted continuing significant shortfalls in policy dialogues with the World Bank. For example, many CSOs have complained that these reviews did not adequately answer their most important concerns. CSOs have generally given reviews (especially in the independent and collaborative formats) high marks for thoughtfully addressing civil society priorities (Dubash *et al.* 2001; Imhof, Wong and Bosshard 2002; BIC 2004; Herz and Ebrahim 2005: App. F; Lawrence 2005). However, many CSOs have felt that the Bank failed to make significant adjustments to its policy framework in response to the review findings and recommendations. For example, the Bank refused to commit to the WCD guidelines for developing large dam projects: it agreed only to assist governments and project developers to 'test' the recommendations in their projects (World Bank 2001b). Similarly, key civil society actors involved in the SAPRI process contend that the Bank ended its involvement in that review after accepting much of the background research, but not revising its policies (SAPRIN 2002: 23–4). For its part, the Bank maintains that the SAPRI findings did influence its approach to poverty and social impact assessment, its Poverty Reduction Strategy (PRS) process and its revised policy on Development Policy Lending (World Bank 2005d: 3). Similarly, while civil society groups believed that the Eminent Person's recommendations in the EIR broadly reflected their concerns, they claim that the Bank adopted only diluted policy changes. In contrast, the Bank claims to have adopted most of the EIR recommendations (Herz and Ebrahim 2005: App. F).

These conflicting perspectives point to two common problems of civil society consultation in World Bank policy reviews. First, the Bank has generally failed to follow through with civil society groups on how it actually uses reviews to revise its practices. Second, the Bank has often failed to set out its goals and priorities in a given review. Civil society groups involved in these reviews suggest that the Bank rarely indicates what it hopes to achieve from a particular consultative process. It seldom clarifies which issues are, and are not, open for consideration, or what policy options are 'politically feasible'. For their part, Bank staff involved in the reviews suggest that CSOs enter the consultation with unrealistic expectations. This issue has arisen particularly in 'collaborative' and 'independent' reviews, which provide greater latitude for departure from World Bank orthodoxies. In the EIR, for example, civil society participants and the independent Eminent Person believed that the review was to consider whether extractive industries investments were an appropriate vehicle for achieving the Bank's mission of poverty alleviation through sustainable development (EIR 2003: 3). However, the Bank was only prepared to consider a narrower set of recommendations on how to improve existing operations. As a result, both management and the Board rejected the Eminent Person's proposal that the Bank phase out certain operations (BIC *et al.* 2004). Similarly, the outcomes of the WCD and SAPRI so thoroughly transgressed the unspoken boundaries of scope that the Bank distanced itself from the processes and refused to adopt their findings or recommendations (SAPRIN 2002: 23–5; World Commission on Dams 2002).

The Bank and CSOs have also often clashed over the design of policy reviews. Each exercise has almost invariably begun with an imbroglio over the structure and process of the review. Since the Bank has no mandatory requirements for whether or how to conduct a consultation of civil society, the terms of engagement must be re-established each time. Moreover, although the Bank's *Consultation Guidelines* recognise that CSOs should have a role in designing the process, staff have rarely tried to develop the framework for a given deliberation in a collaborative way (World Bank 2000a).

Independent reviews have not been immune to controversies over procedure either. In these cases CSOs have often questioned whether the external reviewers would be sufficiently balanced and independent of the Bank to ensure a fair process. For example, a dispute about whether dam-affected people would be represented on the WCD nearly caused the collapse of those discussions (Imhof, Wong and Bosshard 2002: 6; Herz and Ebrahim 2005: App. F, 9–10). In the EIR, CSOs had no voice in deciding who would lead the review and raised concerns about whether the Eminent Person and his staff would have sufficient independence from the Bank. It was only after the Eminent Person took action to assert his independence that CSOs decided not to renounce the process en masse.

SAPRI may be the only World Bank policy review that avoided significant disputes over the initial structuring of the process (SAPRIN

2002: 23). The principle of collaborative design enabled SAPRI to develop a workplan that was acceptable to all parties. Yet in spite of this promising start, substantial disagreements over ideology, methodology and conclusions developed over time, and the collaborative nature of the process ultimately degenerated into mutual distrust and recrimination.

One of the most persistent and sharpest CSO complaints has been that the Bank seems to consider that commitments made to stakeholders in the course of policy dialogues are provisional. In particular, participants have expressed deep frustration with the Bank's failure to enact commitments on issues of overriding importance to them. For example, stakeholders in the Forest Policy Review broadly agreed that the new policy should address the indirect impacts on forests of adjustment and programmatic lending. Bank management declined to address the issue, assuring CSOs (and the Board) that these impacts would be addressed in SAPRI. Towards this end, management committed to revising structural adjustment policy to include a 'transparent mechanism for systematically addressing the environmental aspects, including in particular possible forestry impacts' (World Bank 2002d: 4). Yet, although the revised policy does address forest impacts, it is neither transparent nor systematic. It fails to ensure that adequate environmental assessments will be conducted or that identified impacts will be mitigated (Jenkins and Gibbs undated; World Bank 2004a: para. 11).

The problem of commitment is exacerbated by the fact that the Bank rarely informs CSOs how their inputs have influenced policy development. Bank review processes have not consistently utilised feedback mechanisms to allow participants to understand how they have informed policy outcomes. The Bank's failure to explain how civil society consultations inform policy-making feeds the widespread perception that public inputs do not have a significant influence on policy (World Bank 2005b: 16).

By the end of Wolfensohn's presidency, many World Bank staff and civil society participants alike expressed a sense of fatigue and disillusionment with policy review consultations. However, Bank officials point to more recent global consultations as evidence that the institution has incorporated important lessons from past processes. They argue, for example, that in the 2006–7 consultation on its anti-corruption strategy the Bank was more proactive about posting documents and schedules on the web, translating materials into five languages, providing more lead time for preparation, inviting prominent CSOs such as Transparency International to co-host meetings, and summarising the feedback it received. Similarly, in developing its *Issues and Options* paper in 2004 for improving relations with civil society, the Bank compiled a matrix of all comments and explained how and why each input was or was not addressed in the policy revision. In addition, the Bank has recognised the importance of distributing iterative drafts of policy revisions for feedback prior to board review, so that CSOs can comment on how their inputs have been addressed before final decisions are taken. While the Bank has not consistently used matrices and iterative drafts, these feedback mechanisms appear to be gaining greater currency (World Bank 2005b: 50).

However, there are at least two reasons to be wary of viewing the anti-corruption consultations as indicative of a new approach to civil society participation in policy development at the World Bank. First, several participants viewed the consultations as rushed, particularly in the early stages (World Bank 2006c). Second, the anti-corruption consultations addressed only a general strategy document that lacked specificity with respect to Bank policies or implementation. As such, this exercise is not easily comparable to earlier engagements that considered more specific policy development (WRI undated). Moreover, the framework under discussion did not '*explicitly* lay out consultation principles and strategy for engagement with key external stakeholders' (BIC 2007 – emphasis in the original).

In sum, experiences with civil society involvement in policy reviews have had a debilitating effect on the World Bank's credibility as an institution that is willing to listen to and learn from its constituents. Cynicism and disillusionment have flourished as promises of meaningful participation have given way to perceptions of minimal influence. Negative past experiences prompt many CSOs to question whether it is worthwhile to devote organisational resources to a Bank consultation. Almost invariably they ask how the prospective next consultation will be any more productive than, for example, the WCD or the EIR.

## Civil society and board level accountability

If civil society contributions to World Bank accountability have been noteworthy in respect of projects but less certain in regard to general policies, the impacts have been negligible when it comes to the Board level. 'The Board' here refers to the Board of Governors, which meets once a year, and the Board of Executive Directors (Executive Board), which supervises day-to-day operations of the World Bank. Members of the Board represent the member states of the World Bank. In principle, management and staff are accountable to the member states through the Board representatives, who in turn are accountable to their citizens.

The most common concern with governance arrangements at the World Bank is the disproportionate allocation of voting shares and the inequitable allocation of seats on the Executive Board. Voting shares are apportioned to each member state roughly in accordance with the size of its economy. This weighted voting system decidedly favours the major donor governments. The Group of 7 countries control nearly 43 per cent of the voting shares, and the United States alone holds 16.4 per cent (World Bank 2007a: 57–61). Meanwhile, the 46 countries of Sub-Saharan Africa have a combined voting share of less than 6 per cent. This voting arrangement disenfranchises those with the greatest interest in Board decision-making – namely, the poorest countries that are most affected by Bank decisions (Griffith-Jones undated; Nye *et al.* 2003: 67–8; United Nations 2005: 72).

The problem of skewed votes is compounded by an inequitable allocation of seats on the Executive Board. Only 24 Executive Directors (EDs) represent all 185 member states; 8 of the most powerful states each have their own ED, while the remaining 177 members are grouped into 16 constituencies of 4–24 countries each. Constituencies that include both donor and borrowing countries are almost always represented by an official from a donor country (Calieri and Schroeder 2003: 4). Meanwhile, an ED with a constituency of 24 countries in Sub-Saharan Africa cannot possibly represent these members as effectively as EDs who represent a single country.

Civil society actors have had very little influence in reshaping the voting regime and seat allocations at the World Bank. One reason for this lack of impact is that for a long time CSOs were not as active in respect of Board arrangements as they were on project matters and policy reviews. Moreover, the Board works largely behind closed doors, outside the reach of civil society monitoring, whereas project managers are more exposed to public scrutiny. It is also more difficult to alter the Board structure inasmuch as such reform requires intergovernmental negotiation and possibly changes to the Articles of Agreement of the Bank.

That said, CSOs have in recent years become more active on issues of Board governance at the World Bank. Civil society groups have lobbied Board members in Washington, DC and in their home countries on these matters. Other CSO advocacy on Board reform has been directed at government ministers, bankers and advisors. Some CSOs have developed proposals for alternative models for the Board. The World Bank has so far been slow to respond to these civil society initiatives, although its sister organisation, the International Monetary Fund, opened a consultative process with CSOs in 2009 on matters of institutional governance (IMF 2009b, 2009c; New Rules for Global Finance 2009).

A central civil society concern has been that the disparity in voting power at the World Bank between developed and developing countries creates a substantial problem of moral hazard. Since the donor governments that wield the most voting power do not borrow from the Bank, they are not accountable to citizens who bear the risks of their decisions (Bradlow 2001: 18). As Ann Florini has observed, 'governments, answerable only to domestic electorates, face few incentives to act for the benefit of someone else's constituency' (Florini 2003: 14).

In addition, Board governance is plagued by a dearth of opportunities for citizens to hold their own Executive Director accountable. For one thing, Board secrecy significantly impairs public scrutiny of EDs. Since decisions are usually made by consensus, without formal votes, and since records of any votes and the deliberations that preceded them are not publicised, citizens simply do not know how their ED is representing them (Calieri and Schroeder 2003). Even if citizens were to learn how their representative had voted, in the case of multiple-constituency seats there is little that citizens in one country can do to hold an ED from another country accountable.

Some civil society efforts to address the problem of Board accountability have sought to increase the role of national parliaments in scrutinising the World Bank (Round 2004). On the whole, national parliaments have generally exercised limited oversight on Bank projects and policies; indeed, legislators have often had limited access to major documents about World Bank operations in their own countries. Key decisions in this regard are typically made by the finance and development ministries, with only limited parliamentary involvement. CSO strategies have thus included: (a) publishing the procedures (or lack thereof) used by different countries to hold their directors to account (Round 2004: 4); and (b) working directly with parliamentarians on World Bank activities in their countries, particularly through the Parliamentary Network on the World Bank (PNoWB 2009). Furthermore, many CSOs have argued that privileging finance ministries as the fulcrum of fiscal and development policymaking improperly distorts the balance of power between the ministries and parliament (ActionAid International *et al.* 2005). In this vein, CSOs have recommended that the World Bank Executive Board refrain from approving certain documents (such as the Poverty Reduction Strategy Papers required of heavily indebted poor countries) until they have been reviewed by the relevant national parliament (Rowden and Irama 2004: 39).

Finally on matters of Bank governance, civil society organisations have raised concerns about the accountability of the President of the institution. Many have argued that the United States' informal prerogative to name the President of the World Bank has severely undermined that officer's accountability to the Board and to citizens of member governments.

Since the President has considerable discretion in shaping the agenda, rules and processes of the Bank, this arrangement has greatly enhanced US power within the institution (Kapur 2002: 60). CSOs and other observers have long argued that it is impossible to reconcile this prerogative with basic principles of democratic governance (UNDP 2002; Bretton Woods Project 2003; Bapna and Reisch 2005; IFI Democracy Coalition 2005). Civil society groups have therefore advocated a reform of the selection of the Bank President guided by two basic accountability principles: transparency and competence without regard to nationality (New Rules for Global Finance 2007b).

Many CSOs hoped that the furore over the resignation of former World Bank President Paul Wolfowitz in 2007, under allegations of ethical lapses, would provide a political opportunity to reform the selection process. Nearly a hundred current and retired Bank staff, including several Vice-Presidents, signed a civil society letter calling for change in this matter. Nevertheless, the successor to Wolfowitz, Robert Zoellick, was selected in the same manner as previous Presidents.

In 2008, however, it was announced at the Annual Meeting of the World Bank Board of Governors that:

There is considerable agreement on the importance of a selection process for the President of the Bank that is merit-based and transparent, with nominations open to all Board members and transparent Board consideration of all candidates (World Bank 2009f).

If this apparent relinquishment of the US Government prerogative is indeed enacted in the appointment of the next President, it will mark a significant institutional change for which protracted civil society pressure might claim some credit. The change will, moreover, enhance the public legitimacy of the World Bank President and the institution overall.

On the whole, then, civil society efforts to catalyse greater accountability in the Bank's governance arrangements have had little impact, and have been notably less successful than the efforts to improve accountability in respect of projects and policies. Civil society successes on Bank governance have largely been limited to incremental improvements in Board transparency. Little progress has been achieved on deeper structural problems of Board accountability, i.e. vote allocation proportionate to economy; excessive influence of finance ministries; shortfalls in parliamentary scrutiny; the US prerogative in selecting the President; and the relative voicelessness in the Board of the poorest and most affected constituents.

In part, this failure must be ascribed to the unwillingness of governments that benefit from the current governance arrangements at the

World Bank to relinquish some of their power. In addition, however, civil society efforts to reform Bank governance have been complicated by the recognition that these moves towards greater formal democracy in the Board might not benefit citizens on the ground. Since many borrowing countries lack robust mechanisms for democratic accountability and citizen participation, increasing the vote of their governments in the World Bank Board might not make the institution more responsive to affected citizens. Indeed, donor governments have often supported reforms on issues that CSOs hold dear, such as gender equity, environment, participation and anti-corruption, while many developing country members have opposed such moves. This tension – between more democratic multilateralism on the one hand and more effective issue-oriented advocacy on the other – has perhaps discouraged more concerted and co-ordinated civil society efforts to improve Board accountability.

## Conclusions

Over the course of three decades of advocacy, civil society organisations have achieved some notable successes in improving the accountability of the World Bank to those who are affected by its operations. Improvements have mostly occurred at the project and policy levels, where sustained civil society pressure has been instrumental in the establishment of social and environmental safeguards, greater transparency and consultation requirements, and the creation of the Inspection Panel for purposes of evaluation and redress.

Taken as a whole, however, these CSO successes have been decidedly limited. In particular, persistent problems in the timing, scope, content and quality of consultation processes have often limited their capacity to deliver public accountability. Many of these shortcomings can be attributed to the Bank's inability (or unwillingness) to fully integrate accountability to affected peoples into incentive structures for staff. In addition, as detailed in the latter part of this chapter, CSOs have generally failed to improve accountability of the World Bank Board. These shortfalls of democratic accountability may be the most difficult to address because of their deep roots in power relations of the global political economy. Yet, reforms of Bank governance are among the most crucial for its legitimacy and effectiveness.

The future holds numerous challenges and opportunities for civil society associations in enhancing the accountability of the World Bank, particularly to people who are most affected by its interventions. Potentially the greatest advances could be achieved by focusing civil society attention on the two dimensions most neglected so far: staff incentives and Board governance. Regarding the first of these matters, it is crucial that CSOs better understand the incentive and promotion structures for staff and then seek closer alignment of those arrangements with greater participation of affected people in project cycles and policy reviews. Regarding the second matter, new modes of Board governance, civil society actors may have their greatest advantages at the national rather than the global level. In this vein some CSOs are already usefully working with parliamentarians both to oversee the institution and to become more attentive to how Bank projects affect their citizens. The World Bank is, after all, an intergovernmental organisation, and reform of the institution will be limited unless the member governments are made sufficiently responsive to their own citizens and civil societies.

# 4    Civil society and IMF accountability

*Jan Aart Scholte*

## Introduction

The International Monetary Fund (IMF, also known informally as 'the Fund') is one of the most prominent, influential and, at times, contested agencies in contemporary global governance. Following a relatively sleepy existence in the first quarter-century after its creation at the Bretton Woods Conference in 1944, the IMF greatly enlarged its agenda, resources and membership to become a significant architect of accelerated globalisation, especially in the global south and the former Soviet bloc. In particular the Fund has been a crucial provider of balance of payments support during the recurrent crises that have plagued liberalised global finance since the 1980s. In addition, across the world the IMF is a major source of macroeconomic policy advice, technical assistance, training, policy research, and rules in respect of global financial flows.

From its headquarters in Washington, DC and field offices in over 70 countries and regions, the IMF has extensive involvements in governance of the world economy. In 2009 overall lending capacity of the Fund was raised to US$750 billion. During 2008–9, the IMF approved loans for balance of payments support totalling SDR 67.6 billion (around US$107.3 billion) to 43 national governments (IMF 2009a: 10). In addition, the IMF holds so-called 'Article IV consultations' with all of its 186 member states, on an annual or biennial basis, to monitor and advise

I am grateful to participants in the Gothenburg workshop – especially discussants Jo Marie Griesgraber and Bassirou Sarr – for full feedback on an earlier draft of this chapter. Many thanks are also due to some 500 civil society actors, Fund staff and other officials who have, since 1995, kindly given their time and shared their expertise for my studies of IMF-civil society relations. Many undocumented details in this chapter are taken from those confidential interviews. Funding for the fieldwork that informs this study – undertaken especially in Argentina, Brazil, Canada, Democratic Republic of Congo, Egypt, France, Malawi, Mali, Mozambique, Nigeria, Romania, Russia, Thailand, Uganda, the UK and the USA – has been generously provided by the Economic and Social Research Council, the Ford Foundation, the Independent Evaluation Office of the IMF, the Nuffield Foundation and the University of Warwick.

on national macroeconomic policies. The Fund also conducts surveillance of the global situation (e.g. with its *World Economic Outlook* and *Global Financial Stability Report*) as well as regional developments (e.g. with published surveys on the Asia-Pacific, Europe, Latin America and Caribbean, Middle East and Central Asia, and Sub-Saharan Africa). The IMF despatches several hundred technical assistance missions each year to advise governments and central banks of member states. It furthermore runs training courses for thousands of officials from all over the world at 7 sites on 5 continents. The Fund is also a notable source of rules in respect of the huge expansion of global financial flows that has transpired since the 1970s: in addition to supporting the global monetary regime of floating exchange rates that emerged after 1971, the IMF has taken a leading role in promoting capital account liberalisation, data dissemination standards, and 'codes of good practice' on fiscal, monetary and financial sector policies.

The breadth and depth of IMF activities and impacts have raised considerable demands of accountability on the institution. A wide range of stakeholders – national governments and other governance agencies, commercial companies, civil society associations and general publics – have affirmed that the Fund should answer for its (often highly consequential) actions and omissions. Moreover, many observers have worried that insufficient arrangements are in place to correct IMF performance when it is deficient, with the result that orderly and equitable regulation of today's more global economy could be compromised. A leading veteran official at the Fund puts this point starkly, noting that:

The IMF can be a huge force for good if it has the right kind of accountability. Either we get the accountability right or we lose the opportunity of this institution to make globalisation a fairer process (Interview, 2007b).

Other studies have examined issues of IMF accountability in general terms (Woods 2000; Woods and Narlikar 2001; Stiglitz 2003; Buira 2005; Carin and Wood 2005; IEO 2008). The present chapter assesses the particular role of civil society activities in advancing the democratic accountability of the Fund. Such an analysis can build on earlier investigations of relations between the IMF and civil society (Abugre and Alexander 1998; O'Brien *et al.* 2000: Ch. 5; Scholte 2001b, 2002, 2009; Dawson and Bhatt 2002; Thirkell-White 2004; Griesgraber 2008). However, no research to date has specifically and systematically assessed these interchanges with a focus on IMF accountability. Have civil society groups helped to make the Fund answerable to those whom it affects? In what ways, to what extents, and for what constituencies have civil society associations enhanced the core components of accountability – namely, transparency, consultation, evaluation and correction – in IMF operations?

The argument put forward here is that various types of civil society associations (including NGOs, research institutes, business forums, trade unions, faith groups and informally organised social movements) have used various tactics to advance IMF accountability on various occasions to various constituencies. However, the overall scale of these civil society contributions has remained modest to date, particularly when measured against the substantial accountability gaps that currently exist in respect of Fund activities (on these shortfalls see the literature cited above). More intensive engagement with civil society associations in the future could further enhance IMF accountability.

Yet, in order to advance *democratic* accountability more specifically, certain qualitative improvements in IMF-civil society relations would be needed along with quantitative increases in the interchanges. To date civil society involvement with the Fund has generally tended to promote accountability that is in two significant senses hegemonic in relation to deeper social structures. First, IMF accountability so far secured through civil society channels has, on the whole, flowed disproportionately to dominant countries and social circles, rather than to subordinate countries and social strata. To this degree civil society engagement has reinforced undemocratic structural inequalities at the Fund. Second, and perhaps partly in consequence of this unequal access and impact, the increased accountability so far achieved by civil society initiatives vis-à-vis the IMF has mostly fallen within – and tended to legitimate – prevailing broad policy frames at the institution, rather than more fundamentally challenging the bases upon which the Fund has worked. In other words, civil society influences on IMF accountability have in the main had either a 'conformist' character that reinforces existing priorities and procedures in the agency or a 'reformist' quality that adjusts Fund practices while remaining within dominant patterns of world order (e.g. of capitalism and Western modernity). Civil society interventions in respect of IMF accountability have generally not had deeper 'transformist' implications that subvert and transcend underlying (and often deeply undemocratic) social structures.

To elaborate this argument, the first section below gives a brief general discussion of civil society activity as a means to promote IMF accountability. Then a series of four sections assess where, how far and for whom civil society interventions have and have not made the Fund more answerable, with reference to the respective dimensions of transparency, consultation, evaluation and correction. Hegemonic tendencies in the accountability achieved are highlighted in each case. The conclusion reflects on improved and less hegemonic ways forward in IMF-civil society relations.

## Civil society as a force for IMF accountability

As set out in Chapter 1, civil society can be broadly understood as a political arena where associations of citizens seek, from outside political parties, to shape the rules that govern one or the other aspect of social life. In the present context the 'rules' in question involve IMF governance of global monetary and financial flows as well as macroeconomic policy more generally.

The principal types of civil society associations that have concerned themselves with the Fund are (in roughly descending order of the intensity with which they have considered the agency): research institutes; nongovernmental organisations (NGOs); business forums; labour unions; faith groups; and more ephemeral mobilisations like the Initiative Against Economic Globalization that formed around the 2000 IMF/World Bank Annual Meetings in Prague. Civil society actions have engaged the IMF both at its head offices in Washington and in the field across the planet.

Civil society engagements of the Fund have been both direct and indirect. In terms of direct exchanges, civil society groups have had interchanges with IMF Governors, Executive Directors (EDs), management and staff. In terms of indirect relations, citizen associations have also taken their concerns about the IMF to other global bodies such as the United Nations (including its Financing for Development initiative since 1997); to regional bodies like the Sub-Committee on IMF Matters (SCIMF) at the European Union; to national ministries (especially of economy and finance); to national parliaments (especially their budget and finance committees); to political parties; to the mass media (e.g. with letters to the editor and op-ed pieces); and to the streets.

Notable civil society engagement of the Fund emerged in the 1970s with sporadic demonstrations in various countries of the global south against some of the policy conditions placed on IMF loans. During the 1980s a small number of civil society organisations (CSOs) built up more sustained and systematic advocacy in respect of the Fund. Several global associations – for example the International Confederation of Free Trade Unions (ICFTU) and Friends of the Earth (FOE) – established bureaux in Washington partly in order to pursue closer contacts with the Bretton Woods institutions. The ranks of CSOs engaging the IMF expanded further in the 1990s and the early twenty-first century, for example around the global campaign for debt cancellation and through citizen inputs to Poverty Reduction Strategy Papers (PRSPs) for low-income countries.

By the end of the 1980s civil society activities concerning the IMF had attained sufficient scale and impact for the institution to begin to develop capacities to address these groups. A Public Affairs Division was created inside the External Relations Department (EXR) in 1989, among other things for outreach to CSOs. However, the Fund did not appoint its first specifically designated 'NGO liaison officer' until 1998. Five years later the Executive Board of the IMF took the further step of requesting the preparation of a fairly detailed 'Guide for Staff Relations with Civil Society Organisations' (IMF 2003). Thus, although the Articles of Agreement of 1944 that founded the Fund (and subsequent amendments) have made no provision for interchanges with CSOs, both the institution and its member governments now implicitly accept that civil society activities are part of policy processes at the IMF.

The question at hand here is whether and how this thirty-year accumulation of civil society engagement of the Fund has enhanced transparency, consultation, evaluation and correction at this global governance institution.[1] More particularly, it can be asked how far civil society initiatives have helped to fill the especially severe gaps in IMF accountability with respect to weak states and with regard to citizens, especially those in marginalised social circles. As indicated earlier, the general picture is one of some notable but also limited gains. Moreover, the advances in IMF accountability achieved through CSOs have mainly (though not exclusively) been in response to pressures from more powerful quarters in civil society, and these citizen group inputs have at most refined rather than transformed the broad principles on which the Fund has operated. In these two senses civil society impacts on IMF accountability to date can be qualified as hegemonic.

Of course it is well-nigh impossible to disentangle civil society influences on IMF accountability from the many other forces at play in the multifaceted networks that shape contemporary public policy. Hence no attempt is made here to calculate a precise measure of the civil society role, either on its own or relative to other forces. However, the significance of civil society involvements in respect of IMF accountability can be affirmed on several grounds. First, a conception (as developed in Chapter 1) of global governance through complex public policy networks

---

[1] There is a further question: whether and how IMF relations with civil society might reverberate to enhance the accountability of national governments to their citizens. For example, in countries like Guinea and Mozambique, CSOs have used the opportunity of exchanges with the Fund to open space for increased consultations with, and oversight of, national authorities on matters of macroeconomic policy. However, the present analysis addresses the accountability of the global governance institution rather than that of its member states.

suggests that multiple types of players (including civil society actors) each have some part in shaping outcomes. Second, striking correlations exist between a number of civil society initiatives and various Fund moves on accountability; thus civil society actions have apparently helped in some measure to prompt IMF reactions. Third, numerous witnesses, including many Fund officials themselves, have attributed various developments in respect of IMF accountability at least partly to civil society interventions. Fourth, counterfactual thinking suggests that certain Fund actions on accountability would have been less likely – or would have occurred quite differently – in the absence of civil society involvements. Cumulative evidence of these kinds may not count as definitive proof, but it strongly suggests that civil society activities have made a difference – and could potentially matter a good deal more – in IMF accountability.

Indeed, civil society initiatives have arguably played a significant part in putting the issue of Fund accountability on the political agenda. Several decades of recurrent street demonstrations against the IMF have conveyed an insistent message (often amplified through media coverage) that substantial publics perceive unacceptable shortfalls of accountability in the institution. Such mobilisations have occurred across multiple locations: in dozens of programme countries across the globe; at IMF/World Bank Annual Meetings in Berlin, Madrid, Prague and Washington; at Group of Eight (G8) summits (as covered in Chapter 9 of this book); around the yearly World Economic Forum (WEF) in Davos; and from 2001 at the World Social Forum (WSF). Anti-Fund demonstrations have declined in size and frequency in recent years, arguably in part because of greater IMF consultation of civil society circles, as detailed later.

Alongside the street protests, certain CSOs have for the past two decades specifically lobbied the IMF for greater transparency, consultation, evaluation and correction. Prominent associations in this regard include the Center of Concern (especially its Rethinking Bretton Woods Project) and the New Rules for Global Finance Coalition in Washington, the Bretton Woods Project and the One World Trust in London, the Ottawa-based Halifax Initiative Coalition, and the campaign To Reform the International Financial Institutions, involving some thirty NGOs in France. Several of these advocacy groups have developed close relations with sympathetic Fund officials so that, in the words of one veteran campaigner, 'our initiatives on accountability have helped reformers inside the IMF to press their arguments' (Interview, 2007a).

In sum, then, it seems doubtful that governments as well as IMF management and staff would have begun to reflect more critically on the Fund's answerability to stakeholders if, among other factors, a host of civil society actors had not persistently pushed them to do so. Street protests on the outside and lobbying on the inside have worked in tandem in this regard. In particular, pressure from mass demonstrations has put official circles on the defensive and expanded the political space in which reformers in civil society can promote steps for increased accountability of the Fund.

## Civil society and IMF transparency

Some of those citizen group interventions have, since the mid-1990s, contributed to a number of advances in the public transparency of the IMF. Up to the early 1990s only small circles of central bankers and finance ministry officials could obtain timely and detailed information regarding policy processes at the Fund. Today the IMF practises some of the most extensive public disclosure of any global governance institution. The 2006 *Global Accountability Report* by the One World Trust ranked the Fund fourth among thirty major global organisations in terms of transparency (Blagescu and Lloyd 2006: 26).

Certainly, undue confidentiality continues to mark some aspects of IMF policymaking. For example, while the crucial process of selecting the Managing Director (MD) who heads the organisation is now more open to public scrutiny than previously, it remains substantially secretive. In addition, minutes of Executive Board meetings are normally not released for ten years, and various operational guidance notes for Fund staff are not publicly available at all. Also, governments may overplay their discretion to withhold what they regard as sensitive contents in IMF documents related to their country.

Yet, these limitations noted, the current situation is very different from 1995, when the Fund had never even released an organigram of its basic bureaucratic apparatus. Today, in contrast, the names and contact details of most key IMF staff are readily available. The published *Annual Report* of the Executive Board now provides extensive and more accessible information about the work of the institution. In 1997 the Executive Board began to issue Public Information Notices (PINs) that summarise its discussions of country circumstances and general policy matters. In 2001 it decided to allow a fuller publication of IMF policy papers and, subject to agreement by the government concerned, IMF country documents. Two years later the Board moved further to a presumption of disclosure of these documents unless the government in question specifically objected. IMF transparency has also increased through a burgeoning publication programme of statistical compilations, books, working papers, pamphlets, factsheets, newsletters and more. In 1995 the Fund launched a website that has grown to be one of the most comprehensive of any global governance institution. What role did civil society play in this striking turnaround with regard to IMF transparency?

In a general sense civil society impacts with regard to transparency have come from years of constantly repeated demands on the Fund for greater public disclosure. Starting with a few CSOs (e.g. Friends of the Earth) in the 1980s, calls for IMF transparency spread to many NGOs by the mid-1990s. In a case of specific influence in this matter, lobbying from certain NGOs helped persuade the US Congress in 1994 to withhold three-quarters of a requested US$100 million appropriation for replenishment of the IMF's Enhanced Structural Adjustment Fund (ESAF), subject to greater information disclosure by the institution (CQA 1994). Likewise, a group of development NGOs in Ireland combined forces with opposition members of the Dáil to withhold the Dublin government's contribution to ESAF from 1995 to 1999 (DDC 1997: 24–5, 34–7).

Several notable civil society-led reports have criticised shortfalls in IMF transparency and pressed various recommendations for improvements. For example, in 1997–8 the Center of Concern assembled influential senior figures in a Study Group on Transparency and Accountability in the International Monetary Fund. In addition, the aforementioned Global Accountability Project at the One World Trust has since 2002 highlighted transparency issues at the Fund (Kovach *et al.* 2003; Blagescu and Lloyd 2006). In 2007 a High-Level Panel on IMF Board Accountability convened through New Rules for Global Finance urged greater information disclosure in respect of Board proceedings and staff guidance notes (New Rules for Global Finance 2007a).

In a more extended effort, nine NGOs from five continents joined forces in 2003 to launch a Global Transparency Initiative (GTI) aimed at multilateral financial agencies including the IMF (GTI 2010; also Musuva 2006). A GTI Transparency Charter for International Financial Institutions launched in 2006 has garnered civil society signatories from around the world. The GTI has also issued a guide on access to information at the IMF (GTI 2007). In 2007 the Bank Information Center (BIC) in Washington established a staff position specifically devoted to promote IMF transparency.

Many civil society groups have also made the IMF more publicly visible through their efforts at citizen learning. Countless academic institutions, faith groups, NGOs and trade unions have over the years offered people information about and analysis of the Fund through publications, lectures, workshops, artistic performances, videos, posters, libraries and websites. Some CSOs have also made IMF documentation more accessible to the general public. For example, the Malawi Economic Justice Network (MEJN) and the group Civil Society for Poverty Reduction

(CSPR) in Zambia have produced lay versions (including in local languages) of certain of the respective governments' agreements with the IMF (CSPR 2008).

Of course civil society activities have not been the sole impetus behind moves towards greater transparency at the IMF. Various governments, journalists, legislators, officials from other governance bodies and some of the Fund's own management and staff have also pressed the IMF to become more publicly visible. In addition, the prevailing (often dubbed 'neoliberal') economic policy discourse of recent decades has maintained that markets perform best when producers and consumers are equipped with full information about the situation at hand. In this way the general policy context of the time has encouraged the Fund to follow its own prescriptions. Thus civil society initiatives on IMF transparency have made a difference not so much in their own right, but through relations of mutual reinforcement with other auspicious circumstances.

Having identified this civil society role, certain hegemonic qualities of these politics of transparency can also be observed. Part of the question 'accountability *to whom*' involves the issue 'transparency *for whom*'. The IMF has directed its increased disclosure mainly to English-speaking and economically literate audiences with access to high-speed Internet connections and/or specialist libraries. In contrast, the Fund at present remains largely invisible to non-specialists, even more so when they do not speak English and are offline. Yet these large bypassed circles encompass many of the people whose lives the Fund most deeply affects. Belatedly, the IMF has expanded its translation programme, including through its website since 2007. Resident representative offices of the Fund in sixty-six countries now have their own web page, in certain cases including modest amounts of translated material (IMF 2010). Yet all in all little country-specific documentation is available in relevant local languages. Even the translated material usually remains highly technical and says little that is explicit about the political dimensions of IMF activities. On the whole, then, the Fund has mainly become more transparent for English-speaking elite specialists in the global north. To this extent the greater openness has so far tended to reinforce the dominance of the countries and social circles that were already the most powerful in the IMF.

Civil society activities have – if largely unintentionally – contributed to this hegemonic outcome. Apart from incidental cases like the above-mentioned initiatives in Malawi and Zambia, CSO drives for greater disclosure by the Fund have been concentrated in North America and Western Europe. Moreover, until recently the Northern elite activists who have led the campaigns did little to consult other parts of civil society about needs and priorities as regards IMF transparency. The GTI since 2003 and the High-Level Panel in 2006–7 have involved greater collaboration with parties in the global south, although the co-ordination has still been centred in London and Washington. In 2008 ActionAid USA briefly pursued an economic literacy project in respect of the IMF with civil society associations in Kenya, Malawi and Sierra Leone; yet this initiative to empower general publics in low-income countries is also striking for its exceptionality and tardiness. On democratic grounds it might be urged that CSOs work harder in future to broaden the audiences for greater IMF transparency.

Likewise, civil society campaigners for IMF transparency could reflect more carefully on the purposes that greater disclosure serves. In general the NGO activists concerned have tended to presume somewhat uncritically that more 'openness' ipso facto is a good thing, without more precisely assessing the relationship between particular kinds of transparency and the deeper patterns of world order. Arguably, the types of greater information that the IMF has released, and the forms and channels through which this disclosure has occurred, have mainly served to advance already dominant policy paradigms. In other words, the deeper structural effect of increased technocratic transparency of the Fund could be to make 'markets' (read globalising capitalism) function more smoothly and to make 'knowledge' (read neoclassical economic analysis) more available and influential. In their eagerness to reduce 'secrecy' at the IMF, civil society campaigners have generally not contemplated that the specific ways in which transparency is practised can have different implications for models of 'development'. Far from being subversive, greater openness could in fact consolidate the status quo.

## Civil society and IMF consultation

A similar pattern of notable but incomplete advances in accountability – and on generally hegemonic lines – can be discerned in regard to IMF consultation of civil society associations. The Fund has since the 1980s progressively increased and enhanced its policy deliberations with CSOs, thereby again, as with transparency, de facto broadening its accountability relations beyond governments. However, both the quantity and the quality of these consultations have had limits. In particular, the more substantive IMF discussions with civil society groups have to date predominantly involved organisations in the global north and narrow elite circles in academe, business and better-resourced NGOs. In addition, the discourse in these exchanges has rarely strayed from orthodox macroeconomic analysis.

The Fund began to involve CSOs in its policy deliberations in the early 1980s. At this time IMF staff convened several joint seminars with economic policy think tanks in Washington, initiating intensive dialogues with outside researchers that continue to this day (Killick 1982; Williamson 1983). Concurrently several new business associations, such as the Bretton Woods Committee (BWC), the Institute of International Finance (IIF) and the Japan Center for International Finance (JCIF), opened exchanges with IMF management and staff (Orr 2002). In the late 1980s some NGOs began to meet with Executive Directors of the Fund during the Annual Meetings; however, more regular consultations of NGOs and trade unions by IMF officials did not develop until the mid-1990s.

Today IMF consultation of CSOs occurs, albeit to generally modest extents, at all of the main points in the organisation. For one thing, accredited civil society delegates have since the 1980s obtained access to the Annual and Spring Meetings of the Board of Governors. In 2007, for example, a total of 220 civil society passes were issued for the Spring Meetings in April and 246 for the Annual Meetings in October. The rules allow registered civil society actors to observe (but not address) the plenary sessions of the Board of Governors; however, few groups have exercised this right to sit in on the (usually formulaic) speeches. Instead, CSOs have used their access to the conference area to lobby officials and to stage their own events (in recent years brought together in a so-called Civil Society Policy Forum).

The Annual and Spring Meetings also provide occasions for consultative meetings between CSOs and EDs, although this particular ritual has declined from its peak in the second half of the 1990s. Ad hoc meetings between EDs and civil society actors occur at other times of the year as well, usually at IMF headquarters, but occasionally also when EDs visit their country constituencies. Since the mid-1990s a so-called 'group travel' initiative has on several occasions taken a number of EDs on a joint visit to a particular region, where among other things they have met a few local civil society associations.

The Managing Director, too, has engaged in some consultation of civil society associations since the 1990s. Certain CSOs (e.g. the Brookings Institution, the IIF and Oxfam) have had repeated meetings of a more substantive nature with the MD. In addition, starting in 2002 the MD, together with the President of the World Bank, has jointly convened a biennial summit with labour union leaders from around the world. Also since 2002 the leaders of the two Bretton Woods institutions have held an hour-long so-called 'town hall meeting' with civil society groups at the Annual Meetings. In the field, the MD and Deputy MDs have on their travels held a number of one-off exchanges with local business forums, NGOs, religious leaders and trade unions.

Many IMF staff also pursue policy consultations with CSOs, although practices vary across departments. For example, the Research Department of the Fund has since the late 1980s maintained regular contacts with a host of policy think tanks, university faculties and professional academic associations (nearly all in the field of economics). The Strategy, Policy and Review Department (SPR) – previously Policy Development and Review (PDR) – and the Fiscal Affairs Department (FAD) have since the mid-1990s taken civil society inputs on a variety of questions including debt relief and social expenditure. The Monetary and Capital Markets Department (MCM) has regularly engaged with specialised trade bodies like the IIF and the New York-based Trade Association for the Emerging Markets (EMTA), as well as certain think tanks such as Bruegel, based in Brussels.

Many staff from the IMF's five area departments (African, Asia and Pacific, European, Middle East and Central Asia, Western Hemisphere) also meet with civil society actors. These consultations normally relate to circumstances in the countries where the department operates. The African Department (since 2004) and the European Department (since 2006) have each designated a senior member of staff to co-ordinate external communications, including with civil society groups.

In addition to discussions at Fund headquarters, a number of civil society consultations occur during staff visits to member countries. Programme missions (i.e. staff visits connected with the use of IMF resources) usually set aside at least half a day to meet with civil society actors from the country. Likewise, most Article IV visits for routine Fund surveillance of national economies now meet with a selection of local research institutes, business forums, trade unions and NGOs. Indeed, consultation of CSOs during Article IV exercises was a formal condition of Switzerland's accession to the IMF in 1993 (Chauhan and Gurtner 1996). In addition, country visits connected with the Financial Sector Assessment Program (FSAP), the Policy Support Instrument (PSI), and other technical assistance often meet with civil society bodies like banking associations and think tanks. Briefing papers for IMF missions are now meant to outline plans for interface with civil society, and back-to-office reports are supposed to describe and assess these interchanges. In practice, however, Fund staff generally continue to give scant attention in their paperwork to relations with civil society groups.

A more particular consultation of CSOs concerning IMF-related matters in low-income countries has occurred since 1999 during the formulation of PRSPs. Such documents, which now exist for sixty-two countries, map out a strategy of poverty reduction and form the basis for donor lending, including Fund credits through the Poverty Reduction and Growth Facility (PRGF). Donors have prescribed that the PRSP process should include inputs from civil society, although the record on this engagement has been mixed. In some countries energetic CSO involvement has generated innovative policy measures, while in other cases the process has been limited to a few relatively passive citizen associations (Whaites 2002; Gould 2005). However, in most instances macroeconomic issues that concern the IMF have been kept out of PRSP consultations with CSOs. In any case, PRSP discussions have mainly put civil society groups in dialogue with governments rather than global agencies, in the name of building national ownership of policy.

Between staff visits from Washington additional IMF consultation of in-country CSOs occurs through the resident representative. The Fund has at any one time maintained 'res reps' in up to half of its member countries around the world. The scope and intensity of res rep engagement with civil society groups varies considerably, depending on a number of factors such as the political culture that prevails in the country and the personal predilections of the individuals concerned. In any case IMF res rep bureaux are sparsely staffed and, in contrast to World Bank resident missions and UNDP country offices, lack specially designated civil society liaison officers.

To facilitate and monitor the various management and staff interchanges with CSOs, the External Relations Department of the Fund has since the mid-1990s given more systematic attention to civil society. Certainly, with only 3–4 dedicated personnel (among 2,000 professional staff at the IMF overall) these EXR efforts have remained smaller than those of the Civil Society Team at the World Bank described in Chapter 3 and the various civil society liaison offices at the UN described in Chapter 2. Nevertheless, EXR has taken some noteworthy initiatives, such as producing a Civil Society Newsletter launched in 2002 and reaching around 6,000 addresses in 2007, when it was replaced by a regularly updated 'IMF and Civil Society' page on the Fund's website. EXR also spearheaded the aforementioned staff guide for relations with CSOs and has from time to time undertaken its own visits to the field that include meetings with civil society groups.

In sum, then, the IMF has since the 1980s made gradual but noteworthy advances in consultation of civil society associations; however, the scale of these activities must not be overstated. The Fund's engagement with civil society groups rose noticeably in the dozen years after 1990, but the trend never accelerated into a fast lane and on the contrary has generally stalled since around 2003. Consultations with CSOs do not figure large in the daily work of Governors, EDs, management and staff at the IMF. Many staff visits and resident representatives still give only passing, if any, attention to civil society liaison. As one Fund insider with extensive experience of interchanges with CSOs concedes, 'the rhetoric of outreach does not match what happens on the ground' (Interview, 2007c).

Moreover, the 'consultative' qualities of Fund dialogues with civil society groups can be rather weak. Certainly general attitudes at the IMF towards CSOs have with time become more receptive, as compared with the widespread arrogance and defensiveness that frequently marred exchanges in the 1980s and 1990s. As late as 1999 EXR conceived of contacts with civil society mainly as a public relations exercise that would have little consequence for substantive policy (Edelman 1999). Today EDs, management and staff are on the whole more ready than before to pursue substantive dialogue with civil society groups, in which the officials not only put forward existing IMF positions, but also take information, insight and advice from their interlocutors. Furthermore, in a minority of cases the Fund now engages CSOs early enough in policymaking processes for the inputs to have meaningful effects on outcomes. Thus, for example, the 2007 revision of the *Code of Good Practices on Fiscal Transparency* entailed systematic involvement from civil society organisations such as New Rules for Global Finance, Publish What You Pay, Transparency International and the National Budget Group Azerbaijan (IMF 2007). Likewise, in 2009 Fund management systematically engaged civil society as a 'Fourth Pillar' in its consultations on the reform of IMF governance (IMF 2009c).

Yet, particularly in the field, much IMF 'dialogue' with civil society groups continues to have limited content or consequence. In these situations Fund officials are often poorly briefed on the interlocutors from civil society and give limited if any follow-up to the (frequently sporadic) discussions. The consultations lack written agendas, briefing papers, agreed minutes, or action points. In the light of such shortcomings, a 2007 Independent Evaluation Office (IEO) report on Sub-Saharan Africa still spoke of 'limited and ineffective IMF engagement with country-based members of civil society' (IEO 2007: 25; see also Scholte 2009).

The quality of Fund consultations with CSOs has also suffered when civil society capacities have been weak. Indeed, the circle of civil society associations with long-term, in-depth experience of engaging the IMF is quite small, even in countries like Argentina, Russia and Uganda that have experienced extended and intensive Fund-sponsored programmes. Many civil society actors have held only general intuitions about the workings of the IMF, thereby limiting the possibilities for detailed deliberations with the global agency on specific policies. In these situations many Fund officials are reluctant to devote scarce time to very basic conversations with civil society groups that may only be encountered once.

Yet this reluctance can also feed a deeper hegemonic limitation on democratic accountability in current practices of IMF consultation of CSOs. Not surprisingly, capacities for civil society engagement of the Fund are most concentrated at sites of structural power in the contemporary world order, such as the global north, major urban centres, big business, the professional classes, English-speakers and culturally Western circles. In contrast, CSO inputs to IMF-backed policies have rarely (even in the context of PRSPs) included associations of disabled persons, indigenous peoples, peasants, non-Christian religions, street traders and women. Indeed, technical experts at the Fund have tended to presume that stakeholders with less formal education (such as many shop stewards and small-business people) are not qualified to contribute to policy deliberations. Thus the expansion in IMF consultations of civil society associations has to date predominantly involved geographically and socially privileged quarters. To this extent consultation of civil society has – contrary to a democratic logic that some theorists have assumed and many activists have intended – actually reinforced structural inequalities of voice at the Fund.

Recent years have seen a few steps to counter these hierarchies, particularly as they relate to the North-South axis. For example, in 2007 the IMF at last appointed an official to EXR with a specific brief to upgrade relations with CSOs in the global south. Since 2006 the Fund and the World Bank have jointly sponsored handfuls of civil society delegates from the global south to attend the Board of Governors meetings; a few NGOs have over the years done the same. However, these exceptional initiatives at the margins highlight the prevailing hegemonic patterns of narrow and privileged civil society access to consultations with the Fund.

Moreover, sponsorship and other IMF measures to facilitate consultation of CSOs can encourage a co-optation that blunts the critical edge of the inputs given. Favoured civil society interlocutors have in recent years gained remarkable access to Fund documents, personnel and premises. In some respects these steps by the IMF to facilitate civil society advocacy are welcome; yet comforts and ease can also bring activists to relax their scrutiny. In this vein, one veteran campaigner laments that 'NGOs have been so domesticated in regard to the Fund' (Interview, 2007d). Another observes that 'civil society is now *como Juan por su casa* at the IMF' (Interview, 2007e).

Hegemonic tendencies can also be seen in the range of policy options that IMF-CSO consultations normally cover. Certainly, over the past decade Fund officials have become more flexible in adjusting their recommendations at the level of details. Thus, for example, IMF consultations with civil society groups today often involve genuine deliberations concerning matters such as suitable inflation targets, wage ceilings, budget deficits, social spending plans, liberalisation of the current and capital accounts, and banking standards. To this extent long-heard charges that the Fund rigidly imposes one-size-fits-all blueprints are increasingly out of date.

Yet, in paradigmatic terms, the content of IMF consultations with CSOs has as a rule been confined within prevailing orthodoxies of modern economic and political analysis. Although discussions between the Fund and civil society associations can be searching, creative and even heated, the conversations also rarely transgress certain epistemological boundaries. Discourses beyond neoclassical, Keynesian and liberal-pluralist thought tend to be subtly disallowed, as IMF-CSO dialogues quite systematically (if largely subconsciously) eschew deeper critiques and alternative theoretical frames. Counter-hegemonic propositions from perspectives such as feminism, social ecology, socialism and various forms of religious revivalism are comprehensively excluded from IMF-civil society exchanges. Such silencing of foundational dissent is usually neither deliberate nor aggressive. Rather, the parties implicitly understand that, beyond an invisible frontier of acceptable reformism, more unorthodox ideas are 'out of place' in these conversations. In this sense, then, Fund consultations with civil society have generally had the effect of consolidating and legitimating dominant constructions of knowledge and policy.

### Civil society and IMF evaluation

As in respect of transparency and consultation, civil society activities have since the 1980s contributed some notable advances to IMF accountability with regard to evaluation. For one thing, a number of CSOs have over the years monitored and assessed the execution and results of Fund policies and programmes, often publishing their findings and recommendations for wider consumption. In addition, several well-placed civil society associations promoted the creation of the IMF's own Independent Evaluation Office and have subsequently furthered the operations of that oversight mechanism. Certain other civil society initiatives have sought to enhance parliamentary and media scrutiny of the IMF. Once more, however, CSO involvement in this area of accountability has had some overall hegemonic qualities, in the sense of giving limited voice to peripheral circles and tending on the whole not to question the deeper principles of world order that underpin the Fund's work.

Regarding direct evaluation by CSOs, from the 1970s onwards notable numbers of civil society associations have tracked and analysed the consequences of IMF activities. The results of these assessments have circulated quite widely through newsletters, pamphlets, books and websites. This watchdog role of civil society has been the more important for democratic accountability given the general shortfalls in rigorous scrutiny of the Fund by courts, the mass media, parliaments and (until 2001) an official evaluation unit.

Policy think tanks and university researchers have generated a regular stream of studies that critically examine a wide range of IMF policies and programmes. Prominent sources of such investigations have included the Peterson Institute for International Economics (PIIE) in Washington and the Overseas Development Institute (ODI) in London. In addition, most national capitals and commercial centres have hosted at least one or two research bodies that among other things assess the work of the IMF in that country or region. Examples include the Institute of Higher Studies in Management (IHEM) in Bamako, the Thailand Development Research Institute (TDRI) in Bangkok, the Academy of Economic Studies in Bucharest and the Foundation for Latin American Economic Investigations (FIEL) in Buenos Aires. Studies from such think tanks have usually obtained much less international circulation than work emanating from the Center for Global Development (CGD) in Washington or the University of Oxford, but this local monitoring can obtain a significant hearing in the respective countries.

Indeed, IMF officials have often given evaluative reports from economic research institutes very serious attention. Most professional staff at the Fund hold doctorates in economics and have a deep respect for academic peer review. Many of these officials have held university positions before coming to the Fund, and some continue to present their personal research to academic conferences and journals. In a number of cases IMF staff have exchanged detailed comments with outside scholars on several successive drafts of an evaluative study.

Over the years some NGOs have also built up research capacities that they have applied to assessments of the IMF. For instance, in the mid-1990s the Center of Concern issued several critical studies of policy processes at the Fund (Griesgraber and Gunter 1996). Around the same time the World Wide Fund for Nature (WWF) sponsored research into purportedly harmful ecological consequences of IMF-supported macroeconomic policies (Reed 1996). Several development NGOs such as ActionAid, Oxfam and World Vision have published critical reports on IMF-sponsored policies in low-income countries (Whaites 2002; Oxfam 2003; ActionAid 2007). The Bretton Woods Project has since 1996 circulated a quarterly and then bimonthly newsletter with detailed scrutiny of IMF and World Bank activities (BWP 2008).

A number of business forums and trade unions have also assessed the implications for their members of Fund prescriptions. For example, the International Trade Union Confederation (ITUC) and the ICFTU before it have since the early 1990s released a public letter concerning the effects of the Bretton Woods institutions on workers to the MD ahead of the Annual Meetings (Adaba 2002). The IIF has produced critical evaluations of IMF proposals in the area of debt management and financial regulation.

As well as undertaking considerable external scrutiny of the IMF, civil society initiatives have also figured among the pressures for the creation of a formal evaluation mechanism in the shape of the IEO. The establishment of such a unit, which eventually occurred in 2001, was a primary recommendation of the civil society-led Study Group on Transparency and Accountability in 1998. Activists at Friends of the Earth and the Bretton Woods Project were also prominent advocates of this institutional reform (Wood and Welch 1998). Certainly, forces outside civil society also played a major part in the creation of the IEO: for example the formation of evaluation units in other multilateral financial institutions; pressure from the Fund's own Executive Board; and the arrival of Horst Köhler as MD in 2000. Nevertheless, the persistence of several strategically placed CSOs helped to break staff resistance and get the IEO in place.

Since 2001 civil society associations have furthermore often contributed to IEO investigations. Think tanks and NGOs in particular have provided inputs at all stages: namely, the construction of the IEO work programme; the formulation of preliminary issues notes regarding individual evaluations; the collection and interpretation of data; and finally reactions to, and circulation of, the eventual findings and recommendations of IEO studies. The type and degree of civil society involvement in IEO exercises has varied according to the subject of the evaluation. For example, the IEO examination of the Financial Sector Assessment Program attracted limited civil society engagement, while the evaluation of the IMF and aid to Sub-Saharan Africa drew high civil society interest. More generally, certain well-connected NGOs have regularly urged the IEO to undertake more (and more ambitious) assessments of the Fund's work.

In another supporting role for external evaluation of the IMF, some civil society initiatives have sought to bolster parliamentary scrutiny of the global governance institution. For example, NGOs in France have on several occasions since 1999 scrutinised the Paris government's annual report to the National Assembly regarding the IMF and the World Bank. Similarly, the Halifax Initiative has since 2004 issued a 'report card' on the Canadian Ministry of Finance's annual report to legislators on its actions in respect of the Bretton Woods institutions (Halifax 2008). The Ottawa-based group has also monitored parliamentary actions on the IMF worldwide (Round 2004). In Malawi, the country office of ActionAid and MEJN for a time sponsored a Malawi Parliamentary Committee on the IFIs (MAPCOI).

Certain NGOs have in recent years intensified their promotion of IMF accountability through legislative scrutiny. In 2004–5 a coalition of NGOs organised an International Parliamentarians' Petition for Democratic Oversight of the IMF and World Bank that obtained signatures from over 800 legislators from around the world (IPP 2007). In 2006 the New Rules for Global Finance Coalition and partners launched a project on Democratic Governance and Parliamentary Oversight of the International Financial Institutions. In 2007 the World Development Movement produced a toolkit for legislative scrutiny of the Fund (WDM 2007). Arguably these civil society urgings have reinforced several EXR initiatives of recent years to upgrade IMF outreach to legislators (see IMF 2008), although to date parliamentary surveillance of the Fund remains thin overall, especially in the global south.

Yet, welcome though these many civil society activities to enhance outside monitoring may be for accountability at the Fund, a critical assessment of these efforts must also ask, 'evaluation by and for whom?' As in respect of transparency and consultation, civil society work to evaluate the IMF has, on a hegemonic pattern, emanated mainly from groups based in North America and Western Europe. CSOs in low-income countries have generally lacked the resources either to undertake or to publish their own investigations of the IMF. Meanwhile research institutes in the global north – the civil society bodies that most obtain the Fund's ear on evaluation – have generally made little attempt to involve stakeholders in the global south. Several transnational NGOs have done more to incorporate views from the South in their evaluative research, but even such exercises have usually been led from the North. In another attempt to bolster South-based scrutiny of the IMF, certain NGOs have sponsored a few parliamentarians from low-income countries to attend the Annual and Spring Meetings; yet these initiatives have also been striking for their small scale and infrequency. The Brussels-based European

Network on Debt and Development (Eurodad) once produced 'world credit tables' in an effort to redirect scrutiny from borrowers in the global south to lenders in the global north, including the Fund (Eurodad 1995). However, such deliberate civil society moves to counter North-South hierarchies in public evaluation of the IMF have been the exception rather than the rule.

That said, the past decade has seen a few NGOs based in low-income countries build up their own capacities to scrutinise policies connected with the IMF. For example, the Uganda Debt Network (UDN) has developed a countrywide programme to monitor the use of resources released through multilateral debt relief, with a view to ensuring that government indeed devotes these funds to the intended purposes of poverty alleviation. Other locally based monitoring groups in Africa include the aforementioned CSPR in Zambia and MEJN in Malawi. Even so, such groups remain dependent on donors in the global north to fund their operations.

Other marginalised constituencies have also had little say in civil society scrutiny of the IMF. For instance, a few women's associations have assessed the consequences of Fund-supported policies from a gender perspective, but only occasionally and without a concerted advocacy programme to follow up on critical findings (Dennis and Zuckerman 2006; CIEL/Gender Action 2007). Trade union monitoring of the IMF has almost exclusively considered the formal waged sector, when the workforce is largely informal in many of the countries where the Fund is most active. Likewise, civil society evaluations of IMF policies and programmes have rarely, if ever, explicitly addressed social structures of age, caste, disability, race or religion that are associated with arbitrary disadvantages in many economic contexts. Tendencies at the Fund to overlook these subordinated constituencies are reinforced to the extent that civil society associations do not exert counter-hegemonic pressure to bring these peripheral circles to the centre of attention.

On the whole civil society evaluation of the IMF has also tended to reproduce hegemonic discourses of economy and society. For example, most research institutes have couched their assessments of Fund activities in the same paradigms of neoclassical and, at a stretch, Keynesian macroeconomic analysis that the IMF itself uses. Many NGOs, too, have sought 'credibility' in the eyes of the Fund by aiming to emulate the 'scientists'. To this end some NGOs have, for their research, hired economists with the same general professional training as IMF staff. Similarly, the principal business associations have usually assessed the Fund through a language of 'markets' that the IMF readily dons as its own. In contrast, only a minority of published civil society evaluations of the Fund have started from radically alternative epistemological and methodological premises (see Sivaraksa 1999). Official circles have generally dismissed these unorthodox perspectives – if they encounter them at all – as 'ideological' or 'irrelevant'. Yet these counter-hegemonic understandings might speak powerfully to and for some of the IMF's most affected constituents. On democratic grounds, therefore, these more fundamentally critical evaluations of the Fund could warrant a greater hearing than IMF-civil society relations have accorded them to date.

### Civil society and IMF correction

The thesis that civil society engagement has brought important but generally modest and hegemonic advances to IMF accountability also holds in respect of the fourth aspect, that of correction. On the positive side, civil society actors have, through a combination of street demonstrations and inside lobbying, helped to effect some corrective policy adjustments at the Fund, namely towards more flexible advice, greater attention to poverty, and debt cancellation. Yet pressures from civil society associations have not elicited much redress from the Fund in the form of apologies, reparations, resignations and institutional reorganisations. At most the institution has occasionally issued a public statement to the effect of having 'learned lessons' from involvement in a particular unhappy scenario (such as the Asia crisis of the late 1990s). Meanwhile years of compelling arguments from civil society and other circles for a redistribution of votes on the IMF Board have thus far only achieved several small (and in democratic terms far from adequate) adjustments. The overall slow and limited actions of the Fund in addressing criticisms and shortcomings arguably fuelled a trend in the early years of the new millennium for many member states to retreat from the institution, until a new financial crisis in 2008–9 created new needs for emergency loans.

To begin with the positive, however, the turn at the IMF to more nuanced, context-sensitive and flexible policy advice was noted earlier. Certainly, unsatisfied civil society critics would wish the Fund to become still more responsive and creative in its recommendations; however, the extreme rigidity of a previous generation of structural adjustment policies has receded. For example, in line with urgings from many research institutes, NGOs and trade unions, the IMF no longer promotes capital account liberalisation with all speed and at all cost.

Pressures from civil society have also figured importantly in a gradual policy shift at the IMF towards proactive promotion of poverty reduction. Social concerns were more or less absent from the Fund's lending programmes of the 1970s and 1980s, but in the late 1980s the Fiscal Affairs Department began to examine social aspects of IMF conditionality. In 1992 the MD of the day, Michel Camdessus, publicly conceded that 'the essential missing element [in IMF programmes] is a sufficient regard for the short-term human costs' (Camdessus 1992). By 1994 Fund-backed macroeconomic packages regularly included so-called 'social safety nets' (Chu and Gupta 1998). In 1997–8 IMF support in the Asia crisis gave client governments considerable leeway to run fiscal deficits in order to safeguard crucial social expenditures. In 1999 ESAF was refashioned as the PRGF, and Camdessus declared that poverty reduction was the foremost IMF aim in developing countries. In the subsequent decade the Fund's discussions with governments of low-income countries have continually focused on questions of 'fiscal space' for spending on matters such as primary education and basic healthcare.

Civil society advocacy has not been the only force behind this correct-ive shift in IMF priorities towards poverty concerns, but citizen group action has figured significantly in promoting the rise of a social dimen-sion in the Fund's work. Increasingly through the 1970s and 1980s many trade unions, development NGOs, think tanks and faith groups criti-cised the IMF for attaching macroeconomic conditions to its loans that harmed vulnerable social circles in the borrowing countries. Apart from several UN specialised agencies, prior to the 1990s few players other than CSOs were raising social issues with the Fund; thus civil society activism arguably played a notable part in laying the ground for the turn at the IMF in the 1990s to more socially sensitive macroeconomic advice. As that decade proceeded, other parties also increasingly joined CSOs in promoting this policy reorientation. Since the introduction of the PRGF many NGOs, think tanks and trade unions have continued to press the Fund to keep poverty reduction high on its agenda.

Another instance where civil society mobilisation has helped to prompt a major policy correction at the IMF concerns debt relief (Collins *et al.* 2001; Pettifor 2006). The earliest civil society calls for the cancellation of Third World debts date back to the 1970s. A transnational NGO cam-paign to this end was already active in the mid-1980s. In the 1990s civil society advocacy on debt gave heightened attention specifically to the burdens of loans from multilateral institutions, including the IMF. At the same time the debt campaign broadened beyond development NGOs to include many faith groups, think tanks, trade unions, and even some business associations such as the Bretton Woods Committee. Grassroots Christian congregations constituted the largest component of the global Jubilee 2000 movement for debt cancellation that was pursued in the final years of the last century.

Most Fund officials – even those staff who are reluctant to acknowledge other corrective impacts of civil society on the institution – affirm that co-ordinated citizen group action made a difference to the handling of multilateral debts held in the global south. Civil society pressures helped to prompt both the launch of the IMF/World Bank initiative on Highly Indebted Poor Countries (HIPC) in 1996 and the enhancement of HIPC terms three years later. Persistent advocacy from civil society quarters also helped to elicit agreement at the G8 Gleneagles Summit in July 2005 to write off the multilateral debts of the poorest countries. Initial suggestions from Fund staff that some of the beneficiaries of Gleneagles should first make further improvements to macroeconomic policy and governance prompted a barrage of civil society objections. The Executive Board then hastily passed the Multilateral Debt Relief Initiative (MDRI) in December 2005, with conditions only remaining for Mauritania, and these too were lifted six months later.

Yet, as the cases of policy flexibility, the social dimension and debt relief indicate, corrective actions at the IMF in response to pressures from civil society and other quarters have generally come slowly, belatedly, reluctantly and partially. Weak accountability in this regard has taken its toll on the institution. After 2000 nearly all member states that were able to do so paid off their loans from the Fund and distanced themselves from the agency. Indeed, governments in Asia and Latin America began to explore the possibilities of regional monetary funds as an alternative to the IMF. In this respect the global financial crisis of 2008–9 came to the rescue of an institution that seemed to be in terminal decline. Although IMF balance of payments support has been important in stabilising this latest situation, confidence in the Fund as a purveyor of policy advice and as a regulator of global financial markets is far from fully restored (IEO 2009).

Moreover, regarding correction as much as the other dimensions of accountability one must ask the question, *for whom*? That is, what constituencies have been served by civil society efforts at correction of Fund policies? Certainly, increased flexibility, the social turn and debt relief have directed IMF accountability in good part to the benefit of low-income countries and to impoverished people within those countries. In addition, civil society lobbying in these causes has often involved activists in the global south as well as 'bottom-up' mobilisations in the global north. To this extent, civil society inputs to policy correction at the Fund on matters of poverty have shown counter-hegemonic features.

However, it is also noteworthy that the IMF has mainly adjusted its stance on social policy issues when professional advocates in think tanks and NGOs (as often as not based in the global north) have lobbied the Fund 'on behalf of' marginalised groups. Such was the dynamic, for example, when the IMF relaxed government expenditure ceilings in Mozambique in 2006. True, certain other occasions have arisen (e.g. on food subsidies in Ecuador in 2002) when a Fund mission has altered policy advice principally as a result of interventions from grassroots campaigners in the global south. However, it has been more usual for the IMF to consider poverty without engaging the poor themselves. Thus, for example, Fund officials made no attempt to meet the Assembly of the Poor that for several years around the turn of the century camped outside the Thai parliament flying anti-IMF banners.

Similarly, in the debt campaign, demonstrations at the Bank/Fund Annual Meetings and at G8 summits caught the attention of the major IMF shareholder governments far more than submissions from CSOs such as UDN and the Freedom from Debt Coalition (FDC) in the Philippines. And while Jubilee 2000 encompassed groups in over sixty countries, the campaign was co-ordinated from London and mainly resourced from the global north. Among the regional debt and development networks, Eurodad in Brussels has held the senior position in resources and advocacy co-ordination relative to its Southern cousins Afrodad, Asiadad and Latindad. Hence even on this occasion of major involvement of, and gains for, the global south, civil society efforts to correct IMF policies have still in many ways been centred in the global north.

Moreover, the poverty reduction agenda promoted at the Fund since the late 1990s has amended rather than transformed reigning policy paradigms. What some observers have dubbed the 'Post-Washington Consensus' on a more socially sensitive approach to globalisation could more suitably be termed an 'Augmented Washington Consensus' (Stiglitz 1998; Rodrik 2001). The deeper foundations of policy in mainstream economic analysis at the IMF have not changed. More ambitious anti-poverty strategies (for example, emphasising labour standards as urged by trade unions, gender equality as urged by women's movements, ecological viability as urged by environmental groups, and a new global financial architecture as urged by some think tanks) have made few inroads at the IMF. In short, the Fund has taken modest steps towards promoting a socially accountable global market, but the institution has by no means espoused a vision of global social democracy, let alone a post-capitalist or post-modern order.

### Conclusion

Working through themes of transparency, consultation, evaluation and correction, this chapter has explored in what ways and to what extents civil society activities have and have not contributed to the democratic accountability of the IMF. All in all it has been a tale of cups that are in some respects encouragingly filled and in other respects discouragingly empty. The successes give cause for optimism regarding civil society engagement as a means to promote the public accountability of global governance institutions. The shortcomings give cause for critical reflection on improved strategies for the future.

In a positive vein, civil society activities vis-à-vis the Fund have, as seen above, frequently helped to advance transparency, consultation of non-state constituencies, critical external evaluation and certain policy corrections. However, the extent of these civil society benefits for IMF accountability must not be overplayed. The scale of citizen group interventions in these matters has often been limited. Moreover, other actors and certain systemic trends have also furthered these accountability gains. Nevertheless, it seems most unlikely that, in the absence of the wide range of civil society pressures reviewed above, one would have witnessed the same degree of progress at the IMF regarding information disclosure, citizen consultation, the IEO, parliamentary scrutiny, greater policy flexibility, social measures and debt relief.

As for shortfalls in the record to date, civil society advocacy in respect of the Fund has not – or not yet – achieved certain key transparency gains, systematic and thorough public consultation, binding external evaluations, wider creativity in policy design, comprehensive and deeper social sensitivity, or a final resolution to problems of poor-country debt burdens. Moreover, civil society engagement of the IMF has generally neglected certain important subjects such as ecology, distributive justice (along lines of country, gender, etc.) and regulation of global financial markets in the public interest. These lacunae in civil society pressure have made it easier for the Fund to evade accountability on these subjects.

Looking beyond these gaps at the level of substantive issues, relations between the IMF and civil society have also had deeper structural limitations in terms of *who* exercises and obtains accountable global governance. Certainly, civil society initiatives have increased the attention that the IMF gives directly to citizens, as opposed to states alone. Furthermore, transborder networks within civil society have given some expression to regional and global aspects of citizenship vis-à-vis the Fund. More problematically from a democratic perspective, however, civil society work on the IMF has disproportionately involved players in positions of geographical, cultural and social dominance within world politics. In terms of structural power, therefore, civil society operations have, on the whole, tended to reinforce accountabilities at the Fund that are highly skewed towards dominant countries and social circles.

As also seen above with respect to all four dimensions of accountability, civil society engagement of the IMF has, when taken in sum,
tended sooner to uphold rather than subvert prevailing policy discourses.
In other words, civil society interventions have on balance promoted
accountability in relation to mainstream economic and political analysis,
as well as the deeper structures of capitalism and Western modernity
in which that knowledge is embedded. To this extent, IMF-civil society
relations to date have, in large measure, legitimated the reigning world
order. Counter-hegemonic social movements that might seek accountability on fundamentally different terms (say, of radical democracy, post-
modern ecology, or a spiritual frame) have had next to no entry to the
Fund. Yet, given the far-reaching challenges of human suffering, environmental degradation, arbitrary inequality and violence that confront the
contemporary globalising world, this silencing of deeper critiques would
seem unfortunate – and perhaps dangerous, too.

Hence, looking ahead, the question of enhancing civil society contributions to IMF accountability can be approached at different levels. From a
more immediate 'problem-solving' angle it could be recommended that,
for example, the Fund institute staff training on relations with CSOs. In
addition, job descriptions and performance reviews of EDs, management
and relevant staff could make specific reference to civil society liaison
activities. (As a step in this direction, in 2006 the European Department
made an explicit commitment to reward staff for public outreach activities.) Managers at the IMF could also insist that engagement of CSOs
be seriously and systematically addressed in departmental strategies,
mission plans and back-to-office reports. Resident representatives could
generally intensify their contacts with civil society groups and keep better
records of these exchanges. The IMF arguably also needs more civil society specialists, preferably integrated into the various area and functional
departments, rather than being housed separately in EXR.

On the civil society associations side, too, a number of reforms at
the level of institutional operations could enhance contributions to
IMF accountability. For instance, there could be improved education
of advocates on the workings of the Fund and global governance in
general. In addition, more studies of past civil society engagements of
the IMF could help CSOs learn lessons for future initiatives. Civil society associations could also raise the effectiveness of their campaigns
directed at the Fund by improving communication and co-ordination
amongst themselves. Greater collaboration between civil society and the
'political society' of parliaments and party organisations could further
help in promoting IMF accountability, as could better CSO use of the
mass media.

Shifting to a deeper structural perspective, both the Fund and civil society associations could become more critically conscious of, and take proactive steps to reduce, the hegemonic social hierarchies that have marked their overall accountability relationships. On the IMF side, officials could continually invoke the 'accountability to whom?' question in order to remind themselves of the various constituencies that the Fund affects. This awareness could then encourage deliberate efforts to reach marginalised stakeholders. In civil society, meanwhile, geographically Northern, socially middle class and culturally Western CSOs could become more conscious of, and modest about, their structurally privileged position in civil society relations with the IMF. Acting on this awareness, these citizen bodies could cede some political space to less advantaged groups and at the same time also improve their own accountability vis-à-vis marginalised circles in society. Resource allocations for the development of civil society capacities to engage the IMF could prioritise associations that promote voice for the relatively voiceless. At the same time CSOs from subordinated quarters could more insistently assert their rights to be heard in global politics, rather than acquiescing to the dominance of others in positions of structural privilege.

Finally, in regard to structures of knowledge, IMF officials and civil society advocates alike could cultivate greater awareness of, and respect for, the multiplicity of possible perspectives that can be taken on governing economy and society in contemporary history. More initiatives could be taken to admit these other views into policy debates: on the one hand by opening doors to more critical CSOs; and on the other by loosening self-censorship in respect of unorthodox thinking. As intimated above, this broader range of knowledge would not only promote democratic debate, but could also generate sorely needed creative responses to major global challenges.

In sum, upgraded IMF-civil society relations could significantly enhance future accountability of the Fund. The principal needs are for: (a) more interchanges; (b) more competent and co-ordinated initiatives; (c) more inclusion of marginalised quarters; and (d) more exploration of a wider span of discourses and associated policy options. With these four types of improvement, preferably addressed in tandem, civil society activities could accomplish substantially more to reduce accountability gaps at the Fund. The resultant prize would be greater effectiveness and legitimacy for the IMF and global governance more generally.

# 5 Civil society and the WTO: contesting accountability

*Marc Williams*

I will devote a considerable part of my time after this Conference to try to improve information and dialogue with the civil society, taking into account the point of view of all the WTO Members, and the rules which you have given to me.

(Renato Ruggiero, 1998)

I believe we have made real progress in our efforts to enhance the WTO's image and engage civil society. We are reaching out to NGOs through regular seminars and symposia ... We are also seeking to encourage a greater level of engagement from business leaders, trade unions and other sectors of civil society.

(Mike Moore, 2002)

There can be no doubting the fact that we can improve in all areas of our work including ... improving our links ... with civil society.

(Supachai Panitchpakdi, 2005)

As the Doha Round progresses it is vital that the WTO continue to engage civil society. For me, civil society and governments are both important interlocutors.

(Pascal Lamy, 2005)

## Introduction

As the quotations above indicate, every Director-General of the World Trade Organization (WTO) has made positive rhetorical gestures concerning the importance of civil society. In this respect leaders of the principal global governance agency for trade have spoken much like managers of the UN, World Bank and IMF discussed in the preceding chapters. Nevertheless, the relationship between civil society actors and the WTO has been a contentious matter since the inception of the organisation. From the moment the WTO opened its doors in 1995 it has been a prime target for civil society associations that seek greater engagement

I am grateful to Zsofi Korosy for research assistance and to participants in the Gothenburg workshop for comments on an earlier draft of this chapter.

in, and influence on, the formulation of trade policy. Indeed, civil society mobilisation around the WTO Ministerial Conference in Seattle in late 1999 is widely regarded as the iconic 'anti-globalisation' protest (Millennium 2000).

The WTO is the key body for making and adjudicating rules in the international trading system. As such the institution is subject to intense scrutiny, particularly at a time of deepening international economic integration coupled with widespread perceptions that the nation-state is losing control (Williams 2004: 193–4). Much of this scrutiny focuses on the extent to which the WTO meets standards of legitimacy, democracy and accountability (Bellman and Gerster 1996; Esty 2002; Chimni 2006; Smythe and Smith 2006).

As stressed throughout this book, considerations of accountability under contemporary globalisation must extend beyond a fixation on state actors (Grant and Keohane 2005). Increasing interdependence in the world economy has prompted a shift from an old-style multilateralism based on states alone to a complex multilateralism in which non-state actors also figure as key components (O'Brien *et al.* 2000). Relations with civil society associations therefore unfold as part of the shift to what has been termed a stakeholder model of WTO jurisprudence (Shell 1995; Shell 1996).

This chapter assesses the role of civil society in advancing the democratic accountability of the WTO. While civil society embraces a wide range of actors from grassroots groups to large bureaucratised non-governmental organisations (NGOs), in the context of the WTO the major civil society players have been NGOs (although see Ayres 2003–2004 for an argument which stresses the limitations of a focus on NGOs and calls for greater attention to the activities of direct action groups). Earlier research has examined the general role of NGOs, business actors and public participation in the WTO (cf. Dunoff 1998; Esty 1998; Charnovitz 1996, 2000; Scholte *et al.* 1999; Robertson 2000; Loy 2001; Bonzon 2008). This chapter builds on this work with a systematic investigation of the ways in which and extents to which civil society groups have (or have not) enhanced the core components of accountability in the WTO.

In exploring issues of accountability with respect to the relationship between the WTO and civil society this chapter asks the central question: who is accountable to whom and for what? At the centre of the debate over democratic accountability in the WTO are three separate but interlinked issues. The first is the accountability of the WTO as a policymaking body, in terms of the so-called democratic deficit of its decision-taking procedures. This procedural accountability involves matters such as transparency towards, and consultation of, affected publics. The second key aspect of accountability concerns the WTO as a forum for trade liberalisation and the concrete effects of the policies that it promotes. This substantive accountability involves issues such as monitoring, evaluation, correction and redress. The third major accountability problem (also raised across other case studies in this book) relates to the NGOs who campaign for WTO reform. A number of critics challenge the legitimacy of these associations to speak on behalf of various publics.

The chapter addresses these issues first by describing the WTO as an agency of global governance and exploring general issues of its accountability. It then surveys civil society activities in respect of the WTO, including the types of groups involved and the sorts of strategies and tactics that they employ. The discussion then shifts to a more specific examination of civil society critiques of democratic accountability within the WTO, as well as of the ways that the WTO has responded to demands for increased transparency and greater levels of participation for NGOs. On balance civil society organisations have made a limited contribution to WTO accountability; this is principally because of the intergovernmental nature of the organisation. The penultimate section discusses the limits of engagement to date and explores resistance from official quarters to further increases in NGO participation in WTO governance. The chapter concludes with considerations about the role of civil society in advancing accountability in future global governance of trade.

### The WTO as an institution of global governance

Prior to 1995 global governance of trade was concentrated institutionally in the General Agreement on Tariffs and Trade (GATT). This accord was signed in 1947, in what was meant to be the first step towards the creation of an International Trade Organisation (ITO). The Havana Charter negotiated and signed in 1948 provided the legal basis for the ITO, but it was never ratified by sufficient signatories, and global governance of trade for the next four decades remained limited to the tariff-reduction regime of the GATT.

With a more comprehensive remit over trade issues, the WTO emerged from the Uruguay Round of multilateral trade negotiations conducted in 1986–94. Although the WTO constitutes one of the key institutions of governance in the global political economy, its main organisational features are often misinterpreted, and the nature and extent of its impact on the world trading system remain contested (Wolfe 2005; Steger 2007; Jackson 2008).

The WTO is the legal and institutional foundation of the world trading system. It currently has 153 member states, plus a further 31 (including the Holy See) with observer status. The Marrakesh Agreement, signed in April 1994 at the conclusion of the Uruguay Round, laid the legal basis for the WTO, which began operations on 1 January 1995.

The WTO consists of a series of interlocking legal accords, including most prominently the Agreement Establishing the WTO, the GATT, the General Agreement on Trade in Services (GATS), and the Agreement on Trade-Related Aspects of Intellectual Property Rights (TRIPS). Membership requires acceptance of these agreements as a single undertaking. Further sets of obligations are contained in the Plurilateral Agreements governing trade in civil aircraft and matters of government procurement, but these undertakings are voluntary and adherence to them is therefore not mandatory for WTO membership.

As a mechanism of global trade governance the WTO fulfils three key roles. First, it is a negotiating forum with the explicit objective of liberalising international trade. In this role the WTO is constrained by the willingness of its member states to conclude and implement trade agreements. The WTO also operates a Trade Policy Review Mechanism (TPRM) that facilitates the evolution of trade relations through surveillance of the policies of member states.

Second, the WTO provides the legal framework of global trade. Through its provision of rules, norms and principles the organisation is the main instrument designed by states for the governance of the multilateral trading system. WTO agreements, together with outcomes of negotiations in the organisation, form a set of contractual obligations for the member states under international economic law. The legitimacy of other trade agreements is dependent on the extent to which they are compatible with the framework established by the WTO.

In its third main role, the WTO acts as a site for the resolution of interstate disputes on trade. The WTO's Dispute Settlement Mechanism (DSM) provides a process for resolving members' differences on their rights and obligations in respect of international trade. Through dispute settlement the WTO contributes to the stability and further evolution of the world trading system.

Much like the climate change negotiations (covered in Chapter 11), the WTO process is very much driven by the member states. The sole formal actors in the WTO are the member states, and the Ministerial Conference, involving all member states, is the highest decision-making body in the organisation. It has the authority to make decisions on any issues covered by the WTO agreements. Ministerial Conferences are normally convened every two years and have thus far assembled at

Singapore (1996), Geneva (1998), Seattle (1999), Doha (2001), Cancún (2003), Hong Kong (2005) and Geneva (2009).

In the interval between Ministerial Conferences the day-to-day work of the WTO is undertaken in Geneva by the General Council, the Dispute Settlement Body, and the Trade Policy Review Body. The latter two organs are in practice the General Council convened to undertake different functions. All three bodies are open to the entire membership (usually represented by ambassadors or equivalent) and report to the Ministerial Conference.

To assist the General Council a further three subsidiary bodies have been created, each with a functional area of specialisation. The Council for Trade in Goods, the Council for Trade in Services, and the Council for Trade-Related Aspects of Intellectual Property Rights all report to the General Council. These three organs in turn have their own subordinate bodies that explore specific issues. In addition to these councils and their subsidiary agencies the WTO consists of a number of committees and working groups.

The Ministerial Conference, the General Council and the other WTO bodies and committees are serviced by Secretariat offices in Geneva. Led by a Director-General and four Deputy Directors-General, the staff of 629 persons from 68 countries (as of 2009) is spread across some 20 institutional divisions (WTO 2009b). Although the WTO Secretariat has nearly doubled in size since 1995, it remains quite modest in comparison with the offices of the United Nations (UN), the World Bank, the International Monetary Fund (IMF) and the Organisation for Economic Co-operation and Development (OECD). The WTO Secretariat is closer in size to the central offices of the Global Fund (see Chapter 12), but much larger than the staff of the World Fair Trade Organization (see Chapter 14).

The WTO's organisational structure is based on the principle of formal equality of all members. Every member has access to the main WTO committees and decision-making bodies. Exceptions are the Appellate Body, the Dispute Settlement Panels, the Textiles Monitoring Body and committees covering the Plurilateral Agreements.

The WTO normally operates a consensus mode of decision-making. While the WTO Charter identifies four situations in which the members may take recourse to majority voting, in practice all decisions to date have been taken by consensus. In the context of the WTO, 'consensus' is defined as the absence of a formal objection to a decision by a member present when that decision is reached. This is not to say that all states have an equal voice at the WTO. In the search for consensus members meet in informal groups, and influence in the organisation is a function of a country's importance in world trade and the skills of its government's negotiators.

## The WTO and accountability

There are conflicting views on the actors to whom the WTO should be accountable. Indeed, contending perspectives on the extent to which the WTO meets contemporary standards of accountability constitute an important feature of the relationship between the WTO and civil society. Two broad positions are discernible in this debate: what can be termed the intergovernmental approach and the supranational approach.

### The WTO as an intergovernmental organisation

From an intergovernmentalist perspective the WTO is wholly and solely accountable to its member states. Analysts who adopt a strict intergovernmental approach deny any requirement for the WTO to be accountable to actors other than national governments (Nichols 1996). From this viewpoint civil society associations have no role to play in assuring the accountability of the WTO.

Intergovernmentalists argue that the WTO follows a club model of governance. The club model of multilateral co-operation posits that the democratic legitimacy of global governance organisations is entirely derived from the formal membership, which in the case of the WTO is limited to states (Keohane and Nye 2001). According to this perspective, states engage in global governance on the basis of the legitimate authority delegated to them by their citizens. The key check on accountability in global governance therefore resides in national governments (Robertson 2000). Any government which in its actions on global governance deviates from the preferences of its electorate risks being ejected from office at a subsequent election.

The depiction of the core institutional structure of the WTO in the preceding section supports the contention that the WTO is designed to be a wholly intergovernmental organisation. The principal actors in the WTO are states, and the decision-making processes of the organisation provide all member states with the opportunity to participate in policy formulation. In this view the WTO is principally a forum, and the members (states) take the key decisions. The WTO is limited to supervising a legal order devised by states. Viewed in this way, and in accordance with the theory of trade legalism, the WTO is only accountable to its members (Shell 1995). In these terms the WTO does not have to be inclusive of non-state actors in order to meet the requirements of democratic accountability.

From an intergovernmentalist perspective accountability issues could arise at the WTO in two forms. In one sense an accountability deficit may emerge if the institutional mechanisms prevent some member states from reaping the full benefits of participation. For example, in the context of the WTO it has been argued that informal procedures which reflect the uneven distribution of economic power promote secrecy and a decision-making process that discriminates against developing countries (Kwa 2003). A second form of accountability deficit may arise as a result of the impact of WTO policies on specific populations. For example, intense debate has surrounded the effect of the TRIPS Agreement on access to pharmaceuticals and associated detrimental consequences for healthcare of populations in the developing world (Thomas 2002; Cullett 2003).

Yet adherents of intergovernmentalism deny that accountability deficits of either of these two kinds require the intervention of civil society actors. The answer is to improve internal decision-making procedures of the WTO in order to permit greater equity and accountability among member states. Meanwhile, any adverse impacts of WTO policies on various populations should be addressed through increased accountability measures in respect of national governments, rather than through empowering civil society actors to participate in the global institution (Capling 2003).

### The WTO as a supranational organisation

In contrast to an intergovernmentalist approach, advocates of a supranational perspective contend that the WTO's accountability cannot be adequately secured through its member states alone. Drawing on the sorts of points laid out in the Introduction to this book (see pp. 2–4 above), these analysts argue that the WTO's impact on the global economy transcends a solely intergovernmental approach and that the WTO itself – as something more than a collection of member states – must be held accountable to those affected by its policies. From this perspective the WTO embodies some elements of supranational governance.

Supranationalist arguments regarding the WTO have highlighted three main points. First, they maintain that the WTO process of trade liberalisation restricts the scope of national government action. The Uruguay Round resulted in a significant transformation in the management of world trade (Williams 1999: 155). In comparison with the GATT, the WTO regime is more extensive (including new sectors and issues) and more intrusive in its impact on domestic policies, practices and regulation (Dunkley 2000).

Second, the supranational perspective claims that the WTO has developed processes of surveillance which limit the autonomy of national governments. The WTO redefined the relationship between national regulatory authorities and the management of the global trading system through the construction of mandatory codes for all members, the supervisory functions of the Trade Policy Review Mechanism and the establishment of a strengthened Dispute Settlement Mechanism. The DSM in particular is said to extend supranational surveillance, restrict national decision-making, and significantly influence the behaviour of national governments (Public Citizen 2000). On these lines it has been argued that the WTO is an emerging supranational administrative body, since it 'is no longer a system simply based on consensus, reciprocity, and a balancing of concessions. Rather, it is a system based on rules that reflect the reality of the administrative state' (Ala'i 2008: 802).

Third, the supranational position holds that the normative power of the WTO effectively subverts national policymaking. The WTO embodies a specific set of ideological commitments; it facilitates an open global trading system and deregulation of national economies through its insistence that states remove barriers to trade in goods and services. This process can potentially override domestic legislation enacted to preserve, for example, cultural values, environmental resources and labour standards (Williams 2004).

According to supranationalist perspectives, all three of these processes give rise to accountability deficits at the WTO which states alone cannot correct. Moreover, these changes in the global trade regime bring the WTO into direct engagement with groups (such as consumers, farmers or workers) that may not be adequately represented by national governments. On these grounds civil society actors could have a legitimate role to play in WTO governance, and the WTO should be accountable to relevant civil society groups as well as to member states.

## Civil society engagement of the WTO

Civil society contains a diverse array of actors with an interest in global governance of trade. Civil society groups that address international trade can be grouped in a number of different ways, including in relation to political vision and with respect to constituency.

One way to classify civil society associations relates to the political vision that these groups hold when engaging with trade and trade policy. There is no agreement on the exact terminology to be employed in this regard. Some analysts distinguish between conformers, reformers and rejectionists (Scholte, O'Brien and Williams 1999; Williams and Ford

1999). Others distinguish between supporters, regressives, isolationists and reformers (Said and Desai 2003: 66–72). In each of these cases, however, the central distinction lies between: (a) civil society actors that are broadly supportive of current forms of trade liberalisation; (b) those that are sympathetic to the goals of trade liberalisation but recognise some defects in the present system; and (c) those that are antithetical to the existing trade regime. Demands for accountable governance in the WTO have come primarily from NGOs who seek to reform rather than reject the prevailing trade system.

A different way to classify civil society actors engaging the WTO focuses on the function of the NGO. For example, Bellman and Gerster distinguish between professional associations (such as trade unions and commercial groups), research institutions (such as think tanks and universities) and NGOs (such as consumer associations and development groups) (1996: 35). In terms of specific issue areas the WTO has attracted attention from civil society associations concerned with the environment, labour standards, gender justice, human rights, consumer protection and development.

Civil society groups have devised a number of strategies in their engagement with the WTO. These include lobbying (national governments as well as the WTO organs), educational campaigns, and alliances with developing country governments (e.g. in support of the Cotton Initiative) (Herrick 2006). Civil society associations have also promoted public debate over the benefits of trade liberalisation and the merits of the WTO.

## Contesting accountability

The following pages explore in greater detail how different kinds of civil society associations have used these various kinds of strategies and tactics in campaigns for increased accountability in the WTO. In common with other case studies in this book, the analysis below assesses these accountability effects in respect of transparency, consultation, evaluation and correction. On the whole it is found that CSOs have made limited impact on WTO accountability. While official circles have recognised that the WTO has an obligation to make its operations more transparent, CSOs have still been denied effective engagement with WTO decision-making processes.

### Transparency

Transparency relates to improving the public visibility of WTO proceedings and increasing access to WTO documentation. Greater transparency contributes to more informed public consultations and also enhances outside monitoring and scrutiny of WTO activities.

The WTO is generally rated quite highly in respect of transparency, relative to other global governance agencies (and indeed in comparison with many NGOs as well). An independent review by the One World Trust concluded that 'information on the WTO's trade activities is excellent' (Kovach *et al.* 2003: 15). This positive outcome can be partly attributed to pressure from civil society circles.

Civil society groups have long campaigned for the de-restriction of WTO documents and greater publicity concerning the outcomes of WTO meetings. Activists claim that the absence of such information severely hampers the watchdog functions of NGOs. Similarly, NGOs have demanded increased openness of the WTO dispute settlement process. NGO access to these deliberations would increase their public visibility and thereby enhance confidence in the fairness of WTO decisions (Charnovitz 1996, 2000).

Civil society actors have achieved a degree of success in their efforts for increased transparency at the WTO. At its meeting in July 1996 the General Council adopted *Procedures for the Circulation and De-Restriction of WTO Documents* (WTO 1996a). This decision created a system whereby the circulation of WTO materials depended on the status accorded to the document. Most WTO papers were immediately circulated as unrestricted; others were de-restricted automatically after a sixty-day period; others were in a category that required the consent of a member state to be de-restricted; and still others remained restricted altogether. Having achieved this progress, NGOs then mounted a campaign to increase the speed with which WTO documents are circulated to the public, and in 2002 the General Council agreed to accelerate the release of documents considerably (WTO 2002). This decision has ensured that most WTO documents are now publicly available within six to eight weeks, and the number of exceptions to this early disclosure has been reduced.

Some greater transparency of WTO proceedings has also been achieved around the dispute settlement process. In some respects this is a response to lobbying by NGOs for a greater role in the development of international trade law, and for representation in the DSM (Hernandez-Lopez 2001: 491). It also signals recognition by some influential governments in the global north that increased transparency in the DSM is merited. At the request of the parties involved, some dispute panel meetings and proceedings of the Appellate Body have been made open to the public. In the first case of its kind, panel hearings in September 2005 on the US-EU and Canada-EU disputes over hormones were open to the general public via closed-circuit broadcast (WTO 2005). A further three panel proceedings have since been made open to the public. In July 2008 the Appellate Body for the first time made its proceedings open to the general public, namely, in the Canada-*Continued Suspension* and US-*Continued Suspension* cases (WTO 2008). To date, a further two Appellate Body cases have been made open to the public.

A further innovation in the area of information provision is the WTO website, which makes a wide range of WTO documents, including dispute panel reports, publicly available as soon as they are adopted. Since 1998 the website has also maintained a special section for NGOs which contains general information on WTO activities, relations with NGOs, civil society attendance at Ministerial Conferences, and documents received from NGOs. Civil society groups have not specifically lobbied for these improvements, but in constructing an elaborate website the WTO has arguably been responding in part to NGO pressure for greater transparency.

Finally, civil society associations have also contributed to increased transparency of the WTO through their efforts to raise public awareness of the global trade regime. Indeed, in 1996 the General Council explicitly recognised that NGOs played this important role (WTO 1996b). In this vein, civil society groups have, for example, published pamphlets and studies of the WTO, held workshops about the organisation, maintained information about it on their websites, and drawn public attention to the WTO with street demonstrations.

### Consultation

As indicated above, the WTO is constructed as an intergovernmental organisation, but within this framework a limited space has developed for consultation of civil society groups. The *Marrakesh Agreement Establishing the World Trade Organization* provides in Article V.2 that the agency should make 'appropriate arrangements for consultation and cooperation with non-governmental organisations'. In addition, Article 13.2 of the *Understanding on Rules and Procedures Governing the Settlement of Disputes* opens an avenue for civil society access (WTO 2009c).

These provisions were reinforced in July 1996 when the WTO General Council adopted *Guidelines for Arrangements on Relations with Non-Governmental Organizations* (WTO 1996b). These guidelines made some concession to the roles that NGOs can play in the wider public debate on trade and trade-related issues (Van Dyke and Weiner 1996; Weiner and Van Dyke 1996). The Secretariat was given prime responsibility for liaison with NGOs and was empowered to engage in an expanded dialogue with the non-governmental sector. However, the guidelines also insisted upon the intergovernmental nature of WTO deliberations, noting that 'there is currently a broad view that it would not be possible for NGOs to be directly involved in the work of the WTO or its meetings' (WTO 1996b). In general, official circles around trade policy now broadly accept that enhanced civil society participation in the WTO can be managed and regulated such that it neither impedes efficiency nor compromises legitimate confidentiality concerns (WTO 2004).

The WTO consults with NGOs through formal and informal channels. The *Guidelines for Arrangements on Relations with Non-Governmental Organizations* list four avenues of contact between the WTO and civil society: symposia; the circulation of WTO position papers and information on trade topics; Secretariat responses to requests for information and briefings on the work of the organisation; and the participation of chairpersons of WTO councils and committees in discussions with NGOs (WTO 1996b). The value of these contacts is disputed, with some commentators dismissing them as mere tokenism and others viewing them as evidence of access.

In addition to these four avenues, the most visible form of civil society interaction with the WTO occurs through attendance at Ministerial Conferences. The general trend has been for increased numbers of NGOs to flock to these meetings, although the location of the conference can also influence the levels of participation. At the Singapore Conference in 1996, 108 civil society groups attended (each being allowed up to 3 representatives). This figure rose to 128 associations at the 1998 Geneva Ministerial Conference and 737 organisations at the Seattle Ministerial Meeting in late 1999. The number fell to 366 for the conference in (relatively remote) Doha, which moreover convened amidst the reductions in air travel after 9/11 and involved a range of bureaucratic restrictions that complicated civil society participation. By the Cancún meeting civil society attendance rose again, to 902 organisations, and 812 groups attended the Hong Kong Ministerial Conference in 2005 (WTO 2009a).

Even these large numbers do not reflect the full level of interest from civil society groups in the Ministerial Conferences. For one thing, many more associations register for accreditation (e.g. 1,065 for the Hong Kong meeting) but are in the end unable, for cost and other reasons, to make it to the venue. In addition, a number of governments consult with civil society groups in their home countries before attending the Ministerial Conference.

Geographic representation at the Ministerial Conferences has been diverse, with civil society associations from all the major world regions in attendance. However, the large resources required for travel and accommodation have produced uneven representation, with CSOs from Europe and North America generally predominant in numbers and voice at the conferences. Moreover, accreditation procedures have resulted in privileged access for business associations and international NGOs (Scholte, O'Brien and Williams 1999)

NGO involvement in WTO Ministerial Conferences has been of limited consequence as a mode of consultation. Civil society participation in the official proceedings has been limited to attendance at the plenary meetings, which amount to little more than exercises in general rhetoric by the member states. In contrast to the UN, NGOs cannot make any oral statements or written submissions to the plenary meetings. They are also denied access to negotiating sessions. However, the Secretariat has provided civil society groups with an NGO Centre at the conference, where they have access to communications facilities and WTO officials. Perhaps the most significant impact made by NGOs on a WTO Ministerial Conference occurred when street protests disrupted the Seattle meeting.

Between Ministerial Conferences, public symposia and forums organised by the Secretariat provide another arena for WTO consultation of civil society groups. For example, prior to the Singapore meeting the Secretariat organised a discussion with environmental, development and consumer groups. In the ensuing years other WTO symposia were held on subjects such as trade facilitation, trade and environment, and trade and development. Since 2001 the WTO has facilitated annual symposia or public forums with NGOs. The titles of recent forums have included What WTO for the XXIst Century? (2006), How Can the WTO Help Harness Globalization? (2007), Trading into the Future (2008) and Global Problems, Global Solutions: Towards Better Global Governance (2009). In addition to these gatherings in Geneva, the Secretariat has since 2003 held public symposia in-country with civil society groups and parliamentarians.

The extent to which these symposia present opportunities for a constructive engagement between the WTO and civil society remains open to debate. The events mainly serve to elicit views from NGOs, but without any commitment to meaningful dialogue. The limited participation of officials from WTO member governments further indicates that these events are not an effective exercise in substantive consultation (Van den Bossche 2008: 731). On a more positive note, from 2005 onwards these symposia have been organised on a 'bottom-up' basis, with NGOs selecting the forum theme and the invited speakers. The events have also facilitated NGO networking.

A further channel of WTO consultation of civil society is provided through informal meetings between NGOs and Secretariat officials. Since 1996 the External Relations Division of the WTO has been responsible for managing contacts with NGOs and organising regular briefings for them. In the absence of civil society access to deliberations of the General Council and other bodies, the briefings in Geneva are an important source of information. Yet these meetings do not function as consultation exercises, inasmuch as NGOs only receive reports and do not themselves contribute to WTO operations.

Secretariat briefings for NGOs are supplemented with regular informal meetings with the chairpersons of WTO councils and committees. Again the consequences are limited. The chairpersons can only meet NGOs with the prior consent of the relevant council or committee, and even then they do so only in their personal capacity. Like the Secretariat briefings, then, these meetings are token gestures of consultation that have made a limited contribution to WTO accountability.

Attempts to establish more systematic contact between the Director-General and civil society have met with limited success. Renato Ruggiero failed in his attempt to establish an informal consultative group with civil society. In 2003 Supachai Panitchpakdi established an Informal NGO Advisory Body and an Informal Business Advisory Body, but it is not clear that these consultative mechanisms had any consequence for policy, and they ceased to exist when his term of office expired (Van den Bossche 2008: 735). In any case radical NGOs have refused to engage with such an advisory body (Bello and Kwa 2003).

Civil society groups have not succeeded in going beyond these ad hoc and informal consultations to obtain formal participation in WTO deliberations. Certain NGOs have joined state delegations to WTO Ministerial Conferences, but such participation has depended on the discretion of the government concerned. Nor have NGOs had designated seats on any of the councils, committees and working groups of the WTO, in the way that civil society actors sit on the Board of the Global Fund to Fight AIDS, Tuberculosis and Malaria (see Chapter 12) and certain bodies of the Internet Corporation for Assigned Names and Numbers (see Chapter 13).

A line of consultation in relation to the WTO that has been of particular interest to civil society groups concerns the submission of *amicus curiae* ('friend-of-the-court') briefs to the dispute settlement process. An *amicus curiae* presentation enables a body which is not party to a dispute to provide information on different legal and factual aspects of the case. NGOs have argued that rules and procedures under the Dispute Settlement Understanding allow them to make unsolicited written *amicus curiae* submissions (Hernandez-Lopez 2001). In a landmark ruling in 1998 the Appellate Body in the US-Shrimp case agreed that panels have discretion whether to accept or reject an *amicus curiae* submission. To date practice has been mixed, with some panels admitting *amicus curiae* briefs and others refusing them (Lin 2004: 495; Van den Bossche 2008: 735–43).

Critics from civil society assert that only through systematically integrated participation of NGOs will the WTO become more accountable (Bellman and Gerster 1996; Bullen and Van Dyke 1996; Enders 1998; WWF 1999). These advocates claim that public participation through NGOs would enhance WTO performance with the input of added knowledge and expertise. Proponents argue that formal NGO participation in the WTO would better educate the public about trade policy and its implications. This in turn would result in greater understanding of the need to balance competing interests, and in increased support for the goals of the multilateral trading system. Citizen activists also affirm that formal NGO participation would ensure that WTO decisions are taken in the public interest. In particular, NGOs would provide countervailing power to corporate actors with disproportionate economic sway and thereby assist governments to resist pressures from powerful vested interests (Charnovitz 1996: 342).

However, thus far demands for increased formal civil society participation in WTO proceedings has not resulted in meaningful change. In particular, many WTO member states have resisted increased NGO access by insisting on the intergovernmental status of the organisation. These opponents have argued that civil society actors should lobby on WTO-related matters in their home countries with their national governments. Intergovernmentalists affirm that trade policy is the result of a domestic political bargain; hence NGO advocacy should take place at the national level. Likewise, NGOs who wish to influence the outcome of a case before a WTO dispute settlement panel should engage with their national representatives, removing the need for direct NGO involvement through *amicus curiae* submissions. Intergovernmentalists moreover claim that WTO negotiations demand a high level of secrecy which cannot be guaranteed if participation is granted to non-state actors. Some sceptics have also argued that direct NGO participation in WTO proceedings would encourage the active involvement of protectionist groups and thereby undermine the WTO mission of trade liberalisation (Nichols 1996).

Yet it could be argued that this focus on formal representation overstates the lack of civil society access to the WTO. Some studies have suggested a number of modalities and mechanisms through which NGOs exercise informal influence in the WTO. Murphy (2007) has catalogued the role of NGOs as norm entrepreneurs seeking to frame the terms of debate and generate normative consensus in respect of the TRIPS agreement and discussions on investment policy, and Herrick (2006) has demonstrated a dual role of NGOs in the Cotton Initiative negotiations, as knowledge brokers and public opinion shapers.

*Evaluation*

The WTO has been subject to extensive scrutiny from its inception. A wide range of civil society associations such as NGOs, think tanks, religious organisations and university departments have focused on its policies. Such actors have conducted this watchdog function through studies of the WTO; through monitoring of WTO negotiations and the dispute settlement process; through contacts with mass media organs which cover the WTO; and through lobbying in national parliaments on WTO matters. This scrutiny by civil society has (as documented above and below) performed a critical role in ensuring an ongoing informed debate on developments in the world trading system.

Reputable evaluation of the WTO is provided by civil society organisations too numerous to mention. However, the Geneva-based International Centre for Trade and Sustainable Development (ICTSD), founded by five NGOs in 1995, has developed impressive expertise as an authoritative source of analysis of WTO-related activities. NGOs on other continents that maintain regular detailed scrutiny of the WTO include Public Citizen, the Rede Brasileira Pela Integração dos Povos (REBRIP) (Brazilian Network for the Integration of Peoples) and the Southern and Eastern African Trade Information and Negotiations Institute (SEATINI).

Depending on the country concerned, NGOs have garnered varying levels of access and influence on government regarding the evaluation of WTO policies (Bellman and Gerster 1996). The relative impact of different segments of civil society has also varied, with business associations tending on the whole to have more influence than groups that address consumer, environmental and human rights issues. Likewise, the more business-focused media has normally had greater influence in terms of scrutiny of WTO activities. In contrast, the general media has tended to respond to civil society pressure for scrutiny of the WTO only in the context of spectacular incidents such as the demonstrations in Seattle. NGOs have also on the whole made limited impact in terms of enhancing parliamentary scrutiny of the WTO, and a proposal from the world federalist movement for the creation of a WTO Parliamentary Assembly has made no headway.

*Correction*

The fourth dimension of accountability highlighted in this book – namely, correction and redress – arises with respect to the WTO in terms of the damaging impacts of trade liberalisation policies on affected communities. In addition, civil society critics have argued that the decisions of the WTO Dispute Settlement Mechanism have supported a status quo that is detrimental to various stakeholders.

A key example of NGO action to change damaging WTO policies has unfolded in respect of trade and health, particularly with challenges to TRIPS regarding the provision of anti-retroviral drugs (ARVs) to HIV/AIDS sufferers. A strong coalition of NGOs mounted a vigorous campaign for greater access to life-saving medicines (Murphy 2007). It included large Western-based organisations (such as Health Action International, Médecins Sans Frontières, Oxfam International and the Quaker United Nations Office) as well as organisations based in the developing world (such as the Affordable Treatment and Action in India, the Treatment Action Campaign in South Africa, the Thai NGO Coalition on AIDS, and Third World Network). In 2003 an agreement was achieved through the WTO to improve access to essential medicines, although implementation has been complicated.

NGOs have also pursued campaigns on health-related consequences of trade in genetically modified organisms (GMOs) and WTO agreements in regard to Sanitary and Phytosanitary Measures (SPS) (Epps 2008). Under WTO regulations governments can act to prohibit the import of products that are harmful to their populations even if such action restricts trade. However, it is not always easy to distinguish between the legitimate use of health and safety barriers to trade and the use of such measures to protect and safeguard domestic producers from competition. When such cases have resulted in decisions that appear to support trade liberalisation and restrict national autonomy, civil society critics have accused the WTO of acting as an unelected body that affects stakeholders with no opportunity to seek redress.

In addition to health matters, civil society groups have sought to correct WTO policies in relation to environmental sustainability (see Esty 1998; O'Brien et al. 2000: 134–52). Environmental NGOs such as the Center for International Environmental Law (CIEL), the International Institute for Sustainable Development (IISD), the International Union for the Conservation of Nature (IUCN) and the World Wide Fund for Nature (WWF) have been at the forefront of politicising the trade and environment debate. On balance these efforts to integrate environmental issues into WTO policymaking have met with limited success. On the positive side, this advocacy work has ensured that sustainable development now figures in global trade negotiations, as seen for example in the Doha Declaration. However, such attention to the environmental consequences of trade liberalisation has not translated into effective policy. For example, the WTO Committee on Trade and the Environment has made unsatisfactory progress in devising new trade rules. Certain rulings through the WTO dispute settlement mechanism and the activities of multilateral environmental agreements (MEAs) have been more important in the process of integrating environmental issues into the WTO (Brack 2004).

Civil society efforts to achieve correction at the WTO in regard to labour standards have been unsuccessful (O'Brien *et al.* 2000: 67–108). Trade unions and human rights groups were at the forefront of a campaign to include labour issues in the WTO. The detrimental impact of trade liberalisation on workers' rights and the exploitation of child labour were key issues requiring action. Prominent groups advocating change in the WTO have included the World Confederation of Labour (WCL) and the International Confederation of Free Trade Unions (ICFTU), since 2006 united in the International Trade Union Confederation (ITUC). Human rights groups such as the International Labor Rights Forum (ILRF) and Rights & Democracy were allied with the unsuccessful campaign for the adoption of a social clause that would incorporate core labour rights into the WTO (Scholte 2004b: 150). In what has proved a highly contentious and divisive issue, some trade unions and other civil society organisations have opposed the proposal of a social clause (Chan and Ross 2003). The pursuit of labour rights through the WTO remains an unrealised goal stymied by the opposition of developing country governments and divisions within civil society.

Some of the most persistent NGO efforts to correct WTO policy have concerned investment issues. From the outset the question of investment rules at the WTO has been contentious (Bora 2004). A number of developed country governments have sought to extend the global trade regime to cover matters of foreign direct investment, while many developing country governments and NGOs have questioned the benefits of such an agreement (Smythe 2003–4; Murphy 2007). Prominent opposing NGOs have included Oxfam International, Third World Network (TWN), CIEL, IISD, Friends of the Earth International (FOEI), Public Services International (PSI), the World Development Movement (WDM), and the Institute for Agriculture and Trade Policy (IATP) (Murphy 2007: 10). This coalition was instrumental in building capacity and articulating knowledge about investment issues (Smythe 2003–4: 62). It also successfully supported developing country governments in their opposition to the inclusion of investment issues in the Doha agenda. The failure to achieve consensus on investment (and other Singapore issues) at the Cancún Ministerial Conference in September 2003 was the effective end of efforts by developed country governments to include investment issues in the WTO.

Civil society groups have also attempted to correct flaws in WTO policies regarding development. NGOs in both the global north and south have sought to ensure that WTO rules and policies contribute to a trading system that is fair and equitable for developing countries. The agenda for development reform is broad. Key NGOs who have promoted improved access and greater autonomy for developing countries in global trade include ICTSD, Oxfam International, the Brazilian Institute for Social and Economic Analysis (IBASE), Focus on the Global South, TWN and SEATINI. These civil society organisations have ensured that the relationship between trade and development remains salient at the WTO. The failure of the Seattle conference in 1999 and the necessity to engage meaningfully with the needs of developing countries led to the focus of the Doha Round on development issues. While civil society organisations cannot claim sole responsibility for this outcome, they have, through monitoring and reviewing the impact of WTO policies and ceaseless lobbying activities, nevertheless significantly shaped the current debate (Williams 2005: 40–1).

Inspired by feminist political economy, some NGOs have also raised critical concerns about the gender implications of trade and trade policies. They contend that the existing global trading system is biased against women's interests and requires corrective actions. Civil society groups such as the International Trade and Gender Network (ITGN), Women's EDGE, Women in Development Europe (WIDE) and the Women's Environment and Development Organization (WEDO) have called for the inclusion of gender in analyses of WTO rules and policies. To date these interventions have not brought major correction to the WTO, but a space has been created at symposia and forums for the discussion of gender issues, and a WTO Staff Working Paper has examined this question (Nordås 2003).

Consumer advocates have generally been critical of the WTO in relation to a number of the issues discussed above. In addition, several NGOs have aimed to redress what they perceive as the bias in the liberal trade regime in favour of corporate interests. They argue in support of a multilateral competition policy which would curb the ability of transnational companies (TNCs) to engage in restrictive business practices (Consumers International 2003). Furthermore, these NGOs claim that a binding code of conduct for large firms would curb the power of producers and enhance the public interest. Prominent civil society actors advocating consumer rights vis-à-vis the WTO include Consumers International (CI) and Public Citizen.

In sum, then, civil society organisations have achieved mixed results in their attempts to correct WTO policies. CSOs cannot by themselves effect change in multilateral trade governance. The key decisions rest with states, as attested by, for example, limited progress on environmental negotiations. Nevertheless, NGOs have played important roles as knowledge brokers and policy entrepreneurs. In some cases they have exerted substantial influence, as for instance in the negotiations on an investment agreement and in the battle over access to essential medicines. In other cases, notably gender awareness and consumer rights, NGO campaigns remain at a relatively early stage of development. It is also important to recall the diversity of CSO positions, as evident for example in the deep divisions among CSOs around the issue of labour rights.

### Holding accountability holders to account: the issue of NGO legitimacy

Having established that NGOs and other civil society associations do in various ways shape the public accountability of the WTO, it is pertinent to examine, as several other chapters in this book also do, the accountability of civil society actors themselves. On this subject critics have raised a number of challenges in relation to voice, inequality and politicisation.

On the issue of voice, critics argue that most NGOs lack adequate mechanisms to ensure their own accountability and often make claims to represent constituents with whom they maintain only distant (if any) contacts (Cho 2005). NGOs have in recent years responded to these criticisms with a number of self-assessment initiatives like the INGO Accountability Charter, launched in 2006. These frameworks have attracted adherence from certain NGOs active in respect of the WTO, for example Oxfam International. However, on the whole civil society players in WTO politics have been quicker to assert than to demonstrate their position to speak for the public interest.

In terms of inequality it has indeed often transpired that the civil society which engages the WTO gives more voice to some constituents than to others. With regard to geographic representation, for instance, NGOs based in the global north have generally had greater access to the WTO than civil society actors based in the global south. For example, in the debate over *amicus curiae* submissions officials from developing countries have voiced concerns that well-resourced Northern NGOs will have capabilities to table *amicus curiae* briefs that surpass any likelihood of equivalent Southern NGO influence (Chimni 2004).

In terms of socioeconomic constituency, business associations have generally obtained greater entry to the WTO than other groups. Business actors enjoy more privileged access to national decision-makers and have, in contrast to NGOs, traditionally been perceived as legitimate players in trade politics. Moreover, among non-business actors reformist civil society groups have tended to obtain greater access to the WTO than grassroots organisations and groups that adopt more radical stances. In all of these respects unequal access to the WTO is symptomatic of wider structural inequalities in global politics (Scholte 2004b).

In regard to the third problem, that of politicisation, critics have argued that NGOs misunderstand, misrepresent and mischievously interfere in the process of trade liberalisation. Instead of respecting the WTO as a legal organisation, these detractors say, NGOs deliberately politicise trade negotiations. Thus Cho claims that 'NGOs' activism risks over-representing politics and ... under-representing law' (2005: 396). Yet such a closed view of the WTO fails to recognise the changed nature of trade politics on one hand (Pauwelyn 2008) and on the other the extensive role of private-sector lawyers in WTO legal processes (Dunoff 1998).

### Conclusion: directions for the future

Engagement between civil society and the WTO has not been a dialogue of the deaf. As this chapter has indicated, the exchanges have yielded some accountability increases in respect of all four dimensions of transparency, consultation, evaluation and correction. To this extent the WTO has advanced from mere formal recognition of a relationship with civil society (in Article V.2) to substantive engagement with it.

However, this engagement also remains of limited scope. As noted above, most WTO member states still insist on the intergovernmental character of the institution. While some states, such as the USA, have supported increased civil society involvement in the WTO, others (primarily developing country governments) have taken the view that 'it would be inappropriate to allow NGOs to participate directly even as observers of WTO meetings' (Sampson 2000: 42; Loy 2001: 121–2). Unsympathetic observers claim that engagement with civil society 'tends to further strain the WTO's resources which are already in a sorry state, distract the Secretariat from its main responsibilities, and even run the risk of undermining the integrity of the WTO through unnecessary and even harmful over-politicization' (Cho 2005: 398). Yet such opposition is a minority position. Indeed, Turek (2003) argues that NGO engagement with the WTO can support the interests of developing countries.

While demands from NGOs for increased civil society participation in the WTO are unlikely to be met in the near future, it is apparent that governments are attempting to engage in a more open manner with development and environmental advocates. Defenders of the liberal trade order need allies in order to defeat the ever-present supporters of protectionism. Trade officials are concerned with enhancing the legitimacy of the liberalisation project, and to this end are prepared to relate with NGOs in an attempt to widen public support for increased liberalisation.

To mark the tenth anniversary of the WTO the Director-General of the day, Supachai Panitchpakdi, commissioned a report which included an examination of future relations between civil society and the WTO. The Sutherland Report, as this document was known, reaffirmed the intergovernmental nature of the WTO. While it outlined the benefits of engagement and dialogue with civil society groups, it also noted that 'it is the Member governments themselves that must shoulder most of the responsibility' for developing these relationships (WTO 2004: 41). The value of relations with civil society, stated the report, included increasing transparency, promoting a positive image of the WTO, informing debates on trade policy, increasing the knowledge base of WTO members, and increasing support for trade liberalisation in domestic constituencies. The report also noted the reservations of some governments in the global south about including NGO influence, the burden of parallel track negotiations, the necessity for confidentiality in trade negotiations and the absence of accountability and transparency in many NGOs.

The Sutherland Report offered some limited recommendations in respect of WTO relations with civil society. These included: review of transparency measures; development of a set of clear objectives for the Secretariat's relations with civil society; development of systematic interchange between the Secretariat and certain elements of civil society; capacity-building to assist local civil society organisations specialising in trade issues in the least developed countries; and increased administrative capacity and financial resources directed towards relations with civil society. Yet the modest proposals of the Sutherland Report seem unlikely to enhance WTO accountability. If it is accepted that the dialogue between the WTO and civil society is important, then more is required not only to maintain this dialogue, but also to expand it substantially.

With the demand for more formal recognition of civil society in WTO decision-making effectively blocked, in the short term NGOs can best contribute to greater accountability in global trade politics through their monitoring and evaluation activities and through informal coalitions with developing country governments. As demonstrated above, accountability does not depend on formal representation – NGOs currently perform important roles in scrutinising the impact of WTO policies on affected publics. While civil society organisations cannot by themselves change trade policies, they can ensure that national governments and the WTO are held accountable. Moreover, as the Doha Round negotiations have demonstrated, the activist stance of developing countries and the increasing importance of developing country coalitions have transformed trade bargaining. NGOs in the global north have played an important role in enhancing developing country positions, for example by supporting the research and bargaining strength of the least developed countries. By in these ways redressing unequal power relations, NGOs can contribute to greater accountability in the international trading system.

# 6    Civil society and accountability in the Commonwealth

*Timothy M. Shaw and Pamela K. Mbabazi*

## Introduction

The Commonwealth presents quite a distinctive instance of global governance. It is 'global' in the sense that it draws participating governments and non-governmental groups from multiple regions and highly diverse economic and cultural contexts scattered across the planet. However, in contrast to the global institutions discussed in the preceding four chapters, the Commonwealth does not aspire to, and falls far short of, universal membership of all countries. It mostly links former territories of the British Empire, which often have broadly similar arrangements for education, law, mass media, medicine and government, as well as shared cultures of literature and sport. In addition, nearly all member countries of the Commonwealth share English, the principal global lingua franca, as an official language.

The Anglophone Commonwealth bears broad similarities with the Organisation Internationale de la Francophonie (International Organisation of La Francophonie), which groups governments of fifty-six French-speaking countries, and the smaller Comunidade dos Países de Língua Portuguesa (CPLP) (Community of Portuguese Language Countries), which assembles eight Lusophone states. The Commonwealth and La Francophonie have comprehensive mandates, including development issues, while the CPLP is more narrowly focused on matters of culture and education. Indeed, the formation of the CPLP in 1996 was in part a reaction to the accession of Mozambique to the Anglophone Commonwealth in 1995 (Shaw 2008: 24–7).

The Commonwealth involves 'governance' of a rather soft kind. Unlike the United Nations (UN) or the World Trade Organization (WTO), the Commonwealth has no charter or written constitution (although some of its affiliated institutions do). Instead, the work of the organisation is guided by tradition developed over decades of practice. Furthermore,

The authors thank Daisy Cooper and Rajesh Tandon for their practitioners' feedback to this study.

the Commonwealth generally contributes to governance of global affairs through informal norms and peer pressure rather than with legally binding measures (Weiss 2000; Shaw 2004). Yet this 'soft power' has enabled the institution to have important impacts in matters of democracy, human rights, economic solidarity, peace and security, both among its membership and more broadly. Indeed, as elaborated below, the Commonwealth may and does suspend member states who offend the rules of this 'extended family', particularly in relation to its foremost unifying norm of democracy (Shaw 2007, 2008, 2009).

The Commonwealth network, or 'Commonwealth Plus', takes form not only as an intergovernmental organisation, but also as a network of civil society associations (Shaw 2004, 2008: 1–11). Indeed, the informal, non-state Commonwealth (in the shape of professional bodies and non-governmental organisations) predates the inter-state Commonwealth by more than half a century. Today hundreds of civil society groups engage with the Commonwealth, including through the Commonwealth People's Forum (CPF), a civil society correlate of the biennial Commonwealth Heads of Government Meeting (CHOGM) (Commonwealth Foundation 1999).

This chapter examines how these various civil society associations have and have not pressured the Commonwealth to practise greater public accountability. The discussion begins with an overview of the history, activities and impacts of the Commonwealth. The next part of the chapter reviews the organisations and programmes that make up civil society in the context of the Commonwealth. Then a further section assesses in detail how these civil society activities have and have not made the intergovernmental Commonwealth more accountable, in terms of greater public transparency, more public consultations, more public monitoring and evaluation, and more policy correction (Shaw 2004). In this regard it is argued that civil society engagement has indeed raised the accountability of the intergovernmental Commonwealth, especially around the biennial summits. The last section of the chapter emphasises that accountability is as much a question for civil society quarters as official circles and highlights some of the accountability challenges facing global civil society within the Commonwealth (Commonwealth Foundation 1999).

### History and activities of the Commonwealth

The origins of the Commonwealth go back to occasional conferences in the late nineteenth century between the prime ministers of Britain and self-governing dominions of the British Empire such as Australia and Canada. The Imperial Conference of 1926 adopted the phrase 'Commonwealth of Nations' to denote a voluntary association of states, equal in status, with a shared allegiance to the British crown. In 1949, instigated by the decision of newly decolonised India to declare itself a republic, it was agreed that members of the Commonwealth need not recognise the British monarch as their head of state. Decolonisation brought a great expansion in member states of the Commonwealth through the 1960s and 1970s.

Today the Commonwealth encompasses 53 countries, mostly located in the Caribbean, the Pacific, South and South-East Asia and Sub-Saharan Africa. True, the membership does not include major states such as Brazil, China, Germany, Japan, Russia and the USA. However, Britain, India and South Africa are members, and with a combined population of nearly 2 billion people the Commonwealth is home to around a third of the total world population (Museveni 2007). In addition, the aggregate GDP of Commonwealth members is estimated to be about US$7.8 trillion, or around 16 per cent of the total global economy (Lundan and Jones 2001; CY 2009).

The Commonwealth did not acquire a permanent secretariat until 1965. Its offices are headquartered at Marlborough House in London (Shaw 2005). The organisation has had five Secretary-Generals to date, including Kamalesh Sharma since 2008. With a staff of just over 300 at the end of 2008 and an annual budget in 2008–9 of £45.6 million (US$75 million), the scale of the Commonwealth Secretariat (ComSec) remains modest relative to the global governance agencies discussed in earlier chapters (CY 2009: 90). It is around half the size of the WTO Secretariat and far smaller still than the offices of the UN, the World Bank and the IMF, despite having a wide-ranging remit that encompasses culture, education, finance, gender, health, tourism, youth and more.

Leaders of the Commonwealth meet every two years in a different member country to discuss issues of common concern and to agree on collective policies and initiatives. These summits have been known since 1971 as the Commonwealth Heads of Government Meeting (CHOGM) and are organised by the host government in collaboration with ComSec. The Commonwealth has used its biennial summits to reflect on the development challenges of its member states and to develop courses of action to be pursued collectively and individually through a process of consultations and co-operation. The most recent CHOGMs have taken place in Malta (2005), Uganda (2007) and Trinidad and Tobago (2009).

A semi-detached but well-established dimension of the Commonwealth is the four-yearly Commonwealth Games organised through the

Commonwealth Games Federation (CGF). This event was first held in 1930 in Hamilton, Ontario. The CGF has a somewhat different set of members from ComSec, as the several parts of the UK (including England, Guernsey, Jersey, Scotland and Wales) field separate teams, as do some of the UK Overseas Territories such as Bermuda, the Cayman Islands, Gibraltar and the Virgin Islands. Recent Commonwealth Games have been held in Manchester (2002), Melbourne (2006) and Delhi (2010).

The extensive Commonwealth network includes a number of other affiliated bodies. For example, the Commonwealth Scholarship Commission has sponsored over 20,000 students since it began operations in 1959 (Shaw and Jobbins 2009). Other featured events include Commonwealth Day (the second Monday in March), a Commonwealth Film Festival, a Commonwealth Lecture, and a Commonwealth Writers' Prize. In these ways the Commonwealth has informally shaped intellectual and cultural life in its member countries.

The Commonwealth has also loosely 'governed' global affairs through its facilitation of intercontinental migration and the associated development of diasporas and multiculturalism. The early Commonwealth oversaw much migration from Britain to Australia, Canada, New Zealand and South Africa. Concurrently, major flows within the British Empire took tens of millions of migrants from the Indian subcontinent to the Caribbean, Eastern and Southern Africa, Fiji, Malaysia and Singapore. Global bonds across these countries are sustained to this day through sports such as cricket and rugby, as well as through the English language. The government of India has recently come to encourage diaspora links through its Ministry of Overseas Indian Affairs, while an active Global Organization of People of Indian Origin (GOPIO) has operated in civil society since 1989.

Promotion of English as a lingua franca across the continents is a subtle but highly significant influence of the Commonwealth on global norms. Recent studies into the economic advantages of being within Commonwealth networks and using English have suggested that there may be a 10–15 per cent benefit compared to the use of other languages (Lundan and Jones 2001). Likewise, Anglophone civil society networks such as CIVICUS have had linguistic advantage in much of emergent global civil society. The Commonwealth has also used the advantage of English as its global lingua franca to bring together parties from around the world in order to address a range of global issues (Willis 2009).

The Commonwealth has also concerned itself prominently with questions of economic development, particularly under its longest serving Secretary-General, Sridath Ramphal. Sonny Ramphal captured the mood in global south-north relations by broadly supporting the campaign in the mid-1970s for a New International Economic Order (NIEO). To advance the debate, while at the same time protecting himself and the fledgling Secretariat, Ramphal established a high-powered Group of Experts chaired by a fellow West Indian, Alister McIntyre, whose final report was published in 1977 (Commonwealth Expert Group 1977). Ramphal was the most ubiquitous member of several world commissions in the 1980s concerning development: the Brandt, Palme, Brundtland and South Commissions. On his retirement the Secretariat issued a commemorative overview on *International Economic Issues: Contributions by the Commonwealth 1975–1990* (Hollingdale *et al.* 1990; see also Sanders 1988; Bourne 2008).

Since 1990 the Commonwealth has adopted a lower profile on questions of economic development. In this area the organisation has been most active around issues concerning Small Island Developing States (SIDS) (Commonwealth Secretariat 2009; Cooper and Shaw 2009). In contrast, the Commonwealth has had little visibility around contemporary issues such as the Millennium Development Goals (MDGs), in part because the Secretary-Generals who followed Ramphal have lacked his acute sense of mission. The Commonwealth may yet regain a higher profile on economic development concerns around issues of climate change and SIDS under its latest Secretary-General, Kamalesh Sharma (Shaw 2010).

Overall the Commonwealth has perhaps made its most notable impacts on global governance in the area of democracy and human rights (Weiss 2000). The origins of the organisation lie in the crafting of a post-colonial relationship of equals between Britain and former overseas territories. The Commonwealth was an early site of anti-apartheid politics, prompting South Africa to withdraw from the organisation in 1961, rejoining in 1994 after the end of apartheid. In the late 1970s the Commonwealth was instrumental in facilitating the transition from colonial Southern Rhodesia to Zimbabwe (Commonwealth Secretariat 1986, 1989).

Learning from these nationalist and liberation struggles, analysed further in the next part of this chapter, has led the Commonwealth to have continuing concern for good governance. In the 1990s the third Secretary-General, Emeka Anyaoku, promoted the development of generic Commonwealth values of democracy, human rights and the rule of law. At the 1991 CHOGM members agreed to the Harare Commonwealth Declaration of shared principles (CY 2009: 47–9). In 1998 the so-called Latimer House Guidelines suggested how the Commonwealth and its members could put these values into practice. The Harare Principles and the Latimer House Guidelines are reflected in much contemporary work of the Commonwealth, including election monitoring and good offices missions. Often these activities involve partnerships with civil society organisations. For example, the Commonwealth Foundation currently pursues a project with the London-based NGO, the One World Trust, on accountability and transparency in Belize, India, the Pacific and Uganda (One World Trust 2009).

In promoting democracy, human rights and the rule of law the Commonwealth has sometimes gone so far as to suspend certain of its member governments. It is one of the few global governance institutions to have taken such a step. For example, Fiji was suspended in 1987 following a military coup and rejoined ten years later after adopting a new constitution under civilian rule. Nigeria was suspended from the Commonwealth between 1995 and 1999 in the context of abuses of power by a military government. Pakistan was suspended during a period of unconstitutional military rule in that country from 1999 until 2004 and again during the state of emergency in 2007–8. Zimbabwe was suspended in 2002 for human rights violations and withdrew from the Commonwealth in 2003. Fiji was again suspended after the 2006 coup d'état in that country.

While the Commonwealth has always advocated democracy and economic development, it has tended to have more leverage over the former than the latter. Occasionally the organisation has addressed the two issues together. For example, in 2002 the Commonwealth Secretariat created an Expert Group on Democracy and Development chaired by Manmohan Singh. Characteristically for the Commonwealth, the panel brought together eminent social scientists and policy advisers from throughout the membership (Shaw 2008: 93). In particular the group considered how to secure sustainable development together with democracy, including issues of the balance between the two and the sequence in which they should be pursued. To this end it advocated partnerships between states, civil society associations, multinational corporations and intergovernmental agencies (Commonwealth Expert Group 2003).

In sum, although its institutional size and material resources are limited, the Commonwealth is not inconsequential in global governance. On the contrary, the experience of the Commonwealth shows that a 'voluntary' association of states which operates largely through 'soft' power can have important effects in reinforcing cultural, economic and political norms in the contemporary more global world.

### Civil society in the context of the Commonwealth

What is the role of civil society in these affairs? As noted earlier, civil society associations have been part of Commonwealth developments from the outset. For example, the non-governmental Imperial Federation League was formed in 1884 to advocate for a confederated union of dominions within the British Empire. The non-official periodical *The Round Table*, since 1983 carrying the subtitle *The Commonwealth Journal of International Affairs*, marks its centenary in 2010 (Mayall 2009; May 2010). In the early twentieth century a number of professional associations (e.g. in the areas of education, health, law and parliaments) were also organised on an imperial basis. In the mid-twentieth century anti-colonial nationalist movements and the anti-apartheid struggle helped to create the Commonwealth of legally sovereign states. Thus, much as national civil societies have grown in tandem with nation-states, an unofficial Commonwealth of civil society associations has always paralleled the official Commonwealth of governments.

Also conforming to this pattern of co-development, a Commonwealth Foundation was formed in 1965 to consolidate non-official dimensions of the organisation, in the same year that ComSec was created to co-ordinate the intergovernmental aspects. The Commonwealth Foundation, located alongside the Secretariat in Marlborough House, seeks 'to strengthen civil society organisations across the Commonwealth as they promote democracy, advance sustainable development and foster inter-cultural understanding' (Commonwealth Foundation 2009). Although the Foundation is smaller, poorer and less prestigious than the Secretariat, it has important – and arguably even more extensive – networks across the Commonwealth.

In addition, the Council of Commonwealth Societies (CCS) is an association of civil society organisations that operates under the auspices of the non-official Royal Commonwealth Society (RCS). The RCS is a network that convenes global gatherings at premises on Northumberland Avenue in London. On the annual Commonwealth Day it organises a multi-faith service in Westminster Abbey which reinforces the current Commonwealth focus on cross-cultural respect and understanding.

Meanwhile the London-based Commonwealth Organisations Group (COG) promotes communication among the several official and non-official networks of the Commonwealth. The COG consists of individuals who head major Commonwealth-related institutions. Most of its members come from non-state organisations such as the RCS, the Association of Commonwealth Universities (ACU), the Commonwealth Press Union (CPU) and the Institute of Commonwealth Studies (ICS). The Commonwealth Foundation and the Commonwealth Secretariat are also invited to the COG meetings, which occur several times a year.

Today around seventy pan-Commonwealth civil society bodies are accredited to the organisation (Commonwealth 2009). They include a host of professional associations, covering for example architects, broadcasters, lawyers, local government officials, public administrators, teachers and universities. A Commonwealth Business Council (CBC), formed in 1997, links over a hundred companies across the fifty-three member countries. Organised labour is brought into the picture through the Commonwealth Trade Union Group (CTUG). Issue advocacy groups in Commonwealth civil society include the Commonwealth Association of Indigenous Peoples (CAIP), the Commonwealth Human Rights Initiative (CHRI) and the Commonwealth Women's Network (CWN). The Commonwealth Youth Exchange Council (CYEC) has operated since 1970 and from 1997 has organised a Commonwealth Youth Forum around each CHOGM. Research bodies that focus on the Commonwealth include the Commonwealth Policy Studies Unit (CPSU), the ICS and the RCS.

Each of these heterogeneous institutions has its own genesis, culture and governance structure (including accountability arrangements). For example, the ACU has some 500 member universities with a Council of 25 members holding 2-year terms. The CBC has attracted over 100 members and has a board of 13 persons, including captains of industry from around the Commonwealth such as Rahul Bajaj and Lakshmi Mittal in India and Cyril Ramaphosa in South Africa. The CGF has one of the more extensive and complicated constitutions, which provides for a General Assembly with up to 3 representatives from each affiliate, and an intricately composed Executive Board. Taken together, these myriad forms of institutionalisation, participation and accountability add to the distinctiveness of 'Commonwealth governance'.

In addition, a number of other civil society organisations that are involved in the Commonwealth do not bear its name. Several such as CIVICUS and World Vision are formally accredited to the Commonwealth. Scores of other civil society groups participate in Commonwealth events on an ad hoc basis, including ActionAid, the Aga Khan Foundation, BRAC, Development Alternatives with Women for a New Era (DAWN), the Grameen Foundation, Oxfam, Save the Children Fund (SCF) and Voluntary Service Overseas (VSO). In addition, associations in a CHOGM host country may become engaged with the Commonwealth in the context of the summit meeting. In this vein, the Uganda National NGO Forum and the Uganda Debt Network (UDN) were active around the Kampala CHOGM in 2007.

Civil society associations that relate with the Commonwealth can be arranged on a continuum from enthusiastic supporters to radical critics. Among the more vocal civil society actors in recent years, the CHRI has persistently raised human rights issues. Since 1993 it has published a biennial report, released a few months before the CHOGM, focused on one or two subjects related to human rights (Sanger 2007). Likewise, the Commonwealth Judges and Magistrates Association (CJMA) has insistently addressed matters concerning the division of power in government, while the CAIP has doggedly advocated for the myriad indigenous communities scattered throughout the Commonwealth.

As civil society became more active on a global scale in the last quarter of the twentieth century, the Commonwealth Foundation took greater initiative to encourage civil society engagement. In 1996 it created an NGO Advisory Committee, renamed the Civil Society Advisory Committee (CSAC) in 2000. The CSAC has fourteen members from around the Commonwealth, five of whom sit on the Board of Governors of the Foundation, and two of whom serve on its Executive Committee. Hence, in contrast to other intergovernmental organisations covered elsewhere in this book, the Commonwealth has actually formally integrated civil society organisations into some of its core governing bodies (Commonwealth Foundation 1999).

Since 2005 the CSAC has also taken increasing responsibility for the conception, organisation, animation and delivery of the biennial Commonwealth People's Forum (CPF). First convened in 1997, the CPF is the civil society correlate of the CHOGM, much as NGO Forums have paralleled major UN conferences since the 1970s and, similarly, civil society forums have convened alongside meetings of the Bretton Woods institutions, the WTO, and (to be seen in later chapters) the OECD, the G8 and ASEM. A difference in the case of the Commonwealth is that the CPF meets immediately before CHOGM rather than concurrently with the official meeting. The CPF addresses the same theme as the accompanying CHOGM and typically attracts hundreds of participants. CPFs have convened in Edinburgh (1997), Durban (1999), Brisbane (2001), Abuja (2003), Valletta (2005), Kampala (2007) and Port of Spain (2009). In addition, the Commonwealth Foundation and the CSAC have, for recent CHOGMs (particularly in Uganda and Trinidad and Tobago), sponsored warm-up events for civil society associations in the host country during the twelve months preceding a summit.

Preparations for the CPF are overseen by a steering committee that typically comprises leaders from the government and civil society of the host country. The steering committee meets regularly in a global negotiation – facilitated by the Internet – of the CPF agenda. The committee also maintains communications during its planning operations with the Commonwealth Foundation, the CSAC and the host government. Once the theme of a CHOGM has been decided, at least twelve months ahead of the meeting, a series of sub-themes are developed for discussion in civil society workshops during the CPF.

In the case of Trinidad and Tobago in 2009, for example, government and civil society collaborated in a Summit Office within the Prime Minister's Office. The 2009 CPF theme of Partnering for a More Equitable and Sustainable Future was launched in mid-2008. Eight 'assemblies' were identified for this CPF, and proposals for their content and participation were invited in early 2009, leading to a round of global negotiations that prioritised the issues.

The Commonwealth People's Forum offers a space for civil society organisations across the Commonwealth to engage with each other and shape policies of governments in the Commonwealth context. The CPF has five main aims, namely: to raise the visibility of civil society organisations in the Commonwealth; to promote partnerships in the quest for development and democracy; to strengthen links between Commonwealth civil society organisations; to create opportunities for dialogue between civil society associations and government ministers on priority issues in the Commonwealth; and to provide opportunities for that dialogue to be raised and addressed at the CHOGM.

The Kampala summit of November 2007 featured a CPF that was attended by thousands of people from civil society organisations and the wider public. The forum included multiple panels with the overall theme of Realising People's Potential. In addition, the British Council created a so-called People's Space at the Kampala CPF to enable participants openly to debate and share insights about different issues of common interest and learn from each other. This welcome innovation was repeated, albeit in a different national and global context, in Trinidad in 2009.

In sum, civil society organisations are an increasingly prominent feature of both the Commonwealth as a whole and its individual member countries. This is partly because citizens increasingly feel dissatisfied or disillusioned with traditional formal politics. People therefore look for other ways to have voice in and influence over political processes, locally as well as globally. In the Commonwealth, as elsewhere, governments that previously perceived civil society organisations as a nuisance now increasingly view these groups as one of the most important interfaces between official circles and citizens.

## Civil society and accountability in the Commonwealth

The Commonwealth generally has a strong record on accountability to its constituencies, in comparison with many other global governance agencies. The biennial CHOGM/CPF process in particular constitutes a context for extensive public consultation, evaluation and correction.

ComSec, the Foundation and other Commonwealth-affiliated organisations regularly report to, and take input from, High Commissioners in London, the representatives of the member governments. However, other accountability dynamics of the Commonwealth operate in relation to civil society.

Civil society actors have used a variety of mechanisms to hold the intergovernmental Commonwealth to account for its actions and omissions. As elsewhere in this book, accountability is understood here to have four aspects: transparency, consultation, evaluation and correction/redress. Civil society impacts on the Commonwealth in each of these areas of democratic accountability are considered in turn below.

### Transparency

The issue of transparency can be covered quite summarily, since civil society groups have not pressed the Commonwealth institutions on matters such as the disclosure of official documents and the release of more or better public information. Certain critics have complained that 'the Secretariat moves at a snail's pace on its policy and practice for disclosure of its own documents, when some positive action would prompt member states to follow suit towards greater transparency' (Sanger 2007: 487). However, civil society associations have not pursued specific and concerted demands for increased openness and visibility with the Commonwealth as they have with, say, the Bretton Woods institutions or the WTO.

There would seem to be several reasons for this general reticence. Partly it is not in the culture of the Commonwealth for civil society groups to challenge the official agencies. Also, it is widely assumed that the Secretariat and other Commonwealth institutions have little of public significance to hide. (In contrast, the decision-making and budgets of the CPF could make for much more interesting reading.)

For the rest it might be suggested that the pervasive presence of civil society actors in all areas of the Commonwealth's work helps to make these operations readily visible to any interested party. Public awareness of the Commonwealth would arguably be far more limited if civil society associations were not continually drawing attention to the institution through forums, projects, reports, studies, journals and spectacles.

### Consultation

The Commonwealth has always claimed to be accessible to civil society associations for consultation. In earlier times the institution collaborated with several generations of national liberation movements. However, the Commonwealth was slower than other intergovernmental agencies such as the UN and the World Bank in developing regular consultation processes with civil society groups, partly in view of the more limited resources of its Secretariat.

Nowadays, consultations of civil society associations take place throughout the Commonwealth network. As already noted, from the 1990s the Commonwealth Foundation has spurred more initiatives in this area. Both the Foundation and ComSec regularly generate strategic plans that are open to civil society inputs through their respective websites. In addition, the CBC has come to encourage cross-sectoral dialogues that include civil society, for example in the context of 'corporate social responsibility'. More generally, state and non-state networks within the Commonwealth interact continuously with each other, particularly as facilitated by mobile phones and the Internet, now including Flicker and Twitter along with blogs on the Secretariat website.

However, the most elaborate Commonwealth consultations of civil society have occurred around the biennial CHOGM and its accompanying CPF. Particularly since the Malta meeting in 2005, the Commonwealth has made significant advances in putting in place mechanisms for the consultation of civil society organisations ahead of every Heads of Government meeting. During the two years leading up to each CHOGM the Commonwealth Foundation supports and facilitates a process of civil society dialogue and interaction in national, regional and global spheres. The various consultations in Africa, Asia, the Caribbean and the Pacific culminate in a Committee of the Whole (COW), where civil society representatives meet with senior officials prior to each CHOGM. The outcomes of the COW feed into the CHOGM communiqué.

Other substantial consultation of civil society occurs in the context of the previously described Commonwealth People's Forum. The CPF steering committee, through its ongoing exchanges with CHOGM organisers, is able to have some impact on the CHOGM agenda. Meanwhile outcomes of workshops at the CPF itself, held the week prior to CHOGM, are brought together in a final communiqué of the CPF, which is presented to the Heads of Government. This statement can shape the CHOGM discussions, for example as when interventions from ecology networks at the Kampala CPF helped to generate an official statement on climate change at the ensuing CHOGM.

Since 2005 the Heads of Government meeting has included a formal encounter between Foreign Ministers and the Commonwealth Foundation Civil Society Advisory Committee. These meetings have to some degree enabled Commonwealth member states to consult with various constituencies of civil society. In Kampala in 2007, half a dozen CSAC members along with the Director of the Commonwealth Foundation and one or two leaders of major professional associations participated in a morning session. The setting for the encounter is the same large table where the Heads of Government meet. Whilst the tone of the deliberations is polite, the interaction constitutes another distinctive and symbolic layer of Commonwealth networking.

At the Abuja CHOGM in 2003, consultations of civil society actors made an impact on the so-called Latimer House Guidelines, a framework for implementing the Commonwealth's fundamental principles of responsibility, transparency and accountability in all branches of government: legislative, executive and judiciary. The guidelines reinforce the deliberations of the Commonwealth Ministerial Action Group (CMAG) on suspensions as well as readmissions of member states. The Latimer House Guidelines originated from civil society, especially the well-regarded Commonwealth Magistrates and Judges Association (CMJA). This case provides an excellent example of how Commonwealth civil society can have a key impact on decisions made by heads of government. It also illustrates how ideas initially formulated in civil society circles can work their way into decision-making and help shape government policies.

### Evaluation

Substantial monitoring and evaluation of Commonwealth operations is undertaken by the member states, particularly the High Commissioners in London. The High Commissioners constitute an attentive watchdog over the Commonwealth Secretariat and the Commonwealth Foundation, as well as other London-based Commonwealth associations like the ACU, the CGF, the Commonwealth Local Government Forum (CLGF), the Commonwealth Parliamentary Association (CPA) and the RCS. The ABC group (Australia, Britain and Canada) are especially alert in oversight of financial matters.

However, civil society actors have in various respects complemented governmental monitoring of the Commonwealth. For example, members of the CSAC sit alongside representatives of governments on both the Board of Governors and the Executive Committee that oversee the Commonwealth Foundation. Likewise, civil society actors on the Committee of the Whole take part in its review of the implementation of undertakings made at the previous CHOGM. Civil society groups have also tracked delivery on initiatives such as the Commonwealth Respect and Understanding Commission (Shaw 2008: 93–4; Willis 2009).

*Correction/redress*

Regarding civil society promotion of correction or redress as it relates to democratic accountability, the Commonwealth has arguably fared quite well, although more needs to be done. Civil society impacts in this respect have not related so much to the Commonwealth as a global governance institution. Rather, civil society actors have often used the Commonwealth framework to correct shortfalls of democracy in certain of the Commonwealth member states.

For instance, in late 2005 civil society organisations raised questions about whether Uganda was qualified – in terms of democratic credentials – to host the 2007 CHOGM. As a result, Ugandan President Yoweri Museveni was compelled to meet with and reassure civil society delegates from around the world in the wings of the Malta summit. As a result of this pressure the government of Uganda introduced new rules for greater NGO participation in local governance, facilitated by advice from European Union consultants on best practice. Connections to wider global civil society also gave the local organising group for the CPF more possibilities to moderate any authoritarian inclinations of the government of Uganda. Consequently, during the Kampala CHOGM, President Museveni had to tolerate lobbying activities of local NGOs such as the Development Network of Indigenous Voluntary Associations (DENIVA), the Uganda NGO Forum and UDN, lest he alienate major actors in the Commonwealth.

In addition, as noted earlier, the Commonwealth has through its Ministerial Action Group suspended several member governments who offend its values of democratic government. These actions have often followed pressure from civil society circles, including in the countries concerned. Such civil society pressure was most efficacious in relation to the anti-apartheid movement. Having cut its teeth in the anti-colonial and anti-apartheid struggles, civil society in the Commonwealth has been quite resilient around post-independence challenges to democracy. Professional associations of administrators, lawyers, journalists and parliamentarians have been particularly vigilant. The CHRI has likewise been a consistent, articulate watchdog on human rights violations. Its genesis in 1987 arose from growing concern, especially in the original 'Dominions', that race in Southern Africa was coming to overshadow all other human rights issues in the Commonwealth. Meanwhile diasporas in South Africa and the UK have pressed the Commonwealth on the Zimbabwean case.

Perhaps the most powerful example of civil society pressure through the Commonwealth for correction of a detrimental political situation was the anti-apartheid sports boycott against South Africa, especially in the 1970s and 1980s. The ban included, in particular, the Commonwealth Games themselves. In association with the African National Congress (ANC), the South African Non-Racial Olympic Committee (SAN-ROC) animated a series of boycotts of the Commonwealth Games. As a result, the number of countries competing in Christchurch in 1974 and Edinburgh in 1986 went down rather than up. It was not until the Auckland Commonwealth Games in 1990 that the event featured more than fifty countries (Nauright and Schimmel 2005). Cricket and rugby boycotts also figured prominently (Black and Nauright 1998). Academic, cultural and sports boycotts were particularly telling on the white population of South Africa (Crawford and Klotz 1999).

Looking more broadly, association with the Commonwealth has arguably allowed a number of civil society organisations to bolster their campaigns for correction and redress in wider world politics. Civil society actors connected with the Commonwealth may have a head start in global advocacy given its inheritance of well-developed networks and the English language. In this way Commonwealth links have indirectly furthered such causes as the abolition of landmines through the Ottawa Process, the regulation of the diamond trade through the Kimberley Process, the restriction of flows of small arms and opposition to the use of child soldiers. Civil society in the Commonwealth context has also in recent years promoted a systemic correction of prevailing practices of world politics by encouraging a focus on multiculturalism, inter-faith understanding and inter-racial communication.

### Accountable civil society?

Much as civil society groups try to ensure greater accountability of global governance organisations such as the Commonwealth, these citizen associations also face challenges regarding their own accountability (Scholte 2004a). While civil society actors often demand accountability in others, notably states and corporations within the Commonwealth, they have not always been in the vanguard in terms of their own transparency, their own consultation processes, evaluation of their own operations and correction of their own shortcomings. The findings of the Global Accountability Project at the One World Trust (2009) have been telling in this respect. In four GAP reports since 2003, the accountability performance of global NGOs, many of them engaging the Commonwealth, has often been no better and sometimes, in fact, worse than that of global governance agencies and global corporations (One World Trust 2009).

As in other global governance contexts, civil society groups that engage with Commonwealth institutions claim to be representing certain interests. Yet it is often difficult to determine whether these organisations are genuinely representing the constituencies that they claim to serve. In principle, civil society associations should answer in the first place to their notional beneficiaries. However, in practice, resource dependencies may dictate that civil society bodies more readily answer to official and private funders.

A good example of such flawed accountability relations arose around civil society opposition to the proposed construction by AEG, with funding from the World Bank, of a power project at Bujagali Falls in Uganda. The project was delayed as a result of intensive lobbying from Greenpeace, several local NGOs and companies such as Adrift Water Rafting on the basis that the dam would harm the interests of local people. Yet a subsequent independent study found that the majority of local stakeholders actually favoured the hydro-electric plant as a measure to meet the growing energy deficit in Uganda. The project has since been restarted with funding from the Aga Khan Foundation as well as the World Bank (Bujagali 2009).

Such evidence suggests that civil society organisations generally need to tend more carefully to their own democratic credentials. With this concern in mind the Commonwealth Foundation, as early as 1995, produced a ninety-page document entitled *Non-Governmental Organisations: Guidelines for Good Policy and Practice* (Commonwealth Foundation 1995). More recently, the Foundation has developed collaborative links with the One World Trust on questions of CSO accountability (One World Trust 2009). In particular, the latter initiative has examined prospects for different schemes of self-regulation of NGOs as a means to promote their accountability.

That said, Commonwealth civil society networks score relatively well in terms of their own accountability when it comes to access for Southern groups. The Commonwealth is not marked by a predominance of Northern civil society organisations such as one encounters at the UN (see Chapter 2), the WTO (see Chapter 5), G8 countersummits (see Chapter 9), the climate change negotiations (see Chapter 11) and the Internet Corporation for Assigned Names and Numbers (see Chapter 13). On the contrary, representatives and participants from the global south predominate in, for example, the ACU, the CGF and the CSAC. Civil society input from India and South Africa has been particularly sophisticated and vociferous, as illustrated by CIVICUS and the Treatment Action Campaign (TAC). However, it should be noted that civil society from the South also includes more cautious establishment

NGOs such as the Aga Khan Foundation, BRAC and the Grameen Foundation.

## Conclusion

This chapter has examined an instance of 'soft' global governance through a mainly informally constituted and largely culturally oriented voluntary association of states. It has been seen that this looser mode of global regulation has, in the case of the Commonwealth, attracted civil society attention no less than the 'hard' intergovernmentalism of the UN, the Bretton Woods institutions or the WTO. Important accountability relationships can develop as a result.

As in other cases examined in this book, the history of the Commonwealth reveals a parallel development in which civil society engagement of a global governance body has grown hand in hand with the overall growth of that institution. Indeed, much of the Commonwealth network is comprised of civil society actors, with professional associations having played a particularly prominent role. The intergovernmental Commonwealth and the civil society Commonwealth are in continual interaction, as epitomised by the interplay of ComSec and the Foundation with professional associations and NGOs, as well as that of CHOGM with the CPF. In the case of the Commonwealth Foundation civil society actors even sit alongside state representatives as formal members of the executive organ. It is possible that the Commonwealth holds clues to, and lessons for, future patterns of global governance in which states, global secretariats and civil society actors have become even more pervasively and deeply interconnected than they are today (Shaw 2004, 2005).

These close relationships would appear, in the case of the Commonwealth, to have implications for accountability dynamics in global governance. On the positive side, ubiquitous civil society involvement has helped to make the Commonwealth relatively transparent and consultative vis-à-vis affected publics. The Commonwealth is strikingly responsive to civil society inputs when compared to many of the other global governance institutions examined in this book (Shaw 2004).

Yet caution perhaps needs to be taken in order that the relationship of civil society and global governance does not become overly cosy, such that the civil society engagement comes to lack the sort of critical edge that is vital to a vibrant democracy. In this vein, civil society groups arguably could play a stronger role as watchdogs over the Commonwealth itself (in addition to, and as distinct from, calling to account its errant member states). Civil society associations could in this respect learn from the example of increasing media scrutiny of the Commonwealth. Moreover, weak accountability of civil society groups to their own constituencies might tend to encourage a potentially unhealthy complacency in the Commonwealth. An unhappy outcome of this kind would detract from the substantial capacities of the Commonwealth to contribute to a more global, cosmopolitan world in the twenty-first century (Commonwealth Secretariat 2007).

# 7 The Organisation of the Islamic Conference: accountability and civil society

*Saied Reza Ameli*

## Introduction

The Organisation of the Islamic Conference (OIC) is an instance of global governance where, in contrast to the other institutions examined in this book, religion figures centrally as a unifying factor. Inclusion of the OIC in the present volume is also important as an indication that not all global governance is Western in orientation and dominated by Western countries. Likewise, as the case of the OIC demonstrates, ideas and practices of accountability and civil society do not always adopt a Western pattern.

Established in 1969, the OIC claims to be, and is often perceived as, the 'United Nations' of the Islamic world. Its membership of fifty-seven states across four continents (Africa, Asia, Europe and Latin America) covers most of the world's 1.5 billion Muslims and more than a fifth of the world's total population. Several other states with notable Muslim populations, such as Bosnia-Herzegovina, Russia and Thailand have observer status with the OIC.

The OIC puts its emphasis on Islam as a global religion that transcends ethnic and sectarian differences. That said, the Organisation has a highly diverse membership geographically, socially, linguistically and culturally. This diversity often raises challenges of intercultural communication in forging a unified organisation from a heterogeneous membership.

The OIC embraces issues that touch all countries with Muslim communities. The member states pool resources, combine efforts and speak with one voice in order to safeguard their interests and ensure the progress and wellbeing of their peoples and those of other Muslims the world over. Indeed, the organisation was created as a 'religious reaction' against the attempted destruction of the Al-Aqsa Mosque in Israeli-occupied Jerusalem in August 1969. This event prompted King Faisal of Saudi Arabia to call an Islamic Summit Conference (Ahmad Baba 1994). On this occasion and since, Islamic unity has powerfully motivated Muslims – and in particular Muslim leaders – to stand as a collective global body.

The OIC has received little attention in previous academic research. Ahmad Baba (1994) has examined the circumstances behind the creation of a global institution to support 'Islamic Countries' in an international crisis. He regards the OIC as a reflection of a pan-Islamic inclination among some Muslim leaders. Al-Ahsan (1998) has discussed the OIC as an Islamic political institution. Khan (2002) has presented the agency as an embodiment of the internationality of Islam. Akhtar (2005) has assessed political and economic co-operation through the OIC.

None of this earlier research has analysed the OIC in terms of accountability or civil society, let alone looked at the relationship between the two. The present chapter therefore addresses questions that previous studies have not systematically considered. What does accountability entail in the context of the OIC? For what is this institution accountable and to whom? What counts as civil society in relation to the OIC, and what role does it play in accountability processes of this intergovernmental organisation?

In response to these questions the first section below reviews the history and institutional structure of the OIC. The second part elaborates conceptual clarifications regarding 'civil society' and 'accountability' from an Islamic perspective. The third section relates these concepts to the OIC and assesses how civil society has been relevant to the accountability of the organisation; the effects are found to have been quite limited to date. The conclusion offers a few recommendations for a more functional and productive OIC in relation to political and public participation, citing in particular the potentials of a 'virtual Ummah'.

## The OIC: history and institutional structure

The preliminary meeting of the OIC convened in Rabat on 25 September 1969 in response to the arson perpetrated a month earlier on the Al-Aqsa Mosque. The attack was felt as a deep assault on the honour, dignity and faith of Muslims. This bitter challenge occurred in the holy city of Al-Quds, so dear to Muslims, and moreover involved the third holiest shrine of Islam. The Al-Aqsa Mosque had also served historically as the first Qibla (the direction faced in prayer and other Islamic holy rites), before that centre-point of Muslim faith was reoriented to Mecca and the Kaaba. Leaders at the Rabat Summit seized upon the attack – which evoked worldwide condemnation – to think together of their common cause and muster the force to overcome their differences. They laid the foundations of a grouping of states, the OIC, which they entrusted with liberating Al-Quds/Jerusalem and the Al-Aqsa Mosque from Israeli occupation.

The establishment of the OIC also had deeper roots in the Islamic psyche. As is elaborated below, the notion of the Ummah (the universal community of Muslims) figures centrally in the faith. Yet after the dissolution of the Ottoman Empire following the First World War, there was no governmental expression of Islamic transnationality and brotherhood. The creation of the OIC was a way to reinvigorate, in a modern context, a key Islamic principle.

The OIC convened its first Conference of Foreign Ministers in Muharram 1390 AH (corresponding to February 1970 CE). In February 1972 the Third Session of the Islamic Conference of Foreign Ministers adopted the Charter of the Organisation, whose purpose is to strengthen solidarity and co-operation among Islamic states in political, economic, cultural, scientific and social fields. The first Summit of Kings and Heads of State and Government met in Jeddah later that month.

The Charter begins by enumerating the principles governing OIC activities. These principles include: full equality among member states; the right of all member states to self-determination and non-interference in internal affairs; respect of the sovereignty, independence and territorial integrity of each member state; peaceful settlement of any dispute that might arise among member states; and avoidance of force or the threat of force against member states. Although such language defers to the conventions of modern diplomacy and international relations that underpin other intergovernmental organisations, the OIC also (as is elaborated below) largely rests its work on Islamic norms and the language of Shari'ah (i.e. Islamic Law).

The Charter specifies that the OIC comprises three core bodies. The first of these, the Conference of Kings and Heads of State and Government, is the supreme authority in the organisation and normally meets once every three years; it can also convene whenever the interest of Muslim countries warrants it. Second, the Conference of Foreign Ministers meets once a year (or whenever the need arises) at the level of ministers of external affairs or their officially accredited representatives. Third, the General Secretariat oversees the day-to-day operations of the OIC (see Figure 1). The General Secretariat is headed by a Secretary-General appointed by the Conference of Foreign Ministers for a period of four years, renewable once only. The Secretary-General is responsible for appointing the staff of the General Secretariat from amongst citizens of the member states, paying due regard to their competence and integrity, and in accordance with the principle of equitable geographical distribution. The Conference of Foreign Ministers also appoints four Assistant Secretary-Generals.

In addition to its core organs the OIC encompasses several subsidiary agencies related to finance, education, culture and media. For example, the Islamic Development Bank (IDB) is an international financial

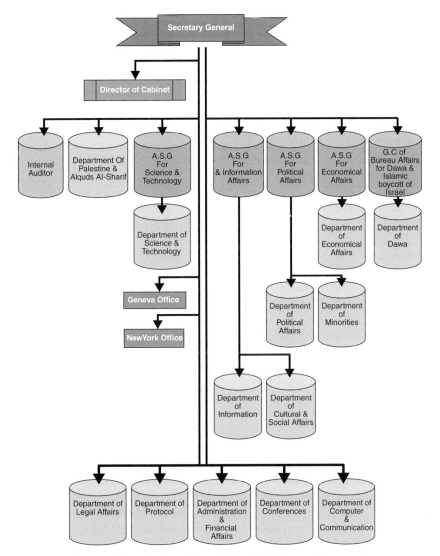

Figure 1: Organisation chart of the OIC General Secretariat

institution instigated by a conference of OIC finance ministers in Jeddah in 1973 and formally opened two years later. The IDB seeks to foster economic development and social progress of OIC member countries and Muslim communities in accordance with the principles of Shari'ah. At present the Bank has fifty-six member states from the OIC (i.e. all but Guyana) that contribute to its capital and accept such terms and conditions as may be decided upon by its Board of Governors. The IDB provides project loans as well as other forms of financial assistance to member countries for economic and social development. The Bank also operates special funds, including one to assist Muslim communities in non-member countries. Over the years the capital stock of the IDB (denominated in Islamic dinars) has grown from US$100 million to US$325 million. States with the largest shareholdings are Saudi Arabia, Libya, Qatar and Iran, who between them hold over half of the subscribed capital. The Bank is authorised to accept deposits and to mobilise financial resources in modes that are compatible with Shari'ah. The IDB is also charged with: promoting trade among member countries, especially in capital goods; providing technical assistance; and extending training facilities for personnel engaged in development activities in Muslim countries in accordance with Shari'ah (IDB 2008).

Another important subsidiary organisation of the OIC is the Statistical, Economic and Social Research and Training Centre for Islamic Countries (SESRTCIC), more commonly known as the Ankara Centre. SESRTCIC has operated since 1978 with the purpose of collating, processing and disseminating socio-economic statistics and information on, and for utilisation by, the member countries. The Centre also plays an important role in the provision of training programmes.

A further subsidiary organ of the OIC is the Islamic Educational, Scientific and Cultural Organisation (ISESCO). Headquartered in Rabat, this body was founded in 1982 following three years of intergovernmental discussions. ISESCO aims: to strengthen co-operation among member states in its fields of concern; to develop applied sciences and advanced technology within the framework of Islamic values; to consolidate understanding among Muslim peoples for the achievement of world peace and security; and to consolidate Islamic identity and solidarity in order to safeguard Islamic civilisation. In the pursuance of such aims ISESCO has held, for example, an international symposium in Cotonou in 2008 on vocational education for persons with special needs. Other events in the same year addressed the educational and developmental role of Arab Islamic schools, the work of mental health institutes, violence against women, training of female journalists, environmental issues and youth policies (ISESCO 2010).

A fourth OIC affiliate, the Islamic States Broadcasting Organisation (ISBO), emerged from a resolution adopted by the Islamic Conference of Foreign Ministers in 1975 and was constituted in 1977. From offices in Jeddah the ISBO aims to disseminate the values of Islam, to familiarise others with Islamic civilisation, to teach Arabic to non-Arabic speakers, and to produce and exchange radio and television programmes (ISBO 2010).

The fifth specialised agency of the OIC, the International Islamic News Agency (IINA), was established in 1972 with headquarters also in Jeddah. The IINA is tasked with enhancing and preserving Islamic cultural heritage, promoting intercultural communication among Muslims around the world, and working for the unification of the objectives of the Islamic world. The IINA distributes daily news reports in Arabic, English and French through the Qatar News Agency. It also sends its news bulletin to agencies in Malaysia, Indonesia, Pakistan, Russia and Central Asia. It further manages projects to inform religious leaders about the conditions of Muslims around the world. The IINA collaborates with the Pan-African News Agency (PANA) and has established co-operation with Islamic centres around the world (IINA 2010).

In terms of subsidiary organs, the OIC has an expert committee called the International Islamic Fiqh (Jurisprudence) Academy (IIFA). This body was created at the Third Islamic Summit Conference with the aim of achieving the theoretical and practical unity of the Ummah around principles of the Shar'ia. The IIFA also seeks to strengthen the link of the Muslim community with the Islamic faith and to draw inspiration from the Shar'ia for the solution of contemporary problems. The IIFA verifies and indexes books published on Islam, prepares books on the Sunna Fiqh Schools to be translated into foreign languages for mainstream society, organises seminars and symposia on the Fiqh, and publishes a journal on Islamic jurisprudence (IIFA 2010).

In addition, the OIC has charitable bodies such as the Islamic Solidarity Fund and its waqf. A waqf is a public Islamic endowment which may involve land, a trust or any other kind of property. The basic regulations governing a waqf are laid down in Shar'ia law, but its interpretation and implementation may vary in different Muslim societies. (One of the purposes of the waqf is to circumvent regulations that do not allow inheritance and cause the wealth of individuals to become the property of the ruler. Rich families donate properties as waqf, naming their sons as trustees. The trustee usually receives 10 per cent of the income, thereby guaranteeing that at least some of the money stays in the family.) The Islamic Solidarity Fund has no governmental contributions. It aims: to raise the intellectual and moral levels of Muslims; to provide required material relief in case of emergencies that may befall Islamic countries; and to assist Muslim minority communities so that they may improve their religious, social and cultural standards (ISF 2010).

In sum, then, the OIC is a multifaceted intergovernmental organisation. In a number of respects it mirrors the UN, with meetings of heads of state and government as well as specialised agencies for finance, education and culture, and communications. However, in contrast to the UN and the other intergovernmental bodies discussed in preceding chapters, the OIC draws no member states from the West. Moreover, the OIC takes its inspiration from religious faith and bases many of its activities explicitly in religious law.

### Current directions: the OIC ten-year programme of action

In 2005 Ekmeleddin Ihsanoglu, a citizen of Turkey, took office as the ninth Secretary-General of the OIC. His tenure has been distinguished by a marked emphasis on long-term strategy and the promotion of Islam as a force of tolerance in the world. To this end Ihsanoglu in June 2006 launched a Ten-Year Programme of Action for the OIC, which had been adopted at the Third Extraordinary Session of the Islamic Summit, held at Mecca in December 2005 (OIC 2005). The Ten-Year Programme of Action reflects a new orientation for the OIC. The strategy gives high priority to matters related to 'civil culture'. In this vein the programme highlights: intellectual and political issues; solidarity and Islamic action; a vision of Islam as a religion of moderation and tolerance; good governance; and human rights, with particular emphasis on women and family rights. The Programme of Action also addresses subjects such as pluralism in Islamic jurisprudence, opposition to terrorism, resistance to Islamophobia, the plight of Palestine and the Occupied Territories, and efforts for conflict prevention and resolution.

Comparing the OIC Charter approved in 1972 with the Ten-Year Programme of Action registered three decades later, a change of discourse is readily apparent. The Ten-Year Programme of Action includes prominent references to good governance and civil society, language which was decidedly absent in the OIC founding document.

To illustrate this shift it is instructive to examine the OIC orientation towards human rights discourse. From its inception the OIC has put serious efforts into articulating an Islamic perspective on the language of universal human rights. Early summit meetings held in Rabat (1969), Lahore (1974) and Mecca-Ta'if (1981) appointed a committee to prepare a text on human rights in Islam. The first version of the statement was published in *The Muslim World League Journal* (*Rabitat al-alam al-islami*) in 1979. The document stated that in our current time 'humanity is in need of religious support and means of self-restraint to protect its rights, and the rights and freedoms in Islam are part of the religion revealed through the Qur'an'. In this text, many issues related to individual freedom, family, freedom of opinion, expression and religious observance were addressed according to the divine inspiration (Jacques 2002).

These introductory steps fertilised an Islamic Charter for Human Rights in January 1981. Since that day the OIC has convened several Muslim Conferences on Human Rights in Islam, the fifth one in Tehran in 1989 (Jacques 2002: 170).

Concurrently the Islamic Council of Europe, based in London, pursued a parallel initiative. It proclaimed a Universal Islamic Declaration of Human Rights in 1981. This declaration is a Muslim response to similar declarations of the UN (1948), the Council of Europe (1950) and the Conference on Security and Co-operation in Europe (1975). So the Islamic Human Rights Declaration is based on the language of European liberal democracy, but at the same time reflects Islamic law according to the Qur'an (the holy book of Islam) and the Sunnah (the sayings and living habits of the Prophet).

Meanwhile the Ten-Year Programme of Action puts more emphasis on human rights and good governance. For example, it is declared in Part VIII that the OIC should (OIC 2005):

seriously endeavour to enlarge the scope of political participation, ensure equality, civil liberties and social justice and ... promote transparency and accountability, and eliminate corruption in the OIC Member States.

The programme also urged the elaboration of an OIC Charter of Human Rights and the establishment of an independent permanent body to promote human rights in the member states. It further mandated the OIC General Secretariat to co-operate with other international and regional organisations in order to guarantee the rights of Muslim communities in non-OIC member states.

With particular reference to civil society activities, the Ten-Year Programme of Action mentions non-governmental organisations (NGOs) several times. For one thing, the strategy urges that Islamic states and Islamic civil society institutions should build co-operation with international civil society organisations in relief efforts (OIC 2005: Part III). In addition, NGOs are described as key partners for governments in the struggle against Islamophobia (OIC 2005: Part VII). The Programme of Action also highlights strengthened relations with officially recognised NGOs in the member states as one of the main priorities for reform of the organisation (OIC 2005: Part XI).

### Civil Society and accountability: some conceptual clarifications

Several important conceptual points need to be considered prior to any detailed discussion about civil society and accountability in relation to the OIC. These points concern: secular and religious notions of civil society; Islamic notions of civil society more particularly; secular and religious notions of accountability; and Islamic notions of accountability more particularly. Attention to these matters elucidates common ground as well as differences between Islamic and Western liberal conceptions of civil society and accountability.

### Civil society: secular or religious?

There is no absolute and permanent definition of civil society. In Western discourse, 'civil society' is a secular concept and related to a particular political philosophy, namely liberal democracy (Hadji Haidar 2008). However, civil society can also be understood and practised in non-Western ways (Hann and Dunn 1996). Thus civil society might take different forms in relation to the OIC as compared with other global governance institutions covered in this book.

In a secular Western liberal vein, Andrew Heywood speaks of civil society as a society alongside the democratic state in which citizens and NGOs are highly effective (2003: 43). Liberal democracy has three central features. One of these is an indirect and representative form of democracy, where political office is gained through success in regular elections that are conducted on the basis of formal equality (i.e. one person, one vote). Second, liberal democracy is based upon competition and electoral choice, as ensured by political pluralism and tolerance of a wide range of contending beliefs, conflicting social philosophies and rival political movements and parties. Third, liberal democracy involves a clear distinction between the state and civil society. This separation is maintained both by checks on government power from autonomous groups and by the organisation of economic life around a capitalist market in the private sector. Liberal democracy also rests importantly on utilitarianism, an 'amoral philosophy ... which equates good with pleasure or happiness, and evil with pain or unhappiness, therefore individuals are assumed to act so as to maximize pleasure and minimize pain' (Heywood 2003: 50).

In the conception just described, civil society is understood in distinctly secular terms. Indeed, as Bryan Turner has suggested, Western secular thinking has in many ways constructed 'citizenship' (and associated ideas of civil society) so as to replace religion as a framework for ethical values (Turner 1994, 1999).

In fact the tenets of secular liberal democracy can be substantially reconciled with religious values in general and Islamic norms in particular. For example, principles of defined expectations, effectiveness, accountability, recognition and responsibility figure strongly in faith-based as well as secular approaches. However, civil society from the perspective of Islamic political philosophy is understood first of all in religious terms and contextualised within the regulation of Shar'ia law. Moreover, as elaborated later, Islam parts from liberal democracy on utilitarianism as a basis for assessing accountability.

### Civil society in Islam

For a Muslim, the ideal civil society should in essence be a land free from all attachments except that to Allah. Civil society would be a society in which Islamic Law becomes the underlying source of social, political and economic measures. Islamic civil society would be a society without injustice, in which previously muted groups have voice and previously oppressed individuals have justice.

The concept of 'Ummah' figures centrally in Islamic notions of 'global governance' and 'global civil society'. 'Ummah' is a Qur'anic term meaning 'the community of believers'. This community encompasses all people of Muslim faith, wherever on the planet they might be located. The Ummah is a transnational society without any territorial or ethnic delimitation. For a Muslim, then, the more that one is among and with the Ummah, the more 'civil' the society is considered to be. Civility means membership in the community of believers and solidarity with the whole Ummah.

The idea of 'Okhovvat' ('brotherhood') falls in a similar framework. Brotherhood is a type of Muslim unity, based on shared values, which creates trust with and sympathy towards others of the faith. According to the principle of universal brotherhood, there are no fundamental differences between Muslims in terms of class, caste, race, nation or territory (Abbas 2005: 48). All members of 'Muslim Society' across the world are considered to be brothers and sisters, meaning that if disaster befalls one, it should alert all.

This is not to suggest that the Ummah and the Okhovvat are exclusionary communities. On the contrary, Islam embraces a very wide universalism that encompasses all believers, whether Muslim, Christian or Jew (Alibabai 1997: 65). The Moghul Empire in India provides an example where the majority did not share the faith of the Muslim rulers. The Sokoto Caliphate in West Africa similarly adopted inclusionary practices towards people of other faiths. Thus history shows that Islamic particularism need not be a force for rejecting others. According to Hadje Haidar (2008: 174), 'although Islamic laws have universal bias, they apply particularly to those who have freely submitted to the faith of

Islam. The term "excused" is used to describe non-Muslims with regard to their disobedience of Islamic Law.' This view corresponds to what Roland Robertson (1992) has described more generally as particularism within universalism under conditions of globalisation.

The socio-ethical principles of Ummah and Okhovvat are key to understanding the operations of the OIC. Indeed, it was an outrage against Islam – the attack on the Al-Aqsa Mosque – that united the Ummah in the creation of the OIC. Muslim identity is a primary criterion for membership in the organisation, and the Charter explicitly highlights the promotion of Islamic solidarity among member states as a core purpose of the OIC. Article II of the OIC Charter pledges members 'to back the struggle of all Muslim people with a view to preserving their dignity, independence and national rights'. To this end the OIC has mobilised the faithful across the world in response to sufferings of fellow Muslims in Palestine, Bosnia and elsewhere. Issues regarding Palestine have been particularly sensitive for the OIC, and the organisation has repeatedly issued declarations to support the struggle of the people of Palestine to regain their rights and liberate their land.

### Accountability: secular and religious

A standard definition of accountability holds that 'A is accountable to B when A is obliged to inform B about A's (past or future) actions and decisions, to justify them, and to suffer punishment in the case of eventual misconduct' (Schedler 1999: 13). In secular conceptions of accountability – as found in other chapters of this book – 'A' and 'B' are always human actors in the physical world. Spiritual considerations and metaphysical forces do not come into play.

Religious life-worlds are different, and accountability processes correspondingly play out differently in religious contexts. As indicated by Gibbon (2008), religious cognition gives believers particular mental tools in approaching social and political issues. As standpoint theory notes, persons interact with others and with the world in accordance with their subjective vantage point. It is therefore essential – when seeking to understand perceptions of society – to take account of a person's or community's internal values and field of experience (Orbe 1998).

A religious approach to civic culture is important in understanding Islamic contexts and the OIC as an umbrella organisation of the Muslim world. OIC members are linked not by geographical proximity or economic mutuality, but by their common faith of Islam. Therefore, we need to examine more closely what accountability means in Islam.

*Accountability in Islam*

Accountability in Islamic political culture is first and foremost towards Allah, who is considered as the Lord of past and present life and the day after. In this conception every Muslim politician and public administrator – including those in the OIC – should answer to Allah for what he or she has done in office.

Primary devotion to Allah does not mean that Muslim governors are not accountable to people. On the contrary, accountability in Islam also exists in respect of society, including individuals, groups, corporations and nations. Accountability for a Muslim consists of two layers: the first to Allah and the second to the people. These two layers by no means have to conflict with one another; in fact, they are very often complementary, each layer strengthening the other. For example, selfless and just action in relation to people (be they individuals, groups, nations or transnational networks) can please the Lord.

That said, Islamic notions of an overriding accountability to Allah can sometimes clash with Western-secular notions of an overriding priority to uphold civil rights. For instance, liberal laws regarding homosexual practices or the consumption of alcohol cause difficulties for the devout Muslim, as they are seen to violate concepts of the good society and thus offend the Lord. Likewise, pressure from some secularists that Muslim women living in Europe should discard the hijab pushes those women into a position where they feel that they violate their primary accountability to Allah. For a Muslim the religious values come first.

Of course these points of difference, while significant, should not be emphasised to the point that they distract from similarities with secular practice. For example, while a Muslim civil society organisation may comprise persons who embrace Islamic values, the degree to which they view their association as a vehicle to spread religious social norms varies. Like many followers of other faiths, a lot of Muslims hold their religious values as private individuals and do not approach, say, disaster relief as a moment to expound an explicitly religious message. In this respect the operations of Muslim and secular civil societies are not polar opposites.

However, in principle, for a Muslim, accountability in social and public affairs is above all to Allah, before accountability to a person, a group or even a nation. A Muslim sees himself or herself to be primarily accountable to Allah because of His will and His expectations. A Muslim acts and reacts towards others, because he or she is responsible to Allah for doing or not doing something. For a Muslim, Allah is the 'ubiquitous observer'. A Muslim sees himself or herself as being first accountable to Allah for every single thing that he or she does in this world. Accountability to Allah works as a benchmark for the purification of action.

Hence there is a key distinction between secular and Islamic approaches to accountability in terms of the cause and motivation of the action. When one acts for the sake of Allah, then the social practice has a certain purity. The action is taken without expecting a reciprocating reaction. A Muslim is supposed to feel accountable, because Allah wants her or him to be accountable. In this respect a Muslim is supposed to have extra motivation to fulfil a social or economic task: thus not only because of civil responsibility, but also and in the first place because of his or her attachment to Allah's orders. There is no inherent contradiction between religious accountability and secular accountability, except that the motivation for accountability is arguably stronger in a religious context than in a secular counterpart.

Thus, in contrast to the other global governance agencies considered in this book, accountability in the context of the OIC is in very significant part about the fulfilment of religious laws and religious values in the practice of the organisation. In addition, the OIC sees as one of its principal objectives the promotion of Islamic values in society at large. In this vein ISESCO, as one of the most important specialised organisations of the OIC, is explicitly tasked with the protection and promotion of Islamic values. To this end ISESCO organises forums, discussion groups and committees of experts to investigate the current situation of Islam in the member countries.

This spirit of religious accountability also forms a backdrop to assessments of accountability in the OIC's work in other social, political and economic affairs. For example, the OIC might be called to account for actions (or inactions) on its declared goal to further the elimination of racism, discrimination and colonialism. Accountability could also be assessed in relation to the Charter objectives 'to consolidate cooperation among Member States in the economic, social, cultural, scientific and other vital fields' and 'to support international peace and security founded on justice'. The OIC (and the IDB more particularly) could in addition be called to answer for their performance (including through a host of development projects) in relation to the declared aim of poverty reduction in member countries.

## Civil society associations and accountability in the OIC

If, as described earlier, civil society is understood in an Islamic sense as a social context pervaded with attachments to Allah, based in Islamic law, and united in Muslim brotherhood, then civil society associations can be understood as those groups outside the state who promote such a society. From an Islamic perspective, civil society organisations (CSOs) give concrete manifestation to the Ummah through non-official channels. Engagement with CSOs is therefore another way that the OIC can relate to the Ummah, alongside its relations with governments.

As in Western liberal civil society, Islamic CSOs come in many forms. In the business arena, for example, the Islamic Chamber of Commerce and Industry (ICCI) has operated since 1977 as a union of national chambers of commerce from OIC member countries. Meanwhile, the Accounting and Auditing Organisation for Islamic Financial Institutions (AAOIFI), established in 1991 with offices in Bahrain, is a non-profit body that develops Shari'a standards for the global Islamic financial industry.

In the field of NGOs the Islamic Human Rights Commission (IHRC), formed in 1997 with headquarters in London, campaigns for justice for all peoples regardless of their racial, confessional or political background. Inspiration for the IHRC derives from Qur'anic injunctions that command believers to rise up in defence of the oppressed. Meanwhile Islamic Relief Worldwide, created in 1984 with head offices in Birmingham, UK, works with poor people across the globe. The Union of NGOs of the Islamic World (UNIW), launched in 2005 with a secretariat in Istanbul, now encompasses some 175 member associations across Africa, Asia and Europe.

In other areas of civil society the previously mentioned International Islamic Fiqh Academy is an example of a think tank based on Islamic principles. Finally, much as Western civil society includes some 'uncivil' elements such as ultranationalist, racist and Islamophobic groups who are rejected by the mainstream, so some self-styled 'Islamic' civil society groups have adopted exclusionary and violent practices that are rejected by the vast majority of Muslims.

The OIC has been quite slow to build relations with CSOs. Non-governmental organisations are not mentioned in the OIC Charter. The agency has developed little institutional apparatus specifically for relations with CSOs: it has no civil society bureau, no guidelines for interaction with CSOs and few organised exchanges with NGOs. To this day – and in contrast with most other global governance institutions covered in this book – the OIC website has no designated pages for CSOs.

That said, the OIC has maintained relations with the IIFA and Islamic universities in Bangladesh, Niger and Uganda as subsidiary organs, as well as the Islamic World Academy of Sciences as an affiliated institution. The OIC affiliated institutions have also included several business associations, such as the ICCI, the Organisation of the Islamic Shipowners

Association (OISA) and the Federation of Consultants from Islamic Countries (FCIC). The ISESCO Charter of 1982 mandates that specialised institution of the OIC to 'encourage non-governmental organizations and local community institutions to work in the fields of education, science, culture and communication' (ISESCO 1982: Art. 15). Since 2003 the OIC has been involved in the development of the Islamic Conference Youth Forum for Dialogue and Cooperation (ICYFDC 2010).

However, the OIC has sometimes had a more testy relationship with NGOs who explicitly challenge its member governments. Expressing such tensions, the Twenty-Eighth Session of the OIC Conference of Foreign Ministers, meeting at Bamako in June 2001, released a declaration on 'slanderous campaigns waged by certain non-governmental organizations targeting a number of OIC member States and the Islamic Shar'ia under the slogan of human rights protection'. Similar points prompted a confrontation with the International Humanist and Ethical Union in 2005 (IHEU 2010). Even the Islamic Human Rights Commission has not succeeded in obtaining recognition from the OIC, although it holds Special Consultative Status with the UN.

Yet some other signs have recently pointed to a prospective growth of links between the OIC and NGOs. The positive language about NGOs in the Ten-Year Programme of Action was noted earlier. In May 2007 the Conference of OIC Foreign Ministers agreed to explore the possibilities of according OIC observer status to NGOs from member countries (OIC 2007). In December 2007 the OIC held a conference with the UNIW to promote the role of NGOs in decreasing the dangers of Islamophobia. In March 2008 the OIC had a three-day meeting in Dakar with representatives from sixty NGOs ahead of its Eleventh Summit. The OIC now has a designated Under Secretary-General responsible for Humanitarian Assistance and Civil Society Relations, and the Secretary-General has also begun to hold meetings with NGOs.

Another noteworthy development in NGO circles is the programme 'Building Bridges: Engaging Civil Society from Muslim Countries and Communities with the Multilateral Sphere', co-ordinated through the Montreal International Forum since 2005 (FIM 2010). This initiative has convened 8 meetings involving over 120 NGOs from 28 OIC countries. It has particularly sought to promote the official accreditation of NGOs to the OIC, although so far the OIC still lacks an official framework of engagement with civil society.

Given the limited links just described, it is not yet possible to identify significant accountability effects of CSOs in respect of the OIC. Arguably the IIFA has brought some enhanced religious accountability to the OIC and its member states (Taskheeri 2007). However, CSOs have accomplished little in the way of enlarging the accountability of the OIC to the populations of the member countries in terms of increased transparency, consultation, evaluation and correction of the kind discussed across the other studies in this book.

## Conclusion: the 'First OIC' and the 'Second OIC'

This chapter has explored the question of civil society and accountable global governance outside a Western context and outside a secularist frame. The analysis has shown that concepts of 'global governance', 'accountability' and 'civil society' – although Western and secular in their origins – can resonate in these different circumstances. However, to acquire that relevance it is necessary to start from the perspective of the other – in this case an Islamic worldview – rather than to impose the notions in an alien form.

With the resultant adaptations, the ideas acquire related but also distinctive meanings. For example, the OIC is an instance of global governance – in the broad sense of a regulatory apparatus whose reach extends across multiple continents; however, the inspiration, the activities and the legitimacy of the institution are largely grounded in religious faith. Likewise, accountability (for what and to whom?) has a different meaning when theorised and practised in an Islamic-religious sense. In addition, civil society in the case of the OIC is substantially rooted in the Ummah and the Okhovvat.

Hence the general discourse of civil society and accountable global governance can – subject to suitable adjustments – work within the context of Islam. The faith is by no means – as some outside observers have assumed – in tension with civil society. On the contrary, Muslims within civil society who express their activities as reflections of their faith often specifically argue that their values and motivation reflect religious dictates Divinely revealed 1,400 years ago.

That said, in concrete terms civil society activities have not yet brought major accountability advances to the OIC. This organisation has so far been slow and rather reluctant to shift from its original intergovernmentalist construction to a multi-actor arrangement in which CSOs also figure significantly. In this respect the OIC experience has been closer to that of the World Trade Organization (WTO) than that of the Commonwealth, the World Bank and the UN. Yet the OIC, too, has moved with the times, as evidenced in the Ten-Year Programme of Action. A transition may indeed be in course from a 'First OIC' born of the modern period to a 'Second OIC' of currently emergent postmodern times. That shift includes, among other things, an increased role in the organisation for

CSOs. Possibly, the transformation might also involve the creation of an OIC Parliament, an OIC Single Currency and an OIC Citizenship. The OIC needs serious changes to increase transparency and participation for improved accountability.

To this end the OIC would do well to consider enhancing its 'virtual environment' and nurturing the development of a 'virtual Ummah'. As Okot-Uma (2000) has argued, new digital technologies can greatly advance good governance with improved public access to information, more public awareness of decisions and policies, enhanced public communication to share experiences, and greater public participation in political processes. These positive accountability results could be realised in relation to the OIC, too.

Significant advances of this kind could be booked with a reconstruction of the OIC website. The capabilities of the OIC in cyberspace are the subject for another study, but even brief reference to the matter here can suggest the possibilities for improved accountability. The current OIC website has functioned relatively well in familiarising visitors with the organisation and its activities, although information is not always adequately updated. However, the site serves more as an online brochure than as an interactive portal. Users are not invited to feed back, to ask questions, and to utter their ideas and comments. Moreover, the website does not equip the OIC to respond quickly and continuously. In these areas the OIC lags well behind most of the other global governance institutions considered in this book.

One hopes, therefore, that the OIC will exploit these possibilities of using cyberspace in order further to unify Muslims throughout the world (Ameli 2009). In addition, other important advances in relations with CSOs can be achieved by developing more formal arrangements through the General Secretariat for these interactions. The Dakar experience of 2008 could be expanded so that each future OIC Summit of Kings and Heads of State and Government is accompanied by a CSO gathering. In these ways and more, relations between Islamic civil society and Islamic global governance could deepen the reality of the Ummah in the postmodern era.

# 8    Civil society and patterns of accountability in the OECD

*Morten Ougaard*

## Introduction

In the late 1990s the Organisation for Economic Co-operation and Development (OECD) became widely known among civil society associations and the general public for its role in the failed negotiations for a Multilateral Agreement on Investment (MAI). The MAI project was heavily criticised, and some depicted the OECD as a remote and secretive body that was concocting ultra-liberal global policies on behalf of transnational capital in isolation from the public interest.

There are several somewhat ironic aspects to this story. One is that the OECD has almost since its inception regularly included some civil society organisations in its work. Another is that the MAI process was an atypical experience, with little resemblance to normal OECD activities. Nevertheless, the affair triggered a process of internal reflection and review of practices, which led to greater civil society involvement in major aspects of the organisation's work (OECD 2006a). Six years later an institution that had been so heavily criticised emerged as one of the top accountability performers among intergovernmental organisations in the 2006 *Global Accountability Report* compiled by the One World Trust (Blagescu and Lloyd 2006: 52).

What role has civil society played in accountability at the OECD? In what ways and to what extent have civil society organisations (CSOs) promoted transparency, consultation, evaluation and redress vis-à-vis affected publics of this Paris-based global governance agency? These questions are more complex for the OECD relative to other institutions examined in the book, inasmuch as this global body performs a particularly wide range of different governance activities and does so with

I want to thank staff in the OECD, BIAC and TUAC interviewed for this study. Particular thanks go to Meggan Dissly of the OECD Public Affairs Division for arranging the interviews and providing much valuable information. Also, special thanks go to Ambassador Steffen Smidt for greatly facilitating my visit to OECD offices.

a variable organisational geometry. Therefore accountability dynamics play out in different ways in different policy areas.

This chapter brings out the above variability by examining civil society engagement of the OECD in five different policy fields: the MAI; the Guidelines for Multinational Enterprises (MNEs); the Model Tax Convention; the Anti-Bribery Convention; and environmental regulation. Experiences in these areas reveal five main patterns of OECD-CSO interaction for accountability:

- a mobilisation-protest-change pattern, found in the MAI case;
- an increased-access-and-voice pattern, found in all instances except the Model Tax Convention;
- a high-institutionalisation pattern, found especially in the OECD's relations with business associations over the Model Tax Convention;
- a broadly accessible complaints mechanism pattern, as found in respect of the Guidelines for Multinational Enterprise;
- a partners-in-implementation pattern, as found in the anti-bribery and environmental areas.

Before detailing these findings, however, a brief account of the OECD and its accountability challenges will help to set the general context.

## The OECD as a global governance agency

The OECD was founded in 1961 as a successor body to the Organisation for European Economic Co-operation (OEEC). (For more on the general history and operations of the OECD, see Ougaard 2004, 2006; Salzman and Terracino 2006; Mahon and McBride 2008.) The OEEC had been created in 1947 to administer US and Canadian aid to post-war Europe under the Marshall Plan. The OECD replaced the OEEC fourteen years later as an agency to promote general policy co-operation among member governments, drawn mainly from the global north.

Over the years the OECD membership has expanded from the starting twenty states to the current (2010) thirty-four. Outside Europe and North America the OECD also counts Australia, Chile, Israel, Japan, New Zealand, South Korea and Turkey as members. Membership negotiations with Russia are ongoing. A further five states (Brazil, China, India, Indonesia and South Africa) have so-called 'enhanced engagement' status with the OECD, with possible future membership in prospect. In addition, the OECD has since 1990 developed relationships with around sixty other non-member governments, including those of many least developed countries.

The work of the OECD covers almost all policy areas that concern its member governments. The organisation addresses a very wide range of issues including agriculture, development co-operation, education, employment, energy, environment, finance, fiscal affairs, industry, investment, monetary policy, science and technology, social policy, trade and transport. The few notable policy fields that have fallen outside the OECD purview include immigration policy and military affairs.

In terms of the forms of global governance discussed in Chapter 1, the OECD is both an intergovernmental organisation and an important meeting point for transgovernmental networks. As an intergovernmental body the OECD is overseen by a Council composed of representatives of each member state. The institution also has a permanent Secretariat in Paris with a staff of 2,500 international civil servants. The Secretariat is organised into a number of 'directorates', 'centres' and other bodies, each focusing on a policy area or specific task. Every directorate serves one or more committees and working groups, and these bodies in turn participate in discussions of the directorates' work. The OECD Secretariat is widely known for its statistical and analytical output, as well as a publication programme that issues some 250 titles per year.

In its extensive committee work the OECD has an important transgovernmental character. Each year some 40,000 senior officials from national administrations come to Paris to participate in the work of around 250 committees, working groups and expert bodies convened by the OECD. To this extent the OECD involves networks of national civil servants as much as – if not more than – government ministers and international bureaucrats.

An important and characteristic aspect of these transgovernmental relations is the process of mutual surveillance and peer review. In this context member governments assess one another's policies. Comparative analyses are made to identify best practices, which leads to the formulation of guidelines and recommendations to national governments. The resultant mutual learning sometimes prompts a convergence of views and policy orientations (Sullivan 1997; Pagani 2002). Arguably the OECD has its most far-reaching impacts in this way, even if these influences are often subtle and largely invisible to the general public.

Occasionally the OECD adopts formal agreements such as the MAI. However, much more commonly the organisation issues recommendations and standards, for instance in the environmental area. The OECD also undertakes broad strategic work, as when during the 1970s it helped develop the new policy orientation of tight monetary and fiscal policies combined with structural reform. More recently the OECD has figured importantly in the formulation of strategies towards sustainable development (Ougaard 2004; OECD 2001a, 2001b).

The OECD has since its creation involved some CSOs in its work (Woodward 2008). Key channels in this regard are the Business and Industry Advisory Committee (BIAC) and the Trade Union Advisory Committee (TUAC). These two bodies are the officially recognised representatives of business and labour through which a large number of employer and worker organisations, national and international, interact with OECD committees and the Secretariat. Other CSOs, for instance associations of agricultural producers and consumer organisations, also have a long history of involvement in OECD work.

It is important in the case of the OECD to include business associations (i.e. non-profit organisations that represent business interests) within the scope of civil society. Not everyone would accept this approach, of course, preferring to depict civil society as an entirely non-commercial sphere. However, inclusion of business forums in civil society is useful in relation to the OECD, because it allows a nuanced treatment of accountability issues in relation to different constituencies that may have varying and conflicting interests.

In sum, then, in any policy area the OECD potentially involves a host of actors: ministers and ambassadors in its Council; staff from its own Secretariat; officials and experts from member national governments (and increasingly non-member governments, too); and civil society organisations. These various actors can interact with each other in a multitude of possible permutations.

### OECD accountability

The organisational features just described pose some complications when discussing the OECD's accountability. Who amongst the various actors involved in this intergovernmental organisation and related transgovernmental networks would be called to account in regard to one or the other issue or outcome? Both the organisation in Paris and the national governments and bureaucracies who participate in OECD work could be included.

Nor is it straightforward to identify the constituents of the OECD: that is, the quarters to which this global governance agency should be accountable. Formally speaking, the constituents of the OECD are its thirty-four member states. However, as noted earlier, the OECD also has relations with – and impacts on – dozens of other governments who are not members. Indeed, with its contributions to policy standards the OECD can significantly impact the world economy as a whole. Arguably, then, the OECD owes accountability to a much wider range of constituents than its member states alone.

Beyond this problem is the further question of whether nation-states are (by themselves) adequate channels to secure accountability for their citizens who are affected by OECD activities. On the one hand, it could be suggested that, since the OECD member states have democratic regimes, their governments can – through elected parliaments and leaders – secure democratic accountability for their citizens. On the other hand, the member governments have no democratic grounds to speak for people that the OECD affects in non-member countries. Moreover, many governments of non-member countries of the OECD have weak democratic credentials. In addition, the many transgovernmental networks that convene through the OECD often operate in the absence of close parliamentary and cabinet scrutiny. Nor is it always clear that national parliamentary processes deliver adequate democratic accountability for all constituents within a country (e.g. ethnic and religious minorities, remote regions, or women).

On various grounds, then, it could be argued that additional pressures beyond the member governments are required to obtain sufficient democratic accountability from the OECD; significant supplementary forces of this kind could be provided from civil society. Hence it makes sense to consider, as the next sections of this chapter do, the contributions to OECD accountability from CSOs.

Owing to the sheer breadth and variety of OECD activities it is not very meaningful to make a blanket assessment of the organisation's accountability performance, such as provided by the One World Trust study cited earlier. What is called for is a careful examination of individual policy areas. Given the limits of this chapter, it is only possible to include a small selection of these issues.

The five scenarios chosen for closer consideration here all concern governance of business activities. The cases of the MAI, the Guidelines for Multinational Enterprises, the Model Taxation Convention, the Anti-Bribery Convention and environmental regulation are arguably not representative of the whole of the OECD's work. On the contrary, they probably represent areas where the institution has been most open to civil society organisations. Thus, for instance, a study of OECD work on New Public Management might lead to rather different and less sanguine conclusions. Moreover, owing to financial and time constraints the research for this chapter has focused data collection on the OECD Secretariat, BIAC and TUAC. Still, the cases illustrate different ways that the accountability equation can play out in a global governance institution.

Each of the following sections first provides some institutional detail regarding governance arrangements in the policy area at hand. The ensuing discussion identifies the key constituencies and assesses the adequacy of accountability provision in that case, including in particular the role of civil society.

## The MAI and its aftermath

Essentially the MAI affair (covered especially in Henderson 1999; Devereaux *et al.* 2006) was an attempt to negotiate a highly ambitious multilateral agreement on the liberalisation of transborder investment flows. The project had to be ambitious, because to be worthwhile it should lead to a significant improvement in the already liberal investment climate among OECD countries. It also should have the potential to expand its scope to non-OECD countries. One reason the OECD was chosen as the venue for this endeavour was that it was difficult to pursue investment liberalisation through the WTO. In contrast, the OECD seemed to offer a much higher degree of consensus on liberalisation matters among its members.

The latter assumption turned out to be mistaken. Instead, it transpired that many member states were loathe to remove the remaining obstacles to full investment liberalisation. The prospective agreement was therefore likely to be filled with national exceptions and escape clauses. In that event little improvement would be offered from a business perspective. Thus the perceived benefits of completing the MAI process declined considerably as negotiations continued, while the political costs grew dramatically.

Formal negotiations on the MAI began through the OECD in September 1995. The first draft agreement text was produced in January 1997. In a marked step to enhance public transparency an NGO, the Council of Canadians, obtained a version of the text a month later and published it on the Internet (Devereaux *et al.* 2006: 161). The release of the document provoked a rapidly snowballing global anti-MAI movement. In the words of Devereaux and co-authors (2006: 140):

The proposed MAI sparked fury around the world, becoming in the words of a European MAI negotiator, 'the focal point for fears about globalisation.' Indeed, according to some observers, the MAI protests marked the beginning of the international anti-globalisation movement ... The MAI negotiations were targeted by hundreds of grassroots environmental, consumer, and development organisations and condemned by critics ranging from labour union leaders to movie actresses, all voicing concern about the harmful impacts of global economic integration ... More than 600 organisations in nearly 70 countries expressed disapproval of the talks.

With the prospects of a strong liberalisation agreement receding, and with the political costs of continuing negotiations rising, the strategic calculations of key actors changed. Main sections of the business community lost interest in the MAI, as did the US government. The French government in effect withdrew from the process in October 1999, leading to the final demise of the MAI in December.

The central question in an analytical post-mortem of the MAI is the cause of death: was the global mobilisation of non-governmental organisations (NGOs) and civil society protests the decisive dragon-slayer; or was the chief culprit the inherent difficulties, disagreements and conflicts of interests among participating governments? Not surprisingly, the first explanation is popular in the NGO world, while both Henderson and Devereaux *et al.* favour the second view. They do not deny the contribution of civil society protests to the result, but they see it more as yet another push to an already badly tilting wagon – and not the most decisive push.

One might attempt to settle this dispute with counterfactual reasoning. On this basis it seems more probable than not that the MAI process would also have broken down in the absence of the global anti-MAI movement. The incompatibility between what was sought and what was possible in the light of deeply entrenched pockets of investment protectionism, even in otherwise highly liberal political economies, was simply too overwhelming. In fact from the outset demand for the MAI was not very strong even in the business community (Devereaux *et al.* 2006: 151–3). Moreover, there was some confusion among supporters of the MAI about the basic rationale for the project (Henderson 1999: 33–47). In contrast, had major sections of international business and major states accorded the MAI strategic importance – comparable for instance to that given to the Agreement on Trade-Related Intellectual Property Rights (TRIPS), which was successfully concluded in the World Trade Organization talks in 1994 – it is not inconceivable that the MAI could have gone through in spite of NGO protests.

Hence the MAI affair is not, as some histories would have it, actually a good case of global governance institutions being brought to account by CSOs. It was a unique event at a specific moment of history, where neoliberalism was riding high and policymakers got overambitious and careless, making the process an unusually easy target for protesters.

However, in a larger perspective the MAI affair clearly played a major role in putting accountability issues much higher on the agenda of global politics. In this sense, CSO involvement in the MAI affair helped to make this particular conjuncture into a turning point in the history of global governance, the magnitude of which it is too early to gauge. So here is another irony: the MAI agreement probably would have failed even in the absence of civil society opposition; yet the affair greatly stimulated the growth of a vigorous transnational NGO community that in multiple ways monitors and seeks to influence global governance arrangements.

In the OECD itself, the MAI story clearly had consequences for relations with CSOs. The MAI process and also civil society disruption of the 1999 Seattle WTO Ministerial Conference inspired the OECD to rethink the situation. From this reassessment the institution concluded among other things that 'openness to civil society is important in the light of the contributions civil society organisations (CSOs) can make to the OECD's work; openness can help to improve understanding by CSOs and the public of the opportunities and challenges of global economic and social change' (OECD 2006a: 3; see also OECD 2005). In this spirit the OECD introduced online public consultations with civil society (OECD 2006b). The Public Affairs Division of the Secretariat was tasked with serving as an internal clearing house for information on civil society (OECD 2006a: 3).

In another specific initiative, in 2000 the organisation launched the OECD Forum as one venue for interaction with CSOs. This annual event is in some ways akin to the better known World Economic Forum at Davos. The OECD Forum is normally held in conjunction with the annual OECD ministerial summit. The Forum 'brings together business and labour leaders, civil society personalities, government ministers and leaders of international organisations to discuss the hottest issues on the international agenda' (OECD 2010). OECD Forums have drawn more than a thousand participants.

In November 2006 the OECD finalised an internal report on contacts with CSOs (OECD 2006a). In this context the Public Affairs Division produced an inventory of contacts between the OECD and civil society organisations (OECD 2006c). This document lists more than a hundred different topics on which the OECD has consulted CSOs at least once and in many cases on a regular basis. It names more than two hundred different NGOs that have been involved. Several times it refers more broadly to, for instance, a 'variety of civil society experts and organisations from OECD and non-OECD countries', or 'umbrella NGO organisations in all DAC member countries'. The inventory thus shows that the OECD now has relations with a broad range of CSOs representing business, labour, consumers, and environmental and development concerns. The report itself concluded that consultations with CSOs have become a regular, systematic and indeed essential part of the work of most OECD committees (OECD 2006a).

## Guidelines for Multinational Enterprises

The OECD Guidelines for Multinational Enterprises were first formulated in 1976 and most recently revised in 1998–2000. They set out a voluntary code of conduct that business is urged to follow and governments are committed to support (OECD 2000, 2001a). The Guidelines state that companies should 'contribute to economic, social and environmental progress with a view to achieving sustainable development'. The document identifies a range of related concerns, including human rights, capacity building and good corporate governance. An associated instrument, the Decision of the Council on National Contact Points (June 2000) is concerned with implementation of the Guidelines (OECD 2001a).

Since the MNE Guidelines are directed towards private companies, business can be seen as an important constituent of this instrument and the OECD as the prime addressee for accountability claims. However, the Guidelines are meant to serve a range of social and environmental purposes that do not always coincide with the main goals of business. Hence the wider public, affected by business behaviour, could be considered the prime constituents in respect of the Guidelines. From this perspective, the addressees for accountability claims would be business and government in their joint responsibility to meet, support and promote the Guidelines.

The 2000 revision of the MNE Guidelines made several changes to 'reinforce the core elements – economic, social and environmental – of the sustainable development agenda' (OECD 2000: 2; also OECD 1999). Among the additions were recommendations on the elimination of child labour and forced labour, encouragements to raise environmental standards, a recommendation on human rights, chapters on consumer protection and combating corruption, and words to 'recognize and encourage progress in enhancing firms' social and environmental accountability' (OECD 2000: 2). Furthermore, with the adoption of a Procedural Guidance the revision of 2000 strengthened the implementation mechanism by 'providing more guidance to the National Contact Points in fulfilling their role' (OECD 2001a: 49).

The revision also recognised the 'crucial' role of business, labour and NGOs in implementing the Guidelines (OECD 2000: 3). Along this line there was, indeed, civil society involvement in the revision of the Guidelines. According to an OECD paper from 1999, 'discussions over the past year have been enhanced by the contributions of the social partners (BIAC, TUAC) and those of NGOs and other interested partners' (OECD 1999: 3). According to another OECD document, the

Guidelines were 'developed in constructive dialogue with the business community, labour representatives and non-governmental organisations' (OECD 2000: 2–3).

These engagements marked the beginning of a more permanent involvement of a broader range of CSOs in OECD work on investment matters. This development became particularly evident with the creation in 2003 of an umbrella organisation, OECD Watch, which was itself an offspring of the anti-MAI mobilisations. OECD Watch groups together NGOs from around the world that share a 'vision about the need for corporate accountability and sustainable investment' (OECD Watch 2007). This CSO monitors the work of the OECD Investment Committee, assesses the effectiveness of the MNE Guidelines, disseminates information to civil society groups, and advises NGOs about filing complaints against companies (OECD Watch 2007). The OECD Committee on International Investment and Multinational Enterprises (CIME, a forerunner of the present Investment Committee) has named OECD Watch 'a partner in implementing the guidelines' and has taken input from the organisation in various matters (OECD Watch 2007). Some talk has even circulated within the OECD about giving OECD Watch a more formal standing, resembling that held by BIAC and TUAC (Interview, 2007a). Thus an enhanced civil society access and voice is clearly evident in the investment area.

When OECD Watch 'advises NGOs on filing complaints against companies', it uses an accountability mechanism that is specific to the MNE Guidelines, namely the system of National Contact Points (NCPs) that each adhering country maintains (OECD 2001a: 44). The new Procedural Guidance dating from 2000 stipulates, among other things, that NCPs must 'respond to enquiries about the Guidelines from: (a) other National Contact Points; (b) the business community, employee organisations, other non-governmental organisations and the public; and (c) governments of non-adhering countries' (OECD 2001a: 46). Furthermore, 'specific instances' can be brought to an NCP by business, employees, NGOs and the public. In short, the various stakeholders can complain to the relevant NCP that an individual company has failed to live up to the Guidelines.

Upon receiving such a complaint the NCP decides whether the issue is relevant to the Guidelines and merits further consideration. If this is found to be the case, the NCP will 'discuss it further with the parties involved and offer "good offices" in an effort to contribute informally to the resolution of issues'. The NCP will, if the parties concerned agree, 'offer or facilitate access to, consensual and non-adversarial procedures, such as conciliation or mediation'. If the parties fail to reach agreement, the NCP will make recommendations on the implementation of the Guidelines. In the words of the OECD commentary on the procedures, this 'makes it clear that an NCP will issue a statement even when it feels that a specific recommendation is not called for' (OECD 2001a: 52). NCPs report to the OECD Investment Committee on the various individual cases. Significantly, however, 'the non-binding nature of the Guidelines precludes the Committee from acting as a judicial or quasi-judicial body', and the committee 'shall not reach conclusions on the conduct of individual enterprises' (OECD 2001a: 53).

The procedure therefore institutionalises a right for all concerned parties to obtain an authoritative statement from a national NCP as to whether a company violates the OECD Guidelines for Multinational Enterprises. It is a concrete accountability measure, a formalised complaint mechanism. Any constituency representative can table an enquiry that the NCP is formally obliged to consider. However, the possibilities of actual redress are limited inasmuch as the mechanism includes no further sanctions. Moreover, the OECD offers CSOs and other stakeholders no channels for complaint and redress regarding the operation of the MNE Guidelines regime itself.

Still, this corporate accountability system is being used and tested. The *2006 Annual Report on the Guidelines for Multinational Enterprises*, while warning of possible double counting as well as underreporting, lists 101 specific instances that had been brought in 5 years since the 2000 revision of the Guidelines (OECD 2006e: 49). These cases involved 27 NCPs and MNE activity on all continents. The complaints covered many principles of the Guidelines, but in particular labour and environmental issues.

TUAC has also analysed its experiences with the NCPs, up to September 2006. Its assessment covers more than 60 cases, again with a proviso against underreporting. The analysis concludes that (TUAC 2006: 33):

the results so far point to both some positive development as well as lack of development in some cases. On the one hand, trade unions are increasingly becoming aware of the Guidelines as a tool to protect workers' rights, cases are raised and significant changes relating to NCPs have been achieved. On the other hand, progress is slow and there are still problems with several NCPs.

From this analysis, as well as several cases discussed in a later document (TUAC 2007), it is clear that the system is far from uniformly effective. Several NCPs have responded slowly and reluctantly to complaints. Yet the regime has also booked successes, and it is reasonable to conclude that the strengthened NCP system has created a potentially strong accountability mechanism, albeit that it is a corrective regime for MNEs rather than for the OECD itself.

## The Model Tax Convention

With the rise of global economic activities, questions of double taxation and tax evasion in relation to territorial jurisdictions have become more pressing. The standard remedy for these problems is a bilateral tax treaty, and a growing number of states need to develop such arrangements with each other. This makes standardisation desirable, and to this end the OECD has developed a Model Tax Convention. As the name says, this instrument serves as a model for a large number of bilateral tax treaties, not only among OECD members, but also between them and non-member countries. The convention has also influenced treaties between non-members.

The Model Tax Convention undergoes continual development. Business practices change, cross-border transactions within companies evolve and become more complex, and new business models emerge, thereby creating new taxation challenges and opportunities for companies and tax authorities alike. Such developments call for regular additions and revisions to the Model Convention, a task that is assigned to the OECD Centre for Tax Policy and Administration (CTP).

In a narrow conception, the CTP is the addressee for accountability claims, and transnational business is the central constituency. Viewed in this way, the Model Tax Convention operates with a high degree of accountability, facilitated by business CSOs such as BIAC and the International Chamber of Commerce (ICC). BIAC or its member organisations often bring issues to the CTP when they find the Model Convention insufficient. Business groups shape the Convention, can initiate revisions to it, and sometimes partly fund analytical work to develop the regime. Indeed, the co-operation is so close that BIAC and the ICC can be described as CTP 'customers' (Interview, 2007b). Thus accountability to a specific constituency is a defining feature of this particular body within the OECD.

Yet this picture needs modification if the scope of the business world is broadened beyond large MNEs. After all, small and medium enterprises (SMEs) are increasingly also involved in transborder activities and are affected, for instance, by questions of taxation of e-commerce. So far the CTP has found it difficult to reach this constituency, partly because existing business CSOs with relations to the OECD do not represent SMEs well (Interview, 2007b).

Indeed, a still broader view of the constituency for OECD work on tax issues would also encompass national tax administrations, which collect the revenue, and citizens at large, who are concerned with the public services that taxation funds. The OECD has attempted to address such wider constituents with its work since 1996 on 'harmful tax practices' such as offshore tax havens that thrive on the facilitation of tax evasion. CSOs that have stressed these matters include the Tax Justice Network and Oxfam.

However, the pattern of civil society access to the OECD has not favoured these wider concerns on taxation. Whereas BIAC and the ICC have had intensive contacts with the CTP, the Tax Justice Network and Oxfam have had no direct relationship (Interview, 2007b). While BIAC has had twice-yearly consultations with the OECD on these matters, TUAC has had a hearing only once every two years. TUAC has since 2007 shown greater concern about the potential negative impacts of economic globalisation on effective taxation of transnational corporations, with consequent risks for public services. Still, on the whole there has so far been little CSO pressure on the OECD to enhance its accountability to broader constituencies in matters of taxation treaties. In these circumstances civil society relations with the OECD have mainly consisted of 'customer service' to (big) business.

### The Anti-Bribery Convention

The OECD Convention on Combating Bribery of Foreign Public Officials in International Business Transactions – in short, the Anti-Bribery Convention – came into force in 1999 (OECD 2003). It is supported by several other instruments, including the 1998 Recommendation on Improving Ethical Conduct in the Public Service (OECD 2006d). The Convention is a binding instrument which requires OECD members and non-members who have joined it to 'implement a comprehensive set of legal, regulatory and policy measures to prevent, detect, prosecute and sanction bribery of foreign officials' (OECD 2006d). For implementation the primary mechanism is systematic two-phase monitoring and review of countries' performance. In Phase 1 it is ascertained whether the relevant legal texts in the country concerned meet the standards of the Convention. In Phase 2 the structures to implement and enforce the Convention are evaluated (OECD 2003: 11–12).

The Anti-Bribery Convention has two main addressees for accountability claims. On one hand, the OECD and its Secretariat can be called to account for the quality of the Convention and its supporting instruments as well as the effectiveness of the monitoring process. On the other hand, participating governments can be called to account regarding their implementation (or not) of the Convention.

CSOs were extensively involved in creating the Anti-Bribery Convention. BIAC, the ICC, TUAC and in particular Transparency International (TI) all played important roles in this regard. According to the OECD itself, CSOs 'helped generate the needed political will to criminalise the bribery of foreign public officials through efficient multilateral action' (OECD 2003: 10–11). CSOs also called attention to issues that in consequence were brought into the Convention and related instruments, for example the solicitation of bribes (thus considering both the demand and the supply side of bribery) and the protection of whistleblowers (OECD 2003; Interview, 2007c).

Civil society has also played a role in implementing the Anti-Bribery Convention. The monitoring process was designed to be maximally transparent, thereby giving CSOs good access to relevant information. In addition, channels were created for civil society representatives to express their views in the monitoring process. Indeed, it is explicit OECD policy to seek civil society participation in implementing the Convention (Interview, 2007c; OECD 2003). Thus CSOs are invited to express their views in writing to the responsible OECD body. CSO views on specific issues can be presented at consultation meetings between country representatives and the monitoring team. CSOs are also formally invited to participate in Phase 2 site visits (OECD 2003: 14). Hence on implementing the Anti-Bribery Convention the efforts of the OECD and CSOs can be described as mutually reinforcing.

CSOs have put these possibilities of engagement with the OECD to good use. In particular the national chapters of TI have in several cases played an important role in shaping national legislation, in contributing to evaluation and monitoring activities, and in calling attention to lacunae and weaknesses in national implementation efforts (OECD 2003: 14–15; Interview, 2007c). Since 2001 BIAC, TUAC, the ICC and TI have coordinated their participation in OECD country visits regarding the Anti-Bribery Convention. These CSOs have helped 'to identify civil society experts from the country being reviewed who will express their views and respond to questions from the examiners' (OECD 2003: 15). Through such mechanisms CSOs can complain to the OECD about a lack of government activity in any particular area, and in turn the OECD can – in the diplomatic language ostensibly used – 'recommend' to the government that it 'raises awareness' on the issue at hand (Interview, 2007c). This involvement of local CSOs from different walks of life has made considerable difference in OECD evaluations of national measures to combat bribery.

Thus CSO participation has had strong accountability effects in the OECD anti-bribery regime. The arrangements are highly transparent, entail considerable consultation of CSOs, involve ample CSO voice in monitoring and evaluation processes, and provide channels for CSO efforts to secure effective implementation. In all four main dimensions of accountability identified in this book, the OECD, on corruption issues, maintains close links to relevant CSOs and is open and responsive to their ideas and suggestions.

Particularly interesting in the anti-bribery regime is the strong partnership between the OECD and CSOs in keeping *national governments* accountable. In this case global governance and civil society team up to exact accountability from the nation-state. As seen in other chapters, similar dynamics also arise in United Nations collaboration with CSOs to promote human rights in national arenas. Likewise, CSOs have partnered with the Global Fund to Fight AIDS, Tuberculosis and Malaria in order to press national governments on questions of health policy.

Yet the successes of CSO participation in the OECD anti-bribery regime should be kept in perspective. The close partnership just described has been much facilitated by the nature of the issue and its very broad constituency. After all, once initial resistance to the Convention was overcome, anti-bribery became a cause that is difficult to oppose in principle. Business, labour and large segments of NGOs all agree that corruption should be fought. Accountability is much easier to achieve when the issue at hand is uncontroversial.

### Environmental policies

The OECD has since the 1970s played an important role in developing common responses among its members to environmental challenges. This work is multifaceted. Some of it relates to specialised technical issues such as good laboratory practices, waste prevention and recycling, and chemical safety and chemical accidents. Other OECD work in the environmental area covers regulatory issues such as harmonisation of regulatory oversight in biotechnology (OECD 2007a). Still further involvements address long-term guidelines such as the 2006 *Strategic Vision* to 'work towards ensuring global economic growth that is environmentally sustainable' (OECD 2006f).

These OECD activities employ the whole range of institutional formats and instruments described previously in relation to other policy areas: analytical work; agreements, decisions and recommendations; and mutual surveillance and peer review of country performance. Although implementation of the measures is the responsibility of member governments, the OECD network itself is also a relevant addressee for accountability claims, particularly in terms of the significant role that the institution plays in the global harmonisation of environmental and safety standards.

The civil society constituencies for OECD work on environmental issues are varied and have cross-cutting interests that are partly overlapping and partly conflicting. Business is a central constituency: as a source of many environmental problems; as a prime target for regulation; and as an important actor in future avoidance or remedy of environmental damage. Labour is another central constituency for environmental policies, being particularly exposed to health hazards in the workplace, as well as to the consequences of environmental regulation for employment and working conditions. In addition, a third large and diverse civil society constituency encompasses a highly visible and very active array of environmental NGOs. Arguably, a general human interest in environmental sustainability cuts across all social, economic and cultural divides (Ougaard 2004).

CSOs have long been closely involved in OECD work on the environment through the access that BIAC and TUAC have had to the Environmental Policy Committee (EPOC). More recently CSO involvement in this policy area has broadened significantly to include NGOs. Both the Committee and the OECD Secretariat broadly recognise that CSOs have a role to play, and the engagement of environmental and other CSOs has become a matter of operational principle.

In this vein, EPOC's *Strategic Vision* of early 2006 pointed to the importance of 'developing successful partnerships with others ... including business, trade unions, environmental NGOs' (OECD 2006f: 7). Another OECD document recognises 'the valuable contribution that civil society can make to the public policy-making process, and attaches great importance to the Organisation's own consultation and dialogue with civil society representatives' (OECD 2007b). On the nature of this involvement, the OECD reported that (OECD 2007b):

Stakeholder representatives participate in a range of activities under ... EPOC, including various conferences, workshops, expert meetings, etc. They participate actively in some of the working parties and expert groups under EPOC in their expert capacity. Representatives of stakeholder groups have participated actively in selected meetings of EPOC in the past, including a High Level Session held in April 2000 and a special stakeholder conference at the start of the Environment Ministerial Meeting in May 2001. The Joint Working Party on Trade and Environment (JWPTE) also holds regular dialogues with civil society representatives.

The involvement of a broader range of CSOs in OECD activities on the environment has been facilitated by the creation, in 2001, of an

NGO umbrella body, the European Environmental Bureau (EEB). This organisation, headquartered in Brussels, has 143 member civil society organisations from 31 countries. They include the national chapters of environmental heavyweights such as Friends of the Earth and Greenpeace (EEB 2007). The EEB co-ordinates NGO interaction with the OECD on environmental matters (Interview, 2007d), much as OECD Watch has done in respect of investment issues. Indeed, the relationship between the OECD and the EEB has developed to a point where EPOC is one of the OECD bodies most open to NGO engagement. Significantly, on environmental matters the OECD has in practice elevated the EEB to a status comparable with that held by BIAC and TUAC (OECD 2007b). It is also telling that the EEB has occasionally obtained high-level access, participating in parts of the 2004 meeting of EPOC at ministerial level and in a consultation at 'the margins' of the 2006 joint development and environment ministerial meeting (OECD 2006c: 42–3).

In short, although formal decision-making power in the environmental area remains with the governmental part of the OECD, the network has become quite open to CSOs. Business groups, trade unions and environmental NGOs have substantial access to information and venues for consultation. An OECD official well-placed in this policy area notes that CSOs generally do not introduce new material, but their contributions of expert knowledge are broadly acknowledged to be valuable (Interview, 2007d).

In addition, CSOs have participated notably in the OECD country review process on environmental affairs (OECD, 2006f). As part of the OECD network, environmental NGOs have become more able to hold national governments accountable for their sustainability performance. In private correspondence with the author, a strategically situated OECD official has described the arrangement as follows (email dated 30 March 2007):

An environmental Performance Review includes a review mission where a group of Secretariat and Government Experts go to the country concerned to interview people and collect information. During these review missions, meetings with civil society are conducted. In addition a 3-hour meeting to discuss the review is done with independent experts from Civil Society. The invitations to these meetings are made by the government and are made to a wide range of Civil Society Groups. The Review Team finds that these meetings are an indispensable source of information. The team also frequently uses NGO sites as an early warning on problems facing the country. The team then digs deeper into the statistics and research to determine if there really is a potential problem.

Thus the OECD works with environmental NGOs to hold national governments accountable in ways similar to the 'partnership-in-implementation' pattern observed earlier in the anti-bribery area.

OECD relations with CSOs in the environmental area also show some features of the 'customer-service' pattern noted previously in regard to the Model Tax Convention. On matters such as chemical safety, for instance, business groups demand global harmonisation of standards and work closely with and in the OECD network on these questions.

## Conclusions

This chapter has assessed how CSO engagement of the OECD has (and has not) furthered the accountability of OECD-centred global governance arrangements. Given that it is impossible within a single chapter to consider adequately the full breadth and variety of OECD activities, this analysis has explored five selected policy areas. While this coverage has not been comprehensive, it has illustrated different ways in which accountability equations between a global governance agency and civil society are configured at the OECD. The five fields examined have suggested several stylised modes of interaction between CSOs and the OECD, each posing the accountability question in a distinct way.

The first pattern is one of mobilisation-activism and is evident in the MAI affair. In this dynamic, widespread demonstrations and petitions on behalf of a broad and heterogeneous set of constituencies contribute to a change in policy and also generate enhanced openness of the global governance institution to CSOs. However, this pattern appeared in a specific historical context and seems unlikely to be repeated often in relation to the OECD.

The second pattern, one of enhanced voice and access, has been evident in all five scenarios except that on taxation. In this pattern, the OECD has created or enlarged more or less formalised arenas and channels of consultation. Here the OECD has provided information to CSOs and allowed them to contribute inputs of information and critique. Such venues can be, and have been, used by CSOs to hold OECD governance networks accountable to their constituencies. These consultations have taken form as regularised real-life consultations (sometimes at high level), as online consultations and as the open OECD Forum. The inclusion (more or less formalised) in the OECD network of two umbrella NGO organisations, OECD Watch and the EEB, is an important example of the broadening of the range of CSOs that have access and voice, beyond the OECD's traditional focus on business and labour groups through BIAC and TUAC.

A third pattern of OECD accountability is the institutionalised complaint mechanism, through the National Contact Points, which has been created to further implementation of the Guidelines for Multinational Enterprises. This arrangement is a 'hard' accountability measure, in the sense that NCPs are obliged to respond to initiatives from any constituency. However, this corrective mechanism is weak inasmuch as it relies entirely on moral and persuasive force, without formal sanctions. Assessments by TUAC indicate that the system has worked in some cases, but far from all.

A fourth pattern of very high accountability to a specific (business) constituency has been seen in OECD work on the Model Tax Convention. In this instance the OECD described business as 'the customer' and treated its own role as being something of a service provider. Signs of such a pattern have also appeared in OECD efforts to harmonise environmental safety standards.

Finally, a 'partners-in-implementation' relationship between the OECD and civil society has been observed in respect of environmental issues and, perhaps most clearly, in regard to anti-bribery initiatives. In these cases CSOs have not only had a high degree of access and voice, but in addition have worked closely with the OECD to hold national governments accountable for the implementation of agreed measures.

Still more patterns of accountability can be identified in other policy fields where the OECD and CSOs interact. For instance, the area of development aid poses wholly different accountability questions, inasmuch as NGOs often serve as a channel through which the assistance flows to recipients. In this area it becomes particularly important to hold CSOs accountable.

In sum, then, the case of OECD relations with civil society highlights that the accountability equation can be configured in many different ways, even in relation to the same governance agency. Hence the manner in which, and extent to which, CSOs advance OECD accountability vary by policy area. The general trend has been towards increased OECD openness to a broader range of CSOs and the development and strengthening of some specific accountability measures. However, this observation does not pertain to all issue areas, and CSOs have much more work at hand in order to open up the OECD across the full range of its operations.

# 9 Civil society and G8 accountability

*Peter I. Hajnal*

## Introduction

The Group of Eight (G8) is an informal transgovernmental forum of what are usually characterised as the major industrial democracies: Canada, France, Germany, Italy, Japan, Russia, the United Kingdom and the United States of America. This global governance mechanism has its origins in 1973 with meetings of the Group of Five (G5) finance ministers from France, Germany, Japan, the UK and the USA. Two years later the heads of state or government of these countries, plus Italy, held a first summit meeting at Rambouillet in France. Canada joined the club in 1976 to form the Group of Seven (G7). The European Union has participated – though not as a member state – since 1977. In 1998 Russia's full membership created the G8. More recently the leaders of five other major regional states (Brazil, China, India, Mexico and South Africa) have joined parts of the summit proceedings in what has been termed the 'G8+5'. In 2007 the '+5' were renamed the 'Outreach 5' ('O5'), and in 2008 the group formed the 'G5', which held its own meeting and issued a separate political declaration.

Despite huge publicity surrounding the G8 summits, this major institution of global governance remains relatively little understood outside specialist circles. In particular, the crucial issue of G8 accountability – especially its democratic accountability – has received scant attention. Two exceptions are recent contributions by Heidi Ullrich (on G8 accountability in respect of trade governance) and Colleen O'Manique (in respect of G8 activities on global health and human rights) (O'Manique 2007; Ullrich 2007).

For their help and insight, I would like to thank Mona Bricke, Sarah Cale, Andrew Cooper, Hugo Dobson, Jenilee Guebert, Peter Harder, Yuri Isakov, Sahar Kazranian, John Kirton, Mika Kohbayashi, Nigel Martin, Kumi Naidoo, Victoria Panova, Muthoni Wanyeki and other civil society activists, academics and government officials, and my research assistant Gillian Clinton.

The present chapter examines the democratic accountability of the G8 with a particular focus on civil society. The discussion that follows first outlines the mandate and activities of the G8, in the process establishing for what and to whom the G8 is accountable. The chapter then analyses how and to what extent civil society engagement has, and has not, promoted G8 accountability. The study considers the motivations for, and range of, civil society interaction with the G8; the accountability effects of this nexus; and factors that have helped or hindered civil society's contributions to G8 accountability.

The chapter concludes that the G8 leaders can be held accountable for actions and inactions across a broad range of economic, political, environmental and other global issues. They are accountable to populations of the eight countries themselves, to the broader global community, to a variety of specific actors, and to each other as peers. In terms of performance on accountability (with reference to the conception developed in Chapter 1), *transparency* of the G8 has increased but remains inadequate; public *consultation* has become common practice; *evaluation* has taken root but continues to have shortcomings; and opportunities for *redress* are largely lacking. Diverse civil society groups have increased the G8's accountability on these four dimensions through a variety of actions, but these effects have not yet reached their full potential.

## The G8: mandate and activities

The G7 emerged against the backdrop of several global economic shocks in the early 1970s. Chief among these were the collapse of the Bretton Woods international monetary system based on fixed exchange rates, as well as the quadrupling of oil prices in 1973–4. Leaders' summits were convened in an effort to forge policy agreements among governments of the major industrial countries in respect of these challenges (Putnam and Bayne 1987: 25–7).

The first summit, at Rambouillet, set out the core values of the club. Its communiqué embraced the vision of 'an open, democratic society dedicated to individual liberty and social advancement'. Indeed, the statement continued, success in the countries of the Group 'is essential to democratic societies everywhere'. Moreover, the leaders affirmed, 'growth and stability of our economies will help the entire industrial world and developing countries to prosper' (G7 1975: para. 2).

After the economic and financial focus of the early years (1975–81), the G7/G8 agenda expanded to embrace more and more topics. Political and security issues became increasingly prominent in the period 1982–8.

From 1989 other global issues joined the agenda, including democratisation, ecology (especially climate change), terrorism, organised crime, development, poor-country debts, infectious diseases, migration, food safety, energy, education, intellectual property, corruption and various armed conflicts.

The functions of the G7/G8 have also expanded over time. The main roles today, according to John Kirton, are deliberation, direction-giving, decision-making, and management of global governance and domestic politics (Kirton 2006: 6). The summit allows the attending heads of state and government to exercise political leadership, reconcile domestic and international concerns, develop collective management, and integrate economics and politics in their negotiations and decisions.

Each G8 leader has a support apparatus led by a personal representative, known in the jargon as a 'sherpa'. The team further includes two deputy 'sous-sherpas' (one for economic affairs and the other for financial matters), a political director and a large retinue of logistical, security and other staff. Since 2001 each G8 leader has also had an Africa Personal Representative (APR).

In the early years of G8 summitry, delegations also included the foreign and finance ministers of each country. Following the organisational innovations of the 1998 Birmingham summit these ministers were detached from the leaders' summits and now hold their own deliberations which feed into the meetings of the heads of state or government. These ministers, as well as others, also convene their own series of G8 meetings throughout the year.

Over its history the G7/G8 has created task forces, expert panels and working groups on a variety of issues. Such committees, like the Digital Opportunities Task Force, are given specific remits and instructed to report back to a future summit. Some of these creations have subsequently expanded their membership beyond the G8 and developed into quite independent entities. Two examples are the Financial Action Task Force on money laundering (FATF), established at the 1989 Paris G7 summit, and the Global Fund to Fight AIDS, Tuberculosis and Malaria, launched at the 2001 Genoa G8 summit (see Chapter 12).

Since the G8 lacks a formal constitutional framework, it has no discrete institutional mechanisms to regulate its interactions with other actors. Nor does the G8 have its own permanent secretariat, so there is no continuing machinery through which civil society players, among others, can interact with the transgovernmental network. However, these institutional limitations have not prevented substantial interchanges between the G8 and civil society associations.

## G8 accountability

As elaborated in Chapter 1, accountability – and, in particular, democratic accountability – entails an actor's answerability for its actions or inactions to those who are affected by such actions and inactions. Among the four key dimensions of accountability identified earlier, the G8 has strongest credentials in respect of consultation and evaluation. Although G8 transparency is greater now than in earlier years of summitry, it remains inadequate. Possibilities of correction and redress in respect of the G8 are weaker still.

The G8 can be held accountable for the mandate and activities described in the preceding section, but to whom does it owe that accountability? The stakeholders include the eight member governments and their citizens, the global community as a whole, financial markets and marginalised groups in society. The G8 also operates mutual accountability, demanding that others answer to it at the same time that it answers to them (Brown 2007).

There is relatively strong internal accountability within the G8 system, as the member heads of state or government answer to their fellow leaders. When, at a summit, they undertake before their peers to accomplish a particular objective, they must again face those colleagues at future meetings should they not comply with their commitments. Can a leader 'look them in the eye' at the following year's summit if he or she has not fulfilled promises made at the previous summit (Kirton 2007)? Moreover, task forces and other working groups must report back to the G8 leaders when asked to do so.

As elected heads of state or government, individual G8 leaders are also (or should be) accountable to their national populations. Positive actions to enact this answerability include regular post-summit reports by the UK Prime Minister to the British parliament, and the Canadian government's follow-up reports to legislators in Ottawa on G8 initiatives concerning Africa. In budgetary terms, host governments are accountable to elected representatives for public money spent on organising summits and other G8-related actions. However, on the whole the practice of G8 accountability through national elected legislators remains underdeveloped.

As a global governance instrument addressing global issues, the G8 is arguably also accountable to the global community as a whole. The G8 leaders have undertaken to provide global public goods for the benefit of all humanity. For example, in 1995 the G7 undertook to 'show leadership in improving the environment' (G7 1995: para. 31). Yet even with the addition of Russia in 1998 and the inclusion of the '+5'/'Outreach 5'/'G5' since 2005, the G8 is anything but representative of overall humanity. Poorer developing countries and a number of important emerging economies remain excluded.

Several recent proposals have sought to remedy this situation (Hajnal 2007b). One suggested reform would turn the G8 into an L20 (Leaders' 20) patterned on the Group of 20 finance ministers' forum, but with a broader global agenda (Carin 2007; Centre for Global Studies 2007; Heap 2008). The 'G20' meetings since 2008 have developed in this direction. The 2009 Pittsburgh G20 summit was especially significant for designating the G20 'to be the premier forum for our international economic co-operation', which in effect appropriates the erstwhile raison d'être of the G8 (G20 2009).

Another proposal to enlarge the G8 would incorporate the 'Outreach 5' as regular members of an enlarged G13 (Elliott and Wintour 2006). A third idea would turn the G8 into a 'G-N' or 'G-XX' that included the G8 as well as middle- and low-income countries (Haynal 2005: 261–74; Stiglitz and Griffith-Jones 2007: 4–5, 14–16, 28). Or the current G8 could be expanded with Brazil, China, Egypt, India, Indonesia, Nigeria and Saudi Arabia to form a G15 (Axworthy 2007). Several former and serving G7/G8 leaders have also called for reform of the mechanism, including Tony Blair, Paul Martin, Nicolas Sarkozy and Helmut Schmidt (Martin 2007; Schmidt 2007: 4–6; President of France 2008). Hence there seems to be broad recognition that the G8 is not sufficiently effective and representative.

The G8 could also potentially fill some accountability deficits to wider humanity by answering to regional and other global governance agencies. In fact, the G8 leaders have for many years invited the administrative heads of certain intergovernmental organisations (IGOs) to the summits for consultation. For example, the 2008 Hokkaido summit saw the presence of the heads of the United Nations (UN), the International Monetary Fund (IMF), the World Bank, the Organisation for Economic Co-operation and Development (OECD), the International Energy Agency (IEA) and the African Union (AU). On issues where the G8 is unable or unwilling to act decisively, it often remits the task to an IGO, for instance by referring unresolved trade problems to the World Trade Organization (WTO). The G7/G8 has also sent quasi-binding requests to the OECD to prepare studies or to facilitate G8-related activities such as the so-called 'Heiligendamm Process' (covering cross-border investment, research and innovation, climate change, energy and development). Yet such transfers of responsibility make for weak accountability on the part of the G8 itself.

The G7's relationship with financial markets has unfolded along similar lines to that with IGOs. The club has had important influences on these markets, through specific initiatives such as reform of the international financial architecture, which has been a concern of many summits. However, no accountability mechanisms have clearly and specifically linked the G8 to the commercial financial sector in respect of these influences. In contrast, the G20 summits have taken certain steps in this direction (G20 2009).

In addition, the G8 has for some years acknowledged its responsibility to extend benefits of globalisation to marginalised groups, and to remedy economic and other inequalities. However, G8 actions in this regard have been uneven. Some benefits have accrued to disadvantaged populations, but many G8 promises to these constituencies have remained partly or wholly unfulfilled. Moreover, some civil society groups have claimed that the G7/G8 governments themselves have, singly and collectively, caused or exacerbated indebtedness and poverty, for example by: irresponsible lending; denial of market access to exports from developing countries; inadequate or inappropriately administered development aid; and unfair exploitation of extractive industries.

In spite of their own weak accountability, the G8 leaders have often expressed expectations of accountability on the part of other actors. For example, at the 1995 Halifax summit the leaders called for 'a more transparent and accountable [UN] Secretariat' (G7 1995: para. 36). Two years later they urged the 'IMF and the multilateral development banks to strengthen their activities to help countries fight corruption' (G7 1997b: para. 25). The 2004 Sea Island summit launched 'Country-led Transparency Compacts' under which 'partner governments [Nicaragua, Georgia, Nigeria and Peru] have specified, in concrete terms, what they intend to do to bring greater transparency and accountability to the management of public resources' (G8 2004).

Meanwhile, a theme of 'mutual accountability' has figured regularly since 2002 in G8 discussions of policies towards Africa. The G8 Africa Action Plan, launched at the 2002 Kananaskis summit, has numerous references to accountability as applied to the New Partnership for Africa's Development (NEPAD), an initiative of African governments. The Gleneagles declaration on Africa includes a section entitled Partnership and Mutual Accountability, calling for monitoring and reviewing progress (G8 2005a: para. 33). At Heiligendamm in 2007 the G8 leaders asserted that the Africa Partnership Forum 'should be established and ... act as a platform for mutual accountability' (G8 2007d: para. 9). The 2008 Hokkaido summit encouraged developing countries to base their efforts in implementing the UN's Millennium Development Goals (MDGs) on mutual accountability with the G8 (G8 2008: para. 40).

In sum, apart from informal accountability to one another, the G8 leaders do not answer systematically and thoroughly to anyone. Internal accountability is reasonably robust both among the leaders themselves and within the broader G8 system. Individual leaders are notionally accountable to their national electorates for their actions taken in the G8. Collectively the G8 owes some accountability to the global community, including marginalised groups within it. On the one hand, this accountability is enhanced by relations with stakeholders such as IGOs, business associations and civil society groups. On the other hand, G8 accountability is compromised by inadequate overall global representation within the club itself.

### Civil society engaging the G8

The definition of civil society set out in the Introduction to this book broadly applies to the case of the G8. One proviso is that the inclusion of business forums within civil society is problematic, because the interests, modus operandi and clout of such associations diverge from those of other civil society actors. Indeed, leaders and other officials of the G8 countries distinguish between business players on the one hand and non-profit civil society organisations (CSOs) on the other.

If business groups are included in civil society, then (much as in the IMF, WTO and OECD cases covered in earlier chapters) the overall civil society impact on the G8 increases. For example, UK Prime Minister Tony Blair, German Chancellor Angela Merkel and Japanese Prime Minister Yasuo Fukuda, the respective hosts of the Gleneagles, Heiligendamm and Hokkaido summits, chose the exclusive business gathering, the annual World Economic Forum, to flesh out their agendas for their forthcoming G8 presidencies (UK 2005b; WEF 2007, 2008). Likewise, the International Chamber of Commerce, another major business interest group, has had a longstanding relationship with the G7/G8 (Hajnal 2007a: 95–6). In April 2008 a G8 Tokyo Business Summit addressed a statement to the G8 leaders on economic matters.

The long history of non-business civil society engagement with the G7/G8 begins with a rather humble letter from a local trade union group to US President Gerald Ford, host of the second summit, held in San Juan, Puerto Rico in 1976. In it, the President of the Puerto Rico Free Federation of Labor asks God to enlighten the leaders in their deliberations and expresses the wish that they should address a whole slew of economic and political issues (Hajnal 2007a: 104). This overture and other early civil society approaches to the G7 had no discernible impact on policy. However, in later years the trade union movement has built up a systematic and focused relationship with the G7 and G8.

Among non-governmental organisations (NGOs) various environmental groups such as Greenpeace, Friends of the Earth and the World Wildlife Fund (WWF) have engaged the G7/G8 for many years. Likewise, human rights NGOs such as Amnesty International and Human Rights Watch have long interacted with the G7/G8. Among development and relief agencies the G7/G8 has attracted attention from Oxfam, Tearfund, ActionAid and the World Development Movement. Several mass campaigns have also targeted the G8, particularly the Jubilee debt campaign, the Global Call to Action against Poverty (GCAP) and the related Make Poverty History movement. Other NGOs to engage the G7/G8 include faith-based groups (across Christian, Jewish, Muslim, Buddhist, Hindu and other traditions) and CSOs focusing on various social and political issues (e.g. Social Watch, the Halifax Initiative, the Montreal International Forum [FIM], Transparency International and Consumers International). Youth groups have figured prominently in the J8 (Junior 8) forum that began around the Gleneagles summit, although the 'civil society' status of this initiative is problematic as it is organised by the United Nations Children's Fund (UNICEF) and the G8 host government. Other civil society assemblies that have specifically focused on the G8 include the 'poor people's summits' (for example, as convened in Mali since 2002) (Sommet des Pauvres 2008), the Civil G8 that functioned during the Russian G8 presidency in 2006 (Civil G8 2007), the G8 NGO Platform under the German presidency in 2007 and the 2008 Japan G8 Summit NGO Forum.

When interacting with the G8, CSOs and civil society coalitions generally concentrate their activities in the summit host country and as close as possible to the summit venue. This has important implications, in that CSOs from other continents and other countries, particularly from the global south, often lack sufficient resources to travel to those locations. In addition, for recent summits visas have been denied to a number of NGO activists who wished to participate in G8-related actions. Although some citizen groups from Africa have been active vis-à-vis the G8 in recent years, civil society around the summits tends to be predominantly local, including local affiliates of large international CSOs. For similar reasons, civil society from the global south is often represented around the summits by diaspora groups residing in the summit country.

Likewise, interaction of women's groups with the G8 has been limited. Many in the women's movement have engaged the G8 on human rights, the environment, development, health and other global issues of concern. One example is the International Council of Women prior to the St Petersburg summit. However, as Dobson has documented, gender equity and women's issues have not figured significantly on the G8 agenda (Dobson 2008). In this regard the G8 experience replicates the sparseness of gender activism seen in respect of most of the other institutions examined in this volume.

In addition to business groups, trade unions and NGOs, professional bodies, research groups and think tanks have played an important role in respect of the G8. Prominent examples include the national science academies of the G8 countries (for instance, The Royal Society in the UK) plus those of Brazil, China, India and South Africa. Also notable are the G8 Research Group at the University of Toronto, the Royal Institute of International Affairs (Chatham House) in London and the Centre for International Governance Innovation (CIGI) in Waterloo, Canada. In 2000–5 a group of former G8 officials and other prominent people convened as a Shadow G8 (originally called the G8 Preparatory Conference). In 2007 a different 'Shadow G8' appeared under the presidency of the economist Joseph E. Stiglitz. Similarly, the InterAction Council of former senior government officials of G8 and other countries has functioned since 1983.

A new kind of civil society actor appeared on the G8 scene in 2008 with a four-day Indigenous Peoples' Summit held in Sapporo ahead of the G8 summit. Indigenous groups from five continents and the Pacific participated. The conference adopted the Nibutani Declaration that detailed various concerns of indigenous peoples and addressed twenty-two proposals to the G8.

In recent years celebrities such as Bono and Bob Geldof, as well as other prominent personalities such as Gro Harlem Brundtland and Stephen Lewis, have played an interesting part. So-called 'Live 8' concerts were held around the world in conjunction with the Gleneagles summit.

Parallel summits are another form of democratic activity by civil society associations in respect of the G8. These events broadly resemble the Commonwealth People's Forum that assembles alongside the Commonwealth Heads of Government Meeting (see Chapter 8) and the Asia-Europe People's Forum that convenes alongside the official Asia-Europe Meeting (see Chapter 10). Parallel summits attract groups that adopt co-operative as well as non-co-operative stances vis-à-vis the G8. In some years the 'engagement' strain has predominated, while in others the 'resistance' mode has figured more strongly. Some parallel summits have transmitted concrete proposals to G8 leaders for consideration.

The first alternative summit convened by civil society groups, called the Popular Summit, took place around the time of the 1981 Ottawa (Montebello) G7 meeting. Subsequently a group known as TOES (The

Other Economic Summit) organised several counter-summits, beginning in London at the time of the 1984 summit. The 1991 London EnviroSummit was an issue-oriented alternative summit. In 2005 a G8 Alternatives Summit met in Edinburgh three days before the Gleneagles summit. In 2007 over forty NGOs held an alternative summit in Rostock, timed to coincide with the Heiligendamm summit (G8 Alternative Summit 2007). In 2008 a People's Summit convened at Lake Toya, some distance from the site of the G8 leaders' meeting.

Parallel summits affect G8 accountability. Participants who collaborate with the official G8 engage in a form of consultation. As is elaborated later, those who reject dialogue (as did the 2006 counter-summit of The Other Russia, for example) can still demand redress from the G8.

## Accountability effects of civil society actions

Civil society activities vis-à-vis the G8 have ranged widely, encompassing for example advocacy, demonstrations, dialogue, analytical reports, performance monitoring, petitions and multistakeholder partnerships (Hajnal 2007a: 130–1). The various types of civil society actions often overlap. For example, dialogue and demonstrations can serve an advocacy function, partnerships can enhance service delivery, and so forth. How has all of this civil society involvement impacted on the democratic accountability of the G8?

Civil society interventions have helped to raise government awareness of citizen concerns regarding the G8 agenda and have stimulated government responses to those concerns. Conversely, civil society groups, in the course of dialogue with official circles, have gained greater appreciation of what is and is not possible for governments in the G8 context. Civil society associations benefit from having channels for advocacy in respect of G8 governments, notwithstanding concerns that, by this engagement, these citizen associations lend those governments, as well as the G8 itself, greater legitimacy than is warranted. Many civil society actors question the legitimacy of the G8, in particular given its restricted membership (Martin 2005: 16–17). So both parties may be using each other while also benefiting their respective constituencies. Given the right conditions, however, this interplay enables CSOs to exact accountability from the G8 and allows the G8 to deliver accountability.

### G8 recognition of civil society

Civil society promotion of G8 accountability is facilitated to the extent that the governments involved acknowledge that citizen groups have a part to play in G8 processes. As positive signs in this direction, summit documents have increasingly recognised civil society, undertaken to work with CSOs and/or urged other institutions to do so. Such statements implicitly accord civil society actors a role as agents of accountability for the G8.

The 1995 Halifax G7 summit was the first to refer to civil society, in the context of promoting sustainable development and reforming international financial institutions (IFIs). Its communiqué promised: 'we will work with others to encourage ... improved coordination among international organizations, bilateral donors and NGOs' (G7 1995: para. 37). Two years later the Denver G7 communiqué 'reaffirm[ed] the vital contribution of civil society' to the environment, democratic governance and poverty eradication (G7 1997a: para. 13). In 1998 summit host Tony Blair paid tribute to the Jubilee campaign for the 'dignified manner in which [the campaign] demonstrated in Birmingham, and for making a most persuasive case for debt relief' (Dent and Peters 1999: 188). The 2001 Genoa communiqué undertook to 'promote innovative solutions [for sustainable development] based on a broad partnership with civil society and the private sector'. At Kananaskis in 2002 the G8 Africa Action Plan and some ministerial documents include explicit references to civil society (G8 2002: paras. 10, I/1.5, II/2.1, VI/6/2).

References by the G8 to civil society have become still more frequent in recent years. For example, the 2005 Gleneagles plan of action on climate change and other G8 documents call for civil society engagement (G8 2005b: para. 14a). In his end-of-summit press conference, Blair acknowledged the positive contributions of civil society, mass demonstrations and celebrities, in particular singling out the Make Poverty History initiative (UK 2005a). At St Petersburg in 2006 (the first summit hosted by Russia), the G8 statement on *Education for Innovative Societies in the 21st Century* and the *G8 Summit Declaration on Counter-Terrorism* both referred to civil society (G8 2006a: para. 17, 2006b: para. 4). Host leader Vladimir Putin stated in his final press conference that 'our discussions took into account recommendations made by two very important forums ... the World Summit of Religious Leaders and the International Forum of Non-Governmental Organisations, the Civil G8 2006' (G8 2006c: para. [2]). At Heiligendamm in 2007, host leader Angela Merkel declared in her *Chair's Summary* that 'we will ... work with all the relevant stakeholders including ... civil society ... to deliver practical steps towards "universal access" [to AIDS medications in Africa]' (G8 2007a: para. 7). Civil society was also mentioned in the Heiligendamm declarations on *Growth and Responsibility in Africa* and *Growth and*

*Responsibility in the World Economy*, as well as in the *Global Partnership Review* (G8 2007c: para. 57; 2007e: paras. 56, 83, 86; 2007b: para. 1). At Hokkaido in 2008 host leader Fukuda, in his final press conference, called for partnership of civil society, governments and the private sector to address contemporary challenges. Other documents of the Hokkaido summit are similarly couched in a multistakeholder frame with explicit references to civil society.

### Transparency

Has this increasing G8 recognition of a role for civil society in global governance had substantive effects on the accountability of this transgovernmental mechanism? On the first dimension of accountability highlighted in this book, namely transparency, not much impact on the G8 can be attributed to civil society activities, in the way that sustained citizen campaigns have helped to open up the Bretton Woods institutions and the WTO to greater public scrutiny (see Chapters 3–5).

Certainly G8 proceedings have become more transparent over time. The amount of publicly released documentation has grown significantly from the rather meagre output of early summits. There has also been a general (though uneven) trend towards the disclosure of more focused and substantial information, including the release of detailed action plans. Media briefings by G8 officials before and during summits are another indication of increased transparency, marking a break from the relative secrecy of earlier years. However, these moves towards greater openness are difficult to attribute specifically to civil society activities.

This minimal civil society impact is not for lack of trying. CSOs have long pressed the G8 on transparency. For example, when the 2003 Evian summit issued a declaration on *Fighting Corruption and Improving Transparency*, Friends of the Earth (FOE) criticised the voluntary compliance provisions in respect of extractive industries and added: 'These eight leaders are more responsible than anyone for the actions of their multinationals' (Friends of the Earth 2003). Likewise, Transparency International (TI) has since 2007 pressed the G8 on anti-corruption measures.

CSOs have occasionally been able to obtain and publicise leaked drafts of G8 declarations in an effort to force greater transparency in G8 proceedings. For example, Reclaim the Commons published a confidential draft of the 2006 St Petersburg declaration on energy security (Reclaim the Commons 2006). In 2007 Oil Change International released a draft Heiligendamm declaration on growth and responsibility in the world economy (Oil Change International 2007).

In spite of this progress, however, the G8 has much more to do before reaching adequate levels of transparency for democratic accountability. For instance, the detailed proceedings of the *in camera* meetings of the leaders remain confidential apart from strategic partial disclosures in off-the-record briefings. The official archives of the member governments that hold the detailed information normally only become publicly available twenty-five or thirty years after the event. As a result even documentation regarding the earliest G7 summits is only now coming to light. Moreover, not every G8 government briefs the public with equal diligence. Thus civil society groups still have much work to do in extracting G8 transparency.

### Consultation

Dialogue of CSOs with leaders and other officials of G8 governments is an important means of exchanging ideas and (sometimes) developing shared positions. Potentially, these consultations give G8 governments and civil society groups alike greater legitimacy in the eyes of the general public. Dialogue implies willingness to co-operate – although not necessarily to agree – with G8 governments. Many civil society groups pay this price of implicitly legitimising the G8 with some reluctance.

Although summit communiqués have referred to civil society from 1995, official consultation of CSOs did not become part of the G8 summit process until the 2000 Okinawa meeting. On that occasion the Japanese host government met with civil society leaders from Europe ahead of the conference. At the summit itself the Japanese Prime Minister exchanged views with representatives of five NGOs to discuss globalisation, the environment, infectious diseases and the importance of partnership between governments and civil society.

Every subsequent G8 summit but one has included an element of direct consultation between official circles and civil society associations. The exception was Sea Island in 2004, when the host (US) government was unwilling to engage in exchanges with CSOs. At Kananaskis in 2002, FIM led a group of CSOs in dialogue with the Canadian government. FIM was again instrumental in convening civil society bodies to engage the G8 process at the 2003 Evian, 2005 Gleneagles and 2006 St Petersburg summits (Martin 2008). In addition, Chatham House organised a series of meetings between government and other stakeholders including civil society associations before and after the Gleneagles summit. In 2006 the Civil G8 coalition organised a year-long series of meetings, including two large NGO forums (one with the participation of President Putin), workshops, and sessions with all nine sherpas (from the G8 countries plus the

EU). At Heiligendamm in 2007 the German presidency of the G8 designated the NGO, *Forum Umwelt und Entwicklung* (Forum on Environment
and Development), as its lead partner in consultations with civil society.
The host government conducted a dialogue in Bonn three months ahead
of the summit, chaired by the Development Minister and involving representatives of German and international civil society as well as the nine
sherpas. In addition, Merkel held her own pre-summit consultation with
the leaders of twenty major NGOs. Similarly, two strands of dialogue
unfolded in 2008: on the one hand sherpa consultations with civil society groups under the aegis of the Japan G8 Summit NGO Forum; and
on the other hand consultations by the host leader of a limited number
of NGOs.

Beyond the annual summits, civil society organisations have also
interacted with G8 ministerial forums, including meetings of the
development ministers and gatherings of the environment ministers.
The G8 has further consulted with CSOs in the context of multistakeholder groups or task forces. One example is the DOT Force (Digital
Opportunities Task Force), which was active between 2000 and 2002.
Another is the Global Fund to Fight AIDS, Tuberculosis and Malaria
(GFATM). Such collaboration between official and civil society circles
on concrete policies can have very positive results, but regrettably has
remained rare to date.

Certainly, these consultations have had their limitations. Some dialogues have been better planned, more carefully organised and more
focused than others. The 2006 St Petersburg process took consultations
to a higher level of quality that will be hard to match, while the 2007
dialogue in Germany was less well prepared, conducted and financed;
the 2008 consultation fell between the previous two years in quality.
Some summit hosts have been more willing than others to engage with
civil society, and discussions have sometimes been confidential meetings with small groups of civil society leaders rather than larger public
forums. Such exclusivity – as seen since 2005 – has caused some tensions among civil society groups. However, it remains the prerogative
of the host leader to restrict engagement to a select group of CSO
leaders.

In addition, civil society associations have not yet fully exploited other
potential channels of consultation in the G8 process. For example, few
groups have targeted members of G8 national legislatures (Harder 2007).
One such avenue exists in the shape of GLOBE International: The Global
Legislators Organisation, a network of parliamentarians from the G8+5.
In February 2006 GLOBE launched a climate change dialogue with
business leaders and civil society representatives (World Bank 2006).

Another channel of consultation that civil society groups have begun to use is the G8 Parliamentarians group, comprised of the speakers of the national legislatures of the eight states.

Yet, these limitations noted, the push by civil society actors for consultation has strengthened G8 accountability. G8 leaders and other officials are now well socialised into a process of interchange with citizen groups. Indeed, leaders, particularly during their summit hosting year, are now expected to consult with CSOs. On their part, many CSOs have found consultation the most efficacious way of bringing their concerns and proposals directly to the G8. Moreover, consultation processes have opened the way for civil society groups to monitor and evaluate G8 performance.

### Evaluation

Evaluative reports and studies are a significant element in civil society efforts to obtain greater accountability of the G8. These investigations assess how far the G8 realises its objectives and complies with its commitments. The reports acknowledge any advances made and, more critically, point up failures to fulfil promises. Some evaluations measure performance in terms of a numerical score or a letter grade, while others present a narrative analysis.

Such assessments from civil society quarters can be used to press the G8 to improve its performance and account to stakeholders for actions and inactions. Clearly, these exercises have had an effect. G8 governments now expect this scrutiny and have indicated some willingness to use the reports in shaping their future actions. Indeed, partly in response to these civil society initiatives, the G8 itself has recently begun to undertake some systematic self-monitoring.

In one prominent civil society initiative to evaluate performance, the G8 Research Group has since 1996 produced compliance reports on summit commitments. For example, the final assessment of implementation in respect of Gleneagles identified 212 distinct commitments and selected 21 for detailed evaluation, including amongst others peacekeeping, good governance, HIV/AIDS, official development assistance, transnational crime, climate change and tsunami relief (G8 Research Group 2006). Some of these issues recur in successive summits, while others appear on the agenda only once.

Another evaluation of fulfilment of the Gleneagles promises has been undertaken since 2006 by the Debt AIDS Trade Africa (DATA) group. In 2008, midway through the MDG process, its third report examined key commitments of G8 governments on development assistance, debt, trade, health, education, water and sanitation, governance, peace and security. The report also assessed progress by African governments in fulfilling their commitments on the MDGs (DATA and ONE 2008). The DATA studies have painted a rather negative overall picture, with progress on track for certain matters such as debt relief, HIV/AIDS and malaria, but off track in most other areas. DATA has presented its findings and recommendations to the hosts of the Heiligendamm and Hokkaido summits.

Another exercise to evaluate the G8 is the scoring system devised by Putnam and Bayne. This approach assigns letter grades to the co-operative achievements of the respective summits. For example, the evaluation gives the Rambouillet summit a mark of 'A–' for advances on monetary reform. The 1978 Bonn summit earns the highest grade ('A') in respect of growth, energy and trade. The 1984 London summit receives 'C–' on debt. The 1987 Venice summit gets 'D' for 'nothing significant'. The Halifax summit receives 'B+' for initiatives on institutional review and reform of the IMF and the UN (Putnam and Bayne 1987; Bayne 2005a, 2005b).

As an example of monitoring a specific G8 issue, Transparency International (TI) has taken a leading role in assessing the G8's performance on corruption. In its pre-summit progress report of 2007, TI concluded that, since the Kananaskis summit when the G8 first took up the question of corruption, rhetoric had exceeded action. TI called for prompt implementation of G8 commitments in this area and for more regulatory efforts to fight corruption in financial markets (TI 2007a: 4–5, 13–14). A few days later, TI's post-summit press release acknowledged some progress, including the ratification by all G8 members of the 2003 UN Convention against Corruption and a 'commitment to keep G8 financial systems from being used to harbor the proceeds of corruption'. However, TI also called for action on these commitments and transparent accounting of how the commitments would be funded (TI 2007b). Ahead of the Hokkaido summit TI issued a detailed assessment of each G8 country's record on fighting corruption. The summit proceeded to produce its own *Accountability Report* on anti-corruption commitments and undertook to update the review annually.

Prodded in part by civil society evaluations such as the above, the G8 has in recent years begun explicit self-monitoring. For example, the Gleneagles final document on climate change calls for a report on progress to the 2008 summit. The aforementioned 'Heiligendamm Process' mandates an interim progress report at the 2008 summit and a final report at the 2009 summit (G8 2007e: para. 97, 2007f). The Hokkaido meeting produced further initiatives on self-monitoring, for example on infectious diseases and corruption. The 2009 L'Aquila summit, in its *Preliminary Accountability Report*, tracked delivery on commitments regarding food security, water, health and education. The report also indicated intentions to establish a working group on accountability in order to share best practices and develop a 'G8 Accountability Framework' (G8 2009). The fact that G8 leaders have (as prodded by a number of civil society forces) increasingly encouraged monitoring and follow-up is itself an accountability benefit.

### Redress

However, have the consultation and evaluation exercises described above also stimulated G8 accountability in respect of redress? In spite of vigorously deploying various tactics (including petitions, media campaigns and street demonstrations), civil society interventions have had relatively little effect on this dimension of accountability vis-à-vis the G8. Such correction of wrongs as has been obtained (for example, substantial debt relief) has been due not only to civil society action, but also other forces such as pressures from governments in the global south and strategic calculations on the part of certain leaders.

An important example of the petition tactic occurred in 1998, when Jubilee 2000 gathered signatures to urge the Birmingham summit to cancel all external debt of the poorest countries by the year 2000. The summit responded to Jubilee's petition in a collective statement, implying some acknowledgement of G8 accountability on debt matters. However, full debt cancellation did not occur by 2000 and, despite significant progress, has not been achieved to this day. In a variation on petition tactics, civil society associations in preparations for the Heiligendamm summit sponsored a letter-writing campaign to achieve just trade policies (Gerechtigkeit jetzt! 2007). In 2008 civil society organisations prepared an anti-poverty petition carrying over a million names (the 'Tanabata Petition') that was handed to the Japanese Prime Minister at his June meeting with civil society leaders.

Media campaigns have long been a staple of civil society action vis-à-vis the G8. News outlets can help bring civil society positions to public and government attention through press releases and opinion pieces. For example, Greenpeace often produces press releases that highlight poor G8 performance on environmental concerns. Sympathetic media coverage of civil society concerns can serve to promote G8 accountability (see e.g. Monbiot 2005). However, journalists often focus merely on the occasional incidents of violence or on 'street theatre' stunts rather than peaceful civil society actions at G8 meetings.

Many civil society groups have also used the Internet in their campaigns for correction of G8 policies. New information and communication technologies have exponentially increased the scope and speed of CSO activity in fundraising, research, advocacy, service delivery, networking and coalition-building. For example, in Germany in 2007 the G8 NGO Platform, a coalition of some forty organisations, used its website to report on demonstrations, conferences, the alternative summit and other activities (G8 NGO Platform 2007a).

The Genoa summit saw another tactic in civil society efforts to correct damaging policies of G8 governments. On this occasion Médecins Sans Frontières (MSF) presented a mobile exhibition of the ravages wrought by neglected diseases and the lack of essential medicines to treat them, especially in poor countries. In another variation of street theatre, the 2003 alternative summit at Annemasse, France – a civil society counterpoint to the Evian G8 summit – featured a 'debt and reparation tribunal'. At the 1998 Birmingham summit Christian Aid convened a 'Poor 7' (P7) of delegates from Sub-Saharan Africa.

Street demonstrations are a familiar mode whereby many CSOs seek redress from the G8. Such protests have been part of the summit scene since the 1981 Ottawa G7 summit when 3,500 demonstrators marched on Parliament Hill (Evans 1981; Holzapfel and Koenig 2002). Demonstrations before and during G8 gatherings have involved the whole gamut of civil society, including groups that prefer co-operative interaction, circles that reject engagement, and a small minority of violence-prone protesters that exploit the situation and can hurt the cause of the peaceful majority. Positive examples of street protest include the Jubilee movement's massive peaceful demonstrations during the 1998 Birmingham summit, and the even larger 2005 march in Edinburgh (250,000 participants) to 'Make Poverty History'. On the negative side, the 2001 Genoa summit saw anarchists disrupt the street protests. The resultant confrontation with inexperienced and combative police resulted in several injuries and the tragic death of one protester. German NGOs staged a mass demonstration in Rostock six days before the opening of the Heiligendamm summit with the *altermondialiste* theme of 'Another World Is Possible' (G8 NGO Platform 2007b). On this occasion, too, smaller groups of 'uncivil society' disrupted the peaceful majority, resulting in clashes with police, several arrests and around a thousand injuries (Dissent! 2007). The Hokkaido summit saw a massive police presence alongside relatively small and peaceful demonstrations.

Other civil society actors have proposed or attempted blockades of G8 summits. During the 2005 summit, for instance, groups of generally non-violent anarchists caused serious delays by blocking the roads leading to Gleneagles and disrupting train services. Two years later the Anti-G8-Alliance for a Revolutionary Perspective staged disruptions before and during the Heiligendamm summit (Anti-G8-Alliance 2007). A group calling itself 'Block G8' pursued civil disobedience by blockading the 2007 summit.

On other occasions authorities in the summit host country have actively discouraged demonstrations. That was the situation at the 2004 Sea Island and 2006 St Petersburg summits. Such official obstruction of street protest detracts from civil society's ability to obtain accountability from the G8.

Apparently, peaceful confrontation has sometimes been necessary to extract redress from the G8. Would debt relief, greater involvement of the 'Outreach 5' and other reforms have occurred without civil society protests? Perhaps even violent confrontation has unwittingly given the peaceful majority more space for consultation with the G8 by contrasting the two styles of action and intimating that violence could grow if 'civil' society is not heard.

In sum, civil society activities have been an important force for greater democratic accountability of the G8, although the impacts must not be exaggerated. The consequences have on the whole been greater in respect of consultation and evaluation, with smaller gains in respect of transparency and redress. Civil society interventions in the G8 process could obtain greater accountability in the future, but such improvements would require that certain challenges are addressed.

### Enabling and disabling civil society engagement of the G8

In order to raise the contributions of civil society action to G8 accountability beyond that which has been achieved to date, it would be useful to identify some of the circumstances that have thus far helped and, more particularly, hindered this dynamic. The following final step in this analysis highlights key factors under three headings: the informal character of the G8 process; the attitudes of member governments towards civil society engagement; and the degree of sophistication in civil society tactics.

#### The perils of informality

The informal nature of the G8 means that its relations with civil society lack constitutional grounding. As a result matters tend to be handled in an ad hoc and superficial fashion. Gradually, more systematic processes for consultation of civil society have taken root in the bureaucracies of at least some G8 governments. Such processes entail liaison with government officials ranging from lower levels to sherpas (who are often deputy ministers) to cabinet members and, in rare cases, with G8 heads of state or government. However, nothing has been formalised.

Just as the G8 has no formal and permanent machinery for consultation with civil society, so global civil society also lacks continuing machinery for engaging the G8. Certain associations, for example FIM or the Shadow G8, could conceivably act as focal points for the co-ordination of civil society engagement of the G8, but no group has in practice fulfilled this kind of role. Such continuity and co-ordination would enhance civil society's ability to influence G8 accountability.

### The crucial role of government attitudes

In the absence of formal mechanisms much depends on G8 government attitudes. Is the government open to civil society and willing to listen to, learn from and give respect to civil society? Positive examples include the Japanese hosts at Okinawa in 2000 (and to a lesser extent Hokkaido in 2008), the Canadian government at Kananaskis in 2002, the French government in Evian in 2003, the British government at Gleneagles in 2005 and the Russian government in St Petersburg in 2006. Some host governments have budgeted funds to promote dialogue with civil society. For example the Japanese authorities in 2000 and 2008 financed a well-equipped NGO centre, and the Russian hosts in 2006 contributed resources to the Civil G8. In contrast, the US G8 presidency in 2004 showed no interest or inclination to engage with civil society, and took measures to discourage even peaceful demonstrations. Post-9/11 concern with security figured strongly in this case, but it has not stopped other more receptive governments from cultivating relations with civil society.

Yet even where attitudes are more receptive, G8 governments tend to use the term 'outreach' for their contacts with civil society. Such vocabulary is problematic inasmuch as it implies a one-way approach by government to civil society. In practice CSOs have been more influential in respect of the G8 when they develop strategies on their own terms, rather than depending on 'outreach'. For example, MSF has shown impressive initiatives in areas of public health and infectious diseases. Thus while G8 government initiatives towards civil society actors are important, CSOs do not have to take their cues from government.

Another important factor concerns the incentives that G8 governments offer their officials to engage with civil society representatives. Not much of substance has been available in this regard. For example, the government officials concerned have received little if any training on building and maintaining relations with civil society groups. In addition, staff rotations and the ebb and flow of a particular government's attention to G8 matters further militate against the development of capacities in official circles for civil society liaison. In the best-case scenario, expertise would be passed on in an organised fashion to successive officials involved in summitry, but in practice such smooth transitions rarely happen.

Another problem in official attitudes is that, with occasional exceptions, G8 governments have felt more comfortable dealing with large, well-established civil society organisations. Most such associations hail from the global north and involve well-connected professional lobbyists. In this situation marginalised social groups – particularly as grouped in smaller NGOs from the global south – are less likely to get a hearing.

A cautionary note on G8-civil society relations has been issued by Stephen Lewis, former Canadian diplomat, a well-known humanitarian and the UN Secretary-General's former special envoy for HIV/AIDS in Africa. Writing about celebrities as well as many NGOs shortly after the Gleneagles summit, Lewis asserted that Geldof's 'incestuous proximity' to the UK government, his membership of Blair's Commission for Africa and his success with the Live 8 concerts made him 'an inescapable member of the Blair team ... [and] a cheerleader for the G8'. In his passionate advocacy for Africa, Lewis was also critical of the reactions of broader civil society to the outcome of Gleneagles, asserting that Blair had effectively co-opted civil society (Lewis 2005: 26, 146–7). This critique highlights the question of 'who is using whom' in civil society relations with the G8, as well as institutions of global governance more generally.

### Sophistication in civil society tactics

A third major set of circumstances that enhance or detract from civil society engagement of the G8 relates to tactical sophistication (or lack thereof). One positive step in this regard is the formation of civil society coalitions. Civil society associations stand a much better chance of having an impact on the G8 when they network with like-minded groups. The whole tends to be more than a sum of its parts. For example, the Global Call to Action against Poverty (GCAP) has brought together a wide array of CSOs and movements. In contrast, the Ya Basta ('white overalls') group has evoked little NGO solidarity and has had correspondingly less impact.

Civil society has also been more effective when it has recognised and exploited linkages among issues on the G8 agenda. For example, the DATA group has highlighted the connections between debt, AIDS, trade and Africa to good effect. It is important for CSOs to resist the temptation to concentrate only on their own single issues; the pro-independence Puerto Rican groups at the time of the 1976 summit adopted a narrow approach of this kind and consequently had little influence.

Flexibility also contributes to civil society effectiveness in exacting accountability from the G8. More successful CSOs have shown themselves ready to be reactive or proactive, according to the situation at hand. In a reactive vein, CSOs have taken advantage when the G8 is preoccupied with issues that are also important to civil society. In a proactive vein, CSOs have lobbied to get other civil society concerns on the G8 agenda. For example, the Civil G8 in 2006 focused on health, energy and education – the centrepieces of the official G8 agenda – but also raised concerns about human rights. In contrast, anti-privatisation activists at the 2005 counter-summit had no purchase on the agenda of the G8 itself.

CSOs can be more successful in their relationship with the G8 if they recognise that the summit is part of a continuum of various major international meetings that take place across the year. Some CSOs overestimate what the G8 can do and neglect to develop adequate relations with other global forums such as the UN and the WTO. In positively co-ordinated actions, NGOs concerned with implementing the MDGs have consistently advocated in respect of the G8 as well as other relevant international institutions.

Thorough knowledge of the G8 system is crucial in order to maximise potential civil society impact on G8 accountability. Better briefed CSOs will know to engage the whole G8 apparatus, including meetings of ministers, task forces and sherpas. More informed activists are aware of the timing and agenda of meetings, and are familiar with G8 member governments' priorities. The 2005 Chatham House multistakeholder consultation demonstrated the advantages of this approach.

Starting dialogue and lobbying early in the summit process is also an essential civil society tactic. The G8 agenda is developed over at least a year, being gradually formulated and honed from one summit to the next. If CSOs are to influence G8 accountability, they can do so more successfully if they get involved in the process early. For instance, preparations under the umbrella of FIM tend to begin a year or more before each summit.

It has been a continuing challenge for civil society engagement of the G8 to isolate potentially violent or disruptive elements (particularly at certain summit venues). The experiences of Genoa, Gleneagles and Rostock show that violence harms the vast majority of civil society activists who use peaceful and democratic methods. After 9/11, it has become even more crucial for civil society to distance itself from violent groups. This calls for vigilance and self-patrolling at G8 summits. Starting after Genoa in 2001, organisers of peaceful demonstrations have made such efforts, thus avoiding or mitigating violent confrontation.

Certain NGOs and other CSOs choose not to engage with the G8. Strategies of co-operation or non-co-operation may be chosen on grounds of resources or ideology. Is it worth expending time and energy on dialogue and other interaction with G8 governments around summits and ministerial meetings? Is it right to refuse engagement with the G8 (and associated insider influence) because the institution is perceived to be illegitimate or not truly powerful? These choices raise difficult questions for civil society. Kumi Naidoo highlighted this dilemma as Secretary-General of CIVICUS, asking: 'Do we walk away from [the G8] because we are not getting what we would like to see ...? Is it better to have miniscule focus because we cannot get the full prize?' (Naidoo 2007).

When a host government is unwilling to interact with civil society, CSOs have other means to influence G8 accountability. They can draft and disseminate policy papers, engage in dialogue with receptive non-host G8 governments, and stage parallel events (including in another country if necessary). Moreover, national NGOs based in G8 countries are in a strong position to lobby their own government. In 2004, even though the host government shunned civil society contacts, African civil society groups were nonetheless active in the USA, advocating for stronger G8 action on debt, development, trade and AIDS.

## Conclusion

This chapter has examined the role of civil society in enhancing the democratic accountability of the G8. The analysis established that the G8, a powerful transgovernmental network, has significant accountabilities but struggles to deliver on them adequately, particularly in respect of correction and redress.

Civil society has had a major role in enhancing G8 accountability, especially as regards the dimensions of consultation and evaluation. However, much more could be done to raise these democratic benefits. The previous section has noted a number of steps that could allow civil society activities more fully to realise their potentials to enhance G8 accountability.

The wider implications of these findings regarding civil society and the G8 are mainly explored in the Conclusion to this book, but already here several observations can be made. For one thing, the principle of 'mutual accountability' that has been articulated in regard to the G8 might have broader applicability to global governance at large. On a different point, the case of the G8 suggests that accountability relations are particularly difficult to consolidate when a global governance institution is informally constituted and operated. In addition, the G8 experience, along with other cases explored in this book, emphasises the importance – in terms of improving accountability – of conducting continuous, substantive and meaningful consultations with civil society groups, as opposed to politically empty ad hoc rituals. Civil society associations engaging other global governance bodies could also learn from the work of citizen groups that have maintained systematic and transparent multi-year monitoring and evaluation of G8 commitments. Further lessons that might be drawn from the history of civil society engagement of the G8 include: the (thus far underdeveloped) use of parliamentary channels to exact democratic accountability from global governance; the positive contributions to be had from such methods as peaceful demonstrations, petitions and mass media campaigns; and the importance of cohesive – if not necessarily integrated – action by civil society vis-à-vis global governance. All of these possible wider implications invite further research, as is partly undertaken in the rest of this book.

Meanwhile history moves on, perhaps beyond the G8. As stressed earlier, it has long been clear that inadequate global representation in the G8 compromises its accountability. Recent developments – notably the emergence of a distinct G5 of the major developing countries and the first G20 leaders summits – present potential opportunities for greater accountability, and new challenges for civil society.

# 10 Structuring accountability: civil society and the Asia-Europe Meeting

*Julie Gilson*

## Introduction

The Asia-Europe Meeting (ASEM) began in 1996 as a biennial summit of heads of state (or their representatives) from the two regions of East Asia and the European Union (EU). In total ASEM now comprises forty-five 'co-operation partners' from the two regions. On the Asian side there are the Association of Southeast Asian Nations (ASEAN) Secretariat, Brunei, Cambodia, China, India, Indonesia, Japan, South Korea, Laos, Malaysia, Mongolia, Myanmar, Pakistan, the Philippines, Singapore, Thailand and Vietnam. On the European side there are the European Commission, Austria, Belgium, Bulgaria, Cyprus, the Czech Republic, Denmark, Estonia, Finland, France, Germany, Greece, Hungary, Ireland, Italy, Latvia, Lithuania, Luxembourg, Malta, the Netherlands, Poland, Portugal, Romania, Slovakia, Slovenia, Spain, Sweden and the United Kingdom.

The ASEM process is an instance of interregionalism. This form of global governance contrasts with the intergovernmentalism and transgovernmentalism that characterise the institutions covered in the preceding case studies in this book. Interregional arrangements bring pre-existing regions together in what might be termed a 'macro-regional' union. Although such constructions have generally remained modest in ambition and accomplishment so far, some analysts regard interregionalism as an emergent new multilateralism that will become increasingly important in the future (Hänggi *et al.* 2006).

In addition to ASEM, other examples of interregionalism include the formal connections that the EU has developed with ASEAN since 1980, the Andean Pact since 1983, the Gulf Cooperation Council (GCC) since 1989 and the Southern Common Market (MERCOSUR) since 1995. Elsewhere the South Atlantic Peace and Cooperation Zone has operated since 1986 and now links twenty-four states of Africa and South America.

I am very grateful to Tina Ebro for her valuable comments.

In another instance of interregionalism, one modelled on ASEM, the Forum for East Asia-Latin America Cooperation (FEALAC) was first convened in 1999 and covers governments from thirty-three countries in those two regions.

Interregionalism through ASEM represents an example of global governance, both in the sense that it draws participants from several continents, and in that it addresses global issues. Thus, for example, the Helsinki Declaration on the Future of ASEM, which issued from the sixth ASEM summit in 2006, expressed the continued goal for ASEM to advance United Nations-led agendas. The Helsinki Declaration also identified a host of global issue areas for co-operation, including climate change, interfaith dialogue and trade (ASEM 2006b).

Like intergovernmental and transgovernmental forms of global governance, interregionalism through the ASEM process has a civil society dimension. The summits, each based on a given theme, formally accommodate representatives from business and trade unions as well as the Asia-Europe Foundation (ASEF). The Foundation, formed under ASEM auspices in 1997, is tasked with promoting intercultural dialogue and social exchange. In addition, on the margins of the official ASEM process is the notable voice of the Asia-Europe People's Forum (AEPF). The Forum has convened an alternative conference of non-state actors alongside every ASEM governmental summit since 1996.

In the context of the present book, then, it is important to ask whether, in what ways, and how far civil society engagement of the ASEM process enhances public accountability in this interregional governance apparatus. The AEPF in particular has highlighted questions about accountability in the actions of ASEM decision-makers. However, the ways in which the AEPF and others have been able to advance accountability within ASEM have been contingent upon the particular structural conditions in which the parties have had to function.

Some of the structural framing of civil society efforts to bring accountability to ASEM has related to the organisation of the summits themselves. Thus, for example, business and trade union associations participate directly in the formal ASEM process, whilst the AEPF has little direct input. In practice, the AEPF has generally obtained better access around those summits held in Europe, where more ministers are willing – and need – to be seen to talk with civil society. In contrast, a number of Asian governments continue to be wary about the participation in ASEM of non-state actors, particularly non-governmental organisations (NGOs) in the AEPF. For instance, when South Korea hosted ASEM in 2000, it located the AEPF quite far from the official venue, and many overseas activists were not permitted into the country. The police were also heavy-handed in their treatment of demonstrators against ASEM (Kim undated).

Other structural impediments to civil society access to ASEM have related to underlying economic and political conditions. For example, it is expensive to run parallel summits, as the AEPF has done. Moreover, NGOs from the global north have traditionally had greater resources, experience and contacts to engage with the ASEM process, whereas some civil society representatives from the global south have simply lacked the means to attend. In this light, many government representatives have questioned the legitimacy of what they regard as self-appointed civil society elites.

Given such considerations this study argues, in line with Marcelo Saguier, that political agency 'cannot be conceived independently from the changing structures of opportunity available to political actors at a given time' (2004: 7). Hence the forms and extent of accountability that civil society can extract from ASEM are shaped by the structural frames of reference of agents, by their (power) relationships with one another, and by both the internal and external mechanisms available to them for ensuring such accountability. Moreover, the chapter asks, in line with Walden Bello, whether meaningful accountability mechanisms can be developed within arrangements such as ASEM whose modes of operation may not be conducive to transparency and scrutiny (Bello 2000).

To elaborate this argument the first part of this chapter outlines the broad mandate and activities undertaken beneath the ASEM umbrella and assesses the constituencies to whom ASEM might be seen to be accountable. The second part examines the challenges faced by ASEM in addressing questions of accountability. Part three describes in more detail the civil society actors and activities that engage the ASEM process. The fourth section examines the results to date of civil society accountability claims on ASEM with reference to transparency, consultation, evaluation and correction. The fifth part looks critically at challenges of accountability facing civil society associations themselves in the ASEM process. The chapter concludes with an assessment of the principal forces that have constrained and facilitated civil society promotion of accountability in ASEM to date.

## The ASEM process in summary

The ASEM process started as a means of redressing a communication gap during the 1990s between the states of the EU and dynamically growing economies in East Asia. (For general accounts of ASEM see

Stokhof and Van de Velde 1999; Gilson 2002; Robles 2008; Yamamoto and Yeo 2006; Reiterer 2009.) ASEM has sought to address many of the matters raised in global fora such as the World Trade Organization (WTO) and the United Nations (UN). Attempts have also been made to broaden ASEM debates to include a range of other subjects.

The inaugural ASEM summit was held in Bangkok in March 1996 and brought together the heads of state or government of the then sixteen members (including the European Commission). That meeting for the first time assembled 'Europe' and 'Asia' (notably without representation from the United States) in a three-pillared dialogue encompassing economic, political and socio-cultural affairs. The Chair's Statement issuing from the Bangkok summit celebrated a new partnership based on a common commitment to: a market economy; a multilateral trading system based on non-discrimination and liberalisation; and what was called 'open regionalism'.

Two years later the second ASEM summit was held in London and focused on how Europe and Asia might jointly address the worst effects of the 1997 Asian financial crisis. ASEM 3, held in Seoul in 2000, coincided with a North-South Korean rapprochement that encouraged leaders to open a broad security dialogue. The fourth ASEM summit, in Copenhagen in 2002, continued the growing focus on the Korean peninsula and a host of other issues. ASEM 5, held in Hanoi in 2004, saw an enlargement of ASEM to thirty-nine states. Myanmar/Burma was only accepted as a member if it sent representation lower than the head of state.

The hosts of ASEM 6 in Helsinki in 2006 developed the theme of 'Ten Years of ASEM: Global Challenges – Joint Responses' in an attempt to revive some of the earlier intentions of the Meeting. Priorities for collective action were deemed to include multilateralism in finance and trade, security threats of all kinds, energy and climate issues, globalisation and global economic changes, and intercultural dialogue.

ASEM 7, held in Beijing in 2008, brought a second round of enlargement, to forty-five countries. As a result, the assembled leaders now represented more than half of the world's population. This summit had to address a growing global financial crisis and also focused on sustainable development (ASEM 2009).

The biennial ASEM summits invariably issue a Chair's Statement to summarise the nature of the discussions. Several summits have also issued additional proclamations, such as the Seoul Declaration for Peace on the Korean Peninsula from ASEM 3 and the Declaration on Cooperation against International Terrorism from ASEM 4. Meanwhile ASEM 7 issued the Beijing Declaration on Sustainable Development and the Statement of the Seventh Asia-Europe Meeting on the International Financial Situation.

Between summits a wide range of ministerial meetings are held in the ASEM framework. For example, an ASEM Finance Ministers' Meeting began in 1997 to discuss issues related to the global economy and the international financial architecture. A meeting of finance deputies usually takes place alongside these gatherings. Meetings of ASEM economic ministers have convened almost every two years since 1997 to discuss the promotion of commerce in the interregional context. Other ASEM meetings have brought together foreign ministers (for the overall co-ordination of the ASEM process), environment ministers, culture ministers and education ministers. Certain other ministerial meetings have convened on an ad hoc basis. In 2009, for instance, special ASEM ministerial conferences were held on subjects including energy security and transport co-operation.

Other ASEM co-operation occurs among ranking civil servants. In this vein Senior Official Meetings (SOMs) are normally held twice a year to provide reports to foreign ministers. In a similar fashion the Senior Officials' Meeting on Trade and Investment (SOMTI) reports to economic ministers. There is also a biennial meeting of customs commissioners from the ASEM countries. With these sorts of networks ASEM is also an instance of transgovernmental relations.

ASEM moreover convenes a range of formal and informal dialogues that offer opportunities for civil society inputs. These discussions have addressed subjects including arms control, disarmament and WMD; welfare of women and children; human resources; development; health; food security and supply; environment and sustainable development; migratory flows; transnational crime/counter-terrorism; globalisation; and human rights. Furthermore, ASEM has sponsored seminars, for example on WTO Trade Facilitation and on Agro Technology and Food Processing. In addition, the Asia-Europe Business Forum and the ASEM Trade Union Forum meet as official components of the ASEM process. Other conferences in the ASEM context that have included civil society input covered education, youth, culture and interfaith dialogue.

Like the Group of 8 (addressed in Chapter 9), and unlike the other global governance institutions covered in this book, ASEM operates without a permanent secretariat. Overall responsibility for the co-ordination of the ASEM process lies with the regular Foreign Ministers' Meetings, which convene twice a year to address issues raised at previous summits and to formulate recommendations for consideration at the next summit. In addition, Coordinators' Meetings bring together four (rotating) ASEM partners, two from Asia alongside the European Commission and the EU Presidency. Set up to compensate for the lack of a secretariat, these co-ordinating mechanisms reflect an ongoing organisational imbalance between the two regions of ASEM. The European Commission can provide institutional memory for the European governments, but Asian states do not use the ASEAN Secretariat in the same way.

In sum, then, ASEM involves considerably more than a biennial summit. True, some critics wonder about the purpose of the process, given its informality, the now unwieldy membership (in terms of both number and diversity) and a distinct lack of commitment on the part of (notably) European heads of government. Yet it can also be argued that ASEM provides a forum for solving common problems and strengthening multilateralism. Indeed, for seasoned observer Lay Hwee Yeo, ASEM is a long-term partnership designed not only to improve general relations between Asia and Europe and to increase trade and investment, but also to develop new rules and standards (Reiterer 2009: 191–2). Thus, whilst ASEM may seem to be primarily a talking shop, it should not be too readily overlooked as a forum in which decisions are formulated, if not formally stamped. Important accountability implications arise as a result.

### Accountability matters

Chapter 1 of this book set out four dimensions of accountability: namely transparency, consultation, evaluation and correction. Both the official and the civil society channels of ASEM face a range of challenges in terms of each criterion. The present section examines how the official ASEM process measures up on democratic accountability. The role of civil society in enhancing ASEM accountability is addressed in the following sections.

The general point to stress from the outset is that ASEM suffers from major shortfalls in democratic accountability, perhaps even more so than the intergovernmental organisations discussed in earlier chapters. ASEM involves global governance through informal, non-binding processes, which makes it all the harder to identify who is accountable to whom, for what and how.

With regard to transparency, few ordinary citizens of any ASEM member state know what ASEM stands for, what it does, or who represents them within it. Despite the fact that EU treaty obligations require member states to account to their citizens for their actions, and in spite of pledges made within ASEM summits for greater visibility, in practice ASEM has operated behind closed doors. As One World Action, a UK-based NGO, notes regarding ASEM: 'The public, the media and national parliaments do not have influence or even obtain detailed knowledge about the content of the discussions' (One World Action 2007).

Low transparency of ASEM has resulted in part from the absence of a regular flow of public information. For years official information regarding ASEM was mostly limited to ad hoc reporting on websites of the government hosting the most recent summit. It was hoped that the inclusion of the ASEAN Secretariat as a partner into ASEM in 2007 would offer greater institutional memory and a record of ASEM activities for all Asian partners. In practice, however, the ASEAN Secretariat has remained a passive participant and does not even mention its ASEM membership on its own website (ASEAN 2009).

Poor public visibility of ASEM has also derived from the relative lack of public persona and media profile around the process, even its summit gatherings. The United States is absent, and many of the participating governments, especially on the European side, accord ASEM little prominence. The mainstream media therefore largely neglect the institution. The annex to the 2006 Helsinki Declaration promises the immediate development of a 'public communication strategy'; however, it is not clear how such a promise can be effectively delivered (ASEM 2006b: 6).

ASEM is also notable for the lack of public consultation in its processes. Many of the constituencies who are implicated in the ASEM agenda – through, for example, policies on trade, poverty eradication, disease control, environmental protection and labour protection – do not have any form of direct participation in the preparation, conduct or follow-up of ASEM meetings. Moreover, in many cases these affected groups lack voice not only within ASEM, but also in their domestic political arenas. The European Parliament, in 2000, regretted the reluctance by Asian states to establish a Social Forum within ASEM that could serve a purpose of wider public consultation to complement activities already involving business and trade unions (Europarl 2000).

Public scrutiny of ASEM through democratic monitoring and evaluation has also been weak. In principle, national parliaments have the power to scrutinise the actions taken by their respective governments in the ASEM context. In practice, however, effective parliamentary oversight of any kind has been decidedly lacking in certain ASEM member states. Even in the working representative democracies national parliaments have given little or no attention to the ASEM process. In the European Parliament, too, ASEM is rarely mentioned, in spite of the existence of an ASEM Inter-Regional Parliamentary Dialogue and a growing role for the European Parliament in discussing ASEM working papers and summit outcomes (Bersick 2008: 252). The final declaration of AEPF 6 (entitled 'People's Vision: Building Solidarity across Asia and

Europe: Towards a Just, Equal and Sustainable World') demanded that the ASEM process become more accountable to national parliaments. ASEM has also not undergone formal independent monitoring and assessment of its actions.

Finally, correction mechanisms are almost impossible in a situation such as ASEM where governance arrangements are so informal and vague. It is unlikely that governments will be removed from office on account of their actions or inactions at ASEM summits. Meanwhile the senior national officials who conduct much of ASEM business are unelected. ASEM has no permanent secretariat or executive director that can be reprimanded, and lacks a legal personality that could make it subject to judicial action. In short, little recourse is available to parties who might be harmed by actions and omissions through the ASEM process.

### ASEM's civil society

What might civil society do to reduce these accountability deficits in ASEM? Before examining civil society impacts on transparency, consultation, evaluation and correction in this interregional manifestation of global governance, it is worth establishing in more detail the character of the civil society that engages the ASEM process. The following paragraphs first describe ASEM's civil society 'insiders', namely the Asia-Europe Business Forum, the ASEM Trade Union Forum and the Asia-Europe Foundation. The discussion then turns to the civil society 'outsiders' of the Asia-Europe People's Forum.

Included in the formal structures of ASEM, the Asia-Europe Business Forum (AEBF) aims to address obstacles and incentives for trade between the two regions, particularly from the perspective of private sector representatives. Over 600 business delegates attended the eleventh AEBF in Beijing, where they called on government leaders to, amongst other things, intervene proactively to address the economic crisis and to initiate a sustainable energy strategy (AEBF 2008).

Similar to the AEBF, the ASEM Trade Union Forum (ATUF) brings together members from Asia and Europe, including umbrella organisations such as the ASEAN Trade Union Council (ATUC) and the European Trade Union Confederation (ETUC). The 2006 Trade Union Forum was organised jointly by the International Confederation of Free Trade Unions (ICFTU), the ETUC, the World Confederation of Labour (WCL), the ICFTU Asian and Pacific Regional Organisation (ICFTU/APRO) and the Brotherhood of Asian Trade Unions (BATU). These bodies jointly called on ASEM 6 to support the multilateral international system and the Doha negotiations, to confront security threats and energy security, and to promote intercultural dialogue (ETUC 2006).

Like the AEBF and the ATUF, the Asia-Europe Foundation (ASEF) has often been criticised for being too closely linked to the governments that sponsor it. In fact the ASEM member states fund ASEF and appoint its Board of Governors. The Foundation is tasked with implementing ASEM proposals and enhancing region-to-region understanding through cultural, intellectual and people-to-people exchanges. Amongst various initiatives, it has developed an Asia-Europe Environment Forum, ASEM Informal Seminars on Human Rights, the Asia-Europe Museum Network (ASEMUS) and the ASEF University Programme. ASEF views its role to be that of an 'interface' between ASEM and its public (ASEF 2009).

Alongside these officially designated channels of interaction, the Asia-Europe People's Forum (AEPF) lobbies from the outside for the rights and representation of groups marginalised within the ASEM project. The AEPF developed on the sidelines of ASEM in the context of a burgeoning NGO sector from the 1980s onwards and the growing presence of civil society representatives at – or at least pressed up against the fences of – a number of major intergovernmental conferences. The agenda of the AEPF is wide, but its core message revolves around 'anti-globalisation', with particular attention to the social inequalities resulting from neoliberal economic policies.

The first Asia-Europe Conference of Non-Governmental Groups, attended by 400 participants, was organised in Bangkok in February 1996 alongside the first ASEM summit. Building on this initiative, the AEPF itself was launched in 1997. Since then the AEPF has organised parallel meetings alongside each ASEM summit.

AEPF gatherings aim to provide a 'space for social actors in each region' to build networks and to develop interregional initiatives. Centrally, the Forum's goal has been to 'provide people's organizations and networks with a channel for *critical engagement* with official ASEM' (italics added). More specifically, the AEPF Charter states that:

The AEPF is an open space for reflective thinking, democratic debate of ideas, formulation of proposals and networking for effective actions by groups and movements of civil society that are opposed to neo-liberalism and to domination of the world by corporate power and any form of imperialism (TNI 2005).

A number of the prominent players in the AEPF illustrate this 'anti-globalisation' orientation. For example, the Transnational Institute (TNI), founded in 1974 and based in Amsterdam, pursues an 'alternative regionalisms' programme from the perspective of social movements in Africa, Asia and Latin America (TNI 2005). The remit of Focus on the Global South, formed in 1995 with its main office in Bangkok, is to 'dismantle oppressive economic and political structures' (Focus on the Global South 2009). Era Consumer, based in Malaysia, campaigns for consumer empowerment among people from all walks of life.

AEPF activities might be regarded as a precursor to the 'participatory regionalism' identified by Acharya (2003: 381) or as a new form of 'social regionalism' (Blackett 2002). The AEPF may be viewed as part of a larger trend – also encompassing initiatives such as the World Social Forum – of building transnational civil society coalitions for social justice.

Co-ordinators of the AEPF are the Institute for Popular Democracy (IPD) in the Philippines, Monitoring Sustainability of Globalisation (MSN) in Malaysia, and TNI in the Netherlands. These bodies sit at the core of an International Organising Committee (IOC), which liaises with National Organising Committees that are based in the countries where the summits are held. Other members of the IOC include Focus on the Global South, Forum Asia, the Vietnam Peace and Development Foundation, Asia House (from Germany) and One World Action.

## Civil society contributions to ASEM accountability

This section examines the ways in which the civil society associations described above – insiders as well as outsiders – have addressed each of the four dimensions of accountability highlighted in this book: transparency, consultation, evaluation and correction. Much of the discussion below focuses on the AEPF, given that it has explicit aims to make the ASEM process more democratically accountable, a task made the more difficult given its status as an outsider group.

### Transparency

Questions of transparency in ASEM have been interpreted differently by the different civil society groups involved. Insiders such as the AEBF, the ATUF and the ASEF have generally exerted little pressure on official circles for greater public visibility of ASEM. In contrast, increased transparency of the ASEM process has been a key concern for outsiders in the AEPF.

Business groups in the AEBF have focused their concerns for transparency in the ASEM context not on the interregional process itself, but rather on government policies around trade and investment. In particular, the AEBF has actively lobbied for a 'fair and transparent market environment for the development of SMEs [small and medium-sized enterprises]' (AEBF 2008). Business cultures differ considerably between Asia and Europe, and where regulatory frameworks lack transparency it is difficult to ensure an even playing field for all.

As for other ASEM insiders, trade unions affiliated to the ATUC have consistently urged that governments make explicit links between economic development and decent treatment of the labour force. However, ATUC advocacy in ASEM has not focused on issues of transparency per se. The ASEF for its part has been tasked by ASEM summits to improve and enhance the public profile and visibility of the interregional process. Through its central remit to foster intercultural relations, the ASEF engages the general public of the two regions, and one of its main purposes today is to ensure that ordinary citizens receive information regarding decisions taken by ASEM leaders. To date, the ASEF has engaged over 14,000 participants in over 350 projects, and it has brought together people from Asia and Europe in particular fields, such as journalism, film, environment and dance (ASEF 2009). Hence the ASEF has raised awareness of ASEM in some circles, although the interregional institution is still unknown to much of the public in most member countries.

Meanwhile transparency of the ASEM process has been a core preoccupation for civil society outsiders in the AEPF. Activists in the AEPF have spent years campaigning for greater access to decision-makers. These critics note that ASEM's aims and objectives are vague. Moreover, the informality of the arrangements can make it difficult for citizens to track ASEM policymaking processes (JCIE 2006). The AEPF also suggests that ASEM's problems with institutional transparency cannot be adequately addressed in the absence of ongoing substantive consultation with civil society actors.

Already the AEPF has, by its vocal presence around the summits, given more public visibility to the ASEM process. The protests have pushed government circles to issue more public declarations of their intentions and to disseminate information about ASEM more widely. In an effort to demonstrate their transparency credentials, leaders also express at least a rhetorical willingness to include civil society in their deliberations.

### Consultation

Consultation is important for all civil society groups involved in ASEM and is closely associated with the issue of access to decision-makers. For some associations consultation is an end in itself, owing to the networks and status that 'participation' generates (Clark *et al.* 1998: 9). For other civil society actors, consultation offers a means to advance advocacy, to exert influence on policy, and to obtain explanations, justifications and redress. In the ASEM context these more substantive purposes have been particularly important for the trade unions and the AEPF.

Consultation of business associations has been fully integrated into the fabric of ASEM through the AEBF since 1996. This grouping has had entry to ASEM plenary sessions involving high-level government figures as well as working group discussions involving senior civil servants. Thus business leaders from both regions have direct access to their counterparts in official circles in order to discuss matters pertaining to global trade in general as well as issues more specifically related to the two regions, such as the enhancement of direct investment between them. Business groups are able to present recommendations directly to official representatives prior to each ASEM summit.

Trade unions have also enjoyed a number of avenues of consultation in the ASEM process. These occasions have included seminars on labour relations and social responsibility, as well as working groups on human rights. The ATUC has actively sought better mechanisms of consultation, for example with proposals that ASEM adapt models from the International Labour Organisation (ILO), the Organisation for Economic Co-operation and Development (OECD), and the EU's social dialogue (ICFTU 2007). The ETUC for its part has stated that 'we need a dialogue mechanism to deal with the social consequences of globalisation that imbeds trade unions in ASEM processes' (ETUC 2006). Collectively, trade union participants successfully lobbied for the establishment of an ASEM Labour and Employment Ministers' Conference in 2006 (ETUC 2006). Advocacy by trade unions also prompted the ASEM Labour Ministers meeting in Bali in 2008 to recognise the need to consult labour representatives more fully, notably through regular meetings with senior officials, greater technical co-operation and the exchange of 'experiences, expertise and good practice' (ASEM Labour 2008).

Union lobbying from the inside also led to the creation in 2006 of the ASEM Social Partners Forum, to deal in general with labour and employment issues. This dialogue brought together 150 labour representatives from more than 40 countries in Asia and Europe. Indonesian and Chinese participants underlined the need to take into account different cultural and political systems when addressing questions of 'decent work'. Nevertheless, the meeting accepted the need for a social dialogue in ASEM and elsewhere to strengthen the social dimension of international institutions. It led to further calls for the formal establishment of a regular Asia-Europe Labour Forum, along the lines of the Asia-Europe Business Forum (ASEM Trade Union 2008).

Like the AEBF and the ATUC, the Asia-Europe Foundation has an automatic right of access to the ASEM process. However, the ASEF is not a consultative body and is used most often as a repository for information. That said, the Foundation does use its position as a convening forum to bring together civil society actors from across the ASEM member countries for deliberations on various topics, and reports from these gatherings are then conveyed to the ASEM governments.

The AEPF, although it has stood outside the formal ASEM process, has nevertheless also provided a channel for public consultation. For example, many Asian and European embassies in Bangkok sent representatives to the NGO conference around the first summit in 1996. The AEPF gained significant access to policy elites in London in 1998 as well as a call from Jacques Santer, then President of the European Commission, for the greater involvement of civil society representatives in the formal ASEM processes (TNI 1998). In 2000 in Seoul, the AEPF obtained hearings with foreign ministry officials and parliamentarians, as well as with the European Commission (TNI 2000). Perhaps surprisingly, the Danish government hosting the ASEM summit in 2002 sent two ministers to meet with the AEBF, but failed to send official representatives to talk with the AEPF (TNI 2002). The Hanoi summit in 2004 did not improve the situation either.

Official consultations with the AEPF were perhaps at their best during the Helsinki summit in 2006. The Prime Minister of Finland had a dialogue with a delegation from the AEPF, and the Foreign Minister participated in the plenary session of the Forum. AEPF participants also had opportunities to lobby a number of national governments. It is no coincidence that the relative success of 2006 was achieved under the auspices of the Finnish hosts, as opportunities for consultation of civil society at ASEM meetings depend largely on the attitudes of the summit organisers. Two years later at Beijing the AEPF once again obtained no hearing in official circles. Access to ASEM for the AEPF therefore remains ad hoc and occasional (JCIE 2006; TNI 2008).

Yet AEPF activism has compelled even reluctant ASEM leaders to acknowledge the value of engaging with NGOs and social movements. Civil society groups have achieved increased media attention on the margins of a number of international meetings. Already at the start of ASEM in 1996, European leaders put their non-democratic counterparts in Asia under pressure to accept the marginal presence of civil society representatives. Leaders of ASEM's Asian states now generally recognise the need to acknowledge, and even to engage with, civil society representatives (Acharya 2003: 386).

Yet greater inclusion in ASEM processes could also carry with it pitfalls for the AEPF. For example, a number of NGOs attending the 2004 Barcelona consultation under the auspices of the Asia-Europe Foundation felt that they had been used to legitimise 'the role of the Foundation as the true representative institution of civil society engagement' in ASEM. That said, the Barcelona Report which resulted from this consultation, and which was subsequently conveyed to ASEM foreign ministers, did signal a serious desire on the part of ASEF to develop 'structures of participatory democracy within the ASEM process', as well as to facilitate the 'democratization of the Asian-European dialogue' (Bersick 2008: 255, 261). In this perspective proximity to the official stratum could advance, rather than hinder, democratic accountability.

Thus in ASEM, as in other institutions discussed in this book, the rhetorical need to recognise and consult with civil society, including its more critical elements like the AEPF, has become a sine qua non of global governance proceedings. However, the structural challenges faced by those involved in parallel summitry in respect of ASEM and other global governance institutions should not be underestimated. NGOs are generally placed in a reactive position of responding to an established agenda and seeking to alter or deflect it, rather than setting the agenda themselves. It can therefore be difficult to widen the debate in ASEM from narrow economic concerns to encompass other issues, for example, human rights or sustainable development.

### Evaluation

One of the roles of both insiders and outsiders in civil society has been to monitor and evaluate the work proposed and implemented in the name of ASEM. However, contributions regarding this aspect of accountability have tended to be less significant than those in respect of consultation (above) and correction (below).

Amongst civil society insiders in the ASEM process, trade union lobbies have consistently reminded official representatives of government pledges to promote and respect peace, democracy and human rights. For example, at the first ASEM Social Partners Forum the General Secretary of the ETUC, John Monks, reminded delegates of the need to keep the issue of Burma on the table (ETUC 2008a). Similarly, the AEBF has evaluated pledges at ASEM in areas from trade to the environment and has made concrete proposals to ensure their implementation. For its part, however, the ASEF has not seen it as its role to monitor and evaluate the actions of ASEM.

On questions of evaluation, as on matters of transparency and consultation, it is the AEPF that has exerted the greatest civil society pressure for a more democratically accountable ASEM process. The AEPF has monitored the continuing democratic deficit within ASEM and has tracked the record of the member states in the pursuit of ASEM's own proclaimed goals, particularly in areas such as human rights and human trafficking. On all manner of subjects – terrorism, privatisation of water, bilateral and regional free trade, and democratisation – members of the AEPF have gathered and collated data, compiled and written reports, and charted the effects and consequences of ASEM decisions. In addition, the AEPF has over the years been consistent and increasingly well organised in lobbying national parliaments to bring greater democratic scrutiny to the ASEM process. However, the lack of available mechanisms for sanction or redress limits the efficacy of AEPF monitoring and evaluation.

### Correction

As Sikkink argues, 'the agency of transnational actors is defined by their attempts to restructure world politics by creating and publicizing new norms and discourses' (2002: 306, cited in Saguier 2004: 15). In relation to ASEM the main correction pursued by civil society groups has been to shift policy discourses away from an economistic neoliberalism and towards greater concern for social issues. (As indicated in other chapters of this book, civil society strivings along these lines have also unfolded in respect of the International Monetary Fund, the Organisation for Economic Co-operation and Development and the World Bank.) Trade unions and the AEPF have figured most prominently in these efforts, which have made some modest advances.

Trade union groups have over a number of years called on ASEM leaders to remedy their 'partial view of the world' and to create adequate mechanisms for welfare provision, public services and social dialogue (ETUC 2008b). The ETUC subscribes to EU aspirations to advance, through ASEM, sustainable economic and social development, and to promote effective multilateralism with a particular aim to realise the UN Millennium Development Goals. However, the union confederation contends that ASEM is hamstrung by a 'mercantilist, limited view of the world' (ETUC 2006, 2008a). Trade, the ETUC maintains, is not an end in itself, and leaders must not lose sight of the core social dimensions involved.

Similarly, the AEPF has since 1996 consistently pushed ASEM to integrate socio-political and cultural factors into its economics-led agenda.

In this spirit the first AEPF conference in Bangkok was themed Beyond Geo-politics and Geo-economics: Towards a New Relationship between Asia and Europe. Four years later AEPF 3 in Seoul brought together over 800 people from 33 countries under the banner of People's Action and Solidarity Challenging Globalisation. ASEM 6 in 2006 called for a new, just and equitable Asia-Europe partnership, one focused on a social dimension and people's rights. In these ways the Forum has consistently rejected the 'geo-economics' of ASEM and pressed the interregional meetings to focus on issues such as human rights, child prostitution, rights of migrant workers, ethical investment, protection of the environment, and the inequitable nature of current world trade agreements (AEPF 2007).

The AEPF and the trade unions have often teamed up in order to promote these social corrections of the neoliberal agenda that has predominated in ASEM. Around ASEM 6 the AEPF and labour organisations issued a joint memorandum that called for the strengthening of the social dimension of globalisation, and policies to promote human and social rights (AEPF 2007). In response, government leaders acknowledged the desirability of establishing a social pillar within ASEM, and several months later ASEM labour and employment ministers convened in Potsdam under the banner of More and Better Jobs – Working Jointly to Strengthen the Social Dimension of Globalisation. In addition, the AEPF and trade unions have lobbied for the promotion of workers' rights within ASEM's Trade Facilitation Action Plan and its Investment Promotion Action Plan.

Civil society activism around ASEM has also reverberated beyond the interregional meetings to encourage political liberalisation in some of the member states. For some civil society actors (such as the Institute for Popular Democracy in the Philippines) engagement in the regional sphere, through ASEM, has expanded political space in national politics. Parallel summitry alongside ASEM has highlighted the significance of civil society voices, especially in relation to Asian states where autonomous civic action is often discouraged or even forbidden. For example, the 1998 'People's Vision towards a more just, equal and sustainable world' was elaborated and endorsed by hundreds of people's organisations across Asia and Europe, thereby illustrating the importance of civil society networks per se (TNI 1998). The final declaration of AEPF 6 demanded that the ASEM process 'recognize and respond to people's needs and rights and become more transparent and accountable to national parliaments' (AEPF 2006). The AEPF has also facilitated space for the emergence of some regional coalitions of NGOs in East Asia (Lizee 2000; see also Acharya 2003: 383).

Notable examples include Forum Asia and Solidarity for Asian People's Advocacy (SAPA).

The preceding examples illustrate how, despite lacking formal powers, civil society groups can have significant bearing on ASEM policies. Nevertheless, on the whole ASEM remains a shadowy forum, and NGOs have difficulties in gaining public support to counter ASEM-derived policies. In particular the inability to impose sanctions has severely constrained the influence of the AEPF and other civil society actors vis-à-vis ASEM.

### Civil society accountability in ASEM

For all that the AEPF has sought to extract democratic accountability from ASEM, official circles in ASEM often resist participation by the AEPF on the grounds that the self-styled 'People's Forum' itself lacks accountability. Certainly, civil society associations in many parts of Asia have been subjected to increased scrutiny, not only from their beneficiaries, but also from donors, partners and their own staff (Kim 2004: 22). Critical questions about the accountability of NGOs and other civil society actors are also increasingly raised in Europe.

In the ASEM context, as elsewhere in global governance, NGOs often have complex accountability relationships with multiple constituencies. Whilst representing the disenfranchised and giving a voice to those who have none, NGOs are often directly accountable to wealthy (usually Western) donors. These civil society actors are therefore prone to tailor their functions to the demands not of the needy, but of the rich. Whilst providing welfare services (often in lieu of the state), NGOs may be bound tightly to the reins of a particular government. In certain Asian countries linkage to the state may form the very basis of civil society, as associations need government approval in order to function as NGOs. These groups may operate few mechanisms for internal scrutiny, and critics from abroad increasingly demand that they 'validate their participation in ... democratic governance in an accountable and effective manner' (Kim 2004: 22). However, Grant and Keohane warn against overly rigid liberal interpretations of NGOs and accountability, and instead advise openness to other kinds of 'opportunities for limiting abuses of power' (2005: 15).

Yet questions do need to be asked about the internal accountability mechanisms of NGOs in the AEPF. Non-state groups certainly can have an important role in mediating the interests of unheard affected communities, but this position demands accountability as well. The People's Forum assembles highly diverse groups with highly diverse constituencies. The organisers of the AEPF tend to be well endowed with funds, expertise and media exposure. These more powerful NGOs issue from environments in which they focus on regional and global issues per se. In contrast, many smaller NGOs simply do not have the capacities to govern the process of civil response. Their priorities and perspectives, perhaps more locally and nationally focused, may be marginalised even within the AEPF. That said, new funding streams from (predominantly Western) donors may be generating new opportunities for international engagement by local Asian NGOs, and the AEPF has increased its visibility as a point of contact for many small NGOs. For example, in preparation for the 2000 AEPF the International Organising Committee and the Korea People's Forum consulted with various NGOs in four Asian and five European countries.

Hence the mere fact of realising positive achievements should not constitute a 'magic wand of accountability' to legitimise the AEPF (Ebrahim and Weisband 2007: 2). As Tian Chua, director of the Labour Resource Centre in Malaysia has observed, 'NGOs have to be much more critical, not just of government *but of ourselves*' (*Bangkok Post*, 17 September 2004). It is clear that the modernisation and professionalisation of NGOs raise a number of issues about the nature of membership and about accountability.

### Conclusion

This chapter has examined the relationship between civil society and accountable global governance in respect of a major initiative in inter-regionalism, the Asia-Europe Meeting. Key questions raised in other chapters of this book concerning other types of global governance have also applied here. How well have civil society activities increased transparency, consultation, evaluation and redress in the ASEM context? How accountable are these civil society associations themselves? What principal forces have constrained and facilitated the promotion of these accountabilities to date?

One key factor, exemplified by the insider-outsider distinction among civil society actors engaging ASEM, is the question of access to formal decision-making processes. The inclusion of business associations and trade unions and the exclusion of the AEPF mean that the structures for ensuring accountability in ASEM are skewed to the advantage of some constituencies and the disadvantage of others. Civil society in ASEM, as elsewhere in global governance, is not a level playing field. Indeed, the AEPF has focused much of its attention on this issue of access. That said, as the AEPF has also demonstrated, formal exclusion from ASEM decision-making processes need not entail a complete lack of access to, or influence on, official circles. Nevertheless, the insider-outsider hierarchy makes a substantial difference.

In spite of unevenness in their levels of access, the various civil society actors in ASEM do now have possibilities of engaging with official summitry. Contestation of a mutually occupied space creates a basis for greater accountability. The summit and its many associated meetings ensure that there are identifiable and sustained nodes of civil society engagement. Through these channels civil society actors can urge transparency, insist upon consultation, conduct evaluation and demand correction.

Civil society groups have achieved relative success in respect of ASEM thanks in part to their common project of incorporating a stronger social dimension into the interregional structure. Many specific objectives can be gathered under this umbrella goal, which speaks to all parts of civil society: business, labour, cultural entrepreneurs and social activists. The social agenda moreover has the advantage of speaking directly to many of ASEM's own declared aims. All of this suggests that a collective civil society response to the institutional failings of ASEM could deliver more accountable interregionalism in the future.

# 11　Civil society and accountability in the global governance of climate change

*Peter Newell*

## Introduction

This chapter uses the lens of accountability to analyse the strategies of a range of civil society groups in their engagement with key actors in the global regime on climate change. It seeks to account for the degree of effectiveness of these strategies in constructing and enforcing mechanisms of accountability in global climate politics. The point of departure is that accountability is constituted by two key elements: answerability and enforceability (Schedler *et al.* 1999; Newell and Wheeler 2006). The chapter shows that while civil society actors have proven adept at demanding answerability from pivotal actors in the global governance of climate change, enforceability has been weak.

The analysis draws on insights gained by the author during fifteen years of following and engaging with different aspects of the climate regime: as an academic; as an activist; as a former employee of an NGO, Climate Network Europe; and as a contributor to policy work undertaken by United Nations agencies (UNDP and the Earth Council) as well as governments (such as those of the UK, Finland and Sweden). The chapter therefore combines personal reflections, interview material, and academic as well as policy and activist literatures.

Climate change has clearly become a matter of high politics. Once considered a marginal issue, a robust political and scientific consensus now prevails that human interference with the climate system presents an unprecedented challenge and that far-reaching global measures are urgently required to tackle it. Intersections between climate change and other issues such as conflict and war have surfaced amid concerns about how drought and resource scarcity – conditions exacerbated by climate change – may fuel violence in Darfur and elsewhere. Some have claimed that 'climate change is arguably the most persistent threat to global stability in the coming century' (Adger *et al.* 2002: 4).

For these reasons climate change is increasingly recognised as one of the most serious threats currently facing humankind – and its poorest members in particular. Indeed, a multi-donor report on *Poverty and Climate Change* acknowledges that climate change is a serious risk to poverty reduction and threatens to undo decades of development efforts (World Bank Group 2003).

The relative lack of action to date on climate change has less to do with the painfully slow diplomatic processes required to secure global agreement than with the vested interests (governments included) that benefit, in the short term at least, from the current patterns of production and consumption that generate climate change. Indeed, action on climate change touches upon some of the most powerful and well-organised interests in the global economy (Newell and Paterson 1998). In this sense an intimate relationship exists between production, power and governance (Newell 2008).

The nature of this relationship has profound implications for the possibilities of effective action in general and for the prospects of accountability politics in particular. Governments are sharply constrained by the nature of their industrial base, the scope for technological change, and the power of business in those sectors where reform is most required. Most governments face conflicting demands: on the one hand from elements of the public (and electorate) who seek immediate stringent action; and on the other hand from businesses whose tax and employment is central to growth strategies and who may demand less or even no action on climate change (Newell and Paterson 2010).

Touching every aspect of life – food, fuel, transport, etc. – the governance of climate change poses immense challenges. Action is required at all levels: individual, local, provincial, national, regional and global. Problems of co-ordination and coherence across these scales – evident in the governance of many global problems – are magnified to extreme proportions in the case of climate change. The terrain of climate politics shifts rapidly, and policy arenas such as the nation-state, where decisions were traditionally made, become less and less relevant. Instead, policy action on climate change resides in a plurality of private and public, formal and informal sites of regulation (Bulkeley and Newell 2010). This altered framework of governance in itself creates accountability challenges, given that traditional channels of representation and participation often do not exist in private and non-state spheres, and rights to information and consultation are not easily applied to private actors.

In terms of the fourfold conception of accountability developed in Chapter 1 of this book, the present case study argues that some elements of civil society have been successful in enhancing the degree of *transparency* of climate change negotiations. This in turn has increased the possibilities of public scrutiny of relevant officials and agencies. With regard to *participation*, civil society groups have raised awareness of climate change among different publics and have increased levels of public engagement with the issue in both national and international politics. In relation to *evaluation*, civil society groups have published newsletters, worked with the mass media, and produced their own assessments of governments' implementation of their commitments to reduce greenhouse gases. With regard to *correction*, recent climate activism shows a growing interest in using human rights tools as a means to obtain redress for victims of climate change.

Of course, the mere presence of civil society in climate change politics does not in itself increase the accountability of the governance actors involved. Moreover, as is elaborated later in this chapter, the range of civil society participants in global climate politics is unrepresentative of global society at large, especially its weaker members.

The chapter is structured as follows. The next section provides an overview of the global regime on climate change. The third section explores the accountability challenges that characterise efforts to hold states and other actors to account for their actions or inactions on climate change. The fourth section details a diversity of civil society engagements with the climate regime and assesses their implications for accountability, particularly in terms of participation, evaluation and redress. The final section summarises key insights and arguments in the chapter, and also raises the issue of civil society's own accountability.

## The global regime on climate change

Global responses to the threat of climate change date back to the late 1980s, when scientific input was organised in the form of the Intergovernmental Panel on Climate Change (IPCC). This body was tasked to provide state-of the-art reviews of the science of climate change to feed into policy deliberations. A succession of four IPCC Assessment Reports on climate change – produced in 1990, 1995, 2001 and 2007 – have repeatedly underscored the need for immediate action (Liverman 2007).

In addition to this knowledge base, UN climate change negotiations are underpinned by an important institutional infrastructure. A Secretariat to support the operation of the United Nations Framework Convention on Climate Change (UNFCCC) has been based in Bonn since 1996 and currently comprises a staff of around 200 people. Led by an Executive Secretary, the Secretariat organises the negotiations, prepares documentation, provides technical expertise and is responsible for overseeing reporting of emissions profiles and projects funded through the Kyoto

Protocol. Its key role in shaping the outcomes of negotiations is often underestimated (Depledge 2005).

The main intergovernmental forum of the climate change regime is the Conference of the Parties (COP) to the UNFCCC and the Kyoto Protocol. The COP meets annually to review progress on commitments contained in those treaties and to update them in the light of the latest scientific advice. This is the ultimate decision-making body in the climate negotiations.

Other agencies related to the UNFCCC include the Subsidiary Body on Implementation (SBI) and the Subsidiary Body on Science and Technological Advice (SBSTA), as well as Ad Hoc Working Groups that take forward negotiations on specific issues. For example, there is currently an Ad Hoc Working Group on Further Commitments for Annex 1 Parties under the Kyoto Protocol. All proposals emanating from these bodies require approval of the COP.

Negotiations towards the UNFCCC began in 1991 and produced an accord in 1992 at the first United Nations Conference on Environment and Development (or 'Earth Summit') in Rio de Janeiro. The UNFCCC identifies the nature of the problem, articulates guiding norms such as the precautionary principle, defines 'common but differentiated responsibilities' (in particular establishing the overriding responsibility of the industrialised global north to act first), and sets in train procedures for the delivery of aid and technology transfer to developing countries to enable their involvement in the collective effort to address the problem. The Framework Convention also required parties to 'aim' towards stabilising their emissions of greenhouse gases (GHGs) at 1990 levels by the year 2000. The UNFCCC entered into force in 1994 after fifty states had ratified the agreement.

As the 1990s progressed and scientific assessments exposed the inadequacy of existing policy responses, momentum grew for a follow-up to the UNFCCC. Negotiations began on a protocol that would set legally binding targets to reduce emissions of GHGs. After a series of tense negotiations, the Kyoto Protocol was concluded in 1997. This global agreement set differentiated targets for industrialised countries, whose collective output of GHGs was to be reduced by an average of 5.2 per cent below 1990 levels in the commitment period 2008–12. The Protocol also set in train processes to elaborate joint implementation schemes, to establish an emissions trading scheme, and to create a Clean Development Mechanism (CDM) (Newell 1998).

Yet progress in global governance of climate change remained slow after Kyoto. A severe blow was the withdrawal from the Kyoto process of the US Government in March 2001 under President George W. Bush.

This move from the country that was then the largest single contributor to the problem undermined the effectiveness of the Protocol and the inclination of other states to ratify it. The Kyoto Protocol did enter into force in 2004 following ratification by the Russian Duma. Nevertheless, with continuing opposition from the Bush Administration many climate activists felt that, in the words of one, 'the chances of our getting anywhere near where we need to be with international diplomacy are grim' (Pettit 2004: 102). Meanwhile, other activists have seen Kyoto as the only game in town and have been unwilling to give up on an agreement they worked so hard to secure.

Following a divisive COP at The Hague in November 2000, accords at the Marrakesh COP in November 2001 sought to establish rules to govern the increasing use of market mechanisms as a means to reduce GHG emissions. Operational details for the CDM were elaborated, and three new funds were created, including the Adaptation Fund. At Buenos Aires in 2004, COP 10 agreed a Programme of Work on Adaptation and Response Measures. COP 11 in Montreal created the aforementioned Ad Hoc Working Group on Further Commitments for Annex 1 Parties under the Kyoto Protocol. COP 12 in Nairobi, dubbed the 'Africa COP', involved significant discussion about financing issues and how to increase the number of CDM projects being hosted by the poorest regions of the world, most notably Sub-Saharan Africa. The Bali Action Plan agreed in 2007 at COP 13 set a path for negotiations on long-term emissions reductions and the means of realising them (Bulkeley and Newell 2010).

Twenty years of global policy development on climate change have witnessed a number of key shifts in the deliberations. For one thing, as each new IPCC report has strengthened the scientific consensus behind climate change, the focus of debate has tended to shift from securing evidence of climate change to constructing rules and institutions for the reduction of GHG emissions. In particular, the emphasis has moved towards evaluating the economic costs of action and who should bear these.

A second shift has seen increased interest in the use of 'flexible' market-based mechanisms to achieve lower emissions of GHGs. Emissions trading schemes have been set up in many countries and regions, and carbon offset schemes exist both within the compliance market overseen by the UN and within private voluntary markets. A large market in voluntary carbon offsets has developed since 2001, growing from 3–5 megatonnes (Mt) of carbon in 2004 to 65 Mt in 2007 (Bayon et al. 2007: 14). Governance of these markets involves a variety of state and non-state actors, which in turn raises issues of accountability, credibility and quality control (Newell et al. 2009).

A third shift in recent years has been increasing demands for emissions reductions from rapidly industrialising developing countries as their contributions to the problem of climate change increase. Indeed, the country that makes the largest aggregate (albeit not per capita) contribution of GHG emissions is now China.

A fourth issue that increasingly features on the agenda is adaptation to the effects of climate change. Amid clear evidence that climate change threatens the livelihoods of many of the world's poorest groups, governments are exploring ways to reduce these vulnerabilities. A key related question is how to generate the vast resources necessary to address this problem.

### Accountability challenges

The question of accountability in global environmental governance has been sorely neglected. Whilst some work has examined issues of transnational accountability with respect to environmental harm (Mason 2005; Elliott 2006), and other reflections have considered closely associated concepts such as responsibility (Pellizzoni 2004), critical thinking about accountability has not been seriously applied to the public and private arenas in which global environmental politics play out. Since I have elsewhere developed a framework for thinking about accountability in global environmental governance (Newell 2008), I confine the present discussion to a few general remarks.

It is also worth noting that many of the general debates about global governance and public accountability also apply to the specific case of climate change. Highly pertinent, for example, is the question that Held and Koenig-Archibugi pose at the start of their book on *Global Governance and Public Accountability*: 'To what extent are those who shape public policies accountable to those affected by their decisions?' (Held and Koenig-Archibugi 2005: 1). Climate change also parallels other issue areas inasmuch as accountability is both *conferred from above* and *claimed from below*. Thus activists seek on the one hand to occupy spaces offered by official institutions and on the other hand to create new spaces of their own. Around climate change, as on other global issues, civil society groups make accountability demands not only of global bodies, but also of regional institutions, nation-states and a range of non-state actors.

Indeed, in the case of climate change, where the Secretariat of the UNFCCC has relatively little direct influence over the climate policies of individual governments, campaigners have understandably directed their advocacy towards other targets, in particular the European Union (EU) and the US Government. It also makes sense for civil society groups to lobby global bodies such as the World Bank and the International Monetary Fund, since these institutions oversee large amounts of financial resources and wield significant power over the governments to which they lend. In contrast, the United Nations Environment Programme (UNEP) and the secretariats of individual global environmental agreements lack such influence and have a weak position within the UN system overall. Civil society organisations can and do submit evidence to these global bodies on governments' progress in meeting their obligations; however, sanctions for inaction tend to rely on national publics or pressure from other states. Thus, in respect of climate change, citizens have most often directed accountability demands towards the national arena (or regional institutions in the case of the EU).

Casting the issue of the global governance of climate change in terms of accountability politics, a number of key points emerge. First, compared with many other global concerns, the politics of climate change has generally been relatively open and transparent. This is in sharp contrast to other issue areas explored in this book and elsewhere, which are marked by sensitivities around commercial confidentiality or state security. Moreover, in other issue areas the nature of bargaining (reciprocal rather than open-ended) and the nature of the knowledge base (subject to elite expertise) have diminished the possibilities for the fuller engagement of civil society as a democratising force.

A second major accountability challenge derives from the fact that governance of climate change is highly dispersed and fragmented. Rights and responsibilities are shared among a multitude of actors operating across numerous scales and at a bewildering number of sites. Relevant actors include global institutions such as the IPCC and the UNFCCC Secretariat, regional bodies such as the EU, national governments (including transgovernmental networks of environmental regulators), groupings of cities, coalitions of corporate actors, and an array of civil society networks. Each is a source of governance in its own right, producing standards and regulations, creating norms of behaviour and developing reporting mechanisms to oversee implementation (Bulkeley and Newell 2010). As noted in Chapter 1, with such a panoply of actors it is often difficult to specify who is accountable for the governance of which aspect of such a multifaceted issue as climate change.

A third critical concern regarding accountability is that the actors who are charged with the main responsibility for action on climate change exercise only limited direct authority and influence over the actors who contribute most to the problem. Geoffrey Heal notes that carbon dioxide is produced as a result of:

billions of decentralised and independent decisions by private households for heating and transportation and by corporations for these and other needs, all outside the government sphere. The government can influence these decisions, but only indirectly through regulations or incentives (Heal 1999).

A fourth major complication from an accountability point of view is the intergenerational character of the problem. In particular, the effects of GHG emissions produced by the current generation will create consequences for future generations over many decades and centuries. Indeed, some effects of climate change that are experienced today have resulted from the build-up of gases going back as far as the Industrial Revolution. The political challenge derives from the obvious fact that future generations – those who will suffer the worst effects of climate change – do not have a voice in current policy deliberations about the issue. These people, as yet unborn, cannot hold present generations to account for their actions and inactions on the global environment.

A fifth key point in the politics of accountability on climate change is *intra*-generational in nature. Here there is a strong North-South element in terms of past and present contributions to climate change and who suffers the worst effects of the problem. Many recent reports, including the 2008 *Human Development Report*, have highlighted a strong social justice dimension to the issue (UNDP 2007–2008). Namely, those who are likely to suffer some of the most severe consequences of climate change not only have historically speaking been the smallest contributors to the problem, but also are least well placed to confront it. The 2007 IPCC report demonstrates quite clearly that poorer and marginalised communities in drought-prone areas, those experiencing water scarcity, and those whose livelihoods depend on agriculture will be the worst affected by climate change and will also have the least capacity to adapt to the consequent disruptions.

A sixth dimension is the intra-national question of accountability between those who pollute most and those who pollute least. Along with the centrality of global north-south relations in climate politics, the geographies of contribution and impact also graft on to patterns of inequality *within* countries. For instance, although India suffers from widespread energy poverty, the $CO_2$ emissions generated by the energy use of the Indian middle class outweigh those of the whole of Australia (ECI 2007). Further climate justice issues arise when the problem is related to cleavages of race and class that cut across national boundaries. Here again social groups that contribute least to environmental problems tend to be most exposed to their worst effects (Newell 2005b).

## Civil society interventions for accountability

Civil society actors have long sought to hold national governments and international institutions to account for their responsibilities to tackle climate change (Arts 1998; Newell 2000; and note parts of this section draw on Newell 2005a). Strategies have included lobbying national governments, seeking access to negotiating delegations, and exposing non-compliance with international agreements. Repertoires of protest have included demonstrations, media work and alternative reporting. Many civil society actors have pursued 'boomerang' effects, whereby pressure in one decision-making arena creates accountability impacts at other sites on other scales (Keck and Sikkink 1998). Environmental NGOs have often sought to attract media attention to global climate conferences through stunts, press conferences and other activities which place the spotlight on a government whose position is stalling progress. The aim of the strategy is to use heightened domestic attention through media exposure as a lever to close accountability gaps which often leave international bureaucrats free from scrutiny by national political institutions and processes.

Of course it should be noted that such 'double-edged' accountability diplomacy – where global politics is influenced by domestic positions and vice versa – can be conducted by social forces that resist environmental action just as easily as by those that promote it. For example, groups opposed to action on climate change tried to hold US negotiators to account for their support of the Kyoto Protocol in the face of significant opposition from a group of US Senators. Industry groups petitioned Senators to reject the ratification of the Kyoto Protocol in the absence of binding emission reduction targets for developing countries, an impossible demand in 1997 and one that sought to tie the hands of US negotiators (Newell 2000).

Meanwhile many other civil society associations have pressed for positive action on climate change, particularly from the 1980s onwards. The World Wildlife Fund (WWF), Greenpeace and Friends of the Earth have been among the most consistently active groups on this issue. In addition, growing acknowledgement of the development impacts of climate change has brought in NGOs such as Third World Network, Oxfam, Christian Aid, Practical Action, and ActionAid.

### Accountability through consultation and participation

Participation from civil society actors in the global climate regime has grown with time. COP 6 in The Hague in 2000 included participants from 323 intergovernmental and non-governmental organisations (Yamin 2001). Seven years later at the Bali COP a total of 4,483 NGO delegates were present. Interestingly, however, while the largest environmental groups made up 2 per cent (WWF) and 1.6 per cent (Greenpeace) of NGO delegates at the Bali meeting, the International Emissions Trading Association (IETA) made up 7.5 per cent of the total, with 336 representatives including lawyers, financiers, consultants, certifiers and emissions trading experts from companies like Shell. The profile of civil society participants has shifted to reflect the increasing role of market-based policy instruments.

In order better to co-ordinate their activities and pool resources, civil society groups have organised themselves into coalitions such as the Climate Action Network (CAN). This grouping was created in 1989 by 63 NGOs from 22 countries under the initial guidance of Greenpeace International and the then Environmental Defense Fund (now Environmental Defense). Today CAN encompasses 430 environmental NGOs from across the globe and maintains regional offices in Africa, Europe, Latin America, and South and South-East Asia (CAN 2008). The network seeks to co-ordinate the strategies of its members on the climate change issue, exchanging information and attempting to develop joint position papers for key international meetings. CAN assembles a broad spectrum of groups who work on various aspects of the climate issue and take different positions on many of the key negotiating matters. The network supports a number of working groups on specific areas of expertise. Gulbrandsen and Andresen suggest: 'Although CAN is more important for the less resource-rich groups than for the major ones, the CAN network is usually an effective way of communicating NGO positions with one voice during the climate negotiations' (2004: 61).

Despite growing cynicism among many civil society actors about the returns from continued engagement with the intergovernmental negotiations on climate change, many groups remain committed to using available channels to influence the future of the Kyoto Protocol. Certainly international environmental law has placed growing emphasis on the importance of public participation. From the 1992 Earth Summit, for example, Agenda 21 calls upon intergovernmental organisations to provide regular channels for NGOs 'to contribute to policy design, decision-making, implementation and evaluation of IGO activities' (United Nations 1992a). Similarly, the Rio Declaration affirms:

Environmental issues are best handled with the participation of all concerned citizens, at the relevant level. At the national level each individual shall have appropriate *access to information* concerning the environment ... and the *opportunity to participate* in decision-making processes. States shall *facilitate and encourage public awareness and participation* by making information widely available. Effective *access to judicial and administrative proceedings, including redress and remedy*, shall be provided. (United Nations 1992b, emphasis added.)

At the same time, it must be recognised that only a fraction of global civil society organisations actively participate in these processes. In particular, groups from the global south are underrepresented in international negotiating processes, because they generally lack the resources required to attend and meaningfully participate in global meetings. Moreover, the global reach of some groups based in the North derives from their access to policymaking processes within powerful states. For example, groups such as the Natural Resources Defense Council (NRDC) and Environmental Defense (ED) have had particular influence on the US Environmental Protection Agency (EPA) and the US Congress (O'Brien *et al.* 2000). Such leverage gives these groups voice and influence which is out of all proportion to the number of people that they represent. As a result, some developing country governments have resisted moves to open up regional and global policy processes on climate change to further participation from civil society. The argument is that well-resourced civil society associations can influence their own government both nationally and within global and regional forums, allowing them 'two bites at the apple' in ways that are not available to less well-resourced groups (Wilkinson 2002).

Better-resourced civil society organisations are indeed able to shape each stage of the policy process on climate change, from agenda-setting through negotiation processes to policy implementation. Some, such as WWF, have greater global reach by virtue of having country offices across the world. This presence puts them in a better position to push governments to ratify agreements. Although civil society is generally considered to be poorly resourced, the finances available to larger environmental NGOs easily exceed the funds available to, say, UNEP. For example, WWF has around 5 million members worldwide and total annual income of around US\$391 million. Greenpeace International has more than 2.5 million members in 158 countries and an annual budget of around US\$30 million. Friends of the Earth has over a million members in 58 countries (Yamin 2001: 151). Resources on this scale are not available to many other civil society groups in climate politics, of course.

Various models have been employed to account for the influence of these NGOs in the climate regime (Arts 1998; Betsill and Correll 2001; Newell 2000). Specific instances where activist pressure has shifted government and corporate positions have been documented elsewhere

(Newell 2000, 2005a). Conclusive attribution of influence remains a daunting task, however, when so many variables and contextual factors are at play. Combinations of direct civil society interventions (drafting text, providing advice, conducting research that informs policy) and indirect pressure (through media and public awareness-raising) can directly shape policy and indirectly create expectations that action is necessary, desirable and morally imperative.

Moreover, civil society activists in different parts of the world have uneven opportunities to engage with and shape state policy and inter-governmental negotiations. For example, some key states whose political positions and climate footprint strongly influence the global climate change regime, most notably China, are subject to less democratic pressure than the other main players in the process. In contexts such as this, activists have sought instead to pressure transnational corporations that operate in the country.

In addition, civil society groups lobbying on climate change tend to have better links with those parts of the state that have least overall power. While many activists have good relations with environment ministries, these departments often find their positions challenged, undermined or reversed by more powerful ministries of trade, industry and finance. Here influence with one part of the state can be dissipated by the veto role of more powerful ministries.

One distinction that is often employed to explain different degrees of civil society influence over the climate negotiations is the division between 'insider' and 'outsider' groups. In practice, the insider-outsider distinction describes a spectrum of access and influence rather than a hard and fast dichotomy. Moreover, groups move between different points on this spectrum over time as they reorient their strategies. Nevertheless, it is the case that some groups have resources, expertise and connections to key government officials that allow them to exert a much greater direct influence upon the decision-making process. Meanwhile other groups, owing to their campaigning agendas, lack of resources and choice of strategy, tend to be excluded from the centres of decision-making power. Such distinctions are often described in terms of North-South divisions. However, some research-based NGOs in the global south have close connections to government delegations, including The Energy and Resources Institute (TERI) in India and the Bangladesh Centre for Advanced Studies (BCAS) in Bangladesh.

Ultimately, 'insider' influence by civil society in climate politics often comes down to key individuals whose experience, understanding of the process and research capabilities mean they are trusted advisors and confidantes of governments. Frequently these personal attributes, rather than the characteristics of the organisation that such individuals represent, determine their degree of access to and impact on the policymaking process. For instance, M. J. Mace and Farhana Yamin, both at different times with the Foundation for International Environmental Law and Development (FIELD) in London, have provided legal advice to small island country delegations since the very start of the climate negotiations. Saleem Huq of the International Institute for Environment and Development (IIED) is a widely respected authority on adaptation issues and is regularly consulted by developing country delegations. Other examples of such individuals include Atiq Rahman of BCAS, Bill Hare of Greenpeace International and Stephan Singer of WWF International.

Nevertheless, the scope for NGO influence in global climate meetings is limited. True, if governments agree, NGOs may attend COPs as observers, on the proviso that they are qualified in matters covered by the UNFCCC. However, NGOs do not have legal rights to put items on the agenda, and opportunities to intervene in proceedings are normally restricted to opening or closing plenary sessions. Even then, possibilities for NGO interventions are subject to the discretion of the chairperson of the meeting. Nevertheless, spaces are provided for position statements to be heard in the plenary sessions from groups claiming to represent different elements of civil society. For example, the Climate Action Network has spoken on behalf of assembled NGOs, and the International Chamber of Commerce has made interventions on behalf of industry. That said, national capitals tend to exercise strong control over their negotiating teams, so that it is difficult for NGO lobbying to achieve meaningful shifts in positions during the meetings themselves.

Indeed, some aspects of the negotiation process are effectively off-limits for NGOs. The more high-level the meeting, the less access NGOs tend to have. As Yamin notes: 'Parties often cite concerns that last minute trade-offs and compromises are more difficult to make if each step is being watched by a large group of observers' (2001: 158). The Secretariat therefore sometimes organises informal encounters where leaders of different blocs of states try to hammer out the basic contours of a negotiating package. Such meetings are off-limits for NGOs unless they have managed to secure a senior place on a leading delegation.

Despite such restrictions on civil society involvement, communication technologies and mobile phones make it increasingly difficult to exclude civil society groups in practice. Yamin notes that, in the waning hours of the Hague COP in 2000:

the 'big' NGOs were able to 'number crunch' the figures and submit their analysis via phones more or less in 'real time'. Because some of the deals being struck were made in the corridors outside the ministerial meeting, some of these NGOs were actually more in touch with what was going on than developing country negotiators in discussion with President Pronk (2001: 158).

In such ways the formal legal rules, which assign NGOs a peripheral role in global environmental governance, are increasingly at odds with the substantial ways that NGOs can in practice shape policy and strengthen institutions.

Membership of delegations remains the most direct way that NGOs are able to participate in the negotiating process and to attempt to influence government positions. NGOs with access to the most powerful delegations can extend their influence further. As Raustiala notes: 'Many US-based NGOs, because of their size, expertise and influence on the government of the US were particularly influential' (1996: 56). At the same time, NGOs can also bolster the negotiating capacity of delegations with fewer resources and less voice. It is now commonplace for weak states to use technical or legal experts from transnational NGOs to support their delegations in complex climate negotiations. In this way FIELD lawyers have assisted representatives of the Alliance of Small Island States (AOSIS). Yamin notes: 'The provision of NGO analysis and recommendation of policy options is … not new … but the degree to which it appears to be relied upon by many governments, without further checks, may be far more widespread than previously.' Diplomats from developing countries and countries-in-transition in particular 'rush from meeting to meeting, often only reading the paperwork on flights, and becoming increasingly reliant on the briefings provided by their favoured NGOs' (Yamin 2001: 157).

Performing this advisory role gives NGOs a position of leverage and a platform from which to launch their own proposals. The AOSIS Protocol of 1995 – thought to have been heavily drafted by FIELD lawyers – is an oft-cited example of such direct influence (Newell 2000). A number of NGOs therefore seek to identify states that could serve as collaborative partners in the negotiations. Even small and seemingly peripheral states can be valuable allies, given that every state has an automatic right of access to committees and working groups from which NGOs are otherwise excluded.

Participation in global meetings can also provide NGOs with opportunities to influence domestic debates on climate change. Activists have used stunts, press conferences and press releases to this end. In this vein, NGOs presented 'Fossil of the Day' awards at COP 10 in Buenos Aires in December 2004, in one case targeting the Netherlands (as reigning EU President) for making too many concessions to the US Government in order to bring it back into the negotiating process. At Bali in 2007, the ECO newsletter proclaimed that 'the US, Canada, Japan and Russia yesterday shared top dishonour for relentlessly blocking any reference to the 25–40 per cent cuts by 2020 in the Bali roadmap' (*ECO Issue 7*, December 2007).

Beyond the public global governance of climate change, many NGOs and other civil society organisations also increasingly participate in private standard-setting aimed at bringing a measure of governance and quality control to private carbon markets. For example, in 2003 WWF International initiated the CDM Gold Standard as an extra set of screening for CDM or voluntary projects on renewable energy and energy efficiency (CDM Gold Standard 2008). In 2006 The Climate Group, the International Emissions Trading Association and the World Business Council for Sustainable Development created a Voluntary Carbon Standard that seeks to provide a 'robust global standard, program framework and institutional structure for validation and verification of voluntary GHG emission reductions' (VCS 2008). In 2007 six non-profit organisations also founded the Offset Quality Initiative to promote best practice in this area.

*Accountability through evaluation*

Once commitments have been secured through intergovernmental agreements, many civil society organisations have directed their attention to monitoring and evaluating the extent to which those accords are implemented and enforced. At this stage of the policy process NGOs can engage in whistleblowing when commitments are being violated and adopt 'naming and shaming' strategies to expose governments that are most guilty of failing to implement their commitments. For example, NGOs have chided parties that buy 'hot air' quotas from Russia and other Central and East European countries in order to meet their commitments under Kyoto (Gulbrandsen and Andresen 2004: 70). To dissuade parties from buying these credits, Greenpeace developed a computer 'loophole analysis' that calculates the country-specific consequences of these actions. Besides such strategies of public exposure, NGOs have also undertaken detailed analysis of national reports on climate change policies, highlighting silences and gaps in data, particularly relating to policies and programmes that might offset projected gains.

Groups from the CAN network have also produced their own reviews of government commitments and whether these are on course to be met. These assessments have been widely distributed at the COP meetings. To some extent, as Arts (1998) notes, the influence of NGO evaluations is revealed by their wide citation in governments' own policy documents. Evaluation work is more difficult for groups such as SinksWatch, CDM Watch and Carbon Trade Watch that have been set up to monitor and assess the environmental quality and social impacts of projects undertaken under the purview of the Clean Development Mechanism and through voluntary carbon markets. The task is formidable given the volumes of activities involved and the geographical scope of the projects (Newell 2008).

Meanwhile, groups such as the Pew Center on Global Climate Change and the Climate Group adopt a different approach. These civil society actors have played an important part in constructively engaging firms, creating incentives through providing positive publicity and performance rankings and providing support for business leaders on the issue. Some of the interventions of these groups have had substantial accountability effects on firms. For example, 2004 saw eight bodies come together to establish the Global GHG Registry: International Emissions Trading Association; Pew Center on Global Climate Change; World Business Council for Sustainable Development; World Energy Council; World Resources Institute; World Wildlife Fund; Deloitte Touche Tohmatsu; and World Economic Forum. The Registry is a potentially powerful tool for holding actors to account for their performance in addressing climate change.

However, as with many such initiatives, enforcement mechanisms are currently weak. Verification is done through checks by the GHG Registry or independent assessors, but the evaluators do not go to sites and stay in head office, taking the facts as given. There are no penalties for withdrawal from the scheme or for using false figures; nor does the GHG Registry comment publicly on withdrawals (Pew Center 2007).

Questions may also be asked about who such civil society organisations represent when they construct these new forms of accountability through evaluation. However, none of these groups makes their claims in terms of accountability. As elite, non-public, membership-based associations, they lack a basis to claim to speak for broader public constituencies. Yet such groups are less likely to attract critical scrutiny about their own accountability, since the question 'who do you represent?' only tends to arise in respect of organisations that claim to represent.

### Accountability through redress

In addition to exacting accountability in the global climate regime through participation and evaluation (which have often also had the effect of enhancing public transparency), civil society actors have brought about accountability impacts through redress. In this regard NGOs have used global fora to hold individual states to account, not just to their own citizens, but also to broader communities affected by their actions (or refusals to take action). Recent years have seen a rising tide of legal activism by NGOs against governments and firms regarding climate change, drawing on human rights instruments in the case of the former and tort law to pursue public nuisance claims in the case of the latter (Newell 2008). The cases brought against corporations form part of a broader suite of strategies of 'civil redress' which include boycotts and shareholder activism, aimed at enhancing the accountability of corporations for their climate change responsibilities (Mason 2005). Here the focus is on a case of redress brought by alleged victims against a leading state contributor to climate change.

In December 2005 the Inuit Circumpolar Conference (ICC), a transnational NGO, submitted a petition to the Inter-American Commission on Human Rights (IACHR) seeking redress for harms suffered owing to global warming caused by actions and omissions of the United States Government. The ICC targeted the USA as the world's then largest contributor to greenhouse gas emissions. Sheila Watt-Cloutier, an Inuk woman and Chair of the ICC, submitted a petition on behalf of herself, sixty-two other named individuals, and 'all Inuit of the arctic regions of the US and Canada who have been affected by the impacts of climate change' (Climate Law 2006). The petition called on the IACHR to investigate the harm caused to the Inuit by global warming and to declare the US Government in violation of the 1948 American Declaration of the Rights and Duties of Man, and other instruments of international law such as the International Covenant on Civil and Political Rights and the International Covenant on Economic, Social and Cultural Rights.

The IACHR rejected the petition as inadmissible, though reasons for the refusal were not given. For Martin Wagner, who helped file the petition, 'it is possible that the Commission weren't ready to tell a government what to do about global warming ... it was uncomfortable demanding specific science-driven remedial steps' (Wagner 2007; and personal communication to the author). Importantly, however, the Commission did not dispute the human rights issues raised by the case.

If the Commission had ruled in favour of the Inuit, it could have referred the US Government to the Inter-American Court of Human Rights for a legal judgment under the American Convention on Human Rights. Though such a ruling would have been largely symbolic, it could have been used in national litigation through the domestic legal mechanism of an Alien Tort Claim, which allows non-US citizens to bring cases in US courts in the instance where a US party has violated international law. One positive outcome of the ICC case was that the Commission invited petitioners to request a public hearing on the matter, which took place in March 2007.

Reflecting on the use of such litigation, one activist lawyer in the US affirms that: 'we try and sue everyone we can. Most cases will fail, but we may just do it anyway' (confidential personal communication to the author). Even failed attempts at large injury claims may have the merit of prompting, for example, the insurance and banking sectors to reconsider their investments in industries and projects that contribute to climate change. The cases also have the educational value of raising awareness of the range of harms being generated by climate change. The prospect of large legal liabilities may also galvanise US Government support for the climate change regime. As a report by the International Council on Human Rights Policy (ICHRP) notes:

Even if law suits cannot themselves provide long-term or far-reaching solutions to the human rights problems raised by climate change, litigation can nevertheless be an effective strategy. At a minimum, a well-constructed case draws attention to harmful effects that might otherwise sink below the public radar – and in particular, puts a name and a face to an otherwise abstract suffering of individuals. Further, legal actions provide impetus and expression to those most affected by the harms of climate change, and can thus become a motor of social or civic mobilisation for policy change ... tort litigation can present polluters with costly trials and the uncomfortable prospect of debilitating damages and reputational costs, all of which encourage behavioural change (ICHRP 2008: 9).

These forms of legal mobilisation are notable for their transnational and multi-actor nature (Newell 2008). They involve coalitions among states, cities, communities and civil society groups. Diverse actors have made accountability demands of governments and corporations regarding process-based issues of transparency and disclosure as well as substantive demands regarding regulation and compensation. An assessment of the effectiveness of these strategies is hindered by the fact that many cases have not yet been settled. Indeed, it is a particular disadvantage of litigation that it requires so much time to work through the complexity of legal claims and to establish causality beyond reasonable doubt. Moreover, the high cost involved inhibits resource-poor groups from bringing cases in the first place (Newell 2001). However, legal activism sends out important signals to polluters for the long term and the prospect of future legal liabilities may provide an incentive for firms to address climate change in their current corporate strategies.

## Conclusion

It is clear from the foregoing analysis that civil society groups have brought a significant and often underestimated degree of democratic accountability to the global politics of climate change. With action on transparency, participation and consultation, evaluation and redress, civil society activism has succeeded in making government officials and key business actors more answerable for their (in)actions on climate change. Owing to civil society interventions, policy action on climate change has undoubtedly gone further than it would otherwise have done.

That said, civil society actors cannot on their own deliver effective accountability from intergovernmental agencies, states and private actors in the global climate change regime. In particular, NGOs lack enforceable sanctions. Such accountability as civil society activism produces on climate change tends to be temporary, tokenistic and subject to publicity cycles.

Indeed, the more civil society actors assume a frontline role in constructing and enforcing mechanisms of accountability in the global governance of climate change, the more they invite scrutiny of their own accountability. In particular, questions arise about whose interests NGOs represent and how. Gaps in civil society's own accountability can lead to failure to reflect, learn from mistakes and adjust strategy accordingly (Scholte 2005a: 107). Without addressing their own accountability to those they claim to represent, NGOs and other civil society actors risk exclusion from policy-making arenas by governments and intergovernmental institutions on the grounds that they are not representative. Thus civil society activism is clearly not an adequate or desirable substitute for other modes of public democratic oversight of power exercised at the international level. Nevertheless, civil society activities play an important role in highlighting accountability deficits and advocating that they be addressed through public regulation. For as long as such stronger public regulation is lacking, civil society engagement can only provide interim, short-term and often isolated forms of accountability.

It is also important to recall, however, that enhanced accountability in itself will not be enough to tackle climate change. The degree of openness and transparency which characterises a political system is a poor indicator of the effectiveness of its strategy for tackling climate change. Indeed, the world's largest and oldest democracies are singularly failing to provide leadership on climate change. Some might even argue that their pluralism and openness to representation inhibits the adoption of more rapid and effective action. Having access to increased spaces of participation and greater levels of transparency about what actions are being undertaken by governments and corporations can make a difference. However, unless transparency is combined with a real political commitment to act, openness in itself will not be a driver of change. Participating in ineffective policy and having access to information about how the problem of climate change is getting worse does not of itself constitute progress without stronger commitments to take action and the means for enforcing compliance. Perhaps the greatest contribution civil society can make is to spur faster and more far-reaching action on climate change, in order to avoid the worst consequences of a problem for which future generations will surely hold us to account.

# 12 Civil society and accountability promotion in the Global Fund

*Carolyn Long and Nata Duvvury*

## Introduction

The debate on civil society and accountable global governance involves two important questions. What role does civil society play in ensuring accountability of global institutions? And to what extent is civil society itself accountable to its own constituencies? This chapter explores these issues in relation to the Global Fund to Fight AIDS, Tuberculosis and Malaria (hereafter abbreviated to 'the Global Fund' or 'GFATM').

In pursuing this analysis, civil society is understood to cover a range of collective actors outside of states and formal political parties, and characterised by the voluntary (non-profit) nature of their association. The range of civil society organisations (CSOs) includes social movements, labour unions and other workers' associations, non-governmental organisations (NGOs), community-based organisations (CBOs), clan and kinship networks, professional associations and any other bodies not motivated by profit. However, recent considerations of the social contract between the state and its citizens in the context of globalisation place particular emphasis on NGOs, especially when they take on the role of providing public services in the place of government.

Accountability is understood here along four dimensions: doing what is right in line with the organisation's goals; doing no harm; taking responsibility for the organisation's policies and actions; and correcting mistakes. The first two aspects of accountability require voice or participation (termed 'consultation' in Chapter 1 of this book), so that a broad spectrum of interests is considered in decision-making. 'Doing right' and 'doing no harm' also require transparency, or making information

We thank Cheryl Morden, a former ICRW staff member, who provided the original impetus for this research; also Helen Cornman, a former ICRW consultant who participated in the first phase of research; and the Kenya AIDS NGO Consortium and the Centre for Advocacy and Research (with facilitation by the HIV/AIDS Alliance in India) who wrote the country case studies. Funding from the Ford Foundation is also gratefully acknowledged.

accessible to scrutiny, so that decisions are clearly understood. The latter two aspects of accountability – taking responsibility and correcting mistakes – further require mechanisms of monitoring and regulation (or 'evaluation', in the language of Chapter 1).

Global governance institutions currently face significant accountability deficits. They are not sufficiently answerable to their stakeholders. They do not adequately accept responsibility for wrong policies, nor do they do enough to assess and correct policies through formal evaluations or policy reviews. As underlined throughout the present book, this lack of accountability can undermine the effectiveness and legitimacy of global institutions.

Given these challenges, there is growing interest in the role that civil society can play in improving the accountability of global institutions. One early exploration of this question suggested that civil society involvement in global governance could potentially raise transparency, increase monitoring, obtain redress for negative consequences of policies, and promote the creation of formal accountability mechanisms (Scholte 2004a). Yet how far have these positive potentials been realised in practice? And what factors influence the ability of CSOs to deliver these benefits?

The intensity and quality of civil society participation is key in this regard. Important factors include the extent of representation, the degree of independence and non-cooptation, the level of hierarchy within civil society networks, and the depth of resources (financial and human). Also vital is the degree to which civil society organisations are themselves accountable to their constituencies.

The latter issue is particularly contentious. Some argue that civil society is not a 'representative instance, but a constituent one' and thus cannot be held to the same accountability criteria as governments with their parliaments and political parties (Peruzzotti 2007: 50). However, there is wide agreement that when NGOs are formally included in governance processes, accountability of non-state actors would in fact be a logical consequence (Edwards 2000; Naidoo 2003; Peruzzotti 2007). In such cases, a civil society actor cannot claim to monitor accountability of the governance mechanism from the outside – as a constituent – since the CSO is part of the regulatory structure. The issue of representation then becomes crucial in order to establish the legitimacy of civil society delegates in the governance apparatus.

Such questions are particularly pronounced in the case of the Global Fund. Like ICANN and the WFTO, covered in the next chapters, but in contrast to the other institutions examined in this book, the GFATM represents a rare instance where certain CSOs have a formal voting role in a global-scale governance mechanism. Civil society delegates have designated seats both on the global Board of the GFATM and in its national Country Coordinating Mechanisms (CCMs). Meanwhile other CSOs engage the Global Fund from positions outside its formal structure, much as civil society groups interact with the United Nations (UN) or the International Monetary Fund (IMF).

From within and from without, CSOs have furthered GFATM accountability to its constituents in several important ways. These gains include: democratising the Board and the CCMs; enhancing transparency; winning the vote on the global Board for people living with one of the three diseases; persuading the Board to promote a strategy of mainstreaming gender concerns into country programmes; and adding value to Board, committee and CCM discussions. At the same time, over the first years of GFATM activities the CSOs concerned have gradually increased their own abilities to be accountable to, and truly representative of, their own constituencies.

The rest of this chapter elaborates these findings, first by describing the workings of the Global Fund and the special role of civil society organisations in these operations. Thereafter, the chapter examines accountability challenges in the GFATM and the ways that CSOs have helped to address them. A further section explores issues of the accountability of civil society actors themselves in relation to the Global Fund, before the conclusion rounds off the discussion with summary thoughts on the way forward.

The chapter is based largely on two research projects conducted by the International Center for Research on Women (ICRW). In the first investigation, undertaken from 2003 to 2005, ICRW examined civil society involvement in the GFATM, with the objective of strengthening CSO participation in Global Fund decision-making processes. The research involved a wide-ranging review of documents, extensive interviews with GFATM staff and civil society actors, and three case studies. Two country-level case studies by local researchers in India and Kenya examined the role of civil society in the CCMs. (For another country case study on the GFATM and civil society in Gambia, see Cassidy and Leach 2010.) A third case study documented the process through which CSO advocacy achieved GFATM Board agreement to two key civil society goals. In 2006–7 the focus of ICRW's research shifted to an examination of civil society promotion of accountability in the GFATM as well as the attention paid by civil society representatives to their own accountability. The authors conducted additional research, and the Kenyan and Indian case studies were updated to analyse the evolving role of CSOs in the respective CCMs.

Throughout this work particular attention has been focused on the ways in which and extents to which Global Fund operations have integrated gender considerations and the role that civil society activities have played in this regard. The focus on gender in assessments of GFATM accountability is critical. The unequal status of women and girls in affected countries means that they lack economic, sexual and reproductive rights and are routinely subjected to violence. This structural subordination renders them particularly vulnerable to the three diseases. Women and girls are most often unable to negotiate sex or to protect themselves from various forms of gender discrimination. They bear the brunt of the effects of the diseases, because even when they are not themselves infected or stricken they are the primary caregivers to the sick and raise children orphaned by the diseases. As of late 2007, 50 per cent of those infected with HIV/AIDs were women and girls, and 60 per cent of adults infected with HIV in Sub-Saharan Africa were women (UNAIDS 2007). Accountability mechanisms that do not recognise these key facts would be severely inadequate.

## The Global Fund

The Global Fund was created in January 2002 in order to increase dramatically the resources available to fight acquired immune deficiency syndrome (AIDS), tuberculosis and malaria. The GFATM does not itself directly implement healthcare programmes, but mobilises and disburses resources in order to make a sustainable and significant contribution to the prevention and treatment of these diseases in countries in need.

Headquartered in Geneva with a Secretariat employing around 500 persons, the Global Fund now supports work in 136 countries in Africa, Latin America and the Caribbean, Central Europe, the Middle East, Central, East and South Asia, and the Pacific. As of August 2009 the GFATM had approved grants in 140 countries to a total of US$15.6 billion. Recipients include governments, NGOs, CBOs, faith-based organisations (FBOs), communities living with the diseases, universities and private sector organisations. Thanks to the GFATM, 2.3 million people with HIV/AIDS were on antiretroviral (ARV) treatment, 5.4 million people had received effective tuberculosis treatment, and 88 million insecticide-treated bed nets had been distributed to fight malaria (Global Fund 2009). A total of US$19.6 billion has thus far been pledged or contributed to the Global Fund. The monies are used to purchase commodities, products and drugs; to provide health infrastructure, equipment, human resources and administration; and to conduct monitoring and evaluation. The largest sums of money in the GFATM have come from governments in Europe (56 per cent), the United States (25 per cent) and Japan and others (14 per cent). The private sector and foundations have contributed 5 per cent of the total raised as of April 2008 (Global Fund 2008a).

Intended as an innovative approach to international health financing, the GFATM encourages a multistakeholder approach to policy processes at both global and country levels. The global Board of the GFATM is comprised of representatives of multilateral and bilateral donors, recipient governments, foundations, the private sector, Northern and Southern NGOs, and affected communities. The Board is responsible for overall governance of the organisation and approves grants. At the national level in grant-receiving countries the GFATM works through CCMs, which are intended to be multistakeholder bodies with the same array of participation as found on the global Board. The multistakeholder approach is promoted to maximise local ownership and planning and thereby to combat the diseases most effectively.

In terms of the GFATM funding cycle, CCMs are responsible for developing and submitting national grant proposals to the global Board. At GFATM headquarters a Technical Review Panel, comprised of independent health and development experts, reviews all proposals and makes recommendations to the Board for decision. Following grant approval the CCM monitors implementation and co-ordinates GFATM-supported work with that of other donors and domestic programmes in the country. Every grant has a monitoring and evaluation component through which recipients report progress to the Principal Recipient and through it to the CCM.

### Civil society in the structure of the Global Fund

The design and implementation of the GFATM has included civil society in an unprecedented manner across its entire institutional structure. This involvement has principally concerned Northern and Southern NGOs, locally based CBOs, and associations of affected communities. Since its creation, the GFATM has committed itself to supporting the participation of CSOs at the heart of its decision-making. The experience of the GFATM has demonstrated that civil society involvement at the core of global policymaking is both feasible and valuable.

The Board of the Global Fund includes specific seats that are designated for Developed Country NGOs, Developing Country NGOs and Affected Communities Organisations. Each of these three groups has a voting member of the Board, an alternate, a Communications Focal

Point (to share information and consult with the particular civil society constituency) and a delegation of seven persons selected by the member who sits on the Board. CSO members of the Board (or their designated representatives) also sit on each of the global Board's committees.

There are some variations in the structures of the CSO delegations to the GFATM Board. The Northern NGOs have a contact group of about forty people from which a core delegation of seven is drawn for each Board meeting, depending on the particular issues to be discussed. The CSO Board member, the alternate Board member and the Communications Focal Point comprise the other three members of the full delegation of ten.

The Affected Communities (AC) core delegation to the GFATM Board works with a support group of ten to twenty people, primarily through email and conferences calls. Members of the AC support delegation must serve for one year before being eligible to join the core delegation. AC core delegates serve for two years, after which they become members of the advisory group that provides guidance and input to the support and core delegations. There is no length of term for the AC advisory group, which serves on an ad hoc basis.

The Developing Country NGO delegation covers countries in four regions: Africa; Eastern Europe and Central Asia; Latin America and the Caribbean; and South East Asia. Until early 2009, the delegation was composed of four people from Africa, and two each from the other three regions. In 2009 it was expanded to forty persons (ten per region), from which a delegation of ten persons would be chosen for each Board meeting. Each region also has a contact group. For example, for Africa the group comprises approximately forty persons who receive regular information from the GFATM Secretariat and from Board meetings, and who are consulted regularly for their views on important issues that will be taken up at Board meetings and in Board committees (personal communication of CSO respondent with co-author, 25 July 2009). Each region now also has its own Communications Focal Point.

Integral CSO involvement in the Global Fund is also mandated with respect to the CCMs. In practice, however, the extent and impact of this civil society participation has varied from country to country, depending on the skills of the particular CSO delegates and the level of respect that they command from other members of the CCM. In the early years of the Global Fund relatively few CCMs had effective involvement of CSOs. However, with time and strengthened requirements from the global Board, CSOs are playing a more effective role in more countries. Ghana, Pakistan and Peru are three examples of countries where CSOs participate actively in CCMs. As of 2007 a CSO representative chaired the CCM in the Gambia, Ghana, Madagascar and Zambia (Interview 2007c).

In addition to involvement in the Board and the CCMs, civil society actors are significant participants in the Global Fund's Partnership Forum (PF). This biennial conference assembles a wide range of stakeholders for discussion of the performance of the GFATM and to make recommendations regarding its strategy and effectiveness. For the most part, civil society participants in the PF come from outside the CSO delegations to the GFATM Board; hence the PF represents a separate opportunity for civil society input to the Global Fund.

Finally, it is also possible for a CSO to become the Principal Recipient (PR) or a Sub-Recipient of a Global Fund grant. CSOs constitute 39 per cent of PRs in Asia and 23 per cent of PRs in Sub-Saharan Africa. Many more CSOs are Sub-Recipients. As time goes on, more countries are using a dual-track financing model where governments and CSOs together act as PRs. Others are using a multiple PR model where government, civil society and the private sector are each involved. At least ten countries are following one or the other of these models, including Bangladesh, Ecuador, Nepal, Ukraine and Zambia. A GFATM report published in late 2007 found that general CSO performance as PRs rates highly in comparison to PRs from other sectors (Global Fund 2007a).

In view of the prominence of civil society in GFATM operations, the Secretariat in Geneva has institutionalised a number of provisions to advance relations with CSOs. In the early years of the GFATM, the Secretariat had just one staff person specifically designated for liaison with CSOs. This number has now risen to three. However, portfolio managers at the GFATM are often so absorbed by their task of overseeing project implementation that they are unable to interact systematically with civil society groups. Moreover, to date, staff of the Secretariat have received no guidance on relating with CSOs; nor has the GFATM recognised interaction with CSOs as a core competency for staff (personal communication to co-author from GFATM staff member, 19 February 2008).

## Accountability challenges for the Global Fund

As each of the case studies in this book indicates, global governance instruments face major challenges of democratic accountability. This general problem also confronts the Global Fund. However, the GFATM differs substantially from older multilateral institutions in some of the concepts and mechanisms that it uses to pursue its accountability.

For one thing, in contrast to intergovernmental constructions of global governance like the United Nations and the World Trade Organization, those involved with the Global Fund do not question that the institution itself has accountability demands to answer. One would never hear a GFATM staff person echo counterparts in the International Monetary Fund or the Organisation of the Islamic Conference who might argue that decision-making powers and associated accountabilities lie entirely with their member states. The Global Fund has always been serious in accepting that the agency itself has direct accountability to the people who are affected by its work.

For what is the Global Fund accountable? Unlike the World Bank, the GFATM does not itself implement projects. Its accountability therefore relates primarily to its mission to generate and channel significant finances to fight the three diseases. This task has become increasingly difficult as the initial enthusiasm of major bilateral donors for the GFATM has waned. CSO lobbying of bilateral donors on behalf of the GFATM has played a key role in obtaining adequate resources for the initiative.

To whom is the Global Fund accountable? First and foremost the GFATM needs to answer to its primary stakeholders, i.e. those infected or otherwise affected by the diseases. In addition, it owes accountability to its other stakeholders: namely, bilateral and multilateral donors, CSOs, foundations and the private sector. Several major challenges have arisen in recognising the GFATM's constituents.

One challenge has involved how best to address gender equity concerns in the context of the three diseases. The requisite expertise has been virtually absent within the GFATM Secretariat, Board and CCMs. At the same time women's organisations, gender experts, and CSO representatives within and outside the GFATM have failed to advocate sufficiently for attention to these concerns. Demand for gender-focused grants has been lacking, and hence the GFATM has not funded such programmes. The GFATM has thereby poorly served a major affected group: women and girls.

Another challenge in regard to accountability to those infected or indirectly affected by the diseases has arisen from the original structure of the GFATM. The Global Fund was designed as a multistakeholder partnership to enable it to operate on the principle of 'local ownership'. The intention was to place the power to conceptualise a proposal in the hands of the recipient country. Thus government, civil society and private sector actors in the country would work together with local affected populations to design an effective approach to fighting one or more of the diseases. Participation of CSOs was key, because they tend to work most closely with the primary stakeholders and in fact often include organisations of people living with the diseases.

In keeping with this principle of local ownership, in the early years the Board of the Global Fund made recommendations to, rather than stipulating requirements of, recipient governments as to the composition and operation of the CCM. As a result, in most countries the Ministry of Health determined the make-up of the CCM and decided on the content and approach of the proposal(s) that would be submitted to the GFATM. Under these circumstances civil society representation on the CCM was largely symbolic and virtually powerless, except in the few countries (such as Zambia) where governments already worked collaboratively with civil society actors. Exacerbating this problem was the fact that few CSOs were knowledgeable about the Global Fund or adequately prepared to demand an active role in their country's CCM. This concentration on government hindered the GFATM's ability to be accountable to its primary stakeholders.

By what means is the GFATM accountable? The principal mechanism is an innovative structure of the global Board. Normally, boards of global governance entities are comprised of representatives of governments and intergovernmental agencies. The governing body of the global institution rarely includes positions for other actors such as civil society associations, foundations or the private sector. In the case of the Global Fund the Board incorporates all of these stakeholders. Hence the GFATM has to chart its course through shared power and joint decision-making across sectors. CSO members of the Board have had to learn 'on the job', since there is little prior experience to draw on from other global governance mechanisms.

The contrast with the board structure of the World Bank is particularly striking. As noted in Chapter 3, power in the Board of Governors and the Executive Board of the World Bank rests inordinately with the governments of donor countries. Their large share of the vote gives them an effective veto. For its part, however, the GFATM Board is constructed so that no single constituency can dominate decision-making. Garrett Brown offers a different perspective by arguing that the wealth and power of donor agencies has undermined the deliberative process of the GFATM. He notes that members of the donor caucus meet prior to GFATM Board meetings in order to solidify their debate strategy, and suggests that they thereby achieve undue advantage to push through various motions or funding decisions (Brown 2009). However, research conducted for this chapter indicates that CSO delegations also meet prior to each Board meeting with other delegations, the Board Chair and Vice-Chair and Secretariat representatives. As one CSO actor affirms: 'Now we have more information, more influence with the other delegations. They want to coordinate their positions with us' (Interview 2007a).

Another challenge for accountability mechanisms at the Global Fund is to be responsive to concerns from primary stakeholders regarding the most effective means of fighting the diseases. The GFATM needs to be nimble in adjusting its policies and procedures to meet changing realities on the ground and to create a truly demand-driven organisation. Local Fund Agents (LFAs) are employed to assess a Principal Recipient's capacity to implement a grant and then to monitor its use of funds. In the early years of GFATM operations the LFAs (most of them accounting firms) were often too rigid in their application of financial oversight. They have subsequently adjusted their approach to suit the modus operandi of GFATM grantees.

## Civil society contributions to GFATM accountability

Measured against the dimensions of accountability discussed in the introduction to this chapter and the challenges noted in the preceding section, civil society associations have contributed importantly in making the Global Fund answer to its constituents better. These positive efforts began in the process of constructing the GFATM. Since its establishment the global Board in particular has had an exemplary record of accountability, and civil society actors have played an important role to this end. For instance, CSOs have enhanced transparency in Board deliberations, promoted a more demand-driven approach to funding projects, secured a gender strategy, and balanced power between Northern and Southern NGOs. As for the CCMs, civil society involvement has sometimes helped to make GFATM-funded programmes more directly relevant and to increase accountability to the primary beneficiaries. Such positive results have occurred more in those countries where CSOs are most active in the CCMs. These general findings are elaborated under the respective headings below.

### Civil society and the creation of the GFATM

CSOs are widely credited for having been an instrumental force in the formation of the GFATM. This involvement clearly promoted accountability to those suffering from, or affected by, the diseases, since the creation of the organisation dramatically increased the level of funding available to fight the three diseases. CSO success in getting seats on the GFATM Board arose especially from civil society efforts to promote and shape the future GFATM at the United Nations General Assembly Special Session on HIV/AIDS (UNGASS), held in June 2001.

CSOs achieved these gains through a mixed inside/outside strategy. At the Organisation of African Unity (OAU) Summit on HIV/AIDS,

Tuberculosis and Other Infectious Diseases, held in April 2001, the UN Secretary-General of the day, Kofi Annan, called for an additional US$10 billion per year to fight HIV/AIDS. Grasping this strategic opportunity, thirty-one NGOs that worked as AIDS service organisations gained access to early documents concerning UNGASS and sent a joint letter with detailed comments and recommendations to the organisers of the Special Session (ICASO 2001). The letter urged UNGASS to take into account the lessons learned by NGOs in their work on the AIDS pandemic, to use a multistakeholder approach in attacking the diseases, and to give civil society a formal role in the governance of the proposed Global Fund.

Once UNGASS began, thousands of people mobilised by NGOs demonstrated in the streets outside UN headquarters in New York City, where the meeting was being held. Meanwhile inside the conference hall NGO delegates succeeded in getting a formal meeting to discuss their recommendations with official delegates to UNGASS, including heads of state or ministers from both donor and recipient countries, other senior governmental representatives, and heads of UN organisations and other international health organisations. NGO participants also spoke on the floor of the Special Session, and lobbied and negotiated in hallways and other informal meetings. Early access to information enabled NGO advocates to create relationships with key actors within the UN system and other donor organisations.

Following UNGASS, NGOs were invited to the Transitional Working Group (TWG), held in November 2001, where representatives of UN agencies, multilateral and bilateral donors, recipient governments, foundations and the private sector met to determine the constitutional framework for the GFATM. NGOs consulted among themselves to develop joint positions prior to the TWG and effectively used these recommendations as the basis of their negotiations during the TWG meeting itself. Two months later the Global Fund was launched with civil society participation at its core.

Over the years since then, civil society representation on the Board and on the CCMs has ensured that the GFATM receives substantial resources from donor governments and that these resources flow to the areas, communities and sectors that require them the most. From the very beginning, CSOs have been the driving force in ensuring that donor governments provide the funds necessary for the GFATM. The GFATM itself acknowledges this contribution of CSOs in its 2007 report on the role of civil society:

The internationally recognized role that civil society played in launching the Global Fund's first funding round and in the conceptualization and design of the Global Fund led to a sense of ownership; the Global Fund was an initiative that they had helped to create, fund and govern (Global Fund 2007a).

### Civil society and Board accountability

Thanks in particular to their seats on the GFATM Board, CSOs have had the knowledge, skills and incentives for effective lobbying to hold governments and other agencies accountable for their commitments to resist the three global diseases. In 2006 most Board members were not anticipating a new grant-making round because of a lack of resources. The Board thought that a new round should only be launched if guaranteed resources were available. However, CSOs put the issue of a sixth round of grants on the agenda of the Board and convinced their colleagues that a new funding round should be pursued each year even when the money was not yet assured. As a result, new rounds are now considered automatic, and the Board must ensure that the necessary resources are raised. In this process the Board relies heavily on CSO advocacy of bilateral donors to contribute to the Global Fund.

The presence of CSOs on the global Board also ensures a greater level of transparency of GFATM operations than would otherwise be the case. The CSO members of the Board have access to a wide array of information and circulate it to their delegations and broader constituencies. These groups, in turn, use this information to formulate strategies regarding issues coming before the Board. Even with information that is confidential (and thus only available to the CSO Board members) such access enables those civil society actors to have more informed policy debates within the Board.

This degree of transparency compares favourably with other multilateral organisations in the field of health. For example, the World Bank's Multi-Country HIV/AIDS Program (MAP) does not make as much information as readily available to CSOs as the GFATM does. Consequently the MAP does not have the same kind of advocacy and push for accountability from CSOs. As one CSO respondent put it: 'They [the Bank] spend a lot of money on consultations with NGOs, but they are not at the same level of accountability as the GFATM because of the GFATM CSOs' access to information' (Interview 2007b).

Over time, CSO members of the GFATM Board have learned how to influence other members through education and negotiation. In this way, also, they have promoted GFATM accountability to those suffering from or otherwise affected by the diseases. Moreover, the expertise of individual CSO representatives has enabled them to play an important role in Board committee discussions on specific issues. As CSO representatives have demonstrated their skill in achieving successful decisions, other Board delegations have increasingly sought them out in order to develop common strategies.

Perhaps the most impressive displays of civil society advocacy skill on the global Board have come in redressing two important accountability lapses by the GFATM. One was to secure a vote on the Board for the representative of the Affected Communities. The other was to obtain strengthened guidelines for CSO involvement in the CCMs. It took nearly two years of persistent CSO pressure to achieve these advances.

At the start of the GFATM only the Northern and Southern NGO members had voting rights on the Board, while the representative of Affected Communities did not. After significant advocacy by CSO representatives, utilising a variety of strategies, the Board agreed in its third year (June 2004) to give this member voting status in both the Board and the CCMs. This step made the Global Fund the first multilateral institution to have primary stakeholders represented on an equal basis in its decision-making bodies.

As for the guidelines regarding CSO participation in the CCMs, these were deliberately vague at the outset, because the Board did not want to dictate to recipient governments how they should run their CCMs, in keeping with the philosophy of 'local ownership' described earlier. However, as research from CSOs demonstrated, in the first years CCMs did not involve civil society in an effective manner. Thanks in good part to CSO pressure, the Board decided in November 2004 to strengthen the CCM guidelines to require each recipient government actively to involve NGOs and representatives of affected communities as members of the CCM and in its decision-making processes. The new requirements mandated that the NGO members of a CCM had to be selected by their own sector through a transparent, documented process developed by the NGOs themselves. The requirements also stipulated that the CCM must maintain a transparent proposal development process that would involve non-CCM members and thereby engage a broad spectrum of stakeholders (Global Fund 2004). These decisions constituted an important step towards creating a veritably demand-driven approach to fighting the diseases. As the GFATM itself states: 'This [CSO involvement in the CCM] has not only become a strong factor in a country's potential sustainability of disease-fighting efforts, but – equally as important – a catalyst for democratic processes where vulnerable and marginalized groups acquire a key voice in national policy' (Global Fund 2007a). That said, many recipient governments have continued to resist the 2004 guidelines.

CSOs have had a more mixed record on GFATM accountability when it comes to matters of gender equity. Following more than five years of inaction, the GFATM Board decided in November 2007 to require the Secretariat to prepare a strategy to mainstream gender concerns into the design and implementation of country programmes. In terms of account-ability, this was a clear case of correcting a mistake. Richard Feachem, former Executive Director of the GFATM, had acknowledged publicly in 2005 that a lack of attention to gender concerns was the single biggest failure of the Global Fund thus far. Responsibility for this failure must be shared by CSOs – including women's organisations – who helped to cre-ate the Global Fund and collectively failed to incorporate requirements for gender expertise at any level of the organisation. Gender balance has always been promoted at the GFATM in regard to membership of the Board and CCMs; however, gender balance without gender expertise is meaningless. Even when the Board strengthened the CCM guidelines in late 2004, the only reference to gender was a weak sentence to the effect that 'representation of a gender perspective in the CCM is desir-able' (Global Fund 2004: 3). CSOs participating in GFATM governance made little or no effort to promote attention to gender concerns and, for the most part, did not see themselves as responsible for this work. As one respondent put it, 'gender expertise is not considered more important or dominant than any other issue … it's not a priority issue' (Interview 2007a).

During the first five years, a few women's organisations outside the Global Fund, including ICRW, advocated for the adoption of a gender strategy. This effort was subsequently intensified with CSO initiatives undertaken for the most part independently of NGOs that hold vot-ing representation on the GFATM Board and in the CCMs. This work involved a three-pronged strategy: (a) to generate demand from coun-tries for grants with a gender-sensitive focus; (b) to lobby the Group of 8 (G8) and donors attending the Global Fund's September 2007 replen-ishment meeting; and (c) to create support within the GFATM Board itself, including among CSO members (Interview 2007d).

To create demand for gender-focused grants, the Global AIDS Alliance (GAA), together with four other NGOs, began working with govern-ment and CSO representatives from several countries and operational GFATM staff on proposals to integrate sexual and reproductive health (SRH) into the HIV and malaria components of the GFATM. Another CSO initiative, Women Won't Wait (WWW), pressed G8 governments at their June 2007 summit to commit substantial resources through the GFATM and other donors to address violence against women and children. The WWW initiative, launched in March 2007 by a coalition of eighteen women's organisations and other NGOs, also issued a report on the lack of donor attention to women and girls in the fight against

HIV/AIDS. The report emphasised the link between gender violence and HIV transmission and noted that donors rarely address this connection when formulating objectives or targets for their grants (Fried 2007). Both the GAA initiative and WWW lobbied Board members and donors at the GFATM replenishment meeting and at the GFATM Secretariat.

The SRH integration work and the initiative to stop violence against women and girls pursued an inside/outside strategy similar to that used by CSOs to help create the GFATM and to gain voting representation therein. The most important inside support was the commitment made by the incoming Vice-Chair of the GFATM Board (who was the representative of the Southern NGO delegation) to 'work towards gender equality, elimination of violence against women and children, and universal sexual and reproductive health rights in my tenure as Vice-Chair' (Mataka 2007).

The German government also played a key role by creating an opportunity at the G8 meeting for the GFATM Board Vice-Chair to make a presentation on the plight of women and girls. As host of the GFATM replenishment conference the German Government supported two side meetings on gender and reproductive health: one held by CSOs and the other by donors. Recommendations prepared at the CSO meeting went to the GFATM Secretariat. In November 2007 the GFATM Board meeting gave priority authorisation to the Secretariat to appoint three senior-level 'Champions of Gender Equality' with appropriate support, in order to develop a gender strategy. In addition, revisions to the guidelines on grant applications encourage submission of proposals that address gender issues (Global Fund 2007b). Subsequently, a senior-level gender advisor was hired in the GFATM Secretariat.

At its eighteenth meeting, in November 2008, the GFATM Board approved a rigorous gender equality strategy for its work on all three of the diseases (Global Fund 2008b). In addition, the Partnership Forum meeting in Dakar in December 2008 put forward recommendations, including one that urged the GFATM to consult with women's organisations and other groups working on gender concerns when preparing the detailed implementation plan for the gender equality strategy (Global Fund 2008c). Thanks in good part to CSO efforts, then, the GFATM has begun to overcome a critical gap in accountability with respect to gender.

### Civil society and CCM accountability

In contrast to their experience with the global Board, CSOs have faced a long and laborious process to get to the table at the CCMs. As a result it has been harder for civil society to promote GFATM accountability at the country level. At the global Board, CSOs are one stakeholder group among several that shape GFATM policy. In the country work of the Global Fund, CSOs are competing for resources with each other and with their government, which often perceives such funding as being rightfully its own. Civil society representatives have sat on most CCMs from the start, but in most instances their involvement was tokenistic during the first four years and continues to remain so in many cases. In some countries, though, CSOs have achieved greater GFATM accountability to primary beneficiaries through: (a) more effective representation of CSOs on the CCM; (b) education of the wider CSO community about the three diseases and the role of the GFATM; and (c) the involvement of many grassroots actors (CBOs, FBOs, NGOs) in the development of proposals to be considered by the CCM.

In Kenya, early efforts by the CSO community to select its own representatives for the CCM in 2002 were hampered by 'political polarization, personal and institutional differences and rivalry' (Kenya AIDS NGO Consortium 2005). However, subsequently CSOs have succeeded in choosing truly representative individuals from NGOs and Affected Communities to be members of the CCM through a countrywide participatory educational process followed by an election of CSO delegates. These new CSO participants in the CCM are drawn from all parts of the country and are in regular communication with primary beneficiaries.

The ways that the civil society sector is structured can promote GFATM accountability in a country. In Zambia, for example, CSO committees for the GFATM exist in nine provinces. When a proposal is to be developed, representatives of these provincial committees, along with district-level task forces, jointly develop the first draft of the document. The draft proposal then goes through an iterative process. Technical experts from the World Health Organisation (WHO) and other multilateral bodies review and edit it. Then the document goes back to the provincial committees for further review and editing. Then it returns to the CCM. The provincial committees in Zambia are comprised of NGOs, CBOs, traditional healers, youth and academics, and CSOs hold 46 per cent of the seats on the CCM (Interview 2007e).

In India, in late 2006, CSOs played an active role in a comprehensive exercise to prepare the National AIDS Control Plan (NACP3). CSOs can now hold the CCM more accountable in terms of drafting proposals on the basis of the national plan (personal communication 2007). For example, civil society pressure led to the prioritising of second-line anti-retroviral treatment in the CCM's proposal to the Global Fund, in accordance with priorities identified in NACP3. Moreover, CSOs, excluding the private sector, held 40 per cent of seats on the Indian CCM in 2009, on parity with government representatives.

Yet these excellent examples from Kenya, Zambia and India are hardly the norm for CCMs. One respondent noted (in confidential correspondence to the authors) that in her country certain NGOs were bribed by government officials so that they would support the proposal that the government wanted to submit to the GFATM and keep quiet about ethically questionable government behaviour in the CCM. Another difficulty present in many countries is the limited human, financial and technical resources available for CSOs to engage with grassroots communities on proposals to the GFATM. A further constraint is limited CSO technical capacity to negotiate effectively with governments regarding the content of proposals for the GFATM. International NGOs generally have significant advantages over local NGOs regarding the last two points. Finally, there are problems with the role of the CCM in monitoring the implementation of GFATM-funded projects. As one respondent put it:

asking people who have vested interests to oversee themselves is a problem. When you ask people who are implementers to also be overseers, you have a clash. Country-driven CCMs with a hands-off attitude by the GFATM are a problem. CCMs can't oversee properly when their members are the same people who have their finger in the pie (Interview 2007e).

## Strengthening CSO accountability in the GFATM

At the same time that CSOs have furthered GFATM accountability to its constituents (through both the Board and the CCMs), they have also worked to increase their own accountability to their constituencies. Since the GFATM began, civil society participation has been evolving. Over time it has moved from giving voice to civil society concerns to becoming more genuinely representative of wider civil society constituencies.

### Improvements in CSO accountability

At the start of the Global Fund, CSOs which had the most experience with fighting the HIV/AIDS pandemic led the negotiation of civil society's 'place at the table'. Some of these associations became the first civil society members of the GFATM Board. Interviews reveal that other Board members and the GFATM Secretariat saw these CSO representatives as speaking for the concerns of the wider civil society community. Yet only as time has passed, and communication and consultation mechanisms have come into place, has more veritable representation of civil society constituencies begun to be realised. Steps in this direction have included: (a) levelling the playing field between Northern and Southern NGOs; (b) formalising the selection process for CSO members of the Board and CCMs; (c) developing a CSO core group at the GFATM, with the institutional memory and capacity for effective advocacy; and (d) maintaining communication among CSOs between meetings of the Board.

Regarding the first of these points, a vote on the Board of the GFATM has helped to equalise the power imbalance in civil society between the global north and the global south. Although the three CSO delegations work well together and rely on one another, both the Southern NGOs and the Affected Communities have built alliances with other representatives on the Board on specific issues when such a step was to their strategic advantage. Multiple and shifting alliances have created space for differences in perspectives and priorities within civil society to be openly articulated and debated. This more level playing field between Northern and Southern NGOs is an important step in enabling civil society as a whole to be more accountable to its wider constituency and potentially more representative.

Other improvements in the accountability of CSOs have come with a more rigorous selection of civil society representatives on the GFATM Board. In the early years the Developed Country NGO Communication Focal Point was responsible for undertaking the selection for all three civil society delegations. Now each delegation handles its own process, indicating a growing sophistication in how the three delegations relate to the GFATM, and greater recognition that their needs are not identical. More rigorous and more participatory processes have also been put in place to choose civil society representatives in some (though not all) CCMs.

The three civil society delegations on the global Board have worked to expand the circle of CSO actors who are knowledgeable about, and actively engaged as advocates to, the GFATM. All three delegations have created a contact group beyond the core delegation of ten people in order to strengthen and support their participation at Board meetings, develop the capacity of future core delegates, and enhance their impact.

Over time civil society representatives on the GFATM Board have made increasing efforts to ensure that they maintain contact with each other between Board meetings. These ongoing communications allow them to track movement on agenda items and to develop advocacy strategies for the next Board meeting. Prior to each meeting the civil society delegations have pre-meetings with each other, with the Board Chair and Vice-Chair, and with Secretariat staff and others. Civil society delegations report back to their wider constituencies following each Board meeting on results achieved, including an assessment of how well the delegation performed regarding key issues, and future work to be done.

### Challenges for CSO accountability

Although CSOs have made progress in becoming more accountable to their constituencies, certain challenges continue to prevent full representation. These problems include limited consultation, lack of understanding of representational roles, limited financial and human resources, and inadequate knowledge and technical expertise to conduct dialogue at both Board and CCM levels.

In spite of the expanded groups of CSOs working with the Northern NGO and Affected Communities delegations, civil society representatives on the GFATM Board still give insufficient attention to consulting more broadly with constituencies at the country level. Instead, the CSO representatives rely on the members of their delegation to represent issues 'from the field'. While interviews regarding the GFATM Board suggest that the majority of CSO representatives have made efforts to communicate effectively with grassroots constituencies insofar as established mechanisms permit, some have neglected to do so.

The extent of engagement with constituencies varies from one delegation to the other depending on available resources, distance, and the ability – and willingness – to communicate. One respondent noted in respect of the Southern NGO delegation that it lacks sufficient human or financial support to get information and report back to constituencies: 'so what we say is not a mandate' (Interview 2007e). This delegation is expected to represent all Southern NGOs worldwide; however, it lacks funds for translations or teleconferences, and many NGOs in the global south have no access to email.

The need for consultations with CSOs at the grassroots is also essential for the CCMs. In this way it can be ensured that CCM discussions are reflective of current needs of the affected communities. As the India case study noted: 'The ground realities, especially in the HIV/AIDS context, are so complex and fluid that NGOs and CBOs involved in information outreach, service outreach and community empowerment are often unable to document their work' (Centre for Advocacy and Research 2005). Consultations of associations working on the ground can ensure that knowledge from the field informs CCM deliberations.

Many CSO representatives still need to learn that their role on bodies of the GFATM is to advocate for the primary concerns of the wider civil society constituency and not simply to advance their personal views or the specific interests of their own organisations. One respondent with experience in several regions noted: '[The CSO delegates] need to meet with their constituencies. This is not going on enough. They have never seen this as part of their role. There are lots of prima donnas, heads of NGOs, who think this role in regard to the GFATM is about them. It's not about them; it's a representative role' (Interview 2007e).

Capacity development of CSOs also remains a major challenge. For example, although CSOs are now required to run their own selection processes for seats on CCMs, the representation becomes an artifice if the CSO delegates thereby appointed are not on a par with government and donor representatives in terms of technical and advocacy skills. These shortcomings are beginning to be addressed in some countries, but by no means all.

To take a positive example, as noted earlier Kenyan CSOs have carried out a countrywide educational process about the GFATM which culminated in an election by secret ballot of a new slate of CSO representatives to the CCM. The four major Kenyan CSO networks working on the three diseases created a training of trainers (TOTS) initiative to develop a core team of regional trainers. The TOTs programme educated the trainers about the three diseases and the GFATM, in addition to issues such as leadership, democracy, transparency, accountability and governance. Once trained, the cadre of forty-four facilitators took the training to eleven regions across the whole country. This training culminated in the election of regional representatives to participate in a national forum which elected six CSO representatives and six alternates to the CCM. These representatives now participate in the CCM meetings and consult their constituencies through regional meetings and workshops, email and newsletters. This ongoing communication ensures input to the CCM from those who are closest to the primary beneficiaries. The CCM has allocated funds for travel and accommodation for CSO representatives from rural areas to facilitate their participation in the CCM meetings. The Kenya CCM considers this work to reflect 'best practice' (Kenya AIDS NGO Consortium 2007).

### Moving forward

The foregoing analysis of progress and continuing pitfalls in CSO accountability at the Global Fund suggests a number of recommendations for future development of this important experiment in civil society involvement in global governance. Five main suggestions are offered here.

*1. Further improve representation and accountability to wider
CSO constituencies*

Civil society activists are truly representative and able to advocate most effectively at Board or CCM meetings when they build their arguments upon data coming from the field. Regular consultations with their constituencies are essential to enable this evidence-based advocacy; hence consultation skills should be a selection criterion for CSO delegates. Work must continue to develop systematic mechanisms to ensure regular input to CSOs from their wider constituencies and to provide subsequent feedback about results of Board and/or CCM decisions. Such efforts must take into account the limitations present in low-income countries regarding access to the Internet and to information more generally.

*2. Raise more resources for CSO participation in the GFATM*

CSO participation in a global governance entity is a long-term commitment. Effective civil society participation in the Global Fund requires adequate financial resources. While the Northern NGO and Affected Communities delegations have succeeded thus far in raising adequate monies for their work in the GFATM, the Southern NGO delegation still lacks a reliable flow of funds. All CSO delegations – for both the Board and the CCMs – need a fundraising strategy to ensure that adequate resources are available for their participation. The strategy must be adaptable, as conditions change over time. Donors supportive of civil society participation in governance need to work closely with CSOs and with each other to ensure a co-ordinated regular flow of the required financial and technical resources.

*3. Value the civil society representatives*

Civil society participation in global governance may be viewed by official circles and others as a privilege. As a result they may undervalue the contributions of civil society representatives, who moreover often do the work on a volunteer basis or in addition to their budgeted tasks. The GFATM Board and at least some of the CCMs have come to value the impressive participation of CSOs in their proceedings, but more appreciation could be shown. Meanwhile the CSOs themselves need to recognise that the selection of a staff person to become a member of the GFATM Board or a CCM requires an adequate allocation of that person's time as well as resources for travel, communication and consultation.

*4. Strengthen capacity for effective CSO participation*

As this chapter has repeatedly indicated, CSO representatives on the global Board and CCMs of the GFATM require a number of skills in order to participate effectively. To enhance capacities the three CSO delegations (especially the Southern NGO group) must continue their efforts to build contact groups. Particular attention is needed for skills in lobbying, negotiating, creating alliances and effectively using field experience.

### 5. Monitor the GFATM gender mainstreaming strategy

The Board decision in late 2007 to develop a gender strategy for the Global Fund requires careful monitoring by CSOs both inside and outside the organisation. The main challenge for the GFATM Board, CCMs and Secretariat is a lack of conceptual understanding of gender issues. Therefore, insider CSO representatives on the GFATM (who are themselves often lacking in full gender sensitivity) need to collaborate closely with relevant CSOs outside the GFATM in order to benefit from their gender expertise.

### Conclusion

This chapter has shown that CSOs are an integral part of accountability dynamics at the Global Fund to Fight AIDS, Tuberculosis and Malaria. Both from within and from outside the institution, civil society actors have expanded GFATM transparency. In terms of consultation CSOs have widened and deepened deliberations with stakeholders on GFATM policies and programmes. With regard to evaluation CSOs have monitored the implementation of promises and projects related to the GFATM. Also, on the accountability dimension of redress CSOs have effectively pressed the GFATM to correct shortcomings in relation to, for example, voting rights for Affected Communities, consultation practices, CCM operations and gender sensitivity.

The case of the Global Fund shows the particular accountability gains that can be available when CSOs are integrated into the decision-making organs of a global governance institution. The principal challenge now before CSOs within the GFATM, in order for them to be truly representative and fully legitimate actors in this important new global institution, is to strengthen accountability mechanisms to their own constituencies.

Accountability in private global
governance: ICANN and civil society

*Mawaki Chango*

## Introduction

The Internet has experienced phenomenal expansion since its introduction to the public in the 1990s, such that it is now commonplace
to observe how global, ubiquitous and basic this medium of communication has become. Yet most users have little idea of how the Internet
operates globally. What and who make the Internet work as effectively
as it does on a global scale? How centralised or diffuse are the relevant
decision-making mechanisms? Who is responsible for what, and how does
that impact the other parts of the network and the various stakeholders,
irrespective of where they reside? Such questions pertain to what is now
widely called 'Internet governance'.

The creation of the Internet Corporation for Assigned Names and
Numbers (ICANN) in 1998 was a key step in the development of Internet
governance. To appreciate the critical importance of ICANN, one might
consider that this institution has the managerial and technical capability
to shut down or severely limit access to, for example, all websites ending
with the suffix '.org' or the Internet domain of a whole country. Such
actions may be extreme and unlikely in the ordinary course of events,
but they are nonetheless within ICANN's reach, and their consequences
would be enormous. Less spectacularly, ICANN could by its decisions
impair the capabilities of some stakeholders on the Internet while fostering those of others. Given these far-reaching capacities it is very important
that effective arrangements are in place to hold ICANN accountable.

The role of civil society in the accountability dynamics of ICANN is
particularly interesting inasmuch as it may be argued that the two – civil
society and ICANN – are not so distinct from one another. In contrast
to most of the other global governance mechanisms examined in this
book, ICANN is itself a non-governmental organisation in terms of its
constitution and membership (although the United States Government
played a pivotal role in its creation and until recently held a formal oversight function). Furthermore, ICANN operations rely heavily on the

participation of private individuals. So by its formal structure and its participants, ICANN could arguably qualify as a civil society entity at the same time as being a governance entity. That said, the notable presence of commercial business among core participants in ICANN suggests that the organisation might be better characterised as a multisectoral (or multistakeholder) organisation.

This multisectoral construction gives civil society actors who operate within ICANN a dual position as regards the accountability of the institution. On the one hand, these players serve as forces that can promote public accountability of ICANN from the inside. On the other hand, civil society actors that work within the institution must also account for themselves as part of ICANN itself. The latter calculation is difficult. Since multiple types of entities participate in ICANN, and since its policymaking procedures are consensus-driven, it is not always easy to document precisely what decisions and impacts can be attributed to civil society elements and what should be attributed to other participants in the organisation.

In the context of *democratic* accountability, civil society has arguably widened space for pluralism within ICANN, although as is elaborated later the institution is riven with complexities and ambiguities. Without civil society ICANN could have been a 'closed circuit' among major governments, powerful business interests (with easy access to those governments), and technology elites (who rarely acknowledge the political bearings of their undertakings). With civil society involvement ICANN has a public and more heterogeneous participation. That said, this multistakeholder construction does not prevent, in some cases, particular groups from driving the ICANN agenda or becoming overly influential in its decision-making processes.

To elaborate on these issues the first section below provides an account of ICANN's mission and organisational structure. The second section examines accountability issues posed by ICANN. The third section appraises the contributions and the constraints of civil society as a force for accountability in respect of ICANN; here matters of transparency, consultation, evaluation and correction are considered in turn. The chapter closes with reflections on the implications of civil society involvement in ICANN for the future of the institution and governance of the information society more generally.

## ICANN: an institutional experiment

ICANN is a private, non-profit public benefit organisation. Its purpose is to manage and co-ordinate the global Internet address systems. The matters under ICANN's purview mainly include: (a) the Internet Protocol (IP) numbers that identify every device connected to the Internet; and (b) the Domain Name System (DNS) that provides the basis for addresses on the World Wide Web (US Department of Commerce 1998). Together these two sets of identifiers enable the stable, reliable and global functioning of the Internet.

DNS implementation is distributed over a global system of servers. Each domain has a 'root', that is, a file containing the primary records necessary to maintain the operation of the top level of the domain. Copies of this 'root zone file' are kept in 'root servers' of the Internet. The initial thirteen servers (almost all located in the USA) are recognised as the authoritative root servers. In addition, over a hundred copies of these root servers are now scattered around the world (Rootserver 2009).

Although the roots are globally dispersed, a centralised authority is required to manage and co-ordinate the overall system of Internet identifiers. The DNS has a hierarchical design, such that any decision enacted at the top impacts the entire related domain. Moreover, if the top-level domain (TLD) is removed from the root, everything that comes under it will eventually disappear from the Internet, as the related records expire from the memory of all host computers on the network.

In contrast to domain names, IP numbers may well be allocated regionally and thus managed in a more decentralised fashion. There are five Regional Internet Registries, respectively for Africa, Asia-Pacific, Europe, Latin America and Caribbean, and North America. Nevertheless, the IP space is still defined by one universal pool of IP numbers. Some homogeneity of underlying IP standards is required, and it is necessary to ensure that an IP number brought into use anywhere in the world is no longer available for allocation elsewhere. For these reasons the regulation of IP addresses also requires a central point of decision-making.

Policy decisions on matters of domain names and protocol numbers may be largely technical, but ICANN is also more than a global technical co-ordinator. Many of its operations have significant political aspects that implicate economic interests, cultural values and power relations. For instance, the agency handles politically sensitive issues such as competition in the domain name operation and registration business, property rights in respect of domain names (Mueller 2002), registrars' handling of user data, and Internet content regulation.

To take a particular example, ICANN periodically decides whether to open bids for the operation of new TLDs. It sets the price of market entry by determining an application fee for firms that wish to participate. That fee reportedly reached US$50,000 in the past and is expected to quadruple in respect of new generic top-level domains (gTLDs), including multilingual script domains (also known as IDN). Far more than by technical considerations, such rules are driven by the power relations of political economy, since they obviously give advantage to those players (mainly established companies in the global north) who can pay the high fee. Particularly with IDN, ICANN's policies lead to a pricing structure that is prohibitive to potential emergent players who actually work in those scripts themselves, while favouring already profitable gTLD incumbents. Another occasion when politics enters into technical questions appears in a glaring political provision from the same new gTLD policy, which states that 'strings must not be contrary to generally accepted legal norms relating to morality and public order' (ICANN GNSO 2007: 20). In the light of such situations, critics have accused ICANN of 'underplaying (and for this purpose camouflaging in technical terms/discourse) its public policy impact' (Singh 2007).

Thus stewardship of the Internet, as provided by ICANN, entails a number of political responsibilities towards a whole array of stakeholders, and fulfilment of those responsibilities requires proper accountability. ICANN activities must be monitored to ensure that the organisation does not usurp public policy power and engage in sweeping policymaking without the necessary checks and balances or the appropriate democratic authority. As is detailed later in this chapter, formal mechanisms for this purpose are often wanting, and one might therefore look to civil society involvements to reduce the accountability deficits.

### ICANN organisational structure

As the title of this chapter indicates, ICANN is a private institution. Although it is a private corporation, it owes its existence to a contractual arrangement with the Department of Commerce (DOC) of the US Government. This relationship emerged because the core set of Internet Protocols, the TCP/IP, resulted from research projects publicly funded by the US Government. As a result, only the US Government was, at the time of ICANN's creation, in a position to decide how to handle and operate the Internet infrastructure as defined by IP resources, complemented by the DNS.

The declared intention has always been to lead ICANN through a transition towards a fully private Internet governance system. For some years a succession of Memoranda of Understanding (MOUs) with the DOC repeatedly deferred the end of the transition period (ICANN 2009c). However, in September 2009 the Joint Project Agreement (JPA) between ICANN and the DOC was replaced by a so-called Affirmation of Commitments that transferred responsibility to monitor ICANN from the US Government to a global review process (ICANN 2009a). At the time of writing it is too early to assess how these new arrangements will operate and in particular how far the role of the US Government will be reduced in practice.

Atop ICANN's own institutional structure is a Board of Directors (see Figure 2). Six directors come from the three Supporting Organizations (SOs) of ICANN. Eight other members of the Board are so-called at-large directors. In addition, the Board includes the President of ICANN, as director ex officio with voting rights, and six non-voting members who are liaisons appointed by various ICANN bodies. Although Board members are variously appointed or elected from lower levels of the ICANN organisational structure, they serve in their individual capacity and are not supposed to represent any particular constituency once seated.

In 2000, during a unique attempt at direct democracy in global governance, some of the at-large directors were elected through an online ballot of Internet users around the world. However, this experiment in accountability through global plebiscite has not been repeated. Nowadays a Nominating Committee (NomCom) slates the candidates to fill the at-large seats.

The ICANN bylaws provide for a minimum balance in geographical distribution on the Board as well as for diversity in skill sets and cultural backgrounds. Each of the five above-mentioned regions with Internet registries must be represented on the Board, and no single region can have more than 5 out of the 15 voting seats. However, the bylaws require that all directors be fluent in written and spoken English.

Apart from the Board, the institutional structure of ICANN includes: the Administration (with around 110 staff led by a President/ CEO), the three SOs, the NomCom and several Advisory Committees. The Governmental Advisory Committee (GAC) is the organ through which nation-state authorities can channel their views on ICANN activities. The three SOs are the primary actors making recommendations for the management of core Internet resources and related policy issues: the Address Supporting Organization (ASO) covers IP policy; the Generic Name Supporting Organization (GNSO) deals with domain name policy; and the Country Code Names Supporting Organization (ccNSO) handles policy on top-level domains related to countries. Bodies such as the Technical Liaison Group (TLG), the Internet Engineering Task Force (IETF), the Root Server System Advisory Committee (RSSAC) and the Security and Stability Advisory Committee (SSAC) deal with the technical operation of Internet infrastructure, from standard-setting to implementation and maintenance. Participation of Internet users and the general public is represented in the ICANN structure through the At-Large Advisory Committee (ALAC).

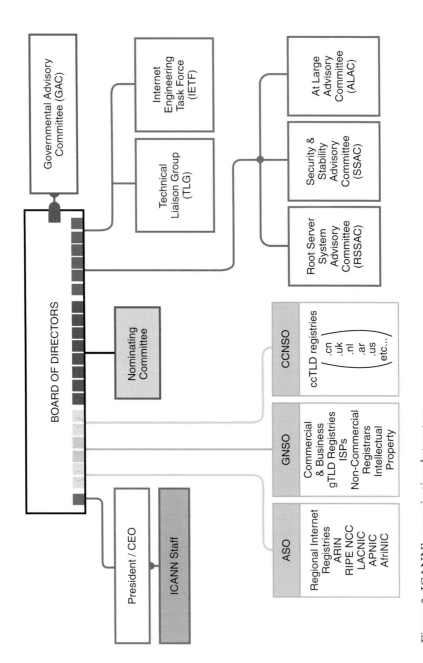

Figure 2: ICANN's organisational structure
(Source: ICANN website (2008), www.icann.org/structure)

In addition to its permanent organs, ICANN has several standing committees and ad hoc groups. Furthermore, its main policy development body regarding domain names, the GNSO, regularly pursues projects that are carried out through ad hoc committees, task forces and working groups.

Like the Global Fund discussed in the preceding chapter, ICANN manifests global governance in a multistakeholder mould. This approach mixes together actors from official, commercial and civil society circles. However, in contrast to the Global Fund, ICANN does not specifically assign seats in its organs to one or the other sector. More often than not, office-holders participate in ICANN as private individuals rather than as representatives of a particular constituency, a practice that creates rather ambiguous accountability relationships.

## ICANN's self-defined accountability

Unlike many other global governance institutions, ICANN openly acknowledges that it faces accountability challenges. Among other things the organisation has an explicit statement of *Accountability and Transparency Frameworks and Principles* (ICANN 2008). The aforementioned Affirmation of Commitments also devotes much attention to accountability arrangements. ICANN furthermore provides appeal and dispute resolution mechanisms such as the Reconsideration Request and the Independent Review (ICANN 2009b). When ICANN's own dispute resolution mechanisms prove insufficient, complainants can always seek redress from the organisation through the US courts.

In its *Frameworks and Principles* document ICANN recognises three levels of constituents to whom it owes three types of accountability, respectively. One is 'public sphere accountability, which deals with mechanisms for assuring stakeholders that ICANN has behaved responsibly'. A second is corporate and legal accountability, 'which covers the obligations that ICANN has through the legal system [of the State of California] and under its bylaws'. A third is 'participating community accountability, which ensures that the Board and executive perform functions in line with the wishes and expectations of the ICANN community' (ICANN 2008: 4).

This threefold conception reflects some confusion as to whom ICANN identifies as its public. In particular the first and third constituencies – and the distinction between them – are not always clear. Greater clarity regarding the scope of ICANN's stakeholders and the nature of its public sphere would be very helpful in facing the challenges of democratic accountability.

The first category, 'public sphere', could be taken to mean the broadest collection of ICANN stakeholders. However, experience indicates that 'stakeholders' for ICANN does not mean all Internet users, but rather refers to formally organised groups of actors who participate in its institutional mechanisms. Some of these stakeholder groups (such as the business constituency and the non-commercial users constituency) are meant to ensure public participation in ICANN. Meanwhile others (such as the domain name registry constituency and the registrar constituency) are commercial partners in ICANN activities.

The third category of stakeholder in ICANN accountability, the 'participating community', is also not clearly circumscribed. Participation in ICANN is voluntary, with no statutory membership. On the one hand, the 'participating community' includes random members of the broader public who have both the interest and the resources to follow, understand and contribute to ICANN processes. On the other hand, the 'participating community' also involves actors who are in a business relationship with the organisation, for example domain name registries (who operate top-level domains) and registrars (who sell domain names to the public).

The *Frameworks and Principles* document confuses matters still further with a claim that ICANN is also 'accountable to the global community' (ICANN 2008: 5). It is not clear what 'the global community' covers and what its relationship is to the 'participating community'. The language seems to imply that ICANN assumes the existence of a global public, albeit undefined and elusive. Nor does ICANN provide a specific mechanism for accountability to 'the global community'.

There are also inherent tensions between the various types of accountability that ICANN has assumed. For one thing, contradictions can arise between corporate legal requirements on the one hand and community expectations on the other. Sometimes corporate legal obligations may run against public trust expectations, for instance, in respect of transparency and information disclosure. The ICANN Documentary Disclosure Policy includes a wide variety of conditions for non-disclosure, some of which appear to be motivated by a wish to protect the corporation's business relationships (ICANN 2008).

Another tension around competing accountabilities in ICANN occurs with respect to the Board. A significant portion of Board members are elected by various stakeholder groups, and these groups may expect such members to advance the particular preferences of the relevant stakeholder circle. Yet the ICANN bylaws require directors to enact duties of 'care, inquiry, loyalty and prudent investment' towards the corporation as a whole and the community at large.

The ambiguities and multidirectional obligations outlined above make it difficult to establish a clear and robust measurement of ICANN's accountability. Koppell (2005) suggests in this regard that ICANN suffers from MAD: 'Multiple Accountability Disorder'. He argues that different notions of accountability are used about ICANN in different contexts with different meanings or nuances. The resulting confusion, he notes, unfortunately leads to competing and conflicting expectations.

However, underlying all of these ambiguities has been the core problem of global accountability that derives from the unilateral control of ICANN by the US Government. Under the MOUs to 2009, ICANN has answered to the US Government as an agent may be accountable to its principal. However, this relationship has not operated in the fashion of other US federal agencies (Froomkin 2000). Until the end of the last iteration of the MOU in September 2009, ICANN regularly reported solely to the US Department of Commerce. In a more ad hoc manner, ICANN has also been compelled to testify in oversight hearings whenever called upon by the relevant committees or subcommittees of the US Congress. Yet most Internet users around the world have no representation in the US Congress. Nor do they have the same access as American citizens to the US DOC or to the US courts. It remains to be seen how far the new Affirmation of Commitments, which replaces the MOU and formally ends the era of unilateral US control, will alter this situation. While the DOC may play a less direct role in supervising ICANN going forward, the Congress may still possibly call on ICANN to respond, albeit not on the ground of the Affirmation of Commitments, but by virtue of ICANN being headquartered and, most importantly, incorporated in the US.

Whatever the case on the US domestic side, the Affirmation only makes ICANN accountable through a periodic review by a team of 'volunteer community members'. Those volunteers include ex officio the Chair of the GAC, the Chair of the ICANN Board, an Officer of the DOC, plus 'representatives of relevant ICANN Advisory Committees and Supporting Organizations and independent experts' (ICANN 2009a). The complete review team must be agreed upon by the Chairs of the GAC and the ICANN Board. Clearly, an explicit and comprehensive framework for accountability standards and enforcement is still lacking.

### Civil society in the ICANN context

Before considering how civil society activities mitigate or exacerbate these accountability challenges at ICANN, it will be helpful to identify who constitutes 'civil society' in respect of this global governance institution. ICANN itself does not in any way officially define or categorise 'civil society'. However, if one adopts the conception taken in this book, where civil society is understood as a political space of public discourse that aims at shaping governance, then it is evident that civil society plays a prominent part in ICANN operations.

Civil society participation within the ICANN institutional structure occurs mainly at two sites: the At-Large Advisory Committee (ALAC) and the Noncommercial Users Constituency (NCUC). Formed in 2002, the ALAC is part of the formal ICANN structure and advises the Board on matters of interest and concern to the end users of the Internet. It has a (non-voting) liaison to the Board of Directors and five other organs of ICANN. Regional At-Large Organisations (RALOs) link local at-large groups and together are meant to form the ALAC community base. 'ICANN At-Large', as this collection of bodies is sometimes called, purports to bring the voice of the individual user to ICANN.

However, in practice the operation of the ALAC as an instrument of democratic voice can be viewed with some scepticism. No doubt these arrangements have provided local user groups with a framework to get involved in ICANN. However, the staff of the corporation have played a prominent role in organising the ALAC community. The development of ICANN At-Large has also followed a top-down dynamic inasmuch as the creation of the central ALAC predated that of the RALOs. Indeed, the ALAC has appeared to function mostly as an outreach programme that brings ICANN's voice to end users rather than the other way around.

For its part the NCUC, created in 2001, seeks to champion public interest concerns in the development of domain name policy more specifically. Its main point of contact in the ICANN structure is the GNSO. As of mid-2009 the NCUC had 142 members from 48 countries, including 73 non-commercial organisations and 69 individuals (NCUC 2009). The NCUC more particularly raises issues of transparency, due process and individual rights (notably of free speech). It plays a role of watchdog over ICANN through its participation in the GNSO, and whenever necessary alerts stakeholders outside the process. NCUC also keeps tabs on ICANN more generally and makes sure that the institution follows predictable, rule-based procedures.

NCUC brings civil society participation into ICANN through the GNSO Council. This body is at the time of writing undergoing substantial reorganisation, with a proposed bicameral structure clustering around commercial stakeholder and non-commercial stakeholder groups. As of mid-2009 the older structure counted twenty-four members: three representatives for each of six constituency groups; three selected by the ICANN Nominating Committee; and three non-voting liaisons and observers from other ICANN bodies. As one of the six constituency groups, NCUC has only had three seats on the GNSO Council, whereas profit-oriented interests – within or outside the domain registration business – have dominated the other five. Sometimes NCUC members can find common cause with the so-called NomCom appointees, whose perspectives can vary widely from one appointee to another. For the rest, however, the civil society members must, if they wish to impact GNSO decisions, form unexpected alliances with representatives of commercial interests. The ongoing reform, if well implemented (e.g. the procedure for appointing the stakeholder group representatives), would have the effect of evenly dividing GNSO seats between commercial and non-commercial interests, although whether interests are homogeneous within each of the two groups remains to be seen.

Apart from the ALAC and the NCUC as the two main channels of formal civil society participation in ICANN, there are also other civil society groupings that engage the institution from outside. The most active civil society players in respect of ICANN can be found in the Internet Governance Caucus (IGC). This loose grouping was initially formed in the context of the World Summit on the Information Society (WSIS), held in 2003 and 2005. Today the caucus comprises around 150 individuals from a variety of civil society associations (IGC 2009). These groups include large NGOs, small local associations interested in Internet access, researchers on Internet policy and related regulations, other professionals such as engineers and lawyers, small-business owners, individuals volunteering their knowledge, and individuals curious to learn. Scholars within the IGC have formed a Global Internet Governance Academic Network (GigaNet), which is dedicated to interdisciplinary research and informed policy dialogue among researchers, governments, global governance agencies, the private sector and civil society.

Another significant civil society player in ICANN affairs is the Internet Society (ISOC). This body was created in 1992 by a group of individuals, including computer geeks, in order to carry out Internet governance in a truly private fashion, albeit with the imprimatur of the International Telecommunication Union (ITU), which they sought. ISOC had to concede its ambition to ICANN after the US Government opposed their initiative, especially the involvement of the ITU (Goldsmith and Wu 2006). With active chapters in around seventy countries across the world, ISOC remains a notable civil society player in Internet politics.

ICANNWatch is a collaborative effort by an unincorporated set of scholars who maintain a forum website and contribute their research expertise in order to shed light on ICANN processes and their impacts. Launched in 1999, ICANNWatch purports to serve as a central point of reference for all persons who seek to make sense of Internet governance and to shape it through informed debate (ICANN Watch 2009).

Another example of informal civil society engagement of ICANN is the Internet Governance Project (IGP), a consortium of academics with scholarly and practical expertise in Internet policy. Founded in 2004, the IGP regularly releases analyses on topics and issues at the core of debates on Internet governance. Some of its members are also actively involved in advocacy (IGP 2009).

Other streaks of civil society, which are not involved in any shape or form in communications policies or management of Internet resources, may still engage sporadically with ICANN matters as relevant. In effect, their focus on other substantive issues may turn out to overlap with ICANN decisions. Some of those actors, based in the USA, have indeed been comfortable with US dominance of ICANN, which has given them leverage over Internet policies through the DOC and the US Congress. For example, as is elaborated later, some conservative civil society associations in the USA have taken their agenda of 'family values' to ICANN regarding the possibility of a new gTLD for adult content. These citizen groups clearly would not have enjoyed such a degree of influence if the Internet were governed through a public multilateral institution firmly rooted in international law.

Some elements outside the USA have shared this satisfaction with the status quo. For instance, many affiliates of the Internet Society, especially those with a strong technological culture, have opposed any suggestion to replace ICANN with a more global arrangement involving other governments besides that of the USA. Thus one sees that the civil society crowd around issues of Internet governance is rather like a harlequin cloth: colourful and patchy in terms of interests, ideas and even values.

As noted earlier, it is difficult to identify and measure precisely the impact of civil society actors on ICANN processes and outcomes. Policy in this institution generally emerges not as the outcome of any one group of actors leading the charge, but from an interchange among business, government and civil society actors. It is therefore hard to attribute one or the other development in ICANN directly or exclusively to civil society groups (or to other sectoral participants in the organisation). Furthermore, changes at ICANN may occur when a handful of well-informed individuals, sometimes spontaneously handpicked by the corporation's staff (regardless of whether they represent business, government or civil society), find themselves in the right place at the right time, coalescing to set the policy agenda or influence a particular outcome. In sum, change may depend on a critical mass of proponents supporting an idea as well as on individual reputation and interpersonal relationships.

## Civil society and ICANN accountability

This general point regarding causality in ICANN policy processes also applies to the more particular question of accountability. Documenting the exact part taken by each actor group (i.e. governments as against corporations as against civil society associations) in improving accountability is not always possible. Hence the following analysis only attempts to illustrate how civil society participants and their allies have tried to tackle some of ICANN's most distinctive accountability shortcomings. The four dimensions of accountability highlighted in this book – transparency, consultation, evaluation and correction – are examined in turn.

### *Transparency*

ICANN's working procedures are officially laid down in its bylaws. Policies are meant to be developed in a bottom-up process, whereby decision-making starts from public participation at the base and ends with sanction given at the top. However, the policy process is far from visible and understandable to all Internet stakeholders. Moreover, sometimes decisions are taken in ways that clash with the established rule or expected good practice. So shortfalls in transparency can be a real issue for ICANN. However, civil society groups have given only sporadic and uneven attention to the problem.

A good illustrative case of transparency deficits in ICANN is the application from the company ICM Registry to hold the '.xxx' top-level domain for hosting websites with adult content. This episode reinforced public suspicions that external powers covertly and unduly interfere in ICANN business. The application obtained initial approval from ICANN in 2005. Negotiations followed in order to work out a detailed formal agreement with ICM Registry. However, the ICANN Board rejected this agreement in May 2006 and confirmed this refusal in March 2007 following a review of a revised draft agreement (ICANN 2007a).

The incident provoked heated debate in civil society circles as to whether the outcome was a legitimate Board decision or the result of pressure outside normal procedures, notably from the US Government and US domestic actors such as the Family Research Council and other conservative groups. Arguably these US-based civil society associations were in effect pressing for government interference in ICANN.

Various other civil society activists raised concerns regarding transparency deficits around the ICM Registry application. However, their complaints in blogs and emails were not followed up with concerted action. As so often occurs in the context of ICANN, the '.xxx' dispute did not generate a large and co-ordinated civil society campaign. Instead, concerned individuals and groups highlight issues of public interest in an ad hoc and generally unsustained fashion.

For its part ICM Registry invoked the US Freedom of Information Act and in early 2008 obtained access to records of communications between the US Government and ICANN regarding the '.xxx' application. These documents did exhibit some evidence of intervention by the DOC to reverse the anticipated approval of the TLD. However, the US authorities still succeeded in concealing contents that would allegedly have provided further insight into the ways that the Department of Commerce exercises US Government power over the root zone, as well as DOC opinions and manoeuvres regarding the '.xxx' application (IGP 2006b). To avoid arbitrary interventions of this kind, some academic voices in civil society have suggested that all stakeholders alongside governments should develop a global framework convention of the sort that the UN has established in respect of climate change (Mathiason 2004; Mueller, Mathiason and Klein 2007).

Other shortfalls in ICANN transparency were evident in the development of a new policy on generic top-level domains (gTLDs). This case shows that, while ICANN prides itself on having bottom-up procedures, the institution does not always facilitate broad participation and upfront inclusion of the public at large. In May 2006 the GNSO Council formed an Internationalized Domain Name (IDN) Working Group to study IDN issues and propose relevant provisions for the new gTLD regime. However, the creation of this group – and its subsequent proceedings and decisions – were given no public notice apart from a mention in the Council minutes (GNSO 2006). Nor were membership criteria or rules for the Working Group specified. As matters transpired the body was populated mostly by affiliates of incumbent registries and registrars, as well as other business-related constituencies. Poor transparency thereby had the result of hindering participation by IDN stakeholders who advocate for non-Roman script user communities. No effective civil society objections to this course of events were heard. Indeed, while civil society voices in the global north have not deliberately opposed the development of DNS infrastructure that supports non-Roman scripts, they have not actively promoted this major step towards increased access to the Internet either.

Greater civil society promotion of ICANN transparency has occurred through urgings from ALAC and the At-Large community for more multilingual documentation, especially in French and Spanish, and if possible in all six languages of the United Nations. The At-Large Secretariat has worked with the At-Large community to increase the availability of such documentation as well as introducing translation tools that can translate papers and webpages quickly and easily, if sometimes imperfectly.

However, to date ICANN has not had the budgetary resources to translate all policy documentation.

CSOs are not the only actors who have pressed ICANN for greater transparency. Business actors have also intervened in this respect, as illustrated by the initiative of ICM Registry noted above, although this was pursuant to their commercial interest. In addition, from a public trust perspective the Canadian Internet Regulatory Authority (CIRA) in March 2006 published an open letter criticising ICANN for insufficient transparency. CIRA advised that the ICANN Board should take fewer decisions behind closed doors, should hold public meetings or make the minutes of these meetings available to the public, and should provide a summary of its deliberations and its rationale for a particular decision on any significant matter (CIRA 2006). Public stances like this have certainly contributed in convincing ICANN to release the minutes of its board meetings for the public record.

### Consultation

ICANN also has shortcomings in respect of the second dimension of accountability highlighted in this book, namely consultation of affected publics. As described earlier, civil society actors can make inputs to the ICANN Board through the ALAC and can engage the GNSO Council through the NCUC. However, as noted before, ALAC operations tend to function in a top-down fashion led by ICANN staff, and active and persistent participation in the NCUC is limited to a few dozen individuals who are more aware of ICANN's operations.

Outside these established institutional mechanisms ICANN has also taken a number of ad hoc initiatives to consult stakeholders. For example, during its general public meetings organised three or four times a year in rotation around the world, ICANN holds open microphone sessions where participants ask questions or make observations and suggestions regarding any issues of relevance to the various ICANN bodies. Furthermore, ICANN regularly provides opportunities for online inputs from the public regarding its ongoing work. The organisation frequently posts drafts of major policy decisions to be made by the Board, including the final draft of proposed policies by lower-level bodies before submission to the Board. The public then has a number of days to submit comments or raise objections.

However, such consultations have not followed any scheme of good practice, and it is not clear how, if at all, the public input has shaped eventual ICANN decisions. A Request for Public Comments posted by ICANN in May 2007 prompted CIRA to criticise the organisation again.

The Canadian agency deplored the lack of sufficient notice as well as the absence of a statement of purpose, background documentation and follow-up procedures. The complaint also noted that the consultation questions were too broad and open-ended, such that each issue could require a whole consultation in itself (CIRA 2007). For improvements, CIRA referred ICANN to the OECD guidelines for online public consultations (OECD 2009).

In any case, the size and scope of the civil society that is likely to submit comments in an ICANN consultation are contingent upon the extent to which the institution reaches out and opens its processes to broader participation. Yet, as already noted with respect to policy on Internationalized Domain Names, vested interests can work to limit wider involvement. The IDN issue was, in fact, a central piece of the new gTLD policy and might have warranted more public attention (GNSO 2007). However, the matter did not gain traction among the mostly Western-centric civil society that invests itself in ICANN processes. Instead, as so often occurs with civil society interventions in respect of ICANN, issues of free speech trumped concerns of equitable access, including opportunities for new entrants from around the world (especially in the global south) to compete in the domain name industry. Hence in ICANN, as in most of the other institutions examined in this book, the dominance of the West in global civil society circles can reinforce the dominance of the West in the global governance agency.

The IDN issue brings out a clear divergence of priorities between the West and others in respect of ICANN. Most Western businesses, governments and civil societies do not see a problem in the exclusive use of Roman script in top-level domain names. However, for users working in Arabic, Chinese, Russian, Sanskrit, Thai and other scripts, the implementation of IDN in TLDs is of crucial importance. As long as participation in ICANN (including civil society inputs) came predominantly from the West, the institution was reluctant to consider implementation of IDN at the top level. After trying without success for nearly a decade to get ICANN to implement IDN, a silenced constituency of IDN entrepreneurs and potential users waiting on the sidelines to engage ICANN on this issue was nearly bypassed by the GNSO Council in its process for developing IDN policy. These actors were nowhere to be found in the GNSO's IDN Working Group when it started its deliberations, and it took a long email battle to get some of them included. Even then they were only observers, with an ability to contribute to the deliberations but not to vote on the IDN policy recommendations. ICANN insiders apparently assumed that participation by outsiders would be disruptive for the simple reason that they were unfamiliar with the ways of the institution;

yet those non-Western participants proved to be very resourceful during the proceedings. More recently, momentum towards the implementation of IDN, with a pilot phase including gTLD in eleven different language scripts, suggests that ICANN may have developed greater sensitivity towards a more global and diverse community of users.

### Monitoring and evaluation

Although civil society advancement of ICANN accountability has not been particularly notable in respect of transparency and consultation, the record shows some more positive impacts with regard to monitoring and evaluation. As noted earlier, several civil society groupings including the NCUC and ICANNWatch have pursued concerted oversight of ICANN. In addition, research initiatives such as the Internet Governance Project have undertaken critical examinations of ICANN operations.

However, as indicated early on in this chapter, until the 2009 Affirmation of Commitments only the US Government has been in a position formally to scrutinise and sanction ICANN. This monitoring has taken place most particularly through public hearings held by the US Congress and through reviews of ICANN conducted by the National Telecommunications and Information Administration (NTIA) of the US Department of Commerce. Civil society groups have participated in both of these processes, albeit with generally modest results.

Civil society players have often participated in US congressional hearings on ICANN with testimony and advocacy. However, they have often been in a reactive position, responding to the priorities of the lawmakers rather than setting the agenda themselves. Indeed, US legislators have tended to focus on what they perceive as a need to protect US interests in ICANN against the rest of the world. Or the congresspersons have responded to their most powerful constituents, who have not generally included socially progressive civil society actors. Moreover, opportunities for congressional testimony have mainly been available for US-based groups, with far less access – if any – for civil society voices from the rest of the world. For these various reasons, then, participation in processes of congressional scrutiny has not been a very effective way for civil society to enhance ICANN accountability. At best, civil society testimonies have raised awareness among US lawmakers of a wider array of concerns to consider in respect of ICANN, instead of pursuing a totally US-centred agenda.

Monitoring and evaluation of ICANN through the NTIA has been more open to inputs from civil society bodies outside the USA. Citizens from around the world have been able to submit opinions through the NTIA website in response to its notices of enquiry into ICANN. In addition, the audience for NTIA public hearings concerning ICANN may also include some civil society participants from outside the USA. However, although civil society groups (both US and non-US) have sometimes been vocal during NTIA proceedings, their influence on the review process has been very limited.

The experience of the NTIA/DOC enquiry in 2006 about a prospective ICANN transition to a fully private governance mechanism is instructive in this regard. On this occasion the Internet Governance Project sought to mobilise the public to submit a template statement, or comments of their own, in favour of ending oversight of ICANN by the US Government (IGP 2006a). Many submissions were made, particularly by contributors from outside the US-based business sector. Nevertheless, the MOU was renewed in September 2006 without any reduction of the unilateral US oversight function. On the contrary, the new version expanded ICANN duties to the US Government, namely around policy on the DNS Whois (discussed further below). Indeed, this DOC intervention effectively subverted an ongoing so-called 'bottom-up' policy development process inside ICANN on the 'Whois' issue (Mueller and Chango 2008).

Civil society actors have also made inputs to the NTIA's mid-term reviews of its MOUs with ICANN (NTIA 2008). For example, in a public meeting convened by the NTIA in February 2008 to assess the then-current MOU, the IGP submitted suggestions for improving accountability at ICANN (IGP 2008). These included, among other things: (a) allowing the Supporting Organisations to take a vote of no confidence against the ICANN Board or the CEO; (b) making the Independent Review Procedure more meaningful by having it examine more than the mere consistency of the organisation's decisions with its own bylaws; and (c) holding a biannual review of ICANN's record and accountability, jointly conducted by ICANN and the United Nations Internet Governance Forum (IGF). Although these specific IGP proposals have not been adopted, years of advocacy on these general lines arguably contributed to the termination of the MOU.

Civil society groups have further promoted monitoring and evaluation of ICANN by contributing to periodic external reviews of the institution, as prescribed in its bylaws. For instance, in 2006–7 ICANN commissioned the One World Trust, an NGO based in London, to assess its accountability mechanisms (ICANN 2007b). In 2006 ICANN asked the Public Policy Group at the London School of Economics to undertake a review of the GNSO (ICANN 2006). The latter evaluation has triggered a number of changes that are expected to make the GNSO Council more effective and to introduce greater fairness into the distribution of votes.

*Correction*

Finally, among the four dimensions of democratic accountability high-lighted in this book, one can examine civil society efforts towards correction and redress in respect of ICANN. In this area, too, civil society actors have found it difficult to make progress in the face of opposition from other powerful interests.

These problems are well illustrated by experiences around the domain name 'Whois' rule. With its Whois policy, ICANN requires that accredited domain name registrars allow anyone to obtain the contact details of the registrant of any given domain name. This practice conflicts with many privacy and data protection legislations, so that a number of registrars, in applying the global ICANN principle, contravene the national or regional law that applies in their jurisdiction. Indeed, unencumbered access to the identification data of domain name registrants can be abused for marketing purposes as well as for private policing without due process.

Civil society actors have, together with the domain name registration business, succeeded in stopping ICANN from adopting an even stricter policy by which registrars would need to guarantee the accuracy of Whois data. In addition, civil society actors have made a decisive case to the GNSO for a limited definition of the purpose of Whois data, rather than an open-ended definition that would make contact details of registrants publicly available to anyone and for any purpose (Mueller and Chango 2008). The NCUC has also alerted privacy advocates and data protection commissioners around the world of the stakes in the Whois debate. However, civil society efforts have so far failed to obtain a revocation of the Whois policy itself.

Not surprisingly, ICANN rarely corrects a policy or procedure merely in response to denunciations by civil society groups. A more effective tactic can be for civil society actors to take their grievances to the US courts. Such an approach was pursued, for example, when one of the individuals elected in the 2000 online public election to the Board, Karl Auerbach, was refused access to ICANN corporate records in his new role as Director. Auerbach's case was taken up by the Electronic Frontier Foundation (EFF), a group of activists, technologists and researchers fighting for consumer protection and civil liberties in respect of digital technologies. The EFF supported Auerbach in suing ICANN in 2002, and he eventually obtained access to the ICANN materials (EFF 2009).

Yet perhaps the greatest correction and redress that civil society forces have advocated in respect of ICANN concerns the lack of underlying democratic legitimacy of this global governance institution so long as it operates at the behest of a single national government (through the

US Department of Commerce). The World Summit on the Information Society was a defining moment in this regard. WSIS brought ICANN into the spotlight of the global public and mobilised civil society energies around Internet governance issues as never before.

Civil society actors took the lead around WSIS in emphasising the democratically unsustainable position in which most of the world's population has no say in governance of one of the principal components of global communications, the Internet. The previously described Internet Governance Caucus was initiated around the WSIS process in February 2003 and five months later issued its first formal statements for a democratisation of Internet regulation (WSIS 2003). Thereafter civil society, through the IGC, set up a plenary platform and issue-specific caucuses, drafted inputs and generally drove the WSIS discussion on issues of Internet governance. Civil society actors also had a remarkable role in drafting the final report of the Working Group on Internet Governance (WGIG) which met between the two summit meetings. The WGIG report provided a working definition of Internet governance and established a number of multistakeholder mechanisms to consider a future replacement of, or complement to, the US-dominated ICANN regime. The WGIG included at least fifteen identifiable civil society actors amongst its forty members (WGIG 2005). At the second WSIS meeting, held in Tunis in 2005, civil society urgings helped to create the Internet Governance Forum under the United Nations to carry forward the multistakeholder dialogue started in the WGIG.

Civil society promotion of debate on Internet governance and the (il) legitimacy of ICANN's governance model and policy lines has persisted since the close of WSIS in 2005. The Internet Governance Caucus has continued to provide a forum for public debate on the subject and has actively engaged both ICANN and the IGF. Arguably these years of pressure from reformers in civil society helped to effect the shift to the Affirmation of Commitments in 2009, under which US Government unilateral control of ICANN is meant to be curtailed.

The civil society Internet Governance Caucus has also had the important corrective effect of raising awareness amongst large constituencies of Internet users who have not been, and cannot be, involved in ICANN's processes. One of the most vocal members of the IGC, Parminder Jeet Singh, has moreover argued that ICANN bases its work on neoliberal ideological fixations with market competition and intellectual property rights. These priorities, he argues, are alien to the needs of the excluded 'development constituency', which is more concerned with public interest, collaboration and access to knowledge. Singh affirms that 'ICANN just doesn't speak the language of these people' and thus limits participation to 'a charmed circle of insiders'. He claims repeatedly to have asked ICANN to define the 'global internet community' to which it claims to be accountable, but without response, and he proceeds to conclude that 'one can't associate with an organization which doesn't clarify its legitimate constituency' (Singh 2007).

## Conclusion

ICANN is certainly open to civil society engagement. However, given the vested interests in play, a large, meticulous and relentless civil society effort is probably required to make the organisation more responsive to the broader public interest. Several obstacles would need to be overcome before such a campaign could be mounted.

For one thing, civil society groups need to become more alert to the major political and economic issues at stake in ICANN. At the moment too many potential activists conclude that, because they experience no obstacles in using the Internet, there is no problem. Most civil society actors apparently believe that ICANN is a highly technical body that has no relevance for them. Or they conclude that engagement with ICANN requires specialist knowledge which is only available to professionals. The discrepancy between the scale of ICANN's impact on the one hand and limited civil society awareness and engagement on the other is puzzling enough to warrant substantial enquiry (Mueller *et al.* 2004).

In addition to countering widespread apathy, greater civil society engagement with ICANN would require that insider activists become more open to wider participation. During the first decade of ICANN operations civil society participation has concentrated on a narrow circle of veteran experts. All too often, anyone whose day job has not intersected with, or does not provide a substantive insight into, Internet governance has been unable to participate meaningfully. In this way ICANN has followed what Robert Michels called an 'iron law of oligarchy', whereby any organisation tends, regardless of its initial level of democracy, to evolve towards the dominance of a small professional elite (Michels 1911). In contrast to ICANN, civil society in the WSIS process opened up a much wider public debate on Internet governance.

Then there is the question of what new governance arrangements for ICANN under the Affirmation of Commitments will mean for civil society engagement of the institution. In recent years ICANN appears to have become more conscious of, and responsive to, the demands of governments. This development needs to be counterbalanced by a significant influx of civil society participation in ICANN policy processes, particularly in order to reinforce conditions of public accountability.

The expansion of the Internet to IDN also raises new concerns for civil society engagement of ICANN. For example, will the institution concur with the views of incumbent domain name registries regarding their de facto 'natural monopoly' over character strings and their alleged semantic equivalence across languages? Or, perhaps with pressure from civil society, will Internet governance be adjusted to enable local communities and businesses to be players in their own markets? Otherwise the domain supply industry will remain a cash cow in the hands of the usual few from the same small quarters of the world, while the rest of the globe merely provides powerless users and consumers.

Important questions such as this will require close scrutiny of ICANN, whose accountability arrangements, as seen in this chapter, remain loose. Clearly, whatever governance formula is ultimately adopted for ICANN, the ways that civil society participation is defined and organised will have significant consequences for the democratic accountability of the institution.

# 14 Civil society and the World Fair Trade Organization: developing responsive accountability

*Heidi Ullrich*

## Introduction

The studies in this book assess the role of civil society in a variety of global governance arrangements. In respect of the first nine institutions examined in earlier chapters, civil society associations have stood as outside parties who intervene in a state-based global governance apparatus. The next three cases (respectively on climate change, global disease control and Internet regulation) have involved hybrid forms of governance, where some civil society actors work inside the regulatory organisation along with official and/or commercial elements. Now this final case study considers a global governance institution with an entirely non-state character, the World Fair Trade Organization (WFTO). Hence this chapter analyses how one civil society actor (the WFTO) has accountability relations with other civil society associations (for example its member organisations and consumer groups).

The fair trade movement is experiencing extraordinary expansion in the early twenty-first century. Growing public awareness of the need for socially and environmentally responsible products is increasing demand for fair trade goods. As a result these articles are now sold not only through specialised fair trade shops, but also through mainstream retail channels. In 2009, consumers in the European Union purchased €1.5 billion in certified fair trade goods, a level 70 times greater than in 1999. In 2007 fair trade sales worldwide totalled more than €2.3 billion, albeit that this figure comprised less than 1 per cent of overall world trade (Commission of the European Communities 2009: 3). It is estimated that approximately 110 million craftspeople, farmers and fair trade producers and suppliers around the world directly benefit from fair trade (WFTO 2009b).

For feedback on earlier versions of this study, I am particularly grateful to Mike Muchilwa, Monitoring Coordinator of IFAT, and Johny Joseph, Director of Creative Handicrafts, a WFTO member organisation.

The fair trade movement encompasses a diverse group of civil society organisations (CSOs). They include business associations, consumer movements, development NGOs, faith-based initiatives and farmer groups. In far-reaching global networks linking the global north and the global south, these actors buy and sell an expanding array of fair trade items produced by various sustainable production methods.

The emergence of the WFTO in October 2008 from its previous identity as the International Fair Trade Association (IFAT) has revitalised this private global governance institution. A 2007 study commissioned by the IFAT Executive Committee found that the organisation was facing a 'great danger that … it will fragment and die' if it did not adapt to changing realities (Myers and Wills 2007: 5). Like IFAT, the WFTO occupies a unique place as the global regulatory body for the certification of fair trade organisations. However, the WFTO has expanded its role relative to IFAT with explicit claims to be the global 'voice of fair trade' and an 'agent for change' (WFTO 2009h).

On three counts the WFTO is more accountable to its members and to other interested parties than its earlier embodiment as IFAT. First, the WFTO has governance arrangements that provide an equitable voice for the organisation's five regions and its members, the majority of which are from the global south. Second, the new institution seeks to provide its approximately 400 member organisations in over 70 countries with a more accessible monitoring and certification system, with fair trade skills training that leads to greater market access opportunities, and with innovative global advocacy activities. Third, the threat that the regulatory functions of the WFTO and its sister body, Fairtrade Labelling Organizations International (FLO), would be taken over by a public body, the International Organization for Standardization (ISO), has been reduced, due in part to increased outreach by the WFTO to key stakeholder groups, including consumer groups and business associations.

The relatively rapid transformation of this global governance institution into a more accountable organisation is noteworthy. This chapter explores in what ways and to what extent civil society activities have played a role in effecting this change. The argument elaborated in this chapter is that pressure from civil society, including member fair trade organisations and transnational consumer associations, played a direct role in the transformation of IFAT into the more accountable WFTO, thereby strengthening the global governance of fair trade. However, although the WFTO has created mechanisms to strengthen its internal accountability (i.e. to members), it has yet fully to develop means of strengthening external accountability (i.e. to stakeholders outside the organisation).

An inappropriate institutional structure and lack of resources resulted in IFAT being unable to respond effectively to the needs of its members, in particular the Southern fair trade producers who comprised two-thirds of its membership. Southern members were therefore constrained from promoting their interests within IFAT and their products to mainstream retailers. In response to internal pressure from its member fair trade associations, the WFTO operates with a decentralised governance system that gives its regions a greater role and responsibility in the operation of the organisation.

Member fair trade organisations have also successfully pressed the WFTO to ensure that its monitoring and certification systems reflect the changing demands of the fair trade movement. After its members cited the need for a more robust system in order to maintain the quality of the 'fair trade' label, the WFTO has made its monitoring and certification system more transparent and trusted by requiring third-party verification of its members' production methods. Meanwhile, as the number of marginalised Southern fair trade organisations has grown, their need for a more flexible fair trade certification system has steadily increased. To this end the WFTO, in consultation with its members, is developing a Sustainable Fair Trade Management System (SFTMS) that replaces the former IFAT/WFTO monitoring and certification arrangements. This scheme adapts fair trade standards so that they are more accessible to Southern fair trade producers and more trusted by Northern fair trade sellers. A key element of this new system is that it uses an integrated supply chain approach to fair trade. The SFTMS thereby covers the entire process by which fair trade goods are produced and distributed, in contrast to the traditional product-specific certification approach (Commons 2008).

External pressure from other citizen action groups, specifically consumer organisations, has prompted the WFTO to increase its outreach activities with wider society somewhat. Consumer associations were concerned at the lack of effective fair trade organisation branding and consumer confusion over a myriad of fair trade labelling schemes, and therefore called for stronger international fair trade standards. In May 2006 the ISO Consumer Policy Committee (COPOLCO) adopted a resolution for the development of a new global standard on fair trade within the ISO. However, after a year of concerted effort by IFAT and FLO, including efforts to institutionalise engagement with consumer organisations, COPOLCO passed a resolution which acknowledged that it was premature to incorporate fair trade certification within the scope of the ISO.

To elaborate the argument set out above, the rest of this chapter first briefly reviews the history and nature of fair trade initiatives. Second, it describes the institutional structure of the WFTO. Third, it identifies the key components of the organisation's accountability. Next the discussion examines WFTO engagement with civil society organisations, with a specific focus on fair trade organisations and consumer groups. The chapter concludes by assessing the extent to which engagement with CSOs has shaped the accountability of the WFTO.

Given the lack of previous research on the WFTO, this study has relied heavily on primary evidence such as interviews and written communications, mainly conducted in 2007 and 2009. Respondents included IFAT/WFTO members (North and South), IFAT/WFTO staff, members of the IFAT Executive Committee and the WFTO Board of Directors, regional forum members and representatives of consumer organisations. IFAT/WFTO documentation, primarily web-based, has constituted a major source of background information. Additionally, the author's participation in the biennial IFAT Conference and Annual General Meeting in May 2007 provided significant insights for the analysis.

### A brief history of fair trade

The contemporary concept of fair trade has evolved as an alternative to the mainstream neoliberal framework. Rather than the maximisation of commercial profit, fair trade puts primary emphasis on economic justice and social equity (Waddell 2002: 21; see also Gutiérrez 1996; Nicholls and Opal 2005; Watson 2006, 2007). A key component of alternative trade is to provide small, and often poor, producers in the global south with means to improve their livelihoods through increased trade with the global north. Alternative trade items are produced, distributed and sold through global networks of producers, importers and retailers. Thus key constituencies of alternative trade include poor and marginalised producers in the South, importers and retailers in the North, and ethically minded consumers worldwide.

The origins of alternative trade lie in civil society. (On the history of free trade see Kocken 2005; Fair Trade Original 2007.) Beginning in the 1940s, the Mennonite Central Committee, a religious relief agency based in the USA, imported and sold handicrafts made in Puerto Rico, in Haiti and by Palestinian refugees as a means to improve the livelihoods of marginalised producers. The idea of alternative trade spread to Europe in the late 1950s, starting in the United Kingdom and the Netherlands. During the 1960s and 1970s the movement was part of wider activism of developing countries on trade issues, for example through the Group of Seventy-Seven (G77), the United Nations Conference on Trade and Development (UNCTAD), and proposals for a New International

Economic Order (NIEO). In the 1980s the range of alternative trade goods expanded beyond traditional handicrafts to include food products such as coffee, tea and cocoa. As demand for alternative food items grew among Northern consumers, conventional market outlets such as grocery chains and coffee shops began to stock these goods. By 2009 over two-thirds of fair trade products were sold in mainstream retail outlets (WFTO 2009c).

Beginning in the mid-1990s, increased demand for alternatively traded food products, coupled with a downturn in demand for alternative traded handicrafts, necessitated a re-evaluation of arrangements. It was highly costly to operate a comprehensive 'alternative trade system' that encompassed the whole production and exchange process. In contrast, it could be competitive to operate 'fair trade' in which only certain key functions such as production were certified as adhering to standards of economic and social justice, while conventional means were used for transport, storage and sale (Waddell 2002: 23). Thus terminology shifted from 'alternative trade' to 'fair trade'.

With the growth in demand came a proliferation of fair trade organisations across the world, particularly in Europe. Initially these organisations met periodically on an informal basis in order to learn from each other and co-ordinate their activities. Concurrently with the transition from 'alternative trade' to 'fair trade', a complex web of global and regional fair trade associations evolved a means to increase effectiveness and face common challenges. In addition to IFAT (launched in 1989), the main umbrella groups are the European Fair Trade Association (EFTA, created in 1990), the Network of European Worldshops (NEWS!, started in 1994), and FLO (founded in 1997). By 2007, these associations collectively represented more than 1 million fair trade producers, over 200 fair trade importers, some 3,000 world shops, and thousands of volunteers (Fair Trade Advocacy Office 2007a). The regional body EFTA is a member of the global body, the WFTO (previously IFAT), while NEWS! merged with the European regional office of the WFTO in 2009 (Myers 2009).

A principal concern for the various associations has been to develop certification and labelling schemes for fair trade. FLO serves as the standard-setting organisation for fair trade products. In 2002 it launched the now widely recognised blue and green International Fair Trade Certification Mark. For its part the WFTO certifies fair trade organisations rather than fair trade products.

As well as advancing standards and certification, the various fair trade umbrella organisations have promoted partnerships between Northern fair trade importers and marginalised Southern producers. In addition, the associations have raised awareness of fair trade among Northern consumers, business circles and politicians. As a result fair trade has become an established and growing feature of world commerce.

## The WFTO as a global governance institution

Before examining the WFTO record on accountability, and civil society contributions in this regard, it is useful to review what the organisation does and with what institutional structure it pursues those activities. Throughout this discussion it bears remembering that, in contrast to other global governance arrangements examined in this book, the WFTO is entirely non-governmental in character.

### Purpose and activities

According to its Constitution, the objectives of the WFTO are to: (a) improve the livelihoods of marginalised producers and workers, especially in the South; (b) change unfair structures of international trade; (c) improve and co-ordinate the co-operation of its member organisations; and (d) promote the interests of, and provide services to, its member organisations and individuals (WFTO 2009m: Art. III).

The Constitution further prescribes that these objectives are to be achieved by: (a) promoting co-operation and exchange of information among members in such areas as marketing, product development and campaigning; (b) co-ordinating international campaigns; (c) advancing co-operation among members in the marketing of goods; (d) pursuing funds for fair trade product development and marketing; (e) issuing a periodic newsletter; (f) convening a conference in combination with the Annual General Meeting; and (g) undertaking any other activities as decided upon by the Annual General Meeting or the Board (WFTO 2009m: Art. IV). In addressing these concerns the WFTO mainly focuses in three areas: market development, global advocacy, and monitoring and certification.

In regard to market development the WFTO works to increase links between Northern fair trade importers and retailers on the one hand and Southern fair trade producers on the other. The WFTO provides forums that bring together Northern retailers and Southern fair trade producers, through global and regional conferences as well as virtually through the WFTO website. In addition, the WFTO offers Southern producers access to business support services that assist them in designing products that meet the demand of Northern consumers. The WFTO also provides members with skills in using new technologies to ensure sustainable production and farming, as well as training in fair trade business and management models (WFTO 2009h). In June 2009 the WFTO established a virtual fair trade shop (www.wftomarket.com) that facilitates online searches for fair trade products and ensures that consumers are purchasing authentic fair trade items (WFTO 2009l).

In respect of global advocacy the WFTO plays an active role in campaigns to raise awareness of fair trade among politicians and the general public. Since 2004 IFAT (and now the WFTO) has co-ordinated advocacy activities with FLO, EFTA and NEWS! (until the latter's absorption into the WFTO) through the Fair Trade Advocacy Office (FTAO). This Brussels-based bureau promotes awareness of fair trade among the various stakeholders. It lobbies regional institutions such as the European Commission and the European Parliament as well as global bodies such as the World Trade Organization (WTO) and the ISO. Achievements of advocacy at the European level include Communications on Fair Trade adopted by the Commission in 1999 and 2009, as well as several European Parliament resolutions concerning fair trade (FTAO 2009). The WFTO also participated in the sixth Ministerial Conference of the WTO in December 2005, where the fair trade movement, represented by IFAT, FLO, NEWS! and EFTA, produced its first joint statement on fair trade (FTAO 2005). Four years later the WFTO delivered a message on the economic sustainability of fair trade to heads of state and government at the G8 Summit in L'Aquila, Italy (WFTO 2009d). More generally, the WFTO plays a leading part in organising events to celebrate World Fair Trade Day, which takes place annually on 9 May.

In addition to market development and global advocacy, the WFTO has devoted considerable energies to certification of fair trade organisations and associated labelling practices. In 1997 IFAT developed a three-step monitoring system to certify fair trade organisations, as a means of increasing trust in fair trade products among consumers and retailers. In 2004 IFAT officially launched a Fair Trade Organization Mark that was granted to bodies which met its established standards and requirements. The mark serves to distinguish fair trade organisations from commercial traders such as Starbucks and Wal-Mart that are involved in fair trade only through the purchase of products labelled under the FLO certification system.

By 2007 many IFAT members were worried that this regime was not sufficiently rigorous, particularly given its lack of external verification. Moreover, Southern IFAT fair trade producers observed that some Northern IFAT importers were not purchasing fair trade items exclusively from IFAT producers. In addition, the complexity and cost of the IFAT labelling system was seen as hampering the promotion of fair trade sales.

In response to these concerns the newly established WFTO began, in 2008, to upgrade the system to certify its members. To be certified under the WFTO an organisation is required to follow the ten WFTO Principles of Fair Trade (detailed at WFTO 2009a and identical to the principles that guided IFAT) (IFAT 2005). Qualifying organisations are deemed to be '100% fair trade' and become members of the WFTO's Fair Trade 100 (FT100) group (WFTO 2009k). The WFTO system for monitoring fair trade organisations entails a four-step process consisting of self-assessments by members, feedback and review by WFTO monitoring staff, approval and external verification. (See WFTO 2009i for full details.) The step of external verification was absent in the IFAT monitoring system. Upon successful completion and verification of the self-assessment review, member fair trade organisations are registered as having met the demands of WFTO certification.

In a more dramatic shift, the WFTO is developing the aforementioned Sustainable Fair Trade Management System (SFTMS). This initiative responds not only to the certification needs of WFTO members, but also to demands from small and medium-sized fair trade organisations, civil society associations, consumers and regulators for a voluntary global fair trade standard (Commons 2008; WFTO 2009j). The SFTMS consists of three parts: (a) a strengthened membership system; (b) a strengthened monitoring system; and (c) a strengthened certification system in which WFTO members may choose to participate (Myers 2010). Members who do not wish to participate in the certification system will receive a single-product certification. Members who wish to participate in the certification system must complete the requirements of the SFTMS Standard, which is based on criteria developed by the International Social and Environmental Accreditation and Labelling Alliance (ISEAL) in order to guarantee credibility in the marketplace (Myers 2010). Upon completion they will be given an organisational certification mark (rather than one for a single product) backed by the WFTO (Myers 2010). The key feature that distinguishes the SFTMS from the WFTO Monitoring System for Fair Trade Organizations and the product-specific certification of FLO is that it is a 'lean, process and performance oriented standard, customized to the needs of small and medium sized organisations' (WFTO 2009j: 0.4). The SFTMS uses an integrated supply chain approach to fair trade which certifies that practices across the production process adhere to fair trade principles. The system offers a transparent and independently monitored global certification regime that allows marginalised fair trade organisations to guarantee that their processes and products conform to the Principles of Fair Trade (WFTO 2009j: 0.5).

*Governance structure*

As noted earlier, the WFTO (launched in 2008) is a reincarnation of IFAT (formed in 1989). This transformation was instigated at the Annual General Meeting of IFAT in May 2007 when members overwhelmingly adopted a 'New Strategic Plan' to reconfigure the institution (Wills 2007). This programme of action addressed several challenges that IFAT was facing due to changes within the organisation as well as the fair trade movement since the mid-1990s.

The New Strategic Plan prescribed that the organisation would decentralise in order to provide the five regions of IFAT with greater influence and responsibility in terms of capacity building, identifying market access opportunities, monitoring, communication and membership recruitment. The regions would henceforth take the lead in specific global activities, and regional representatives would make up the majority of the new Board of Directors. The decentralisation reflects the balance of the WFTO's membership and thus increases the democratic nature of its governance as well as the accountability to its Southern members.

In addition, the New Strategic Plan updated the organisation's mission and vision statements in order to reflect greater scope and ambition. Also, a review of the certification and monitoring system (as described above) took place so as to respond to the needs of the majority of member organisations.

The WFTO has a tripartite structure consisting of its Members, the Board of Directors and the WFTO Global Office. The members include fair trade producers, Southern exporters, Northern importers and 'world shops' retail outlets. The WFTO Constitution identifies three types of members: (a) Fair Trade Organisations, comprised of companies, partnerships or other legal entities whose primary activity is fair trade; (b) Fair Trade Networks, consisting of national or international associations of fair trade producers and fair trade organisations; and (c) Fair Trade Support Networks, made up of organisations that provide technical, financial and other activities to promote fair trade (WFTO 2009m: Art. V). The WFTO also recognises Provisional Members, consisting of organisations that are not yet in the position to undertake the registration audit or have not passed the audit. Associate Members are individuals and groups who wish to promote fair trade. Finally, Honorary Members are those who have played a significant role in the fair trade movement (WFTO 2009m: Art. V). It is implied that consumers who purchase fair trade products could also qualify as Individual Associates.

The WFTO membership is divided into five regions: Africa, Asia, Europe, Latin America and a combined region of North America and the Pacific Rim. In recent years several other regions have joined Europe (with EFTA) in establishing regional chapters. They include Cooperation for Fair Trade in Africa (COFTA), the Asia Fair Trade Forum (AFTF), and the Asociacion Internacional de Comercio Justo Latinoamerica (International Fair Trade Association in Latin America, IFAT-LA). Prior to the adoption of the New Strategic Plan, these regional chapters were autonomous bodies with no institutional link to IFAT, and directors of the regional bodies did not take part in the governance of IFAT. In contrast, elected regional representatives do sit on the Board of the WFTO and serve as the point of contact between the regions and the global organisation (WFTO 2009e).

The Board of Directors has the responsibility to manage the activities of the WFTO (WFTO 2009m: Art. XI). Its members are responsible for the development of policy as well as the implementation of decisions agreed by the membership at the Annual General Meeting. The Board serves as guardian of the WFTO Constitution and the Principles for Fair Trade Organisations (WFTO 2009e). It also decides which fair trade organisations are allowed to become members of the WFTO.

According to the WFTO Constitution, the Board has a minimum of five and a maximum of eleven directors elected for staggered terms of four years (WFTO 2009m: Art. XI). Board directors may serve two consecutive terms. Five Board directors are nominated by each of the five WFTO regions and elected at the WFTO Annual General Meeting. This meeting also elects a President and three additional Board directors, who are required to be current or past officers or staff of a member of the WFTO or to have played a significant role as a WFTO volunteer. The Board may co-opt up to three additional directors, depending on budget restrictions, to ensure regional and gender balance or to replace a director who has resigned, died or whose organisation has been suspended from WFTO membership (WFTO 2009m: Art. XI: 5). However, unlike elected directors, co-opted members of the Board are required to step down at the next Annual General Meeting. The Board itself elects a Vice-President, a Secretary and a Treasurer. Board Directors are expected to represent the interests of the entire WFTO membership rather than those of only their region or organisation.

The WFTO Global Office, formerly the IFAT Secretariat, serves as the WFTO Secretariat. This bureau, based in Culemborg, the Netherlands, has eight staff members on site, while another three persons work remotely from elsewhere in Europe (WFTO 2009f). The Global Office serves as a point of contact for WFTO Members, assists them in implementing their initiatives, and facilitates global networking among them (WFTO 2009f). The Global Office also works with the Fair Trade Advocacy Office to support wider lobbying for fair trade.

The highest decision-making body in the WFTO is the Annual General Meeting. All registered members have equal voting rights. In the early years of IFAT, Northern members outnumbered Southern members, but over time this balance has shifted so that Southern members now make up 65 per cent of the WFTO membership (WFTO 2009g). All major policy decisions require approval among members, including on issues of market access, advocacy and monitoring.

### Accountability at the WFTO

As noted in Chapter 1, accountability is a contested concept open to multiple interpretations. In keeping with the approach of this book as a whole, the present study of the WFTO highlights questions of demo-cratic accountability through processes of transparency, consultation, evaluation and redress. The following paragraphs describe and assess general accountability arrangements at the WFTO.

A key prior question is, of course, *to whom* is the WFTO accountable? Obviously the institution must answer to its members, both organisa-tional and individual. In addition, the WFTO has an implied particular accountability to marginalised fair trade producers and workers, with an emphasis on those operating in the global south. These circles have a fairly direct link to the WFTO inasmuch as the majority of member producer organisations are co-operatives that work with poor and unskilled work-ers. A further WFTO constituency is consumers, including as grouped in consumer associations.

The WFTO record on transparency, consultation, evaluation and redress can be considered both internally (i.e. in terms of relations of the executive and secretariat with the membership) and externally (i.e. in terms of WFTO relations with parties outside the organisation). In general, the WFTO has developed fairly robust arrangements for internal accountability, but has rather neglected provisions for external accountability.

In terms of transparency, IFAT had a mixed record. On the posi-tive side, the Executive Committee (IFAT's governing body) and the Secretariat provided regular information to members in the form of a bimonthly newsletter on activities, issues of interest and enquiries from businesses about fair trade products. There were also regular flows of ad hoc communications among Members, the Executive Committee and the Secretariat. The Secretariat directly contacted individual fair trade organisations when a particular issue of interest arose. However, respondents in interviews for this research also indicated that much more could have been done to increase internal transparency in terms of adequate and timely information, as well as discussion of shared challenges and strategic plans.

Moreover, neither IFAT nor the successor WFTO have yet given full attention to providing transparency beyond the membership, for example to other civil society organisations and the general public. The WFTO has developed a useful website. However, the organisation has thus far not made public key governance documents such as its constitution or bylaws. Only two annual reports (for IFAT in 2006 and 2007) are posted on the website. The WFTO also offers only very limited translation from English of its website and other documentation.

Both the WFTO and IFAT before it have performed adequately with respect to consultation of the membership. For example, the preparation of the New Strategic Plan involved an open and inclusive deliberation within the IFAT membership. The Secretariat and the Executive Committee explained why such an action was necessary, co-ordinated the development of several options that were distributed to members, and detailed the implications prior to the vote at the 2007 Annual General Meeting.

That said, IFAT and, until recently, the WFTO, have lacked a regular process for consulting non-member stakeholders such as consumer associations and the general public. In principle, external parties could respond to items posted on the WFTO website, and there has been some informal communication between the secretariats of the WFTO and Consumers International. However, neither IFAT nor the WFTO have had any regular institutionalised process for consultation (especially on policy matters) with Consumers International, its member associations and the wider public.

The WFTO is itself an accountability mechanism, inasmuch as monitoring and evaluation to ensure compliance with fair trade principles form two of its principal tasks. The fair trade certification system – and in particular the new SFTMS Standard regime – validates that WFTO Members are '100% fair trade' and meet the organisation's ten Principles of Fair Trade. As for monitoring and evaluation of the WFTO's own operations, one of the responsibilities of the Board of Directors is to act as guardian of the body's constitution. As noted earlier, the absence of external verification was a major shortcoming in the IFAT certification and labelling scheme; however, evaluation of WFTO operations in this area is bringing improvement. Under the new arrangements an organisation that wishes to remain certified must submit, every three years, to a full site audit of its management system by an accredited external auditor recognised in the global marketplace (Gent 2010). In addition, to remain certified organisations need to prepare a Sustainable Fair Trade Management System Report on an annual basis. This report must be evaluated by an independent external auditor to ensure that the organisation is meeting SFTMS certification requirements. A system to train accredited external evaluators from the various WFTO regions is being developed.

Regarding the fourth dimension of accountability highlighted in this book, correction and redress, the WFTO Constitution provides for sanctions of member fair trade organisations as well as of members of the Board of Directors. Article IX defines grounds for the termination of WFTO membership, including non-compliance with the Constitution and violation of WFTO principles (WFTO 2009m: Art. IX). Members of the WFTO also have the ability to remove a member of the Board of Directors from office through the adoption of a resolution (WFTO 2009m: Art. XI: 6.1). No specific sanctions exist in respect of failures by Global Office staff members, but the Board of Directors is responsible for all matters relating to staff under Dutch employment laws (Myers 2009). The WFTO also has no formal arrangements (such as an ombudsperson) through which parties outside the WFTO can bring complaints to the organisation and obtain redress for any harms suffered.

In sum, then, the fact that the WFTO is a civil society operation rather than a public sector body has not in itself ensured that the organisation has overcome the accountability problems of global governance. Although accountability arrangements work fairly well amongst the parties who are internal to the WFTO, provisions for transparency, consultation, evaluation and correction in respect of outside stakeholders are generally weak. In this regard the civil society-run WFTO is not necessarily more publicly accountable than the state-run WTO.

## Civil society engagement of the WFTO

Civil society is defined in this book as *a political space where associations of citizens seek, from outside political parties, to shape societal rules*. This study of the WFTO focuses on the engagement of civil society organisations such as Southern fair trade producers, Northern fair trade importers and world shops with consumer associations.

Civil society engagement within the fair trade movement has consisted primarily of the activities of fair trade organisations, including producer co-operatives and associations, importers and retailers (i.e. world shops), as well as to a lesser extent co-operative financial institutions. Fair trade organisations – in particular volunteer associations of retailers, importers and producers of fair trade products – have shaped the evolution of fair trade from its origins as an alternative trade system through its transition to the fair trade movement.

The continued expansion of demand for fair trade goods and the growing trend towards an integration of alternative trade into mainstream commercial trade have had significant repercussions for the fair trade movement. With these changes different types of civil society associations have chosen to engage (or not to engage) in the regulation of fair trade. This shifting profile of civil society involvement has been largely responsible for the need to transform IFAT into the WFTO, and for the accountability challenges that this global governance organisation continues to face.

In earlier days, when the alternative trade movement operated on a small scale and at the margins of the global economy, the scope of civil society that engaged with the issue was mainly limited to the producer groups and retailer associations directly involved. Other sectors of civil society such as consumer organisations, environmental groups, business forums and trade unions were notable for their absence from activities regarding global fair trade standards and certification mechanisms. However, with the growth in fair trade and increased interest in ethical trade and corporate social responsibility, these other civil society groups have started to dedicate greater attention to fair trade matters.

At the same time, fair trade umbrella groups and fair trade organisations have historically been deficient in proactive outreach to stakeholders in wider civil society. In 2002 an analysis of IFAT noted that, although within the organisation 'participation of stakeholders is a highly valued quality ... the stakeholder definition appears under-developed' (Waddell 2002: 25). As a result, engagement with stakeholders beyond the immediate fair trade community tended not to be forthcoming (Waddell 2002: 18).

The lack of outreach was sufficiently problematic for, in May 2006, the ISO Consumer Policy Committee (COPOLCO) to adopt Resolution 23/2006 inviting the global consumer organisation, Consumers International, to 'develop a proposal for new technical work in fair trade, including certification' (INNI 2007). This step pointed towards an eventual global standard on fair trade within the ISO. The initiative arose due to concern on the part of consumer organisations about growing confusion among shoppers regarding the various alternative approaches to conventional trade (including fair trade, ethical trade and social accountability), as well as numerous fair trade labelling schemes. Consumers

International pointed out that consumers need to be able to make purchasing decisions based on clear information about the claims of fair trade, and stressed the need for greater recognition of fair trade organisations (IHS 2007).

In response, IFAT and FLO argued that 'social and environmental standards are by their very nature substantially different from the technical standards ISO traditionally works on' (ISEAL 2007). FINE – an informal association that derives its name from the first letter of its original four members, FLO International, IFAT, NEWS! and EFTA – was concerned that such standards would likely be less ambitious than IFAT and FLO standards. Moreover, meeting and monitoring ISO standards is a lengthy and expensive process that would adversely affect the small and marginalised organisations that make up the majority of fair trade producers. As a result an ISO regime would be less able to serve the interests of fair trade producers.

There followed a year of concerted efforts by the Fair Trade Advocacy Office and a small number of IFAT members against future ISO standardisation of fair trade. A statement was issued announcing that the international fair trade movement was eager to engage in dialogue with consumer associations and other interested stakeholders to improve participation in fair trade (FTAO 2007a). In May 2007 members of COPOLCO passed Resolution 10/2007 Fair Trade, which acknowledged that it was premature to incorporate fair trade certification within the scope of ISO. In order to develop greater understanding of the 'potential for problems associated with accurate unreliable claims concerning the ethical dimension of consumer products and services' (COPOLCO 2007), a joint ethical trade fact-finding process was established to study the issues of concern (IFAT 2007). This process included representatives of IFAT, FLO, Consumers International and other interested stakeholders.

The ruling of COPOLCO reduces the immediate threat of a transfer of responsibility for fair trade monitoring and certification from the WFTO to the ISO. However, this development also provides the WFTO with a window of opportunity to institutionalise engagement with a wider scope of civil society, in particular consumer organisations and global standard-setting bodies, and to address their concerns related to fair trade certification.

In a move towards greater engagement with consumer groups and other stakeholders, IFAT and FLO issued a statement in April 2007 which recognised 'the need to protect consumers against misleading ethical and "fair" claims' and invited 'interested stakeholders to participate in a dialogue on how to improve transparency, accessibility and participation within Fair Trade'. Such a dialogue would 'improve Fair Trade, to make it a more open system, more transparent for consumers and with a wider participation from other sectors of the society, and at the same time strengthen Fair Trade contribution to sustainable development and poverty reduction' (Fair Trade Advocacy Office 2007b).

Further evidence that the WFTO and its members will deepen their engagement with civil society organisations such as consumer and environmental groups is found in the Charter of Fair Trade Principles, which notes the need for increased consumer awareness of fair trade principles and continuous improvement in environmental sustainability. This document was published in January 2009 by the WFTO and FLO, in conjunction with ISEAL, after three years of consultations with fair trade stakeholders. A key objective of the charter is to 'set the foundations for future dialogue and co-operation among Fair Trade Organisations – and between those organisations and other actors – in order that Fair Trade fully develops its potential to secure greater equity in international trade' (WFTO and FLO 2009: 3). Notably, the charter incorporates a definition of fair trade stakeholders that includes an explicit reference to consumers (WFTO and FLO 2009: 4).

The activities described above show that the WFTO is recognising the importance of greater interaction with a broader array of relevant civil society organisations. Paul Myers, President of the WFTO, notes that the organisation is now in conversation with consumer associations in a number of different venues (Myers 2009). Regular and effective implementation of dialogue with these groups will contribute to the WFTO making further progress in its accountability.

### Conclusion

This study has analysed the extent to which engagement by civil society groups, including member fair trade organisations and consumer groups, has shaped the accountability of the WFTO. Internal pressure from its member fair trade groups contributed to the transformation of the IFAT into the WFTO. This institutional change and the new SFTMS Standard offer a new, more accessible, monitoring and certification system. It uses the process-oriented integrated supply chain approach to certify fair trade products, a strengthened governance structure (including the establishment of a Board of Directors), and an increased voice for the regions. It also rebrands the WFTO as the global voice of fair trade. At the same time, as part of its response to external pressure from other civil society groups, including consumer and environmental associations, the WFTO has made progress in institutionalising its outreach to, and dialogue with, these other stake-holders. Such developments provide evidence that this global govern-ance organisation is addressing matters of transparency, consultation, evaluation and redress, and making some progress towards broadly responsive accountability arrangements.

# Conclusion

*Jan Aart Scholte*

This book opened with a puzzle. It was noted that human society has in recent times become qualitatively more global. More global relations have elicited more global governance. For that transplanetary regulation to be effective and legitimate it must, amongst other things, be democratically accountable. Such accountability is not available through states alone. Analysts and activists have often suggested that civil society could substantially correct the accountability shortfalls in contemporary global governance. But is this proposition tenable? In what ways and to what extents have civil society activities made global regulatory institutions more answerable to the people whose lives and livelihoods are affected?

Prior to this book, no conceptually systematic and empirically wide-ranging research had focused on this important question of global politics in the twenty-first century. To address the gap the book has: (a) elaborated a conceptualisation of 'global governance', 'accountability' and 'civil society'; and (b) related that analytical framework to thirteen diverse arrangements for transplanetary regulation. Now, in this Conclusion to the book, it is possible to return with firmer grounding to the overarching question of the study.

So, how far is civil society engagement an answer to accountability deficits in contemporary global governance? The following pages first consider, in the light of the thirteen case studies, the merits or otherwise of the conceptual approach set out in Chapter 1. A second section then synthesises evidence from the thirteen empirical chapters to make broad assessments of the nature and degree of civil society contributions to accountable global governance, once again in terms of the four highlighted dimensions of transparency, consultation, evaluation and correction. A third section draws on the case studies to offer broad reflections concerning factors – personal, institutional and deeper structural – that have promoted or hindered civil society efforts to improve the

My thanks to the authors of the other chapters for comments and corrections on earlier versions of this Conclusion.

accountability of global governance. This explanatory framework in turn suggests ways forward in civil society activities to enhance democratically accountable global governance.

### A framework of analysis

This summary of findings can begin by confirming the viability of the conceptualisation that has united the book. Certainly, other notions of 'global governance', 'accountability' and 'civil society' are available and may well bring their own coherence and insights. However, the thirteen case studies herein have between them shown that the framework of analysis set out in Chapter 1 has a sustainable logic, applies well empirically, promotes searching normative assessments of the status quo, and generates innovative proposals for improving future conditions.

The case studies have certainly confirmed the proposition that contemporary global governance comes in diverse forms. In part, as seen in Chapters 2–7, rules and regulatory processes with global application continue to emanate from traditional intergovernmental apparatuses such as the United Nations (UN), the World Bank, the International Monetary Fund (IMF), the World Trade Organization (WTO), the Commonwealth and the Organisation of the Islamic Conference (OIC). However, as evidenced in Chapters 8–14, much other global governance now transpires through different kinds of multilateralism. For example, important transgovernmental networks operate inter alia through the Organisation of Economic Cooperation and Development (OECD), the Group of Eight (G8) and the Asia-Europe Meeting (ASEM). The case of ASEM moreover illustrates incipient interregionalism within global regulation in the twenty-first century. The studies of climate change and the Global Fund to Fight AIDS, Tuberculosis and Malaria (GFATM) have shown the substantial trans-sectoral quality of much contemporary global governance, where the regulatory arrangement rests on collaboration among governments, intergovernmental organisations, business and civil society actors. Finally, chapters on the Internet Corporation of Assigned Names and Numbers (ICANN) and the World Fair Trade Organization (WFTO) have revealed that important parts of global governance are private in character, rooted in both business and civil society circles.

Arguably the book should, for more complete coverage, also have included a case study on translocal global governance through transplanetary networks of substate authorities such as municipal and provincial governments. In addition, the book could also have examined global governance in further substantive areas such as education where civil society activity has also figured importantly (Gaventa and Mayo 2010). As ever, no work is complete.

Nevertheless, the thirteen case studies presented here have between them confirmed the polycentric character of contemporary governance, such that a given public policy issue is handled by multiple regulatory institutions at the same time. Thus, for example, governance of climate change was seen in Chapter 11 to involve agencies operating on local, national, regional and global scales. Moreover, the global elements alone included various UN bodies as well as multilateral financial organisations and private sector actors. Similarly, global governance of finance was seen to be addressed not only in the IMF, but also in ASEM, the G8, the OECD, the UN, the OIC and the World Bank – plus a host of other institutions not examined in this book. The case studies have likewise shown that global governance of health, human rights, security and trade are dispersed in a polycentric fashion. The more empirical chapters have therefore illustrated the argument put forward in general terms at the outset, namely that the diffuse nature of governance in today's more global world raises particular challenges of co-ordination (often poorly met).

In addition, the involvement in each issue area of multiple players with overlapping mandates raises major complications of specifying the respective accountability of each actor. In today's global governance it is often not clear who is answerable for what, and to what degree. For example, which amongst the many agencies involved should be called to account for regulatory failure in the recurrent crises of contemporary global finance? Accountability becomes all the more elusive in instances such as ASEM and the G8 where global regulatory processes have been mostly informal. The OIC case highlighted cultural complexities of global accountabilities.

Yet in whatever way one establishes the precise extent of a global governance institution's accountability, it is evident from the thirteen case studies in this book that the general picture on delivering accountability is poor. To one degree or another, all of the transplanetary regulatory organisations examined here have suffered from significant shortcomings in respect of transparency, consultation, evaluation and redress. Several of these bodies, including ICANN and the WFTO, have become more self-critically conscious of the complex accountability issues that they face, even if this reflexivity has landed ICANN in something of a muddle with 'multiple accountability disorder'. However, most of the global governance institutions covered in this project have given little if any systematic attention to thinking through their own accountability challenges and constructing procedures that adequately respond to them. In particular, some quarters of some intergovernmental organisations such as the WTO continue to cling to an obsolete Westphalian notion that they only owe accountability to member states.

Nor, judging from the sample of thirteen case studies presented here, have global governance agencies given adequate attention to ensuring accountability to their weaker constituents. The most striking exception in this regard is the WFTO, which as seen in Chapter 14 has undergone comprehensive reconstruction in order to answer better to poor producers in the global south. In addition, the GFATM has sought to involve persons affected by its focal diseases, including (belatedly) women in particular. The Commonwealth for its part has given some priority to answering to smaller member states and their citizens, and the World Bank has – albeit unevenly – consulted impoverished and marginalised people affected by some of its projects. On the whole, however, accountability in global governance (to the degree that institutions have offered it at all) has generally favoured dominant states and dominant social groups. Hence one key question for this book has been the extent to which civil society involvement in global governance might expand space for disadvantaged constituencies.

Regarding civil society, all of the case studies have confirmed the starting premise of this book that many citizen groups today engage not only the state, but also a host of regulatory institutions with global jurisdictions and constituencies. The history of all thirteen regimes covered here shows a parallel growth of the global governance arrangement on the one hand and of civil society activities that engage it on the other. Indeed, civil society organisations (CSOs) were instrumental in the very creation of the UN, the WTO, the Commonwealth, the GFATM and the WFTO. Increasingly since the 1970s, civil society gatherings have convened alongside major official meetings of the UN, the Bretton Woods institutions, the WTO, the Commonwealth, the G8, ASEM, Conferences of the Parties (COPs) on climate change, and of late also the OIC. In more recently created global regulatory agencies such as the GFATM, ICANN and the WFTO, civil society actors have moreover occupied ex officio positions at the heart of policy processes.

As anticipated in the conceptual framework set out in Chapter 1, 'civil society' in relation to global governance institutions encompasses a wide range of actors, including but not limited to non-governmental organisations (NGOs). Certainly NGOs have figured in all thirteen case studies, albeit that their focal issues have often varied between one agency and the next. For example, NGOs concerned with health have particularly engaged the Global Fund, while groups concerned with democratisation have sooner targeted the Commonwealth. In addition, however, the case studies have continually shown that the civil society which relates to global governance stretches well beyond public-interest advocacy NGOs. For instance, nearly all of the global regulatory agencies examined in this book have had notable contacts with research institutes and policy think tanks. The case studies have also indicated that business lobbies such as chambers of commerce, employer groups and banking associations have sometimes played prominent civil society roles in global governance, particularly in relation to the IMF, the WTO, the OECD and the climate change regime. Meanwhile labour unions have actively engaged the UN, the Bretton Woods institutions, the WTO and the OECD. Faith-based organisations (FBOs) have been prominent civil society elements in relation to the UN, the OIC and campaigns for debt cancellation vis-à-vis the World Bank, the IMF and the G8. Indeed, as the OIC study indicated, adoption of a religious perspective can substantially alter ideas about the nature and purpose of civil society. Finally, more loosely organised and ephemeral civil society activities, including street protests, have at one or the other juncture played an important part in citizen engagement of around half of the global governance institutions studied in this book. In sum, then, the evidence from Chapters 2–14 has well vindicated the conception in Chapter 1 that civil society extends beyond NGOs to a full range of citizen groups that seek, from outside political parties, to shape societal rules and governance apparatuses.

As the case studies have also shown, civil society associations are not of one mind (or indeed always very clear) when it comes to their visions for the preferred future course of global governance. In broad terms many CSOs aim to make global governance more socially just, culturally sensitive, morally decent, ecologically sound and politically democratic. However, their elaborations of these principles can diverge widely. Whereas many development NGOs and trade unions have espoused 'progressive' agendas, the case studies also indicate that 'conservative' ideologies have informed anti-abortion groups in their engagement of the GFATM, as well as the Family Research Council in its advocacy regarding ICANN. Meanwhile other CSOs, such as many business associations, have been most concerned that global governance fosters favourable market conditions, with only secondary, if any, regard for social and environmental issues. As seen in Chapter 11, some commercial lobbies have even lobbied against cuts in greenhouse gas emissions.

The case studies have, in addition, demonstrated that civil society associations adopt large repertoires of tactics in relation to global regulatory arrangements. From the inside CSOs have held formal positions in certain global governance bodies, supplied research, provided advice, drafted resolutions and assisted in policy implementation. From the outside, CSOs have pressed a given global regulatory institution via national states (their ministries, legislatures and courts), other global bodies (e.g. the IMF via the UN), regional governance agencies, local governments, political parties, the mass media, companies, celebrities, public education schemes and street protest. Often CSOs have pursued insider and outsider tactics in tandem.

All of the global governance agencies examined in this book have made arrangements of some kind to address this civil society pressure. Many (though not all) of their charters provide a formal mandate for relations with CSOs. The UN has developed an elaborate accreditation scheme for NGOs. The World Bank has undertaken joint policy assessments with CSOs. The UN, the World Bank, the IMF, the WTO, the Commonwealth, the OECD and ICANN have all appointed civil society liaison officers. A number of state delegations to WTO Ministerial Conferences, the Conferences of the Parties and other UN meetings have included civil society actors. The Commonwealth Foundation and the Asia-Europe Foundation have nurtured civil society networks across the member countries of the Commonwealth and ASEM, respectively. Host governments of G8 summits have developed a routine of meeting with a delegation of NGOs. The Board of the Global Fund (and all of its committees) include designated seats for Developed Country NGOs, Developing Country NGOs and Affected Communities Organisations. ICANN has created an At-Large Advisory Committee (ALAC) and a Noncommercial Users Constituency (NCUC) as channels for civil society input. In the case of the WFTO the global regulatory agency itself is a civil society body. Sometimes these institutional 'openings' to civil society have tamed resistance towards global governance among certain CSOs, although other groups have used channels of access to pursue an unwavering strategy of subversion.

The degree to which the secretariats of global governance arrangements are important sites of civil society intervention varies across the institutions. In some cases – especially the UN, the World Bank, the IMF, the OECD and the Global Fund – CSOs regard the bureaux of global agencies as important places to lever for influence. In other cases, including the WTO, the Commonwealth and ICANN, civil society engagement of the global secretariat has been relatively less pronounced. In contrast again, CSOs have rarely taken advocacy to the offices of the OIC and the secretariat of the United Nations Framework Convention on Climate Change. For their part the G8 and ASEM have lacked a permanent global secretariat in the first place.

Taken together, the thirteen case studies suggest that, since the late 1990s, a general consensus has prevailed that CSOs are rightly involved in transplanetary regulation. Statements by successive Directors-General at the WTO, cited at the opening of Chapter 5, and recurrent declarations at G8 summits, recorded in Chapter 9, have well illustrated this point. The degree to which authorities have genuinely welcomed civil society involvement may be debated, of course, as might the legitimacy of certain civil society groups. However, the underlying principle of civil society participation in global governance is today broadly accepted.

## The record to date

Now that civil society involvement has become a well-established aspect of global governance, what are the implications of these citizen group activities for the accountability of transplanetary regulatory institutions, including in particular to their more disadvantaged constituents? As several chapters have already emphasised, it is notoriously difficult to determine conclusively the precise causal impacts of CSOs (or any other forces for that matter) in the complex dynamics of polycentric governance. No methodology of social enquiry is entirely secure in this respect.

Nevertheless, there are four quite solid general grounds for the present study to conclude that civil society matters for democratic accountability in contemporary global governance. First, the conceptual frame – in relation to transparency, consultation, evaluation and correction – has offered a logically coherent base for analysis across the various case studies. Second, evidence of manifold correlations between civil society inputs and global accountability outputs has accumulated across the thirteen empirical chapters. Third, many policymakers and activists have affirmed, from their own direct experience of these affairs, that civil society has made a difference in promoting accountable global governance. Fourth, counterfactual ponderings in relation to many (though certainly not all) scenarios suggest that an absence of civil society involvement would have reduced or postponed various advances in global governance accountability. Taken together, these conceptual, empirical, testimonial and counterfactual considerations provide something approximating to 'proof' of CSO significance.

Certainly, the record across the thirteen case studies is not uniform. Civil society effects on transparency, consultation, evaluation and redress have on the whole been more pronounced in relation to the Commonwealth, the GFATM and the WFTO. At the other end of the spectrum, CSO accountability impacts have generally been more limited in respect of ASEM, the G8 and the OIC. On this somewhat crude comparison, experiences related to the other seven institutions examined have tended to fall somewhere in between. As is elaborated in the third section of this concluding chapter, a variety of circumstances have encouraged greater accountability outcomes in some situations of civil society involvement in global governance.

Nevertheless, as the rest of the present section will detail, the overall extent of civil society influence on democratic accountability in global governance must not be overestimated. Although the case studies show that CSOs have regularly played an important role in highlighting problems of accountability deficits in global governance, citizen group action has generally had a more modest record in terms of generating responses to those problems. CSO impacts in making transplanetary regulation more answerable to constituents have sometimes been limited, slow or absent altogether. In particular, with few powers of (mostly moral) sanction at their disposal, it has often proved difficult for CSOs to obtain correction and redress from global agencies. Moreover, CSOs have rarely advanced accountability in transplanetary regulation by themselves. Usually concurrent pressure has figured: from national governments, other global and regional governance bodies, political parties, business enterprises, mass media and/or other actors.

Yet while civil society has not been – and shows no signs of becoming – a panacea for accountability problems in global governance, CSO activities clearly have made a difference. Thanks in part to citizen group interventions, transplanetary regulation is today more publicly visible, more consultative, more externally monitored and more liable to corrective action than it was prior to the 1990s. That said, as is elaborated under other headings below, critical questions remain regarding which constituencies and what purposes these civil society impacts have most served. Indeed, CSO interventions in respect of global governance have in many situations tended to reinforce arbitrary power hierarchies in global politics and to legitimate rather than challenge global governance arrangements that may be significantly flawed.

*Transparency*

In general, global governance has become considerably more visible to affected publics over the past several decades. Most regulatory agencies with transplanetary remits have released more documentation and developed more elaborate public information operations (e.g. with websites, publications and press visibility). As a result, more people are more aware of the nature and significance of global regulatory apparatuses in contemporary society. Of course, still more transparency of global governance would be welcome, as many of the investigations in this book have made clear. However, the widespread invisibility of global regulatory arrangements that prevailed prior to the 1990s has been substantially overcome.

As indicated in the case studies, civil society actions have sometimes played an important role in this shift. For example, the World Bank consulted closely with CSOs in 2001, 2005 and 2009 regarding its information disclosure policies. CSO-sponsored investigations of IMF transparency in 1998, 2006 and 2007 gained some attention from the management of that institution. Civil society pressure also figured in WTO moves of 1996 and 2002 towards larger and faster release of official documents. Greater transparency has also been a consistent demand – if only partly met – of the Asia-Europe People's Forum in respect of ASEM. Civil society initiatives to promote transparency have been more sporadic in regard to the OECD and the G8, but CSOs have occasionally obtained and released a confidential official document from these institutions. Thus CSO publication of the OECD's confidential draft Multilateral Agreement on Investment drew much attention in 1997. Meanwhile, civil society pressure has encouraged ICANN to publish the minutes of its board meetings, and the Electronic Frontier Foundation (EFF) supported a successful lawsuit in 2002 that allowed an elected director of ICANN to access the corporate archives.

In contrast, CSOs have not given particular attention to transparency issues in relation to the UN, the Commonwealth, the OIC, the climate change regime, the GFATM and the WFTO. In several of these cases, such as the Commonwealth and the COPs, policy processes have already been sufficiently visible as to elicit relatively little civil society pressure for greater public openness. Moreover, in these two cases, as well as in the Global Fund and the WFTO, the ubiquitous presence of CSOs in institutional operations has arguably contributed to making the respective agencies more readily visible to affected constituencies. For example, it was seen in Chapter 12 that CSO involvement in GFATM activities has often brought relevant policy information into the public domain.

In another contribution to greater transparency, some (though far from all) CSOs have pursued citizen learning initiatives that raise the public visibility of global governance arrangements. For example, ongoing civil society activities such as forums, studies and spectacles have brought the Commonwealth, the IMF, the UN and the WTO considerably more into public view. The Asia-Europe Foundation has had a specific mandate to raise public awareness of ASEM and has organised multiple events to that end.

Yet all in all the case studies provide little evidence that CSOs have been particularly attuned to questions of *effective* transparency for *all* affected groups, especially less advantaged circles of society. One exception in this regard surfaced in the IMF study, where it was noted that several NGOs in Africa produced lay versions (including in local languages) of some of their respective governments' agreements with the Fund. In another push for transparency to marginalised circles, certain civil society activists in the global south have pressed ICANN to promote Internationalized Domain Names, so that the Internet becomes more accessible to people who do not work in Roman script. In general across the thirteen institutions, though, CSOs have done little to address issues of *meaningful* transparency, such as timely release of information, multi-lingual documentation, equitable Internet access and ready public availability of global governance officials. Many civil society activists have apparently seen information disclosure per se as the goal, neglecting to look more carefully at the conditions of those releases, as well as whom those conditions benefit or disadvantage.

Perhaps this blind spot regarding effective transparency has resulted in good part from the social privilege that has tended to predominate in civil society engagement of global governance to date. That is, most activists who have lobbied for greater openness in these institutions have been university-educated, English-speaking, computer-literate, middle-class professionals – in other words, the sorts of people who are more adept at navigating websites and technical documents. Such advantaged actors can readily neglect the different transparency needs of other social circles that have been less well represented in civil society relations with global governance.

### Consultation

Regarding the second core component of accountability identified in this research, the various case studies have shown that a degree of consultation with civil society has become a *sine qua non* of contemporary global governance. All thirteen of the institutions examined in this book have made some kind of arrangements to discuss their policies, programmes and projects with civil society associations. However, most of the case studies have also found that these consultations are seriously wanting in one way or another.

Certainly, most global governance institutions today wish to appear receptive to exchanging information and insights with civil society. Sometimes this openness extends to the highest levels of decision-takers. For instance, meetings under the so-called Arria Formula have since 1997 allowed CSOs to brief members of the UN Security Council. The President of the World Bank and the Managing Director of the IMF have since 2002 convened so-called 'town hall meetings' with CSOs during the Bank/Fund Annual Meetings. Both Bretton Woods leaders also engage with civil society groups on many of their country visits. Supachai

Panitchpakdi, as Director-General of the WTO, formed his own advisory bodies of business groups and NGOs, albeit that they played little policy role in practice. High-level exchanges between government leaders and selected CSOs have occurred at ASEM gatherings since 1996, G8 summits since 2000 and the Commonwealth Heads of Government Meeting (CHOGM) since 2005.

In addition, several global governance institutions examined in this book have staged major consultation events involving their staffs and CSOs. For example: the IMF and the World Bank have organised a Civil Society Policy Forum at their Annual Meetings. The WTO has sponsored periodic public symposia and forums with CSOs. The Commonwealth has undertaken elaborate exchanges with CSOs in the planning and execution of CHOGMs. The Global Fund has hosted a biennial Partnership Forum with significant civil society participation. ICANN has convened several public meetings per year around the world with an open microphone for civil society input.

Yet these and other global regulatory agencies have established relatively few permanent organs for ongoing consultation with CSOs. For this purpose the UN has a small Non-Governmental Liaison Service (NGLS) that maintains contacts especially with the more than 3,000 CSOs that are accredited to the organisation. The OECD and ASEM each have formally institutionalised engagement with business associations and trade unions, albeit not with other quarters of civil society. ICANN has permanent channels for interchange with civil society through its At-Large Advisory Committee and Non-Commercial Users Constituency. Meanwhile the Commonwealth Foundation and the GFATM maintain continual consultation with civil society by including seats for CSOs on their executive boards, while the WFTO is itself a civil society organisation. In addition, the GFATM operates an elaborate CSO consultation network of delegations, advisory teams and contact groups. However, permanent formally institutionalised consultation with CSOs has been absent altogether at the IMF, WTO, OIC, G8 and UNFCCC. An NGO-World Bank Committee operated in the 1980s and 1990s, but it petered out after 2000.

Indeed, after several decades of growing relations between CSOs and global governance agencies, many consultations remain ad hoc. The World Bank has encouraged its staff and borrowing governments to engage with civil society actors throughout the project cycle, but the form and frequency of such consultations has not been prescribed. The IMF has since 2003 had a guide for staff relations with CSOs, but its application has not been monitored. From 1998 CSOs have in principle had the right to submit *amicus curiae* briefs in WTO dispute settlement cases, but acceptance of these inputs has lain at the discretion of individual panels. CSOs have been actively involved across the spectrum of Commonwealth institutions, but often without a deliberate pattern or programme. OECD committees and working groups have manifold exchanges with CSOs, but without any particular system. ICANN has regularly invited civil society feedback on policy proposals via its website, but it is not clear what, if any, use is made of this input.

The largely improvised character of many global governance consultations of CSOs has had significant negative implications for democratic accountability. One major downside has been to favour better resourced and more powerful quarters of civil society, to the relative neglect of more peripheral groups. With their systematic arrangements for thorough consultation of civil society, the Commonwealth, the GFATM and the WFTO have deliberately promoted the inclusion of disadvantaged constituents, for example from the global south and among women and patient groups. In contrast, the other global institutions examined here have mostly omitted proactive steps to consult circles that might otherwise be overlooked. As a result CSOs from impoverished countries, underclasses, indigenous peoples and other marginalised circles have been largely left out of the exchanges. Instead, the field of global governance consultation has generally been disproportionately occupied by CSOs with bases in the global north, metropolitan cities and professional classes. As ever, laissez-faire tends to favour the strong.

Ad hoc approaches have also generated various problems with respect to the process of exchanges with CSOs. One shortfall noted in several case studies is a neglect to consult CSOs throughout a policy cycle, particularly in the early stages when issues and options are initially framed. Too often global governance bodies only engage with civil society associations later in the cycle, after the general policy direction has already been set. In addition, global regulatory institutions have often convened consultations with CSOs at short notice and with poor preparation, for example in the absence of clear objectives, a formal agenda and briefing papers. The conduct of the meetings themselves can be wanting as well, for example with shallow content, inadequate listening and a lack of mutual respect. Some case studies also note that global governance officials have neglected to provide feedback and follow-up on consultations with CSOs.

A particular complaint, voiced in relation to several of the institutions examined in this research, concerns the ritualistic quality of some purported 'consultations' of civil society. For example, many meetings at senior level with CSOs (e.g. around summit conferences) appear to be carefully choreographed public relations exercises, with little substantive discussion of specific concerns. Meanwhile some operational staff of global governance agencies have treated encounters with CSOs as a pro forma 'tick-the-box' affair, with no measurable consequence for concrete policy. Perfunctory approaches of this kind have discouraged some CSOs from devoting scarce time and energy to further interaction with global regulatory bodies.

Also especially problematic are occasions where officials have approached 'consultations' of civil society as one-way briefings rather than two-way dialogues. In these situations the global governance agency has used meetings with CSOs mainly to disseminate information and analysis rather than to acquire new data and insights that could raise the effectiveness and legitimacy of policy. Instead of seeking views and advice from civil society actors, officials have tended with what is often termed 'outreach' merely to notify CSOs of decisions already taken. Staff have, on these occasions, sought to validate the institution's pre-established position rather than to deliberate with CSOs in ways that might prompt adjustments to policy. A unilateral briefing approach was noted especially in the case studies on the World Bank, the IMF and ICANN.

If ritual and briefing predominate, there is a risk that 'consultation' of civil society can become an uncritical legitimation process for global governance. In these situations, neatly staged CSO involvement provides a veneer of public participation that deflects more searching and demanding scrutiny of the global regulatory apparatus. In the worst cases such 'engagement' of civil society can actually undermine accountability and prop up an ineffective and undemocratic institution. Case studies of the IMF, the G8 and ASEM specifically noted this risk, although the danger arguably also exists in relation to other global governance agencies.

Rejectionist opposition to certain global governance institutions and policies can exert an important counterweight to tendencies to turn civil society consultation into a process of co-optation. As seen in several of the case studies, some CSOs take to the streets rather than, or as well as, engaging in consultations with global regulatory agencies. Such mass protests have surfaced from time to time, for example around G7/G8 summits since 1981, around IMF/World Bank Annual Meetings since 1987, and around WTO Ministerial Conferences since 1998. Officials can become more inclined to pursue veritable consultations when they realise that the alternative is highly visible public demonstrations of dissent. Arguably, such a logic played a part in the IMF/World Bank turn towards greater exchanges with civil society in the context of Poverty Reduction Strategy Papers after 1999.

Thus, as with transparency, it is important when examining consultation of CSOs in global governance to ask probing questions regarding 'who' and 'for what purpose'. Which constituencies are – and as importantly are not – consulted by global regulatory bodies through CSOs? And does the consultation which is undertaken serve to enhance democratic accountability or to promote hegemonic legitimation? The record from the thirteen case studies suggests that disabling as well as enabling tendencies have surfaced to date, so that it cannot be assumed that consultation of CSOs has a democratising logic.

### Monitoring and evaluation

Conclusions from the thirteen case studies are also mixed in respect of civil society impacts on the third dimension of accountability, namely that of providing external scrutiny and assessment of global governance institutions. Numerous examples across the various chapters have shown that CSOs can act as vigilant watchdogs vis-à-vis global regulatory bodies. The various tactics in this regard include ad hoc surveillance, research reports, creation and use of official evaluation mechanisms, pressure on national authorities to examine global governance more carefully, and promotion of media investigations. However, taken in sum these accountability benefits have been modest. Moreover, civil society monitoring and evaluation of global governance has to date been undertaken disproportionately by actors from more advantaged countries and social circles, thus again raising the crucial democratic question of 'accountability for whom?'

Many CSOs have issued reports regarding the performance of global governance arrangements in delivering on policies and commitments. For instance, Social Watch and other civil society players have monitored the implementation of action plans adopted at a succession of UN conferences. Think tanks and NGOs have prepared countless studies on the impacts of UN operations, World Bank activities, IMF prescriptions, WTO rules and ICANN arrangements. ICANN has in fact commissioned several civil society actors to conduct its own internal evaluations of policy and process. OECD Watch has maintained ongoing scrutiny of the effectiveness of the OECD Guidelines for Multinational Enterprises. A number of civil society groups have prepared scorecards on government follow-up of commitments undertaken in the G8 and in climate change negotiations. On greenhouse gas emissions in particular, CSOs have adopted 'name and shame' tactics to expose poorly performing governments. Meanwhile the One World Trust has since 2003 assessed and compared the accountability practices of several dozen global governance agencies, including several of the institutions examined in the present book.

In other cases CSOs have monitored the implementation of undertakings in global governance without producing published studies on these matters. With respect to the Commonwealth, for example, CSOs have reminded official circles of their promises in CHOGM communiqués and certain ad hoc commission reports. Similarly, the main civil society players in the ASEM process have tracked the implementation of summit pledges in that interregional framework. A loose watchdog function could also be ascribed to CSOs in relation to the GFATM and the OIC, although the impacts have been limited, particularly in the latter case.

On several occasions CSOs have played a role in the creation and subsequent use of formal evaluation mechanisms within global governance institutions. For example, civil society groups called for the establishment of an Inspection Panel at the World Bank and have taken a lead in some of the cases brought before it. Similarly, certain CSOs pressed for the establishment of an Independent Evaluation Office for the IMF and have thereafter contributed to its assessments of various Fund policies and practices. It was also suggested in Chapter 9 that the G8 has begun to undertake some systematic self-monitoring, partly in response to performance evaluations by CSOs. However, the other global governance institutions examined in the case studies (GFATM, OECD, UN, etc.) still lack permanent formal mechanisms for outside evaluation of their work, and civil society actors have generally neglected to press for the creation of such instruments.

On the whole CSOs have also not fully exploited possibilities to enhance scrutiny of global governance by national governments. True, certain civil society associations have pushed foreign ministries to exert more oversight on the UN. Similarly, some CSOs have urged finance ministries to watch the IMF more carefully. Other citizen groups have taken their concerns about the WTO to national trade ministries. In addition, several CSOs have participated in reviews of ICANN by the National Telecommunications and Information Administration (NTIA) of the US Department of Commerce. However, such civil society attempts to intensify monitoring of global governance institutions via national government ministries have been fairly rare, which is somewhat surprising given the influence that those state bodies can exert.

Likewise, the thirteen case studies have uncovered relatively few instances of concerted civil society efforts to upgrade oversight of global governance arrangements by national and regional parliaments. CSOs have engaged certain national legislatures (e.g. in Britain, Canada, France and the USA) on their governments' involvements in the Bretton Woods institutions and the G8. Several civil society groups have also contributed to US Congress oversight of ICANN and EU

Parliament work on the WTO. Yet such instances have been relatively exceptional. It is as if CSOs and legislators have had an implicit agreement not to mix the 'participatory democracy' of civil society with the 'representative democracy' of parliament. Yet joint efforts by the two sets of actors could arguably achieve much more effective scrutiny of global governance.

Nor have CSOs on the whole booked much success in promoting scrutiny of global regulatory arrangements through the mass media. The case studies have presented only a few instances of notable CSO impact in generating increased press attention to global governance. One relative success story arose in respect of climate change, where a number of CSOs have pursued concerted public communications strategies including media campaigns. Debates of global issues at the yearly World Economic Forum in Davos have also attracted cameras and reporters. In general, however, civil society groups have tended to draw the attention of major media outlets to global governance issues mainly by staging street protests or theatrical stunts.

Not only has scrutiny of global governance by CSOs remained on a modest scale overall, but in addition this evaluation – like the promotion of transparency and consultation – has been most concentrated in more privileged quarters of civil society. It is mainly professionalised CSOs in the urban global north which have done the studies on global governance, used the official evaluation mechanisms, lobbied the ministries and parliaments and pursued the media campaigns. Yet how far can these elite actors interrogate global governance in ways that reflect and promote the views, experiences and interests of other, less advantaged, groups? The question 'evaluation for whom?' is crucial in this regard, and the issue becomes the more acute when (as is currently so often the case) the CSOs involved have inadequately developed their own accountability vis-à-vis underprivileged constituencies.

Finally, as with transparency and consultation, it is important to consider the purposes that civil society monitoring and evaluation of global governance has served. In particular, have the assessments been undertaken with a view to improving existing regimes or with a view to creating fundamentally different regimes? Both tendencies have shown themselves in the case studies, and in some instances a single civil society evaluation exercise can show both qualities. However, on the whole, reformist civil society monitoring that supports existing global governance has carried greater weight than transformist civil society scrutiny that challenges underlying structures of global order. To this extent evaluation activities through CSOs have, overall, tended to be part of a status quo that legitimates prevailing global governance arrangements.

*Correction and redress*

The same broad conclusion – that civil society has had some important, but on the whole modest, accountability effects on contemporary global governance – also applies to the fourth dimension highlighted in this book, namely that of correction and redress. Many civil society initiatives on global governance have been motivated by a determination to right perceived wrongs in the work of these regulatory agencies. As the case studies have shown, various civil society actions have brought instances of harmful global governance to public attention and debate. In addition, certain campaigns have generated substantial institutional and policy changes, although these successes have normally been booked when interventions from civil society have combined with pressures from other quarters. However, many other CSO strivings for correction and redress have had little impact, particularly when they have sought to change deeper structures of global governance. Thus – as with other aspects of accountability – it is, as ever, pertinent to ask the questions 'correction for whom?' and 'redress for what purpose?'

Certainly, civil society pressure has generally failed as a mechanism to remove poorly performing leaders of global regulatory institutions. The thirteen case studies provide only one example of successful civil society agitation for the resignation of a flawed global governance chief. Yet it required extreme ethical lapses before CSOs could, together with other actors, drive Paul Wolfowitz from office as President of the World Bank in 2007. Meanwhile CSOs have generally put little pressure on the many global governance executives who survive in office on a record of low ambition that in effect obstructs urgently needed initiatives on transplanetary problems. Hence civil society interventions have not so far filled the corrective role in respect of global leadership that parliaments and plebiscites are meant to play vis-à-vis national executives.

An area where CSOs have accomplished somewhat more corrective change in global governance is institutional reform. Indeed, the advances described above in relation to transparency, consultation and evaluation can be seen as civil society contributions to organisational improvements in global governance. In addition, sustained objections from some civil society quarters have helped to bring modest steps in 2007, 2009 and 2010 towards a more equitable alignment of votes on the boards of the IMF and the World Bank. Similarly, civil society critiques of unrepresentative Northern dominance of the global economy through the G8 have arguably played some part in encouraging the rise of the G20. Civil society pressure has also contributed to the democratising shift at ICANN in 2009 from unilateral US Government oversight to a global review process.

In contrast, civil society advocacy has failed to advance other proposed institutional reconstructions of global governance, such as reform of the UN Security Council or the creation of a fully-fledged World Ecological Organisation in place of the weak environmental commissions and programmes that are currently scattered about the UN system.

Another way that civil society has had corrective impacts on global governance is in revising agendas. In this regard CSOs have helped to put neglected issues on the global governance table and/or to raise their relative priority. For example, NGOs have been largely responsible for getting environmental and consumer concerns on the WTO agenda and keeping investment issues off it. Trade unions and human rights groups have played a key role in raising matters of labour standards and 'decent work' in governance of the global economy. It is hard to imagine that, in the absence of civil society pressure, global regulatory agencies would so substantially have increased their attention to poverty alleviation. Likewise, CSOs have been prime promoters of greater attention in global governance to matters of corruption and democracy.

Not only has civil society engagement of global governance affected the political agenda; in addition, as the case studies have repeatedly shown, CSOs have promoted reassessments of a number of policies and projects that flow from this agenda. For example, civil society actors eventually booked success in their long-running campaign, vis-à-vis a number of global regulatory agencies, for the cancellation of unsustainable bilateral and multilateral debts of poor countries. Civil society advocacy also figured prominently in generating the 2003 accord at the WTO to improve access to essential medicines. However, CSOs have thus far failed in their broader ambition to incorporate a social clause into the WTO agreement. Global governance measures to counter climate change – however inadequate they may have been to date – arguably would not have emerged without unflagging pressure from CSOs. Meanwhile civil society interventions at ICANN have limited violations of data protection and privacy in the context of the Whois policy. CSOs have also played a prominent role in moving to correct shortcomings at the GFATM concerning gender sensitivity. At the World Bank, civil society groups have successfully pushed for the adoption of various project safeguards in respect of, for example, environmental concerns, indigenous peoples and resettlement.

Regarding another type of correction, some CSOs have, in 'boomerang' fashion, used global governance institutions as an avenue to counter violations of democracy and human rights by member states. For instance, many CSOs have brought complaints of human rights abuses by national governments to relevant UN bodies, sometimes thereby prompting corrective action, for example on the status of women. Civil society actors have likewise pushed the Commonwealth – periodically with effect – to suspend member governments that have taken an authoritarian turn. In relation to ASEM, the Asia-Europe People's Forum has expanded political space for some CSOs that they could not find in their respective national contexts.

More broadly than individual agenda items and specific policy positions, civil society interventions have also contributed significantly in shifting some general discourses of global governance. Across the world countless NGOs, trade unions, FBOs, more critical think tanks and more socially minded business associations have objected to harms associated with the neoliberalist policy frame that predominated in global governance between the early 1980s and the late 1990s. When coupled with changes of government in various major states and policy breakdowns such as recurrent financial crises, these civil society pressures helped to turn the tide away from the so-called Washington Consensus on laissez faire to a reformulated dominant discourse of the 'social market'. Since the turn of the century it has become the prevailing wisdom in global governance to advocate interventions from official and civil society quarters in order to correct 'market imperfections'. Thus global governance agencies now regularly promote manipulations of markets by non-market actors in order to combat societal ills such as poverty, environmental degradation, digital inequality, disease and corruption.

True, CSOs have not (yet) moved the overall policy orientation in global governance further beyond market capitalism. For example, citizen groups that advocate global social democracy, with a focus on progressive redistribution of planetary resources, have so far made little impact on global regulatory agencies. (Initiatives at the OECD to counter tax evasion and steps at the WFTO to promote fair trade have been exceptional in this regard.) Nor have more transformational visions (such as deep ecology, radical feminism and religious revivalism) that reside in some quarters of civil society come close to centre stage in contemporary global governance. However, these more far-reaching challenges arguably have encouraged ruling elites to shift the focus of global governance from neoliberalism to a reformist discourse of socially and environmentally sensitive markets.

The overall modest quality of the corrections so far achieved by CSOs in global governance again raises the question of who is served by these strivings for accountability. On the whole, the corrections made have involved changes within the existing broad parameters of global governance rather than changes to those parameters themselves. For example, the move from neoliberalism to a social market discourse has occurred within a persistent overall framework of market capitalism. Sometimes CSOs, in pushing for policy corrections, have successfully challenged certain deeper structures of global governance, for instance by advancing measures to counter the subordination of women and the marginalisation of indigenous peoples. However, the various case studies have also shown strong tendencies towards an undemocratic dominance by the global north and professional elites in the civil society that engages global regulatory agencies. On balance, then, corrective actions by civil society on global governance have accomplished more in the way of smoothing problems that arise from underlying principles of global order, as opposed to altering those deeper structures or indeed in many cases even calling them into question. To this degree civil society action on global governance has in general reinforced and legitimated primary features of contemporary global order such as market capitalism, technocratic rationalism and an array of arbitrary social inequalities.

### Explaining the record and moving forward

Having set out the important, but also in key respects limited, contributions of civil society to accountable global governance, a crucial question remains, i.e. to identify the circumstances that have promoted the achievements and/or prompted the failings. Such explanations not only add to academic knowledge, but they can also inform future political action. Explanations hold within them prescriptions for how citizen activists and officials could raise the gains from, and reduce the shortfalls in, civil society strivings for accountable global governance.

Broadly speaking, the circumstances that have variously promoted and/or inhibited civil society advancement of accountable global regulatory processes can be classed as personal, institutional and structural. Personal factors relate to the characters and efforts of individual activists and officials. Institutional conditions relate to attributes of the organisations involved: global governance agencies as well as civil society associations. Structural circumstances relate to more generic framing principles of global politics, such as arbitrary social inequalities (related to class, country, etc.), capitalist production and rationalist knowledge. The personal, institutional and structural forces are deeply interrelated and co-determining. It is their particular combinations that in each situation enable and/or frustrate civil society activities to bring greater transparency, consultation, evaluation and correction to global governance arrangements.

*Personal attributes*

The present account of causal dynamics mainly elaborates on institutional and structural factors, inasmuch as these forces generally have a wider span, a longer duration and a deeper influence in respect of global politics than the energies of individuals. Thus attention to – and changes in – institutional and structural conditions would in most instances bring larger and more lasting impacts to accountable global governance than shifts in personalities. It is perhaps telling in this regard that the thirteen case studies in this book have rarely referred to the specific characteristics and initiatives of named individuals (e.g. pp. 190, 202, 236–7).

That said, social and political action does not happen in the absence of individuals, and the qualities of those persons have, as in any other area, also made a difference to civil society involvement with global governance. At least five broad personal features (or their absence) have affected the record of civil society efforts to have global regulatory agencies answer to their affected publics. These key traits are charisma, passion, acumen, persistence and reflexivity.

As in other political actions, charismatic leadership can be important in mobilising civil society strivings for accountable global governance, as well as official responses to those initiatives. Indeed, the personal appeal of certain activists, such as Walden Bello of Focus on the Global South, José Bové of Vía Campesina, the writer Naomi Klein, and Wangari Maathai of the Green Belt Movement has considerably energised broad alter-globalisation campaigns. A number of NGOs have also drawn on the charisma of media celebrities to motivate supporters for campaigns on, for example, human rights, debt cancellation and landmines (Cooper 2007). However, in most cases grinding civil society efforts for transparency, consultation, evaluation and redress in global governance have struggled for the lack of profile and broad backing that charismatic direction can generate.

Likewise, general deficits of charismatic leadership in global governance agencies have made it more difficult to mobilise institutional change towards greater accountability. The personal dynamism of Michel Camdessus as Managing Director of the IMF in 1987–2000, James Wolfensohn as President of the World Bank in 1995–2005, and Kofi Annan as Secretary-General of the UN in 1997–2007 helped to open those three organisations to more exchanges with civil society circles. Yet more usually global governance bodies have, to date, been led by rather faceless managers who do not energise staff with an agenda of increased democratic accountability.

Another general personal attribute that has, by its presence, frequently advanced efforts for accountable global governance (and weakened them by its absence) is passion. Collective anger, devotion, indignation and inspiration have often helped to overcome the very substantial institutional and structural obstacles (elaborated below) to more accountable global governance. Many advances, particularly in the area of correction and redress, have occurred when large numbers of individuals have combined their passions in collective mobilisation for climate action, debt cancellation, access to essential medicines, fair trade, and so on. In contrast, widespread apathy, disillusion and cynicism can act as powerful brakes on civil society promotion of accountable global governance. Such indifference can figure especially among seasoned global governance bureaucrats, though it also affects some CSO careerists.

Regarding acumen, time and again civil society strivings for accountable global governance have been advanced because individual activists have had an astute tactical bent. Civil society efforts have generally had greater results when pivotally placed campaigners have promoted their respective causes with clever publicity ploys, shrewd manipulations of institutional procedures and/or perceptive insights into the psychologies of others. Charisma and passion can have all the greater effect when they are linked with adroit calculations regarding types of pressures to apply, when and where. The many examples of such ingenuity include the above-mentioned EFF suit against ICANN and the creation by the One World Trust of a global accountability index. In addition, a number of reform-minded officials have skilfully manoeuvred from inside global governance bodies to support civil society efforts for greater transparency, consultation, external evaluation and redress in these institutions.

Yet in many cases accountability advances in global governance have required sheer persistence on the part of at least a core of committed civil society advocates and their allies within the regulatory agencies. In the face of widespread official bureaucratic inertia, strivings for more transparency at ICANN, more consultation at the G8, more evaluation at the World Bank, and more correction in the climate change regime have required dogged determination and immense patience. Many civil society initiatives for accountable global governance have faltered when individual activists and officials have been unable to sustain the required long-term resolve. Thus, for example, modest progress on ecological accountability at the IMF petered out after the mid-1990s when the principal activists involved shifted their emphases to other causes. Yet behind the success stories of civil society promotion of accountable global governance one generally finds certain individuals – their exploits often unsung – who have stayed the course, sometimes for up to several decades.

Finally, in particular to avoid slippage into hegemonic modes of accountability, it is important that the individuals engaged in relations between civil society and global governance have well-honed reflexivity. Accountability outcomes often end up disproportionately serving dominant social groups and dominant political discourses when the campaigners involved neglect continually to ask probing questions about who is and is not benefiting from their efforts. Certainly, proponents of accountable global governance generally face obstacles enough without in addition having to subject their own actions to constant critical scrutiny. Understandably, many advocates of change depend on convictions of self-rectitude to sustain them in an adverse political climate. However, complacency regarding one's own virtues can allow hard-won gains in accountable global governance to take an (often unintended) hegemonic turn that favours established power structures. For example, many North-based and middle-class activists considerably underestimate the extent to which they themselves enact and reproduce inequalities in global politics.

In sum, then, a number of personal qualities of citizen activists and officials can have a notable effect on civil society promotion of democratically accountable global governance. The implication of the preceding analysis is that campaigns for transparency, consultation, critical scrutiny and correction in global governance are generally furthered when they:

- are spurred with charismatic leadership;
- tap individual and collective passions for change;
- draw on creative tacticians;
- maintain a core of long-term committed support; and
- build upon self-critical reflexivity among the activists and officials involved.

### Institutional circumstances (global governance agencies)

Of course personality traits are far from all-determining in politics. The various case studies also show that the realisation or frustration of civil society contributions to accountable global governance depends in good part on conditions that are prevailing at the global regulatory institution in question. In this regard (lack of) resources, (in)competence of personnel, (absence of) incentives for staff, and (type of) organisational attitudes towards CSOs can make a substantial difference to accountability outcomes.

Just as with any other policy activity, global governance actions to engage civil society tend to yield larger accountability results to the extent that these initiatives are backed with resources. Money does not resolve all difficulties, of course, but a lack of funds can debilitate the hardest of resolves. Thus, for example, civil society can normally extract greater transparency in global governance to the degree that – as in the case of the Bretton Woods institutions – the agency allocates a substantial budget to communications activities. Likewise, efforts to consult with civil society groups have better chances of yielding substantial results when – as at the Commonwealth and the World Bank – the organisation specifically allocates resources for that purpose. Conversely, elaborate consultation procedures – for example as developed at the GFATM – can generate disappointing concrete results when the policy is not supported with adequate resources for full implementation. Some host governments of G8 and ASEM summits have supplied more resources than others for civil society involvement in those meetings. This irregular provision has made it difficult for these two global processes to build substantive and sustained exchanges with CSOs. Thus, although it is perhaps to state the obvious, nothing – including meaningful civil society contributions to accountable global governance – comes for free.

Another resource issue for global regulatory agencies that can aid or hamper the development of more substantive accountability relations with CSOs is availability of information on civil society. Apart from the UN, which maintains its roll of NGOs with consultative status, none of the institutions examined in this book has kept a systematic and regularly updated catalogue of relevant civil society contacts. A global governance official's 'database' for civil society typically consists of a haphazardly accrued stack of visiting cards and/or a casually assembled electronic mailing list. All too often global civil servants have limited awareness of the full range of potential civil society contacts and instead focus their interactions on a smaller circle of more prominent players, usually professional advocacy groups and usually disproportionately based in the global north.

A further institutional circumstance in global governance that has often constrained substantive engagement of civil society relates to staff competence. As the case studies note, many global regulatory agencies have, starting in the 1980s, appointed specifically designated civil society liaison officers. For example, the UN has its Non-Governmental Liaison Service (NGLS), and the World Bank has its Civil Society Team as well as a Participation and Civic Engagement Team. Yet these staff contingents are usually very small and of relatively junior rank. The secretariats of the IMF, the WTO, the Commonwealth, the GFATM and ICANN have no more than three persons each specially devoted to relations with CSOs. For their part the OIC, the G8 and ASEM have no permanent office to pursue contacts with civil society associations. Clearly it is difficult for global governance bodies to undertake substantive exchanges with civil society in the absence of a sufficient number and seniority of co-ordinating staff.

These personnel problems are exacerbated when, as in all of the global governance institutions examined in this book, the main bulk of officials have little if any expertise in respect of civil society. In fact even some of the civil society liaison officers have come to their posts without academic or practical experience in the subject. Meanwhile most other global governance personnel struggle even to define 'civil society', let alone to engage with CSOs in a professional manner. Several institutions, such as the IMF and the World Bank, have prepared written staff guides for relations with CSOs; however, it would seem that officials rarely actually consult these documents. Among the thirteen agencies covered in this study, only the World Bank has offered staff specific training on civil society liaison, and that provision has been modest and optional. As a result of these weak underpinnings, many global governance consultations of civil society associations have an ad hoc and rather amateur quality that undermines their potentials for enhancing accountability.

Nor, judging from these thirteen case studies, have global governance agencies given staff direct and substantial incentives to develop substantive accountability relations with CSOs. This problem is explicitly emphasised in the chapters on the World Bank and the GFATM. In both of these institutions the core of officials are most concerned to move money and often regard engagement with civil society as a delaying distraction. Moreover, almost nowhere in these thirteen global bodies do personnel reviews and promotion decisions highlight an official's record in respect of civil society liaison. Many global governance staff appreciate, in the abstract, that substantive relations with CSOs could spill over to raise their job performance. However, this understanding of a principle does not normally translate into concrete initiatives towards civil society in their day-to-day work. Meanwhile senior managers may from time to time issue general exhortations for staff to engage with civil society, as the quotations from WTO Directors-General at the opening of Chapter 5 well illustrate. However, these broad rhetorical declarations, unconnected with specific incentives for the individual staff member, do not generally motivate officials to upgrade their own relations with CSOs.

A generally weak lead from management on building global governance links with CSOs forms part of a wider issue of institutional attitudes towards civil society. Potential advances in accountable global governance from relations with CSOs are more likely to be realised when officials appreciate the contributions that these citizen groups can bring. Indeed, CSOs can provide global regulatory agencies with valuable information, cultural contextualisation, sharpened analysis, alternative perspectives, advice and political support. Yet negative attitudes in official circles – of reluctance and arrogance towards civil society actors – can readily obstruct constructive accountability relations. Full institutional receptiveness to CSOs has not been apparent in any of the global regulatory bodies studied here. However, some organisations, such as the Commonwealth and the WFTO, have shown themselves more ready than others to listen to, learn from and accord respect to civil society groups. In contrast, wary attitudes towards CSOs in some host governments of ASEM and G8 meetings have severely limited the possibilities of engagement.

In sum, then, a number of institutional factors on the side of the regulatory agencies concerned condition the effectiveness of civil society interventions as a means of advancing democratic accountability in global governance. To improve these accountability benefits in the future would, correspondingly, require attention to the main points identified above, namely:

- more funds in global governance budgets for relations with CSOs;
- larger and better maintained databases of relevant CSOs;
- higher number, quality and seniority of specialist staff for CSO liaison;
- greater guidance and training on relations with CSOs for other global governance personnel;
- clearer and more substantial incentives for officials to engage with civil society;
- stronger lead from management to promote relations with CSOs; and
- more cultivation of positive institutional attitudes towards civil society.

Pursuance of more inter-institutional learning in respect of civil society liaison could also be recommended. To date the various global regulatory agencies have developed their interchanges with civil society in relative isolation from one another. The project that has produced the present book has provided a rare occasion when officials from different global governance institutions have come together to compare experiences of relations with civil society. More regular exchanges of this kind could improve everyone's practices.

### Institutional circumstances (civil society associations)

Some of the same institutional factors that affect the capacities of global governance bodies to engage with civil society also affect the CSOs themselves. For example, civil society groups can lack adequate resources and competences to develop effective efforts to exact accountability from transplanetary regulatory bodies. Attitudinally, more CSOs could give more priority to sustained engagement of global governance institutions. In addition, CSO credentials to demand accountability of global governance agencies are strengthened or weakened to the extent that these citizen groups are themselves accountable to the constituents on whose behalf they claim to act.

To begin with, then, sustained civil society engagement of global governance institutions can demand levels of resources that many citizen groups lack. Much more than a shoestring is generally required for CSOs to be able to: examine a plethora of disclosed information; participate across the range of consultation opportunities; conduct well-grounded evaluations; and campaign for correction and redress. Major and predictable flows of funds are needed in order for civil society associations to support, for example, substantial and qualified staff contingents, large travel budgets, and advanced computing and communications technologies. Certain CSOs working on global governance matters have benefited from substantial membership contributions and/or philanthropic grants; however, most of these citizen action groups limp from one poorly financed initiative to the next.

Much as global governance agencies can struggle to build staff competence for relating with civil society, so CSOs can struggle to have sufficient staff capacity to engage effectively with global regulatory bodies. Certainly, laypersons' knowledge can provide an important base for many advocacy campaigns, including for example strivings to promote project reviews at the World Bank; to champion national democracy through the Commonwealth; to further gender equity in health care through the GFATM; or to pursue fair trade through the WFTO. However, CSO activities to advance accountable global governance often also require substantial levels of expertise, developed over a number of years, regarding the technicalities of the policy issue, the operations of the institution in question and the workings of global governance in general. Such specialist knowledge is often lacking, for instance, in civil society engagement of the IMF on macroeconomic policy, of the COPs on climate change, or of ICANN on Internet engineering. In addition, extensive field experience is normally needed for activists to hone tactical skills in lobbying, negotiating and building alliances. Yet, as noted in the preceding section, so far only relatively few civil society actors have had the priorities, the aptitudes, the resources and the stamina to develop this greater expertise for advocacy on global governance matters.

As several case studies have illustrated, CSOs have on various occasions countered problems of shallow financial and human resources by forming hubs and coalitions. In relation to the IMF and the World Bank, for instance, civil society actions have coalesced around co-ordinating bodies such as the Bretton Woods Project in Britain, the Halifax Initiative in Canada, the European Network on Debt and Development (Eurodad) in the EU, and 50 Years Is Enough in the USA. The ASEM study shows that trade unions and NGOs have combined forces well in order to advance a social agenda at that interregional body. In addition, civil society groups have joined together to form powerful issue-based coalitions, for example: in opposition to a Multilateral Agreement on Investment (MAI) through the OECD; in support of access to essential medicines under the WTO; in the Global Call to Action against Poverty (GCAP); in the Climate Action Network (CAN); and in mobilisation for the cancellation of poor country debts. These issue-focused alliances have often had a further advantage of engaging the entire polycentric apparatus that governs a given global issue, rather than concentrating on a single regulatory institution on its own. Of course CSOs must be ready, for the sake of building and sustaining such coalitions, to adapt their tactics to wider campaigns and perhaps also to engage issues that lie beyond their immediate priorities.

While such flexibility and the informality of ad hoc coalitions can encourage spontaneous and creative combinations of civil society forces, CSO efforts to advance accountable global governance have perhaps also suffered from the lack of more formal co-ordination mechanisms. In the absence of systematic approaches from the civil society side, many potential exchanges with global regulatory bodies are overlooked and/or many voices (especially from more marginalised circles) are excluded from the conversations. To address these problems the present author has explored ideas for a 'Global Civil Society Forum' that could better regularise and upgrade citizen group engagement of transplanetary governance agencies (Scholte 2008b). However, such propositions have so far gained no traction – neither among global regulatory institutions nor among CSOs – and improvisation remains the order of the day.

A final major organisational feature of civil society associations that conditions their contributions to accountable global governance concerns their own accountability. The framework chapter at the beginning of this book, as well as most of the case studies, have all noted that, in order to advance democratically accountable global governance, civil society must itself be an arena marked by transparency, consultation, evaluation and correction vis-à-vis affected people. The more that CSOs take a leading role in demanding and extracting accountability from global regulatory institutions, the more their own accountability comes under scrutiny, and rightly so.

Yet, as different case studies have noted, the record on accountability in civil society can be as mixed as the record on accountability in global governance. Successive reports by the Global Accountability Project have suggested that the performance of global NGOs on accountability measures generally does not exceed, and in some cases lags strikingly behind, the performance of global actors in the official and corporate sectors (Kovach *et al.* 2003; Blagescu and Lloyd 2006; Lloyd *et al.* 2007, 2008). To the extent that civil society associations neglect in their own practices to enact the sorts of accountability that they demand of official circles, they become vulnerable to charges of being self-appointed voices without democratic legitimacy. Indeed, failure to address questions of CSO accountability can lead to contractions of space for civil society participation in global governance.

Concerns about accountability deficits in civil society involvement in global politics have prompted some notable corrective initiatives. For example, as documented in Chapter 6, the Commonwealth Foundation as early as 1995 issued *Guidelines for Good Policy and Practice for NGOs*. In addition, the case study on the Global Fund noted extensive efforts to improve the accountability to constituents of CSOs that hold seats on the Board and the Country Coordinating Mechanisms (CCMs). In the 1990s the NGO Steering Committee of the United Nations Commission on Sustainable Development created an elaborate self-regulatory framework for promoting accountable civil society involvement in UN work on environment and development, although this process became increasingly burdensome and fractious until it collapsed in 2001 (Dodds 2001).

Broader initiatives to promote accountable civil society involvement in global affairs include the Humanitarian Accountability Partnership (HAP), established in 2003, and the International Non-Governmental Organisations Accountability Charter, launched in 2006. On a national scale the Philippine Council for NGO Certification has operated a code of conduct since 1998, and CSOs in India formed a so-called 'Credibility Alliance' in 1999. Also notable are accountability frameworks set up within individual civil society associations. Examples include the self-regulatory Code of Ethics implemented through the Canadian Council for International Co-operation since 1995 and the Accountability, Learning and Planning System (ALPS) operated by ActionAid International (ALPS 2006).

In spite of such initiatives, however, significant shortfalls remain in the accountability of civil society associations that engage with global governance processes. Many of these citizen groups do not subscribe to a code of practice that holds them to standards of transparency, consultation, evaluation and redress. Indeed, to this day some civil society actors continue to show considerable reluctance to communicate with, and answer to, their notional beneficiaries. Even where explicit guidelines are in place to improve CSO accountability, many associations lack resources for full implementation of the prescribed practices.

Meanwhile certain CSOs have also become so closely aligned with a given global governance agency that they can act more as uncritical promoters of the institution than as scrutinising watchdogs. Cosy relationships of this kind have arguably developed: between many United Nations Associations and the UN; between some economic policy think tanks and the Bretton Woods institutions; between much of the non-official and the official Commonwealths; and between the Asia-Europe Foundation and ASEM. In such cases the CSOs may end up serving more as instruments of the global governance agency's outreach than as levers of accountability for affected publics.

Thus a number of institutional improvements could be pursued on the side of CSOs in order to increase the contributions of civil society activities to accountable global governance. In summary, helpful steps for the future would include:

• greater priority on the part of CSOs to issues of global governance;
• more, and more reliable, funding of CSO programmes on global governance;
• expansion of CSO staff expertise to engage global regulatory apparatuses;
• fuller development of CSO coalitions on global governance matters;
• more formalised co-ordination of CSO engagement of global regulatory agencies; and
• greater attention by CSOs to their own accountabilities in global politics.

### Deeper social structures

Yet adjustments in personal attributes and institutional practices cannot alone overcome all of the shortfalls in civil society promotion of democratically accountable global governance. Concurrent attention to certain features of the deeper structures of global politics is also needed. The notion of 'deeper structures' refers here to underlying principles of social order, to the main frameworks of social action that shape relations among people on a global scale. These systemic patterns can, depending on their character, open up or constrain possibilities for CSOs to exact accountability from global regulatory agencies. Such structures can also affect which constituents obtain greater or lesser accountability in global governance, as well as the purposes which that accountability serves.

One deeper structure that has often complicated contemporary civil society initiatives to advance accountable global governance is the statist legacy of modern international relations. History may well be moving beyond a statist past (where national governments were the sole agents of accountability in world politics) to a polycentric condition (where accountability dynamics can involve multiple kinds of actors, including civil society associations). Nevertheless, embedded structures are slow to wane and can hamper the development of new patterns. In particular, intergovernmental organisations whose original constitutions date from statist times can find it difficult to reorient their accountability processes to include CSOs as well as nation-states. Moreover, some politicians and officials can still invoke a traditional discourse of sovereign statehood in order to resist – or at least place on the defensive – civil society initiatives to extract accountability from global governance. Even when, as is nowadays usually the case, national governments do not explicitly object to and obstruct civil society engagement of global regulatory bodies, state authorities generally do not actively promote these contacts either. Among the institutions examined in this book, the heritage of statism has perhaps most hindered the development of relations with CSOs at the IMF, the WTO and the OIC. In contrast, post-statist practices and mindsets that readily include civil society actors in global governance have made particularly notable headway at the GFATM, ICANN and the WFTO.

A second deeper structure – or rather group of structures – with major consequences for civil society promotion of accountable global governance involves embedded social hierarchies. A person's access to civil society engagement of global regulatory agencies is substantially conditioned by accidents of history related to factors such as caste, class, (dis)ability, faith, gender, nationality, race and sexuality. People who find themselves on the privileged end of each of these axes of dominance and subordination have better chances to use civil society to obtain accountability in global governance. Conversely, those on the low end of these social hierarchies generally have much more limited possibilities to obtain transparency, consultation, evaluation and redress in respect of transplanetary regulatory institutions. In this way embedded structural inequalities largely shape who is (and is not) served by CSO actions for accountable global governance.

Owing to hierarchies among countries, for example, CSOs based in the global north have tended to enjoy greater opportunities to obtain accountability from global governance agencies than CSOs based in the global south. This North-South discrepancy in resources, experience and contacts is seen especially starkly in the case studies of the IMF, the WTO, the OECD, the G8, climate change negotiations and ICANN. North-South inequalities have been relatively less marked in respect of the Commonwealth, the GFATM and the WFTO. All three of these latter institutions have reserved specific roles in their policy processes for CSOs from the global south. In addition, the Commonwealth has held most of its summits in the global south, enabling CSOs from the surrounding region to have greater possibilities of accessing the proceedings. The Global Fund has devolved many of its implementation activities to CCMs in the global south. The WFTO has arranged its constitution so as to spread civil society voice equitably across five regions of the world. However, in the absence of such proactive measures to counter North-South inequalities, prevailing structures of global politics have mostly favoured civil society actors from more privileged parts of the world. Indeed, on the whole the distribution of civil society involvement in global governance has sooner reproduced than challenged Northern dominance of existing regulatory institutions.

Similarly, civil society engagement of global governance agencies has widely manifested and reinforced class hierarchies. Thus professional and wealthy social circles have generally obtained greater accountability from global governance through CSOs than underclasses. For example, the case studies indicate that business associations have ranked among the largest civil society contingents at WTO Ministerial Conferences and climate change COPs. Organisations of big business have also been a favoured civil society interlocutor for the IMF and the OECD. Likewise, business groups have enjoyed privileged access to civil society engagement of ASEM and the OIC relative to NGOs and social movements which advocate for marginalised classes. Associations that assemble impoverished people have had little say in climate politics, even though these underclasses are set to suffer the greatest harms of drought, sea level rise and more volatile weather. True, the case studies have uncovered situations where, as in certain projects of the World Bank and certain CCMs at the Global Fund, concerted efforts have been made to involve CSOs that maintain close links with marginalised classes. On the whole, however, civil society relations with transplanetary governance agencies have to date mainly confirmed elite dominance of global politics. As a result, transparency, consultation, evaluation and redress in global governance have generally flowed disproportionately to those classes who have the most resources and power to demand voice.

Likewise, embedded inequalities have normally made it more difficult for women, people of colour, persons living with disability, and other subordinated social groups to find voice and impact in the civil society that engages global governance. The case studies show only isolated instances – such as UN Conferences on Women and gender reviews at the GFATM – where CSOs have effectively put the spotlight on gender hierarchies in global politics. Questions of race are mentioned in four of the thirteen empirical investigations in this book: in respect of the Commonwealth on apartheid; and with passing remarks in the chapters on the IMF, the OIC and climate change. The case studies also reveal but one instance (namely, with seats for Affected Communities at the Global Fund) where civil society action has promoted direct account-ability in global governance to disabled people.

In general, then, CSO engagement of global regulatory bodies has more often conformed to, rather than resisted, structures of social inequality. This tendency ought not to be so surprising. After all, civil society is part of – and tends to reflect – society as a whole. As a result, CSOs have usually found it easier to obtain transparency for privileged circles, con-sultation of dominant social groups, evaluation by those in advantaged quarters, and correction for more powerful interests. To achieve more equitable accountabilities in global governance would require high levels of critical awareness (i.e. the reflexivity mentioned earlier) and persistent struggle on the part of CSOs. Greater equality would also demand that civil society groups which occupy structurally strong positions relinquish some of their arbitrarily acquired prerogatives in favour of structurally weaker parties.

Such redistribution of resources and power within civil society engage-ment of global governance is the more difficult to accomplish given the deeply embedded capitalist structure of contemporary political economy. By capitalism is here understood a circumstance where social relations are pervasively and thoroughly oriented to the accumulation of surplus (i.e. resources in excess of subsistence needs). Capitalism lies at the heart of contemporary globalisation and has deeply shaped the rules that gov-ern expanded transplanetary connections in the twenty-first century (Scholte 2005b: Ch. 4).

Capitalism has tended to reinforce and intensify social inequalities inasmuch as arbitrary hierarchies associated with country, class, gender, race and other social categories can be readily harnessed to further the extraction of surplus from some quarters and its concentration in others. The historical causes of social hierarchies are more complex than capital-ism alone, of course, but reversing such inequalities in today's world – for example to obtain more equitable accountabilities in global governance – cannot be accomplished without challenging deeply entrenched capitalist interests. Needless to say, resistance to the prevailing mode of production is no small matter, and most CSOs that engage global regulatory institutions have avoided such a direct confrontation.

The centrality of capitalism in global relations has far-reaching implications for the nature of accountabilities that CSOs are likely to pursue or be able to achieve in global governance. Transparency, consultation, evaluation and correction that facilitate or refine the workings of surplus accumulation – for example with corporate social responsibility schemes – are far more readily accomplished than accountabilities on non-capitalist terms such as feudal relations, a care economy or the Gaia principle. Thus CSOs that pursue accountable global governance in line with the deeper rules of capitalism – for example by not questioning the law of contract, private property rights and monetised social relations – can generally make greater headway. In contrast, social movements that seek accountability through a structural transformation beyond capitalism have usually remained at the margins of global politics. In this way, business associations, orthodox trade unions, mainstream think tanks and reformist NGOs have generally obtained greater accountability from global governance than anti-capitalists in peasant associations, radical environmental movements and certain faith groups. The structural power of capitalism has the consequence that (hegemonic) accountability which sustains processes of accumulation tends to prevail over (counter-hegemonic) accountability that would subvert accumulation.

Whether or not one regards this outcome as a good thing depends on one's judgement of capitalism as either furthering or frustrating the realisation of a good society. On the one hand, reformists in civil society and elsewhere contend that capitalism, for all its shortcomings, is a progressive force that can be managed – for example through global governance – to advance material welfare, social justice, individual liberty, cultural vibrancy, democracy and peace. On the other hand, some transformists in CSOs and elsewhere argue that capitalism is an incorrigible source of harm in terms of generating arbitrary inequalities, atomisation, moral degradation, violence and ecological destruction.

Whereas capitalism is perhaps the deepest structure of global politics in terms of material circumstances, rationalism is arguably the deepest organising principle of ideational conditions in the contemporary more global world. By rationalism is here meant a frame of knowledge marked by secularism, anthropocentrism, techno-scientism and instrumentalism. In a modern rationalist frame, the highest truth values are assigned to knowledge that: (a) focuses on the physical (and not metaphysical) world; (b) centres on human concerns and control; (c) grasps and applies laws of nature and society; and (d) delivers tools to solve immediate problems of everyday life. In a rationalist logic, knowledge is constructed with the overriding aim of harnessing natural and social forces to advance human wellbeing in life on earth. Much as capitalism as a mode of production sets the predominant frame of what is normal, expected and accepted in the global economy, so rationalism as a mode of knowledge defines the prevailing 'common sense' in global affairs.

The power of rationalism in contemporary global politics is well illustrated by the difficulties that indigenous peoples, animal rights activists and religious revivalists experience to obtain a hearing in global governance institutions. Such civil society groups – which seek accountability for harms that are allegedly inherent in rationalism – are generally branded by the mainstream as 'irrational' if not 'crazy' and then locked out of global governance proceedings. Indeed, the case studies in this book barely mention such silenced actors, apart from a few references to occasional audiences for aboriginal peoples at the UN and the World Bank, and the heavy involvement of churches in the campaign for debt relief. In contrast, CSOs that seek accountability within a secularist, anthropocentric, scientific, instrumentalist frame of 'solving problems' (such as hunger, disease, banking crises, digital access and greenhouse gas emissions) have had far easier entry into global regulatory processes. Hence civil society strivings for accountable global governance have generally fared better when they advance modern rationalism than when they challenge it. It is easier to achieve (hegemonic) accountability which sustains rationalist knowledge than (counter-hegemonic) accountability that affirms alternative grounds of understanding.

Whether or not one welcomes this situation in current civil society engagement of global governance depends on one's assessment of the promises and pitfalls of modern rationalism. Reformists in civil society work on a premise that policy adjustments – for example through global governance – can overcome negative potentials of rationalism in relation to, say, ecological destruction in a consumerist society, violations of privacy in a surveillance society, or moral decay in a godless society. However, certain transformist elements in civil society would argue that rationalism itself is the core problem of global governance, for instance through its generation of an arrogant and dangerous disregard of nature, by its fostering of shallow preoccupations that suppress fuller meanings of life, and/or by its propensity to cause offence to a supreme deity.

In sum, then, a number of structural forces play a key part in determining who does and does not obtain accountability from global regulatory institutions through civil society. Structures also figure significantly in determining what purposes are served in civil society promotion of more accountable global governance. Unless deliberately countered, many of these structural forces can work in undemocratic ways to impose arbitrary subordinations and to silence dissent. Steps to confront these tendencies could include:

- avoidance of, and resistance to, statist thinking that is both obsolete and counterproductive in today's more global world;
- proactive measures by global governance institutions to broaden access for CSOs with close links to peripheral geographical areas and subordinated social circles;
- redistributions of resources within civil society in favour of associations that offer direct voice and influence to marginalised groups; and
- greater political space and more respectful hearing for radical critics of predominant capitalist and rationalist structures of contemporary global politics.

### A conclusion's conclusion

And so, at the close, this book makes a final return to its overarching concern: in what ways and to what extents have civil society activities made global regulatory institutions more answerable to the people whose lives and livelihoods are affected? In summary, several hundred pages have demonstrated that the question is not open to a simple unqualified answer. Nevertheless, it is possible to draw the findings together in several brief points.

First, accountability is not an unproblematic good in global politics. It is always necessary to ask 'accountability for whom?' and 'accountability for what purpose?' Not all accountabilities in global governance are *democratic* accountabilities.

Second, civil society activities have over recent decades made some important contributions to more accountable global governance. Thanks in part to interventions from CSOs, global regulatory institutions today offer more transparency, consultation, evaluation and correction than was the case before the 1990s. CSO campaigns on these matters have usually yielded the greatest results when associations have worked collectively in coalitions.

Third, the overall scale of civil society promotion of transparency, consultation, evaluation and correction in global regulatory bodies has to date remained modest, both in absolute terms and relative to the needs. Moreover, civil society contributions to accountable global governance have not served all constituencies and purposes equally. Indeed, in relation to the deeper structures of global politics the accountabilities achieved have sooner had a hegemonic character than a counter-hegemonic force.

Fourth, these limitations in civil society advancement of democratically accountable global governance can be ascribed to a combination of personal, institutional and deeper structural conditions. On the personal side, accountability promotion has been compromised to the extent that the activists and officials involved have lacked charisma, passion, acumen, determination and reflexivity. On the institutional side, both CSOs and global regulatory agencies have often suffered from problems of funding, staffing, information, attitudes, procedures and leadership. On the structural side, the contributions of civil society to democratically accountable global governance have generally been qualified by lingering statism and entrenched social hierarchies, as well as forces of capitalism and rationalism that marginalise certain kinds of civil society associations and messages.

Fifth, this diagnosis of the sources of the problems also suggests a forward programme of action, encompassing measures identified with bullet points at the close of the respective sections above. Many of the corrective measures require a substantial commitment of resources. Democracy does not come cheap. Yet inaction on this matter could be even more costly. Pressing global challenges are crying out for more global governance. That expansion of global regulation is substantially dependent on the development of adequate accountability mechanisms. When properly resourced and practised, civil society engagement of global governance is one of the principal feasible ways to deliver that accountability. The case is clear – and pressing. Now for the requisite political action ...

# Bibliography

Abbas, M. (2005) *Civilization in Islam*. New Delhi: Reference Press.

Abugre, C. and Alexander, N. (1998) 'Non-Governmental Organizations and the International Monetary and Financial System', in UNCTAD, *International Monetary and Financial Issues for the 1990s – Volume IX*. New York: United Nations, pp. 107–25.

Acharya, A. (2003) 'Democratisation and the Prospects for Participatory Regionalism in Southeast Asia', *Third World Quarterly*, vol. 24, no. 2, 375–90.

ActionAid (2007) *The IMF's Policy Support Instrument: Expanded Fiscal Space or Continued Belt-Tightening?* Johannesburg: ActionAid.

ActionAid International, Bretton Woods Project, The Development Gap, Christian Aid, One World Trust, AFRODAD and World Development Movement (2005) *Kept in the Dark: A Briefing on Parliamentary Scrutiny of the IMF and World Bank*.

Adaba, G. (2002) 'Trade Unions and the Promotion of Socially Sustainable Global Finance', in J. A. Scholte and A. Schnabel (eds.), *Civil Society and Global Finance*. London: Routledge, pp. 181–98.

Adger, N., Huq, S., Brown, K., Conway, D. and Hulme, M. (2002) *Adaptation to Climate Change: Setting the Agenda for Development Policy and Research*. Tyndall Centre Working Paper No. 16, April.

AEBF (2008) 'Chairman Statement', available at www.aebf11.org/files/up2008128111335.pdf. Accessed 18 August 2009.

AEPF (2006) 'People's Vision: Building Solidarity across Asia and Europe', 6 September, available at www.tni.org/detail_page.phtml?page=asem-helsinki_final-declaration. Accessed 15 September 2009.

(2007) 'AEPF Address to ASEM at 10', available at www.tni.org/detail_page.phtml?page=asem-helsinki_santiago. Accessed 18 August 2009.

Aggarwal, V. (ed.) (1998) *Institutional Designs for a Complex World: Bargaining, Linkages, and Nesting*. Ithaca: Cornell University Press.

Ahmad Baba, N. (1994) *Organisation of Islamic Conference: Theory and Practice of Pan-Islamic Cooperation*. New Delhi: Sterling Publishers Private Limited.

Ahrne, G. (1998) 'Civil Society and Uncivil Organizations', in J. C. Alexander (ed.), *Real Civil Societies: Dilemmas of Institutionalization*. London: Sage.

Akhtar, S. (2005) *The Organisation of Islamic Conference: Political and Economic Co-operation*. Pakistan: Research Society of Pakistan.

Al Ahsan, A. (1998) *The Organisation of the Islamic Conference (OIC): An Introduction to an Islamic Political Institution*. Washington, DC: International Institute of Islamic Thought.

Ala'i, P. (2008) 'From the Periphery to the Center? The Evolving WTO Jurisprudence on Transparency and Good Governance', *Journal of International Economic Law*, vol. 11, no. 4, 779–802.

Alibabai, G. R. (1997) 'OIC: Overview of its Failures and Achievements', in C. Ghulam Sarwar (ed.), *OIC: Contemporary Issues in the Muslim World*. Rawalpindi: A Friends Publication.

ALPS (2006) *Alps: Accountability, Learning and Planning System*. Johannesburg: ActionAid International, available at www.actionaid.org/assets/pdf/ALPSENGLISH2006FINAL_14FEB06.pdf.

Ameli, S. R. (2009) 'Virtual Religion and Duality of Religious Spaces', *Asian Journal of Social Science*, vol. 37, 208–31.

Anti-G8-Alliance for a Revolutionary Perspective (2007), previously available at www.g8-alternative-summit.org (website no longer active).

Archer, A. (1983) 'Methods of Multilateral Management: The Interrelationship of International Organizations and NGOs', in T. Trister Gati (ed.), *The US, the UN and the Management of Global Change*. New York: UNA-USA, pp. 303–26.

Arts, B. (1998) *The Political Influence of Global NGOs: Case Studies on the Climate and Biodiversity Conventions*. Utrecht: International Books.

ASEAN (2009) 'Association of Southeast Asian Nations', available at aseansec. organisation. Accessed 19 August.

ASEF (2009) 'History, the Beginning', available at www.asef.org/index.php?option=com_content&task=view&id=17&Itemid=62. Accessed 24 August.

ASEM (2006a) 'Chairman's Statement of the Sixth Asia-Europe Meeting, Helsinki 10–11 September 2006', available at www.aseminfoboard.org/content/documents/060911_ChairmanStatement.pdf. Accessed 30 August 2009.

(2006b) 'Helsinki Declaration on the Future of ASEM', available at www. aseminfoboard.org/content/documents/060911_FutureAsem.pdf.

(2008) 'The Second ASEM Labour and Employment Ministers Meeting', Bali, 14–15 October, available at ec.europa.eu/external_relations/asem/docs/declaration_2_asem_labour_en.pdf. Accessed 15 September 2009.

(2009) 'Asia-Europe Meeting InfoBoard', available at www.aseminfoboard. org. Accessed on 18 August.

ASEM Trade Union (2008) 'Trade Union Statement to the VII ASEM Leaders Summit', 13–15 October, available at www.ituccsi.org/IMG/pdf/FINAL_statement_Bali_Oct_2008.8_Oct.final.pdf. Accessed 15 September 2009.

Ashman, D. (2002) *Seeing Eye to Eye? InterAction Member Agencies and World Bank Staff Assess their Operational Collaboration on Policy Engagement for Poverty Reduction and Sustainable Development*. Washington, DC: The World Bank and InterAction.

Aston, J. (2001) 'The United Nations Committee on Non-Governmental Organizations: Guarding the Entrance to a Politically Divided House', *European Journal of International Law*, vol. 12, no. 5, 943–62.

Axworthy, T. (2007) 'Eight Is Not Enough at Summit' [Helmut Schmidt's keynote speech to the 25th anniversary of the InterAction Council], *Toronto Star*, 8 June.

Ayres, J. M. (2003–4) 'Global Governance and Collective Action', *International Journal of Political Economy*, vol. 33, no. 4, 84–100.

Bank Information Center (BIC) (2004) *A Civil Society Analysis of the World Bank's Response to the Extractive Industries Review*. Washington, DC: Bank Information Center.

(2007) *Comments on the World Bank's Governance and Anti-Corruption Strategy*. Washington, DC: Bank Information Center.

Bank Information Center, Bretton Woods Project, Campagna per la Riforma della Banca Mondiale and Third World Network (2004) *60 Years of the World Bank and the International Monetary Fund: Civil Society Strategy Meeting Summary Report*. Prepared by the co-organizers of the Penang Conference.

Bapna, M. and Reisch, N. (2005) 'Making the World Bank More Democratic Is Just as Important as Appointing a New Chief', *Financial Times*, 13 January, available at www.bicusa.org/en/Article.1865.aspx.

Bayne, N. (2005a) 'Overcoming Evil with Good: Impressions of the Gleneagles Summit, 6–8 July 2005'. Gleneagles and London: G8 Research Group, 18 July, available at www.g8.utoronto.ca/evaluations/2005gleneagles/bayne2005–0718.html.

(2005b) *Staying Together: The G8 Summit Confronts the 21st Century*. Aldershot: Ashgate.

Bayon, R., Hawn, A. and Hamilton, K. (2007) *Voluntary Carbon Markets*. London: Earthscan.

Bellman, C. and Gerster, R. (1996) 'Accountability in the World Trade Organization', *Journal of World Trade Law*, vol. 30, no. 6, 31–74.

Bello, W. (2000) 'From Seattle to Seoul: The Struggle for a Deglobalized World', ASEM 2000 People's Forum Conference, 'People's Action and Solidarity Challenging Globalisation', Seoul, 17–21 October. Reproduced at www.tni.org/detail_page.phtml?page=archives_bello_struggle. Accessed on 26 September 2007.

Bello, W. and Kwa, A. (2003) 'The Stalemate in the WTO', *CorpWatch*, 11 June, available at www.corpwatch.org/article.php?id=7089.

Bendell, J. (2006) *Debating NGO Accountability*. Geneva: United Nations Non-Governmental Liaison Service Development Dossier.

Bersick, S. (2008) 'The Democratization of Inter- and Transregional Dialogues: The Role of Civil Society, NGOs and Parliaments', in J. Rüland, G. Schubert, G. Schucher and C. Storz (eds.), *Asian-European Relations: Building Blocks for Global Governance?* London and New York: Routledge, pp. 244–70.

Betsill, M. and Correll, E. (2001) 'NGO Influence in International Environmental Negotiations: A Framework for Analysis', *Global Environmental Politics*, vol. 1, no. 4, 65–85.

Bichsel, A. (1996) 'NGOs as Agents of Public Accountability and Democratization in Intergovernmental Forums', in W. Lafferty and J. Meadowcroft (eds.), *Democracy and the Environment – Problems and Prospects*. Cheltenham: Edward Elgar, pp. 234–55.

Black, D. and Nauright, J. (1998) *Rugby and the South African Nation.* Manchester: Manchester University Press.

Blackett, A. (2002, printed 2004) 'Toward Social Regionalism in the Americas', *Comparative Labor Law and Policy Journal*, vol. 23, no. 4, 910–66.

Blagescu, M. and Lloyd, R. (2006) *2006 Global Accountability Report: Holding Power to Account.* London: One World Trust.

Blagescu, M., *et al.* (2005) *Pathways to Accountability: The GAP Framework.* London: One World Trust.

Bohman, J. (2007) *Democracy across Borders: From Demos to Demoi.* Cambridge, MA: MIT Press.

Bonzon, Y. (2008) 'Institutionalizing Public Participation in WTO Decision Making: Some Conceptual Hurdles and Avenues', *Journal of International Economic Law*, vol. 11, no. 4, 751–77.

Bora, B. (2004) 'Investment Issues in the WTO', in B. Hocking and S. McGuire (eds.), *Trade Politics.* London: Routledge.

Bourne, R. (ed.) (2008) *Shridath Ramphal: The Commonwealth and the World.* London: Hansib.

Brack, D. (2004) 'Trade and the Environment', in B. Hocking and S. McGuire (eds.), *Trade Politics.* London: Routledge, pp. 223–37.

Bradlow, D. D. (2001) 'Stuffing New Wine into Old Bottles: The Troubling Case of the IMF', *Journal of International Banking Regulation*, vol. 3, no. 9, 9–36.

(2004) 'Development Decision-Making and the Content of International Development Law', *Boston College International and Comparative Law Review*, vol. 27, no. 2, 195.

Bretton Woods Project (2003) 'Open Statement on Steps to Democratize the World Bank and IMF'. London: www.brettonwoodsproject.org/art-16202.

Brown, G. W. (2009) 'Multisectoralism, Participation, and Stakeholder Effectiveness: Increasing the Role of Nonstate Actors in the Global Fund to Fight AIDS, Tuberculosis and Malaria', *Global Governance*, vol. 15, no. 2 (April–June), 169–78.

Brown, L. D. (2007) 'Multiparty Social Action and Mutual Accountability', in A. Ebrahim and E. Weisband (eds.), *Global Accountabilities: Participation, Pluralism, and Public Ethics.* Cambridge University Press, pp. 89–111.

Buira, A. (ed.) (2005) *Reforming the Governance of the IMF and the World Bank.* London: Anthem.

Bujagali (2009) Website of the Bujagali Hydropower Project, www.bujagali-energy.com. Accessed on 26 August.

Bulkeley, H. and Newell, P. (2010) *Governing Climate Change.* London: Routledge.

Bull, B. and McNeill, D. (eds.) (2007) *Development Issues in Global Governance: Market Multilateralism and Private-Public Partnerships.* London: Routledge.

Bullen, S. and Van Dyke, B. (1996) *In Search of Sound Environment and Trade Policy: A Critique of Public Participation in the WTO.* Geneva: Center for International Environmental Law.

BWP (2008) 'Bretton Woods Update', archived at www.brettonwoodsproject.org/update/index.shtml. Accessed on 15 February.

Calieri, A. and Schroeder, F. (2003) 'Reform Proposals for the Governance Structures of the International Financial Institutions: A New Rules for Global Finance Briefing Paper'. Paper prepared for www.new-rules.org.

Camdessus, M. (1992) IMF Speeches 92/14.

CAN (Climate Action Network) (2008) www.climatenetwork.org. Accessed 7 May.

Capling, A. (2003) 'Democratic Deficit, the Global Trade System and 11 September', *The Australian Journal of Politics and History*, vol. 49, no. 3, 372–79.

Carin, B. and Wood, A. (eds.) (2005) *Accountability of the International Monetary Fund*. Aldershot: Ashgate.

Carin, B., Scholte, J. A., Smith, G. and Stone, D. (eds.) (2007) 'Global Insights: A Symposium: Global Summit Reform and the L-20', *Global Governance*, vol. 13, no. 3, 299–323.

Carin, B. *et al.* (2006) 'Global Governance: Looking Ahead, 2006–2010', *Global Governance*, vol. 12, no. 1 (January–March), 1–6.

Carlsson, I. *et al.* (1995) *Our Global Neighbourhood: The Report of the Commission on Global Governance*. Oxford University Press.

Cassidy, R. and Leach, M. (2010) 'Mediated Health Citizenships: Living with HIV and Engaging with the Global Fund in the Gambia', in J. Gaventa and R. Tandon (eds.), *Citizen Engagements in a Globalising World*. London: Zed.

CDM Gold Standard (2008) www.cdmgoldstandard.org/objectives.php. Accessed 17th November.

Centre for Advocacy and Research (2005) *India Case Study*. New Delhi.

Centre for Global Studies (2007) *L20: A Leaders' Forum*. Victoria, BC: Centre for Global Studies, University of Victoria. See www.l20.org.

Chambers, S. and Kopstein, J. (2001) 'Bad Civil Society', *Political Theory*, vol. 29, no. 6 (December), 837–65.

Chan, A. and Ross, R. J. S. (2003) 'Racing to the Bottom: International Trade Without a Social Clause', *Third World Quarterly*, vol. 24, no. 6, 1011–28.

Chandhoke, N. (2003) *The Conceits of Civil Society*. New Delhi: Oxford University Press.

Charnovitz, S. (1996) 'Participation of Nongovernmental Organizations in the World Trade Organization', *University of Pennsylvania Journal of International Economic Law*, vol. 17, no. 1, 331–57.

(1997) 'Two Centuries of Participation: NGOs and International Governance', *Michigan Journal of International Law*, vol. 18, no. 2 (Winter), 183–286.

(2000) 'Opening the WTO to Nongovernmental Interests', *Fordham International Law Journal*, vol. 24, 173–216.

Chauhan, S. and Gurtner, B. (1996) 'NGO Participation in Article IV Consultations of the IMF', *Swiss Coalition News*, No. 9 (September), 2–6.

Chiang, P. (1981) *Non-Governmental Organizations at the United Nations: Identity, Role and Functions*. New York: Praeger.

Chimni, B. S. (2004) 'International Institutions Today: an Imperial Global State in the Making', *European Journal of International Law*, vol. 15, no. 1, 1–37.

(2006) 'The World Trade Organization, Democracy and Development: A View from the South', *Journal of World Trade*, vol. 40, no. 1, 5–36.

Cho, S. (2005) 'A Quest for WTO's Legitimacy', *World Trade Review*, vol. 4, no. 3, 391–9.

Chu, K.-Y. and Gupta, S. (1998) *Social Safety Nets: Issues and Experiences*. Washington, DC: International Monetary Fund.

CIEL/Gender Action (2007) *Gender Justice: A Citizen's Guide to Gender Accountability at International Financial Institutions*. Washington, DC: Center for International Environmental Law and Gender Action.

CIRA (2006) 'Open letter to the Internet Corporation for Assigned Names and Numbers (ICANN) from the Canadian Internet Registration Authority (CIRA)', 17 March 2006, available at www.icann.org/correspondence/cira-to-icann-17mar06.pdf.

(2007) 'Response to ICANN's Request for Public Comments', 11 May 2007, available at www.cira.ca/response-to-icann-s-request-for-public-comments/ (searchable from www.cira.ca/news/, and last accessed 31 August 2009).

Civil G8 (2007) Website of the Civil G8, www.civilg8.ru (in Russian) and www.en.civilg8.ru (in English).

Clapham, A. (2000) 'UN Human Rights Reporting Procedures: An NGO Perspective', in P. Alston and J. Crawford (eds.), *The Future of UN Human Rights Treaty Monitoring*. Cambridge University Press, pp. 175–98.

Clark, A. M. (2001) *Diplomacy of Conscience: Amnesty International and Changing Human Rights Norms*. Princeton University Press.

Clark, A. M., Friedman, E. J. and Hochstetler, K. (1998) 'The Sovereign Limits of Global Civil Society: A Comparison of NGO Participation in UN World Conferences on the Environment, Human Rights, and Women', *World Politics*, vol. 51, no. 1, 1–35.

Clark, D., Fox, J. and Treakle, K. (2003) *Demanding Accountability: Civil-Society Claims and the World Bank Inspection Panel*. New Delhi: Rainbow Publishers (first published by Rowman & Littlefield, USA).

Clark, J. D. (ed.) (2003) *Globalizing Civic Engagement: Civil Society and Transnational Action*. London: Earthscan.

Climate Law (2006) www.climatelawsuit.org/. Accessed 15 August.

Coate, R. A. and Murphy, C. (1995) Editorial, *Global Governance*, vol. 1, no. 1.

Cohen, J. L. and Arato, A. (1992) *Civil Society and Political Theory*. Cambridge, MA: MIT Press.

Cohen, R. and Rai, S. M. (2000) 'Global Social Movements: Towards a Cosmopolitan Politics', in R. Cohen and S. M. Rai (eds.), *Global Social Movements*. London: Athlone Press, pp. 1–17.

Coleman, W. and Porter, T. (2000) 'International Institutions, Globalization and Democracy: Assessing the Challenges', *Global Society*, vol. 14, no. 3, 77–117.

Collins, C. J. L. *et al.* (2001) 'Jubilee 2000: Citizen Action across the North-South Divide', in M. Edwards and J. Gaventa (eds.), *Global Citizen Action*. Boulder: Lynne Rienner, pp. 135–48.

Commission of the European Communities (2009) 'Contributing to Sustainable Development: The Role of Fair Trade and Nongovernmental Trade-Related Sustainability Assurance Schemes'. Communication from the Commission to the Council, the European Parliament and the European Economic and Social Committee (COM(2009) 215 final, 5 May), available at www.fairtradeadvocacy.org/images/communfairtrade. pdf. Accessed 25 July.

Commons, M. (2008) 'IFAT and FLO Agree on Charter of Generic Fair Trade Principles', *The Organic Standard*, Issue 86 (June).

Commonwealth (2009) 'List of CSOs Accredited to the Commonwealth', at www.thecommonwealth.org/Internal/174739/142018/143215/8/, accessed 18 June.

Commonwealth Expert Group (2003) *Making Democracy Work for Pro-Poor Development: Report of the Commonwealth Expert Group on Democracy and Development*. London: Commonwealth Secretariat.

Commonwealth Experts' Group (1977) *Towards a New International Economic Order: A Final Report by a Commonwealth Experts' Group*. London: Commonwealth Secretariat (Economic Affairs Division).

Commonwealth Foundation (1995) *Non-Governmental Organisations: Guidelines for Good Policy and Practice*. London: Commonwealth Foundation, available at: www.commonwealthfoundation.com/uploads/documents/NGO_ Guidelines1.pdf.

(1999) *Citizens and Governance: Civil Society in the New Millennium*. London: Commonwealth Foundation.

(2009) 'Mission and Values', available at www.commonwealthfoundation. com. Accessed 25 August.

Commonwealth Secretariat (1986) *Mission to South Africa: the Commonwealth Report*. London: Penguin.

(1989) *South Africa: the Sanctions Report*. London: Penguin.

(2007) *Civil Paths to Peace: Report of the Commonwealth Commission on Respect and Understanding* (Amartya Sen Commission).

(2009) *Sustaining Development in Small States in a Turbulent Global Economy*.

Consumers International (2003) *Consumer Policy and Multilateral Competition Frameworks: A Consumers International Discussion Paper*, available at www. wto.org/english/tratop_e/dda_e/symp03_ci_disc_paper.pdf.

Cook, H. (1996) 'Amnesty International at the United Nations', in P. Willetts (ed.), *'The Conscience of the World': The Influence of Non-Governmental Organisations in the UN System*. London: Hurst, pp. 181–213.

Cooper, A. F. (2007) *Celebrity Diplomacy*. Boulder: Paradigm.

Cooper, A. F. and Shaw, T. M. (eds.) (2009) *The Diplomacies of Small States: Between Vulnerability and Resilience*. London: Palgrave Macmillan.

COPOLCO (2007) *29th Meeting of COPOLCO, Salvador de Bahia, Brazil, 24–25 May 2007: Resolutions*, No. 14504741, May, p. 4.

Cosbey, A. *et al.* (2004) *The Rush to Regionalism*. Winnipeg: International Institute for Sustainable Development.

CQA (1994) 'Foreign Aid Bill Clears Easily', *Congressional Quarterly Almanac*, vol. 50, 505–12.

Crawford, N. and Klotz, A. (eds.) (1999) *How Sanctions Work: Lessons from South Africa*. London: Macmillan

CSPR (2008) Website of the Civil Society for Poverty Reduction network, www.cspr.org.zm. Accessed 15 February.

Cullet, P. (2003) 'Patents and Medicine: the Relationship between TRIPS and the Human Rights to Health', *International Affairs*, vol. 79, no. 1, 139–60.

Cutler, A. C. *et al.* (eds.) (1999) *Private Authority in International Affairs*. Albany, NY: State University of New York Press.

CY (2009) *Commonwealth Yearbook 2009*. London: Commonwealth Secretariat.

DATA and ONE (2008) *The Data Report 2008: Keep the G8 Promise to Africa* Website no longer active.

Dawson, T. and Bhatt, G. (2002) 'The IMF and Civil Society: Striking a Balance', in J. A. Scholte and A. Schnabel (eds.), *Civil Society and Global Finance*. London: Routledge, pp. 144–61.

DDC (1997) *Common Cause: Challenging Development Strategies: The International Monetary Fund and the World Bank*. Dublin: Irish Mozambique Solidarity/ Debt and Development Coalition.

Dennis, S. and Zuckerman, E. (2006) *Gender Guide to World Bank and IMF Policy-Based Lending*. Washington, DC: Gender Action.

Dent, M. and Peters, B. (1999) *The Crisis of Poverty and Debt in the Third World*. Aldershot: Ashgate.

Depledge, J. (2005) *The Organisation of the Global Negotiations: Constructing the Climate Regime*. London: Earthscan.

Devereaux, C., Lawrence, R. C. and Watkins, M. D. (2006) *Case Studies in US Trade Negotiations, Vol. 1: Making the Rules*. Washington, DC: Institute for International Economics.

Dewey, J. (1927) *The Public and its Problems*. New York: Holt.

Diehl, P. F. (2005) *The Politics of Global Governance: International Organizations in an Interdependent World*, 3rd edn. Boulder, CO: Lynne Rienner.

Dissent! Network of Resistance (2007) *Spin and Rumours at the G8*, 3 July, available at www.dissent.org.uk.

Dobson, H. (2008) 'Where Are the Women at the G8?', 9 July, available at www.g8.utoronto.ca/scholar/dobson-2008.html.

Dodds, F. (2001) 'From the Corridors of Power to the Global Negotiating Table: The NGO Steering Commmittee of the Commission on Sustainable Development', in M. Edwards and J. Gaventa (eds.), *Global Citizen Action*. Boulder, CO: Lynne Rienner, pp. 203–13.

Dubash, N., Dupar, M., Kothari, S. and Lissu, T. (2001) *A Watershed in Global Governance? An Independent Assessment of the World Commission on Dams*. World Resources Institute, Lokayan, and Lawyers' Environmental Action Team.

Dunkley, G. (2000) *The Free Trade Adventure: The WTO, the Uruguay Round and Globalism – A Critique*. London: Zed Books.

Dunoff, J. D. (1998) 'The Misguided Debate over NGO Participation at the WTO', *Journal of International Environmental Law*, vol. 1, 433–56.

Ebrahim, A. and Weisband, E. (eds.) (2007) *Global Accountabilities: Participation, Pluralism and Public Ethics*. Cambridge University Press.

ECI (2007) 'Commodifying Carbon: The Ethics of Markets in Nature', Workshop Summary, 16 July. Oxford: Environmental Change Institute.

Edelman (1999) *Moving the IMF Forward: A Plan for Improving the Fund's Communications with Critical Audiences around the Globe*. Chicago/New York: Edelman Public Relations Worldwide.

Edwards, M. (2000) *NGO Rights and Responsibilities: A New Deal for Global Governance*. London: Foreign Policy Centre.

Edwards, M. and Gaventa, J. (eds.) (2001) *Global Citizen Action*. Boulder, CO: Lynne Rienner.

Edwards, M. and Hulme, D. (1996) 'Too Close for Comfort? The Impact of Official Aid on Non-Governmental Organizations', *World Development*, vol. 24, 961–74.

EEB (European Environmental Bureau) (2007) 'How the EEB Works', www. eeb.org/how_the_EEB_works/Index.htm. Accessed 11 May.

EFF (2009) 'Auerbach v. ICANN Archive', available at w2.eff.org/ Infrastructure/DNS_control/ICANN_IANA_IAHC/Auerbach_v_ICANN/.

EIAS (2006) 'ASEM and Trade Unions', available at www.eias.org/luncheons/ 2006/asemunions310806.html. Accessed 18 August 2009.

Ekdawi, A. (2010) 'The World Bank's New Disclosure of Information Policy: How Can Civil Society Ensure Its Proper Implementation?' Washington, DC: Bank Information Center. Available at www.bicusa.org/en/Article. 11848.aspx.

Elliott, L. (2006) 'Cosmopolitan Environmental Harm Conventions', *Global Society*, vol. 20, no. 3, 345–63.

Elliott, L. and Wintour, P. (2006) 'Blair Wants Developing Nations in New G13 to Help Secure Key Deals', *Guardian*, 13 July.

Enders, A. (1998) *Openness and the WTO*. Winnipeg: a Draft IISD Working Paper.

Epps, T. (2008) 'Reconciling Public Opinion and WTO Rules under the SPS Agreement', *World Trade Review*, vol. 7, no. 2, 359–92.

Esty, D. (1998) 'NGOs at the World Trade Organization: Cooperation, Competition, or Exclusion', *Journal of International Economic Law*, vol. 1, no. 1, 123–47.

(2002) 'The World Trade Organization's Legitimacy Crisis', *World Trade Review*, vol. 1, no. 1, 7–22.

ETUC (2006) 'ASEM Trade Union Summit', available at www.etuc.org/ a/2786. Accessed 18 August and 14 September 2009.

(2008a) '1st ASEM (the Asia-Europe Meeting) Social Partners Forum', Brussels, 30 June to 1 July, available at www.etuc.org/a/5188?var_ recherche=asem. Accessed 22 August 2009.

(2008b) 'International Trade Union Confederation (ITUC) Working for the Social Dimension of the Asia-Europe Meeting (ASEM), Background Document to the ASEM Trade Union Summit 2008', 12–14 October, Bali, available at www.ituccsi.org/IMG/pdf/ASEM_Background_ document_2008.final.pdf. Accessed 22 August 2009.

Eurodad (1995) *World Credit Tables: Creditor-Debtor Relations from Another Perspective*. Brussels: Eurodad.

Europarl (2000) 'Debates', 2 October, available at www.europarl.europa. eu/sides/getDoc.do?type=CRE&reference=20001002&secondRef= ITEM-007&format=XML&language=EN. Accessed 14 September 2009.

Evans, D. (1981) '"Popular Summit" Calls for World Disarmament', *The Citizen* (Ottawa), 20 July, 3.

Extractive Industries Review (2003) *Striking a Better Balance: The World Bank Group and Extractive Industries*. Washington, DC: The World Bank, available at go.worldbank.org/T1VB5JCV61.

Fair Trade Advocacy Office (2005) 'Last Minute Compromise Offers Little for the World's Poor: WTO Fair Trade Statement after Hong Kong', December 2005, available at http://fairtrade-advocacy.org/images/stories/publications/fine_wto_dec05.pdf.

(2007a) *Is There a Need for an ISO Standard on Fair Trade?* Brussels, May 2007.

(2007b) *An ISO Norm on Fair Trade?* Brussels, April 2007.

(2009) EU Official Texts, available at www.fairtradeadvocacy.org/index.php?option=com_content&view=article&id=5&Itemid=5. Accessed 9 May.

Fair Trade Original (2007) 'History', available at www.fairtrade.nl/main_en.php?item_id=656. Accessed 3 May.

Falk, R. and Strauss, A. (2001) 'Toward Global Parliament', *Foreign Affairs*, vol. 80, no. 1 (January/February).

Farrington, J. and Bebbington, A. (1993) *Reluctant Partners? Non-Governmental Organizations, the State and Sustainable Agricultural Development*. London: Routledge.

FIM (2010) 'Building Bridges', at www.fimcivilsociety.org/en/building_en.htm. Accessed 5 February.

Fisher, E. (2004) 'The European Union in an Age of Accountability', *Oxford Journal of Legal Studies*, vol. 24, 495–515.

Fisher, W. F. (1997) 'Doing Good? The Politics and Antipolitics of NGO Practices', *Annual Review of Anthropology*, vol. 26, 439–64.

Florini, A. (ed.) (2000) *The Third Force: The Rise of Transnational Civil Society*. Tokyo/Washington, DC: Japan Center for International Exchange and Carnegie Endowment for International Peace.

(2003) *The Coming Democracy*. Washington, DC: Island Press.

Focus on the Global South (2009), available at www.focusweb.org. Accessed 24 September.

Foster, J. W. and Anand, A. (eds.) (1999) *Whose World Is It Anyway? Civil Society, the United Nations and the Multilateral Future*. Ottawa: United Nations Association in Canada.

Fox, J. (2000) 'Civil Society and Political Accountability: Propositions for Discussion'. Paper presented at a conference on 'Institutions, Accountability and Democratic Governance in Latin America', the Helen Kellogg Institute for International Studies, University of Notre Dame, 8–9 May.

Fox, J. and Brown, L. (eds.) (1998) *The Struggle for Accountability: The World Bank, NGOs, and Grassroots Movements*. Cambridge, MA: MIT Press.

France, Présidence de la République (2008) 'Conférence de presse', 8 January.

Fraser, N. (2007) 'Transnationalizing the Public Sphere: On the Legitimacy and Efficacy of Public Opinion in a Post-Westphalian World', *Theory, Culture and Society*, vol. 24, no. 4, 7–30.

Fried, S. T. (2007) *Show Us the Money: Is Violence Against Women on the HIV & AIDS Funding Agenda?* Women Won't Wait Campaign, Washington, DC: ActionAid, 2007.

Friedman, E. J. *et al.* (2005) *Sovereignty, Democracy and Global Civil Society: State-Society Relations at UN World Conferences.* Albany, NY: State University of New York Press.

Friends of the Earth (2003) 'G8 Declaration Puts Bad Business First', *Evian*, 2 June, available at www.foe.co.uk/resource/press_releases/g8_declaration_puts_bad_bu.html.

Froomkin, A. M. (2000) 'Wrong Turn in Cyberspace: Using ICANN to Route around the APA and the Constitution', *Duke Law Journal*, vol. 50, no. 1 (October), 17–186.

G7 (1975) 'Declaration of Rambouillet'. Rambouillet, 17 November, available at www.g8.utoronto.ca/summit/1975rambouillet/communique.html.

(1995) 'Halifax Summit Communiqué'. Halifax, 16 June, available at www.g8.utoronto.ca/summit/1995halifax/communique/index.html.

(1997a) 'Communiqué'. Denver, 22 June, available at www.g8.utoronto.ca/summit/1997denver/g8final.htm.

(1997b) 'Confronting Global Economic and Financial Challenges: Denver Summit Statement by Seven'. Denver, 21 June, available at www.g8.utoronto.ca/summit/1997denver/confront.htm.

G8 (2002) 'G8 Africa Action Plan'. Kananaskis, 27 June, available at www.g8.utoronto.ca/summit/2002kananaskis/africaplan.html.

(2004) 'Fighting Corruption and Improving Transparency' under 'Public Financial Management and Accountability Strengthened'. Sea Island, 10 June, available at www.g8.utoronto.ca/summit/2004seaisland/corruption.html.

(2005a) 'Africa'. Gleneagles, 8 July, available at www.g8.utoronto.ca/summit/2005gleneagles/africa.pdf.

(2005b) 'Gleneagles Plan of Action: Climate Change, Clean Energy and Sustainable Development'. Gleneagles, 8 July, available at www.g8.utoronto.ca/summit/2005gleneagles/climatechangeplan.pdf.

(2006a) 'Education for Innovative Societies in the 21st Century'. St Petersburg, 16 July, available at www.g8.utoronto.ca/summit/2006stpetersburg/education.html.

(2006b) 'G8 Summit Declaration on Counter-Terrorism'. St Petersburg, 16 July, available at www.g8.utoronto.ca/summit/2006stpetersburg/counter-terrorism.html.

(2006c) 'Press Statement Following the G8 Summit'. St Petersburg, 18 July, available at en.g8russia.ru/podcast/001/246/115/putin4_en.mp3.

(2007a) 'Chair's Summary'. Heiligendamm, 8 June, available at www.g8.utoronto.ca/summit/2007heiligendamm/g8-2007-summary.html.

(2007b) 'Global Partnership Review'. Heiligendamm, 8 June, available at www.g8.utoronto.ca/summit/2007heiligendamm/g8-2007-gp-review.html.

(2007c) 'Growth and Responsibility in Africa'. Heiligendamm, 8 June, available at www.g8.utoronto.ca/summit/2007heiligendamm/g8-2007-africa.html.

(2007d) 'Growth and Responsibility in Africa, Annex: Summary of G8 Africa Personal Representatives' Joint Progress Report on the G8 Africa Partnership'. Heiligendamm, 8 June, available at www.g8.utoronto.ca/summit/2007heiligendamm/g8-2007-apr.html.

(2007e) 'Growth and Responsibility in the World Economy'. Heiligendamm, 7 June, available at www.g8.toronto.ca/summit/2007heiligendamm/ g8-2007-economy.pdf.

(2007f) 'Joint Statement by the German G8 Presidency and the Heads of State and/or Government of Brazil, China, India, Mexico and South Africa'. Heiligendamm, 8 June, available at portal3.sre.gob.mx/groupfive/ images/Heiligendamm/presidenciaalemana-G5.pdf.

(2008) 'G8 Hokkaido Toyako Summit Leaders Declaration'. Hokkaido, 8 July, available at www.mofa.go.jp/policy/economy/summit/2008/doc/ doc080714__en.html.

(2009) 'G8 Preliminary Accountability Report'. L'Aquila, 8–10 July, available at www.g8italia2009.it/static/G8_Allegato/G8_Preliminary_ Accountability_Report_8.7.09,0.pdf.

G8 Alternative Summit (2007) 'The Call', previously available at www.g8-alternative-summit.org/en.

G8 NGO Platform (2007a), available at www.g8-germany.info/english/index. htm.

(2007b) 'Rally', available at www.g8-germany.info/english/rally.htm.

G8 Research Group (2006) 'Gleneagles Final Compliance Report'. Toronto, 12 June, available at www.g8.utoronto.ca/evaluations/2005compliance_ final/2005-g8compliance-final.pdf.

G20 (2009) 'Leaders' Statement: The Pittsburgh Summit'. Pittsburgh, 25 September, available at www.pittsburghsummit.gov/documents/ organization/129853.pdf.

Gaer, F. (1996) 'Reality Check: Human Rights Nongovernmental Organizations Confront Governments at the United Nations', in T. G. Weiss and L. Gordenker (eds.), *NGOs, the UN, and Global Governance*. Boulder, CO: Lynne Rienner, pp. 51–66.

Gaventa, J. and Mayo, M. (2010) 'Spanning Citizenship Spaces through Transnational Coalitions: The Global Campaign for Education', in J. Gaventa and R. Tandon (eds.) (2010) *Globalizing Citizens: New Dynamics of Inclusion and Exclusion*. London: Zed, pp. 140–62.

Gaventa, J. and Tandon, R. (eds.) (2010) *Globalizing Citizens: New Dynamics of Inclusion and Exclusion*. London: Zed.

Gent, C. (2010) Author's personal communication with Christine Gent, External Affairs, WFTO, 28 January.

Gerechtigkeit jetzt! (2007) 'Letter to the Chancellor', previously available at wto.gerechtigkeitjetzt.de/index.php?option=com_content&task=view& id=99&Itemid=120.

Germain, R. and Kenny, M. (eds.) (2005) *The Idea of Global Civil Society: Ethics and Politics in a Globalizing Era*. London: Routledge.

Gibbon, J. (2008) 'God is Great, God is Good: Teaching God Concepts in Turkish Islamic Sermons', *Poetics*, vol. 36, 389–403.

Gilson, J. (2002) *Asia Meets Europe: Inter-Regionalism and the Asia-Europe Meeting*. Cheltenham: Edward Elgar.

Global Fund (2004) *Revised Guidelines on the Purpose, Structure and Composition of the CCMs and Requirements for Grant Eligibility*. Geneva: Global Fund, 18 November, p. 3.

(2007a) *An Evolving Partnership: The Global Fund and Civil Society in the Fight Against AIDS, Tuberculosis and Malaria*. Geneva: Global Fund.

(2007b) 'Board Decisions', Sixteenth Board Meeting, Kunming, 12–13 November 2007, archived at www.theglobalfund.org/en/files/boardmeeting16/GFATM-BM16-Decisions.pdf.

(2008a) 'Monthly Progress Update', April 2008, archived at www.theglobalfund.org/documents/publications/update/progressupdate.pdf.

(2008b) 'Decision Point GFATM/B18/DP18, Eighteenth Global Board Meeting', 7–8 November 2008, available at www.theglobalfund.org/documents/board/18/GFATM-BM-18-DecisionPoints_en.pdf.

(2008c) 'Partnership Forum 2008: Recommendations to the Board of the Global Fund'; see www.theglobalfund.org/partnershipforum/2008/PF2008_Recommendations.pdf, p. 2.

(2009) Home page, www.theglobalfund.org/en/. Accessed 15 August.

Global Policy Forum (2000) 'NGO Working Group on the Security Council – Information Statement', December, available at www.globalpolicy.org/security/ngowkgrp/statements/current.htm. Accessed 20 May 2007.

(2007) 'Arria and Other Special Meetings between NGOs and the Security Council Members', available at www.globalpolicy.org/security/mtgsetc/brieindx.htm. Accessed 20 May 2007.

Global Transparency Initiative (2009) 'Model World Bank Policy on Disclosure of Information', available at www.ifitransparency.org/uploads/7f12423bd48c10f788a1abf37ccfae2b/GTI_WB_Model_Policy_final.pdf. Accessed 20 July 2009.

GNSO (2006) 'GNSO Council Teleconference Minutes', 18 May 2006, available at gnso.icann.org/meetings/minutes-gnso-18may06.shtml.

(2007) 'Board Report: Introduction of New Generic Top-Level Domains', 11 September, available at: gnso.icann.org/issues/new-gtlds/council-report-to-board-pdp- newgtlds11sep07.pdf.

Godsäter, A. (2006) 'Civil Society and SADC – Regional Responses'. Paper delivered at the conference 'Civil Society and African Regional Integration: a Nordic Research Conference', Centre for Comparative Integration Studies, Aalborg University, Denmark, 6–7 November.

Goldsmith, J. and Wu, T. (2006) *Who Controls the Internet? Illusions of a Borderless World*. New York: Oxford University Press.

Goodman, P. S. (2007) 'Bush to Pick Zoellick for World Bank', *Washington Post*, 30 May, pp. A1, A6, available at www.washingtonpost.com/wp-dyn/content/article/2007/05/29/AR2007052900760.html.

Gordenker, L. and Weiss, T. G. (1996) 'Pluralising Global Governance: Analytical Approaches and Dimensions', in T. G Weiss and L. Gordenker (eds.), *NGOs, the UN, and Global Governance*. Boulder, CO: Lynne Rienner, pp. 17–50.

(1998) 'Devolving Responsibilities: a Framework for Analysing NGOs and Services', in T. G. Weiss (ed.), *Beyond UN Subcontracting: Task-Sharing with Regional Security Arrangements and Service-Providing NGOs*. London: Macmillan, pp. 30–48.

Gould, J. (ed.) (2005) *The New Conditionality: The Politics of Poverty Reduction Strategies*. London: Zed.

Grant, R. W. and Keohane, R. O. (2005) 'Accountability and Abuses of Power in World Politics', *American Political Science Review*, vol. 99, no. 1, 29–43.

Grasso, P. G., Wasty, S. S. and Weaving, R. V. (eds.) (2003) *World Bank Operations Evaluation Department: The First 30 Years*. Washington, DC: World Bank.

Griesgraber, J. M. (2008) 'Influencing the IMF', in J. W. St. G. Walker and A. S. Thompson (eds.), *Critical Mass: The Emergence of Global Civil Society*. Waterloo: Wilfrid Laurier University Press, pp. 153–67.

Griesgraber, J. M. and Gunter, B. G. (eds.) (1996) *The World's Monetary System: Toward Stability and Sustainability in the Twenty-First Century*. London: Pluto.

Griffith-Jones, S. (undated) *Governance of the World Bank*. London: UK Department for International Development (DfID).

Grugel, J. (2006) 'Regionalist Governance and Transnational Collective Action in Latin America', *Economy and Society*, vol. 35, no. 2, 209–31.

Grugel, J. and Piper, N. (2006) *Critical Perspectives on Global Governance*. London: Routledge.

GTA (2005) Discussion of the Grupo de Trabalho Amazônico (Amazon Working Group) with Jan Aart Scholte, Manaus, 17 August.

GTI (2007) *Transparency at the IMF: A Guide for Civil Society on Getting Access to Information from the IMF*. London: Bretton Woods Project.

   (2010) Website of the Global Transparency Initiative, www.ifitransparency. org. Accessed 5 February.

Gulbrandsen, L. and Andresen, S. (2004) 'NGO Influence in the Implementation of the Kyoto Protocol: Compliance, Flexibility Mechanisms and Sinks', *Global Environmental Politics*, vol. 4, no. 4, 54–75.

Gutiérrez, A. (1996) *NGOs and Fairtrade: the Perspectives of Some Fairtrade Organisations*. Trieste: La Città Invisibile.

Gutmann, A. and Thompson, D. (2004) *Why Deliberative Democracy?* Princeton University Press.

Habermas, J. (1962) *The Structural Transformation of the Public Sphere: An Inquiry into a Category of Bourgeois Society*. Cambridge: Polity, 1989.

Hadji Haidar, H. (2008) *Liberalism and Islam: Practical Reconciliation between the Liberal State and Shiite Muslims*. New York: Palgrave Macmillan.

Hajnal, P. I. (2007a) *The G8 System and the G20: Evolution, Role and Documentation*. Aldershot: Ashgate.

   (2007b) 'Summitry from G8 to L20: A Review of Reform Initiatives', CIGI Working Paper 20.

Halifax (2008) 'Annual Report Cards on Canada and the IFIs', available at www. halifaxinitiative.org/index.php/canada_and_the_ifis. Accessed 5 February.

Hall, R. B. and Biersteker, T. J. (eds.) (2003) *The Emergence of Private Authority in Global Governance*. Cambridge University Press.

Hänggi, H. *et al.* (eds.) (2006) *Interregionalism and International Relations*. London: Routledge.

Hann, C. and Dunn, E. (eds.) (1996) *Civil Society: Challenging Western Models*. London: Routledge.

Harder, P. [former Canadian sherpa] (2007) Interview with Peter Hajnal, Ottawa, 14 August.

Haynal, G. (2005) 'Summitry and Governance: The Case for a G-XX', in D. Carment, F. O. Hampson and N. Hillmer (eds.), *Setting Priorities Straight: Canada among Nations 2004*. Montreal: McGill-Queens University Press, pp. 261–74.

Heal, G. (1999) 'New Strategies for the Provision of Global Public Goods: Learning From International Environmental Challenges', in I. Kaul, I. Grunberg and M. Stern (eds.), *Global Public Goods: International Cooperation in the Twenty-first Century*. New York: Oxford University Press.

Heap, P. C. (2008) *Globalization and Summit Reform: An Experiment in International Governance*. Springer/IDRC.

Held, D. and Koenig-Archibugi, M. (eds.) (2005) *Global Governance and Public Accountability*. Oxford: Blackwell.

Held, D. *et al.* (1999) *Global Transformations: Politics, Economics and Culture*. Cambridge: Polity.

Henderson, D. (1999) *The MAI Affair*. London: Royal Institute of International Affairs.

Hernandez-Lopez, E. (2001) 'Recent Trends and Perspectives for Non-State Actor Participation in World Trade Organization Disputes', *Journal of World Trade*, vol. 35, no. 4, 469–98.

Herrick, A. (2006) 'NGOs as Intervening Variables in WTO Trade Governance: A Case Study on the Cotton Initiative', available at www. institut-gouvernance.org/fr/analyse/fiche-analyse-80.html.

Herz, S. and Ebrahim, A. (2005) 'A Call for Participatory Decision Making: Discussion Paper on World Bank-Civil Society Engagement'. Civil Society Members of the World Bank-Civil Society Joint Facilitation Committee (JFC). Available at www.civicus.org/new/media/World_ Bank_Civil_Society_Discussion_Paper_FINAL_VERSION.pdf or at siteresources.worldbank.org/CSO/Resources/World_Bank_Civil_Society_ Discussion_Paper_FINAL_VERSION.pdf.

Hewson, M. and Sinclair, T. J. (eds.) (1999) *Approaches to Global Governance Theory*. Albany, NY: State University of New York Press.

Heywood, A. (2003) *Political Ideologies: An Introduction*, 4th edn. London: Palgrave Macmillan.

Hill, T. (2004) *Three Generations of UN-Civil Society Relations: A Quick Sketch*. Geneva: NGLS.

Hollingdale, A. *et al.* (1990) *International Economic Issues: Contributions by the Commonwealth 1975–1990*. London: Commonwealth Secretariat.

Holzapfel, M. and Koenig, K. (2002) 'A History of the Anti-Globalisation Protests', *Eurozine*, available at www.eurozine.com/articles/2002–04–05-holzapfel-en.html.

Holzner, B. and Holzner, L. (2006) *Transparency in Global Change: The Vanguard of the Open Society*. University of Pittsburgh Press.

Hood, C. and Heald, D. (eds.) (2006) *Transparency: The Key to Better Governance?* Oxford University Press.

ICANN (2006) 'A Review of the Generic Names Supporting Organization', available at www.icann.org/en/announcements/gnso-review-report-sep06. pdf.

(2007a) 'Adopted Resolutions from ICANN Board Meeting, 30 March 2007', available at www.icann.org/en/minutes/resolutions-30mar07.htm.

(2007b) 'Independent Review of ICANN's Accountability and Transparency – Structures and Practices', available at www.icann.org/en/transparency/ow-report-final-2007.pdf.

(2008) 'ICANN Accountability and Transparency Frameworks and Principles', January, available at icann.org/transparency/acct-trans-frameworks-principles-10jan08.pdf.

(2009a) 'Affirmation of Commitments by the United States Department of Commerce and the Internet Corporation for Assigned Names and Numbers', available at: www.icann.org/en/announcements/announcement-30sep09-en.htm#affirmation. Accessed 12 October.

(2009b) Bylaws as amended 20 March 2009, available at www.icann.org/en/general/bylaws.htm. Accessed 1 July.

(2009c) 'Memorandum of Understanding/Joint Project Agreement with US Department of Commerce', available at www.icann.org/en/general/agreements.htm. Accessed 1 July.

ICANN Watch (2009) Website of ICANN Watch, www.icannwatch.org/. Accessed 10 July.

ICASO (2001) 'Letter from the International Council of AIDS Service Organizations (ICASO) on behalf of 31 NGOs to the HIV/AIDS Special Session facilitators', April.

ICFTU (2007) 'Trade Union Statement on the Agenda for the 6th Summit of the Asia-Europe Meeting', available at www.icftu.org/displaydocument.asp?Index=991224959&Language=EN. Accessed 18 August 2009.

ICYFDC (2010) Website of the Islamic Conference Youth Forum for Dialogue and Cooperation, www.icyf.com. Accessed 5 February.

IDB (2008) Website of the Islamic Development Bank, www.isdb.org. Accessed in September.

Idris, K. and Bartolo, M. (2000) *A Better United Nations for the Millennium: The United Nations System – How It Is Now and How It Should Be in the Future.* The Hague: Kluwer Law International.

IEO (2007) *The IMF and Aid to Sub-Saharan Africa.* Washington, DC: Independent Evaluation Office of the International Monetary Fund.

(2008) *Governance at the IMF: An Evaluation.* Washington, DC: Independent Evaluation Office of the International Monetary Fund.

(2009) *IMF Interactions with Member Countries.* Washington, DC: Independent Evaluation Office of the International Monetary Fund.

IFAT (2005) *The Ten Standards of Fair Trade*, as approved at the Quito AGM, available at:www.ifat.org/index.php?option=com_content&task=view&id=2&Itemid=14. Accessed 7 January 2007.

(2007) *IFAT Annual Report.* Culemborg: IFAT.

IGC (2009) Website of the Internet Governance Caucus, www.igcaucus.org/. Accessed 8 July.

IGP (2006a) 'Comments of the Internet Governance Project', available at internetgovernance.org/pdf/ntiacomments-igp-final.pdf.

(2006b) 'Review of Documents Released under the Freedom of Information Act in the .XXX Case', Internet Governance Project, Paper IGP06–003, 19 May, available at internetgovernance.org/pdf/dist-sec.pdf.

(2008) 'Comments of the Internet Governance Project', available at inter-netgovernance.org/pdf/IGP-JPA-08-comments.pdf.

(2009) Website of the Internet Governance Project, www.internetgovern-ance.org/. Accessed 10 July.

IHEU (2010) 'IHEU Responds to Accusation of Islamophobia by the OIC', available at www.iheu.org/uncampaign/iheuresponse. Accessed 5 February.

IHS (2007) 'ISO COPOLCO Workshop Addresses Fair Trade', available at engineers.ihs.com/news/iso-copolco-fairtrade.htm. Accessed 18 May 2009.

IIFA (2010) Website of the International Islamic Fiqh Academy, www.fiqhacad-emy.org.sa/. Accessed 8 February.

IINA (2010) Website of the International Islamic News Agency, www.islamic-news.org.sa. Accessed 8 February.

IMF (2003) 'Guide for Staff Relations with Civil Society Organizations', 10 October, posted at www.imf.org/external/np/cso/eng/2003/101003.htm.

(2006) *Annual Report 2006*. Washington, DC: International Monetary Fund.

(2007) 'Transcript of a Conference with the Media and Civil Society Organizations on the Launch of the Revised IMF Fiscal Transparency Code', 15 May, available at www.imf.org/external/np/tr/2007/tr070515.htm.

(2008) 'Legislators', available at www.imf.org/external/np/legislators/index.htm. Accessed 15 February.

(2009a) *Annual Report 2009*. Washington, DC: International Monetary Fund.

(2009b) 'Reforming the International Financial System', available at www.imf.org/external/np/exr/key/quotav.htm. Accessed 20 July.

(2009c) 'The Fourth Pillar: IMF Consultations with CSOs on Governance Reforms', available at thefourthpillar.ning.com.

(2010) 'IMF Resident Representative Offices', available at www.imf.org/external/ns/cs.aspx?id=57. Accessed 8 February.

Imhof, A., Wong, S. and Bosshard, P. (2002) 'Citizen's Guide to the World Commission on Dams', in L. Jordan and P. van Tuijl (eds.), *NGO Account-ability: Politics, Principles and Innovations*. London: Earthscan, pp. 43–58.

INGO (2007) Website of the INGO Accountability Charter, www.ingoac-countabilitycharter.org/. Accessed 23 February.

INNI (2007) 'ISO Assesses Whether to Undertake Standardization on Fair Trade' (INNI Online Update, Issue no. 14), May 2007, available at inni.pacinst.org/inni/inni_online_update_14.htm. Accessed 14 September.

International Council on Human Rights Policy (ICHRP) (2008) *Climate Change and Human Rights: A Rough Guide*. Geneva: ICHRP.

International Finance Corporation (IFC) (Undated) *Lessons Learned: Pangue Hydroelectric*. Washington, DC: Environment and Social Development Department, International Finance Corporation.

International Financial Institutions Democracy Coalition (2005) 'Democratizing the World Bank and IMF: Statement of the IFI Democracy Coalition' (endorsed by over 50 NGOs), available at www.financialpolicy.org/IMFDemocracy/imfdemwbgovernors.pdf.

International Social and Environmental Accreditation and Labelling Alliance (ISEAL) (2007) 'Letter to Consumers International, COPOLCO, and the ISO Secretariat', 10 May.

IPP (2007) Website of the International Parliamentarians' Petition for Democratic Oversight of the IMF and World Bank, www.ippinfo.org. Accessed 15 March.

ISBO (2010) Website of the Islamic States Broadcasting Organisation, www. isboo.org. Accessed 8 February.

ISESCO (1982) *Charter of the Islamic Educational, Scientific and Cultural Organisation*, available at www.isesco.org.ma/english/charter/charter. php?idd=TDD_REF.

(2010) Website of the Islamic Educational, Scientific and Cultural Organisation, www.isesco.org.ma/. Accessed 8 February.

ISF (2010) Website of the Islamic Solidarity Fund, www.isf-fsi.org/. Accessed 2 February.

ITFGPG (2006) *Meeting Global Challenges: International Cooperation in the National Interest*. Stockholm: International Task Force on Global Public Goods.

Jackson, J. H. (2008) 'The Case of the World Trade Organization', *International Affairs*, vol. 84, no. 3, 437–54.

Jacques, J. (2002) *Islam: Historical, Social and Political Perspective*. Waardenburg: Walter de Gruyter.

JCIE (2006) 'ASEM in Its Tenth Year: Looking Back, Looking Forward', available at www.jcie.org/researchpdfs/ASEM10/europe.pdf. Accessed 15 September 2009.

Jenkins, B. and Mainhardt Gibbs, H. (undated) 'BIC Comments on Draft OP 8.60 "Development Policy Lending"'. Washington, DC: Bank Information Center, available at www.bicusa.org/bicusa/issues/BIC_comments_8.601. pdf.

Joachim, J. M. (2007) *Agenda Setting, the UN, and NGOs – Gender Violence and Reproductive Rights*. Washington, DC: Georgetown University Press.

Jönsson, C. and Tallberg, J. (eds.) (2010) *Transnational Actors in Global Governance*. Basingstoke: Palgrave Macmillan.

Jordan, L. and van Tuijl, P. (eds.) (2006) *NGO Accountability: Politics, Principles, and Innovations*. London: Earthscan.

Kaldor, M. (2003) 'Civil Society and Accountability', *Journal of Human Development*, vol. 4, no. 1, 5–23.

Kaldor, M. and Muro, D. (2003) 'Religious and Nationalist Militant Groups', in Kaldor *et al.* (eds.), *Global Civil Society Yearbook 2003*. Oxford University Press, p. 151.

Kapur, D. (2002) 'The Changing Anatomy of Governance of the World Bank', in J. R. Pincus and J. A. Winters (eds.), *Reinventing the World Bank*. Ithaca: Cornell University Press.

Kaul, I. *et al.* (eds.) (1999) *Global Public Goods: International Cooperation in the 21st Century*. New York: Oxford University Press.

(2003) *Providing Global Public Goods: Managing Globalization*. New York: Oxford University Press.

Keane, J. (2003) *Global Civil Society?* Cambridge University Press.

Keck, M. E. and Sikkink, K. (1998) *Activists Beyond Borders: Advocacy Networks in International Politics*. Ithaca: Cornell University Press.

Kelly, R. (2007) 'From International Relations to Global Governance Theory: Conceptualizing NGOs after the Rio Breakthrough of 1992', *Journal of Civil Society,* vol. 3, no. 1, 81–99.

Kenya AIDS NGO Consortium (2005) 'Kenya Case Study', Nairobi.

(2007) 'Kenya Case Study Update', Nairobi.

Keohane, R. O. (2002) *Global Governance and Democratic Accountability.* Miliband Lecture, London School of Economics, Spring.

Keohane, R. O. and Nye, J. S. (2001) 'The Club Model of Multilateral Cooperation and the World Trade Organization: Problems of Democratic Legitimacy'. John F. Kennedy School of Government, Harvard University, 'Visions of Governance in the 21st Century' Working Paper 4, available at www.ksg.hardard.edu/visions/publication/keohane_nye.pdf.

(2003) 'Redefining Accountability for Global Governance', in M. Kahler and D. A. Lake (eds.), *Governance in a Global Economy: Political Authority in Transition.* Princeton University Press.

Khagram, S., Riker, J. V. and Sikkink, K. (eds.) (2002) *Restructuring World Politics: Transnational Social Movements, Networks, and Norms.* Minneapolis: University of Minnesota Press.

Khan, S. S. (2002) *Reassessing International Islam: A Focus on the Organization of the Islamic Conference and Other Islamic Institutions.* Oxford University Press.

Killick, T. (ed.) (1982) *Adjustment and Financing in the Developing World: The Role of the International Monetary Fund.* Washington, DC: International Monetary Fund.

Kim, I. (undated) 'How an NGO-Union Partnership Suffocated the Anti-ASEM Struggle in Korea', available at links.org.au/node/126. Accessed 24 September 2009.

Kim, J. (2004) 'Accountability, Governance, and Non-Governmental Organizations: A Comparative Study of Twelve Asia-Pacific Nations'. The International Society for Third-Sector Research (ISTR), 'Contesting Citizenship and Civil Society in a Divided World'. Ryerson University and York University, Toronto, 11–14 July, available at www.istr.org/conferences/toronto/workingpapers/kim.junki.pdf. Accessed 12 May 2007.

Kimble, M. (2010) 'Mobilizing Civil Society in the Interest of the Global Public Good'. Paper for the Annual Convention of the International Studies Association, New Orleans, 18 February.

Kirton, J. J. (2006) 'A Summit of Significant Success: The G8 at St. Petersburg'. G8 Research Group, Toronto, 19 July, available at www.g8.utoronto.ca/evaluations/2006stpetersburg/kirton_perf_060719.pdf.

[director of the G8 Research Group] (2007) Interview with Peter Hajnal, Toronto, 8 July.

Klein, H. (2001) 'The Feasibility of Global Democracy: Understanding ICANN's At-Large Elections', *Journal of Policy, Regulation and Strategy for Telecommunications Information and Media,* vol. 3, no. 4, 333–45.

Kocken, M. (2005) 'Fifty Years of Fair Trade: A Brief History of the Fair Trade Movement'. Prepared for IFAT, and available at www.ifat.org/index.php?option=com_docman&task=cat_view&gid=67&Itemid=106. Accessed 14 September 2007.

Kopecky, P. and Mudde, C. (eds.) (2002) *Uncivil Society? Contentious Politics in Post-Communist Europe*. London: Routledge.

Koppell, J. G. S. (2005) 'Pathologies of Accountability: ICANN and the Challenge of "Multiple Accountabilities Disorder"', *Public Administration Review*, vol. 65, no. 1, 94–108.

Korey, W. (1998) *NGOs and the Universal Declaration of Human Rights*. New York: St. Martin's.

Kovach, H., Neligan, C. and Burrall, S. (2003) *Power Without Accountability?* London: One World Trust.

Kwa, A. (2003) *Power Politics in the WTO*. Bangkok: Focus on the Global South.

Lamy, P. (2005) Speech at the NGO Roundtable Forum: The WTO's Sixth Ministerial Meeting, Hong Kong, 16 October.

Lawrence, S. (2005) 'Retreat from the Safeguard Policies: Recent Trends Undermining Social and Environmental Accountability at the World Bank'. New York: Environmental Defense, available at www.environmentaldefense. org/documents/4279_RetreatSafeguardPolicies_0105.pdf.

Lewis, S. (2005) *Race against Time*. Toronto: House of Anansi Press.

Lin, Z. (2004) 'An Analysis of the Role of NGOs in the WTO', *Chinese Journal of International Law*, vol. 3, 485–97.

Liverman, D. (2007) 'Review: From Uncertain to Unequivocal: The IPCC Working Group I Report: Climate Change 2007 – The Physical Science Basis', *Environment*, vol. 49, no. 8, 28–32.

Lizee, P. (2000) 'Civil Society and Regional Security: Tensions and Potentials in Post-Crisis Southeast Asia', *Contemporary Southeast Asia*, vol. 22, no. 3, 551–70.

Lloyd, R., Oatham, J. and Hammer, M. (2007) *2007 Global Accountability Report*. London: One World Trust.

Lloyd, R., Warren, S. and Hammer, M. (2008) *2008 Global Accountability Report*. London: One World Trust.

Long, C. (2001) *Participation of the Poor in Development Initiatives: Taking Their Rightful Place*. London and Sterling, VA: Earthscan and Institute for Development Research.

Loy, F. (2001) 'Public Participation in the World Trade Organization', in G. P. Sampson (ed.), *The Role of the World Trade Organization in Global Governance*. New York: United Nations University Press, pp. 113–35.

Lundan, S. M. and Jones, G. (2001) 'The "Commonwealth Effect" and the Process of Internationalisation', *World Economy*, vol. 24, no. 1, 99–118.

MacKenzie, H. (ed.) (2009) *Democratizing Global Governance: Ten Years of Case Studies and Reflections by Civil Society Activists*. New Delhi: Mosaic.

Mahon, R. and McBride, S. (eds.) (2008) *The OECD and Transnational Governance*. Vancouver: University of British Columbia Press.

Martens, J. (2006) 'The Future of NGO Participation at the United Nations after the 2005 World Summit'. Bonn: Friedrich-Ebert-Stiftung Briefing Papers, 'Dialogue on Globalization'.

Martens, K. (2002), 'Mission Impossible? Defining Nongovernmental Organizations', *Voluntas*, vol. 13, no. 3, 271–85.

(2004) 'Bypassing Obstacles to Access: How NGOs Are Taken Piggy-Back to the UN', *Human Rights Review*, vol. 5, no. 3, 80–91.

(2005) *NGOs and the United Nations: Institutionalization, Professionalization and Adaptation*. Basingstoke: Palgrave Macmillan.

Martin, N. (2005) 'Not Representative, but Still Legitimate', *Alliance*, vol. 10, no. 2, 16–17.

(2008) 'The FIM G8 Project, 2002–2006: A Case Analysis of a Project to Initiate Civil Society Engagement with the G8', in J. W. St. G. Walker and A. S. Thompson (eds.), *Critical Mass: The Emergence of Global Civil Society*. Waterloo: Wilfrid Laurier University Press, pp. 183–209.

Martin, P. (2007) 'Breaking Deadlocks in Global Governance: The L-20 Proposal', *Global Governance*, vol. 13, no. 3, 301–5.

Mason, M. (2005) *The New Accountability: Environmental Responsibility Across Borders*. London: Earthscan.

Mataka, E. (2007) 'Acceptance Statement', Geneva, 26 April.

Mathiason, J. (2004) 'A Framework Convention: An Institutional Option for Internet Governance', *Internet Governance Project*, Paper IGP04–002 (21 December), available at internetgovernance.org/pdf/igp-fc.pdf.

May, A. (ed.) (2010) *The Commonwealth and International Affairs: the Round Table Centennial Selection*. London: Routledge.

Mayall, J. (ed.) (2009) *The Contemporary Commonwealth: An Assessment 1996–2009*. London: Routledge.

McGee, R. and Norton, A (2000) 'Participation in Poverty Reduction Strategies: Synthesis of Experience with Participatory Approaches to Policy Design, Implementation and Monitoring'. IDS Working Paper No. 109.

McKeon, N. (2009) *The United Nations and Civil Society: Legitimating Global Governance – Whose Voice?* London: Zed.

McKeon, N. and Kalafatic, C. (2009) *Strengthening Dialogue: UN Experience with Small Farmer Organizations and Indigenous Peoples*. New York: United Nations and UN Non-Governmental Liaison Service.

Meyer, D. S. and Tarrow, S. (1998) 'A Movement Society: Contentious Politics for a New Century', in D. S. Meyer and S. Tarrow (eds.), *The Social Movement Society*. Lanham, MD: Rowman and Littlefield Publishers, pp. 1–28.

Michels, R. (1911) *Political Parties: A Sociological Study of Oligarchical Tendencies of Modern Democracy*. Glencoe, IL: Free Press, 1958.

Millennium (2000) *Millennium: Journal of International Studies*, vol. 29, no. 1.

Mittelman, J. H. (2000) *The Globalisation Syndrome: Transformation and Resistance*. Princeton University Press.

Monbiot, G. (2003) *The Age of Consent: A Manifesto for a New World Order*. London: Flamingo.

(2005) 'Africa's New Best Friends', *Guardian*, 5 July, p. 21.

Moore, M. (2002) 'Director General's Farewell Speech to the General Council', 31 July.

Mueller, M. (2002) *Ruling the Root: Internet Governance and the Taming of Cyberspace*. Cambridge, MA: MIT Press.

Mueller, M. and Chango, M. (2008) 'Disrupting Global Governance: The Internet Who Is Service, ICANN, and Privacy', *Journal of Information Technology and Politics*, vol. 5, no. 3.

Mueller, M., Kuerbis, B. and Pagé, C. (2004) 'Reinventing Media Activism: Public Interest Advocacy in the Making of US Communication-Information Policy, 1960–2002', *Information Society*, vol. 20, no. 3, 169–87.

Mueller, M., Mathiason, J. and Klein, H. (2007) 'The Internet and Global Governance: Principles and Norms for a New Regime', *Global Governance*, vol. 13, no. 2, 237–54.

Müller, J. (eds.) (2006) *Reforming the United Nations: The Struggle for Legitimacy*. Leiden: Martinus Nijhoff.

Murphy, H. (2007) 'NGOs, Agenda-Setting and the WTO', Paper presented to the Australasian Political Studies Association Conference, Monash University, 24–26 September.

Museveni, Y. K. (2007) 'Social Transformation of the Commonwealth Societies', speech to the Opening of the Commonwealth Heads of Government Meeting, Kampala, 23 November, available at www.thecommonwealth. org/shared_asp_files/gfsr.asp?NodeID=172950andattributename=file.

Musuva, C. (ed.) (2006) *Behind Closed Doors: Secrecy in International Financial Institutions*. Cape Town: IDASA.

Myers, P. (2009) Heidi Ullrich's personal communication with Paul Myers, President of the WFTO, 23 October.

(2010) Heidi Ullrich's personal communication with Paul Myers, President of the WFTO, 11 January.

Myers, P. and Wills, C. (2007) *IFAT: An Agenda for Change*. Kolkata: EKTA Trust.

Naidoo, K. (2003) 'Civil Society Accountability: Who Guards the Guardians?' Lecture delivered at the United Nations, New York, available at www. gdrc.org/ngo/accountability/ngo-accountability.pdf.

(2007) Interview with J. Garcia of Transparency Watch, Heiligendamm, 8 June, available at www.civicus.org/new/media/TransparencyWatch-KumiNaidoo-Interview-The-Month.doc.

Narayan, D. (1999) *Voices of the Poor: Can Anyone Hear Us? Voices from 47 Countries*. Washington, DC: World Bank.

Nauright, J. and Schimmel, K. (eds.) (2005) *The Political Economy of Sport*. London: Palgrave Macmillan.

NCUC (2009) Website of the Noncommercial Users Constituency, www.ncd-nhc.org. Accessed 10 July.

New Rules for Global Finance (2007a) 'High-Level Panel on IMF Board Accountability: Key Findings and Recommendations', April.

(2007b) 'Leadership Selection Reform at the World Bank and International Monetary Fund'. Washington, DC: www.new-rules.org/docs/imf_wb_leadership_selection051107.htm.

(2009) See www.new-rules.org. Accessed 20 July 2009.

Newell, P. (1998) 'Who "CoPed" Out at Kyoto? An Assessment of the Third Conference of the Parties to the Framework Convention on Climate Change', *Environmental Politics*, vol. 7, no. 2, 153–60.

(2000) *Climate for Change: Non-State Actors and the Global Politics of the Greenhouse*. Cambridge University Press.

(2001) 'Managing Multinationals: The Governance of Investment for the Environment', *Journal of International Development*, vol. 13, 907–19.

(2005a) 'Climate for Change? Civil Society and the Politics of Global Warming', in M. Glasius *et al.* (eds.), *Global Civil Society Yearbook 2005/6*. London: SAGE.

(2005b) 'Race, Class and the Global Politics of Environmental Inequality', *Global Environmental Politics*, vol. 5, No. 3, 70–94.

(2008) 'Civil Society, Corporate Accountability and the Politics of Climate Change', *Global Environmental Politics*, vol. 8, no. 3, 124–55.

Newell, P. and Paterson, M. (1998) 'Climate for Business: Global Warming, the State and Capital', *Review of International Political Economy*, vol. 5, no. 4, 679–704.

(2010) *Climate Capitalism: Global Warming and the Transformation of the Global Economy*. Cambridge University Press.

Newell, P. and Wheeler, J. (eds.) (2006) *Rights, Resources and the Politics of Accountability*. London: Zed Books.

Newell, P., Jenner, N. and Baker, L. (2009) 'Governing Clean Development: A Framework for Analysis', *Development Policy Review*, vol. 27, no. 6, 717–39.

Nicholls, A. and Opal, C. (2005) *Fair Trade: Market-Driven Ethical Consumption*. London: Sage Publications.

Nichols, P. M. (1996) 'Realism, Liberalism, Values and the World Trade Organization', *University of Pennsylvania Journal of International Economic Law*, vol. 17, no. 3, 851–82.

Nordås, H. K. (2003) *Is Trade Liberalization a Window of Opportunity for Women?* Geneva: World Trade Organization Staff Working Paper ERSD-2003-03.

NTIA (2008) 'NTIA Seeks Public Comments Regarding Joint Project Agreement with ICANN', available at www.ntia.doc.gov/ntiahome/domainname/jpamidtermreview.html.

Nye, J. S. (2001) 'Globalization's Democratic Deficit: How to Make International Institutions More Accountable', *Foreign Affairs*, vol. 80, no. 4, 2–6.

Nye, J. S., Einhorn, J. P., Kadar, B., Owada, H., Rubio, L. and Young, S. (2003) *The 'Democracy Deficit' in the Global Economy: Enhancing the Legitimacy and Accountability of Global Institutions*. Washington, DC: Trilateral Commission.

O'Brien, R., Goetz, A. M., Scholte, J. A. and Williams, M. A. (2000) *Contesting Global Governance: Multilateral Economic Institutions and Global Social Movements*. Cambridge University Press.

O'Donnell, G. (1999) 'Horizontal Accountability in New Democracies', in A. Schedler, L. Diamond and M. F. Plattner (eds.), *The Self-Restraining State: Power and Accountability in New Democracies*. Boulder: Lynne Rienner, pp. 29–52.

O'Manique, C. (2007) 'Global Health and Universal Human Rights', in A. F. Cooper, J. J. Kirton and T. Schrecker (eds.), *Governing Global Health: Challenge, Response, Innovation*. Aldershot: Ashgate, pp. 207–26.

Ochwada, H. (2004) 'Rethinking East African Integration: From Economic to Political and from State to Civil Society', *Africa Development*, vol. 29, no. 2, 53–79.

OECD (1999) *Review of the OECD Guidelines for Multinational Enterprises: Framework for the Review*, 21 May. Paris: OECD.

(2000) *The OECD Declaration and Decisions on International Investment and Multinational Enterprises: Basic Texts* (DAFFE/IME(2000)20). Paris: OECD.

(2001a) *The OECD Guidelines for Multinational Enterprises: Text, Commentary and Clarifications* (DAFFE/IME/WPG(2000)15/Final). Paris: OECD.

(2001b) *OECD Environmental Strategy for the First Decade of the 21st Century.* Adopted by OECD Environment Ministers, 16 May. Paris: OECD.

(2003) *Fighting Corruption. What Role for Civil Society? The Experience of the OECD.* Paris: OECD.

(2005) 'Civil Society and the OECD', *Policy Brief*, November. Paris: OECD Observer.

(2006a) *OECD's Co-operative Work with Civil Society* (C/INF(2006)24). Council Committee on Public Affairs and Communications.

(2006b) 'Guidelines for On-line Public Consultation', Annex I to OECD (2006a) above.

(2006c) 'OECD and Civil Society: An Inventory of Current Contacts', Annex III to OECD (2006a) above.

(2006d) *The OECD Fights Corruption.* Paris: OECD.

(2006e) *Annual Report on the OECD Guidelines for Multinational Enterprises: Conducting Business in Weak Governance Zones.* Paris: OECD.

(2006f) *Strategic Vision of the OECD Environment Policy Committee.* Approved by the OECD Environment Policy Committee, 30 January.

(2007a) *OECD Work on Environment.* Paris: OECD.

(2007b) 'The OECD's Stakeholder Partners', available at www.oecd.org/document/61/0,3343,en_264937465_2387261_1_1_1_1,00.html. Accessed 14 May.

(2009) 'Guidelines for Online Public Consultation', available at www.oecd.org/document/40/0,2340,en_2649_34495_37539752_1_1_1_1,00.html. Accessed 10 July.

(2010) OECD Forum 2010, details at www.oecd.org/site/0,3407,en_215713 61_44354303_1_1_1_1_1,00.html. Accessed 26 January.

OECD Watch (2007) 'Background', available at www.oecdwatch.org/419.htm. Accessed 5 May.

OIC (2005) *Ten-Year Programme of Action to Meet the Challenges Facing the Muslim Ummah in the 21st Century*, available at www.oic-oci.org/ex-summit/english/10-years-plan.htm.

(2007) Resolution No. 1/34-Org on Requests from Member States' NGOs for OIC Observer Status, available at www.oic-oci.org/34icfm/english/resolution/34ICFM-ORG-RES-FINAL.pdf.

Oil Change International (2007) *Growth and Responsibility in the World Economy: Draft Summit Declarations – February 2007*, available at priceofoil.org/wp-content/uploads/2007/04/Draft%20G8%20Feb%20 2007%20Version.pdf.

Okot-Uma, R. W. O. (2000) *Electronic Governance: Re-inventing Good Governance.* London, Commonwealth Secretariat.

One World Action (2007) www.oneworldaction.org/_uploads/documents/WhatisASEM.pdf. Accessed 28 September.

One World Trust (2009) 'CSO Accountability Project', available at www.one-worldtrust.org/index.php?option=com_content&view=article&id=83&Itemid=70. Accessed 19 August.

Orbe, M. P. (1998) *Constructing Co-Cultural Theory: An Explication of Culture, Power, and Communication*. Thousand Oaks, CA: Sage.

Orr, J. C. (2002) 'Business Associations and Global Financial Governance', in J. A Scholte and A. Schnabel (eds.), *Civil Society and Global Finance*. London: Routledge, pp. 199–212.

Ougaard, M. (2004) *The Globalization of Politics: Power, Social Forces, and Governance*. Basingstoke: Palgrave Macmillan.

(2006) 'The Organisation for Economic Co-operation and Development', in R. Robertson and J. A. Scholte (eds.), *Encyclopedia of Globalization*. New York: Routledge.

Oxfam (2003) 'The IMF and the Millennium Goals: Failing to Deliver for Low Income Countries', Oxfam Briefing Paper 54 (September).

Pagani, F. (2002) 'Peer Review: A Tool for Co-operation and Change. An Analysis of an OECD Working Method' (OECD SG/LEG(2002)1), 11 September.

Panitchpakdi, S. (2005) 'The WTO after 10 Years: The Lessons Learned and the Challenges Ahead', speech given to the Council on Foreign Relations, New York, 11 March.

Parliamentary Network on the World Bank (PNoWB) (2009). See www.pnowb.org. Accessed 7 August.

Paul, J. (2003) 'The Arria Formula' (October), available online at www.globalpolicy.org/security/mtgsetc/arria.htm. Accessed 30 January 2005.

Pauwelyn, J. (2008) 'New Trade Politics for the 21st Century', *Journal of International Economic Law*, vol. 11, no. 3, 559–73.

Pellizzoni, L. (2004) 'Responsibility and Environmental Governance', *Environmental Politics*, vol. 13, no. 3, 541–65.

Peruzzotti, E. (2007) 'Civil Society, Representation and Accountability: Restating Current Debates of Representativeness and Accountability of Civic Associations', in L. Jordan and P. Van Tuijl (eds.), *NGO Accountability: Politics, Principles and Innovation*. London: Earthscan.

Pettifor, A. (2006) 'The Jubilee 2000 Campaign: A Brief Overview', in C. Jochnick and F. A. Preston (eds.), *Sovereign Debt at the Crossroads: Challenges and Proposals for Resolving the Third World Debt Crisis*. New York: Oxford University Press, pp. 297–317.

Pettit, J. (2004) 'Climate Justice: A New Social Movement for Atmospheric Rights', IDS Bulletin *Climate Change and Development (Special Issue)*, vol. 35, no. 3, 102–6.

Pew Centre (2007) www.pewclimate.org/docUploads/WEF%5FGHGR%5FFAQ%2Epdf. Accessed 13 July.

Powell, J. and Baker, L. (2007) *Programme Conditions, Project Safeguards: Quo Vadis World Bank? At Issue*, Update 57. London: Bretton Woods Project, available at www.brettonwoodsproject.org/art-557489. Accessed 20 July 2009.

Public Citizen (2000) *Harmonization Handbook: Accountable Governance in the Era of Globalization: the WTO, NAFTA, and International Harmonization of Standards*. Washington, DC: Public Citizen.

Putnam, R. D. (2000) *Bowling Alone: The Collapse and Revival of American Community*. New York: Simon & Schuster.

Putnam, R. D. and Bayne, N. (1987) *Hanging Together: Cooperation and Conflict in the Seven-Power Summits* (rev. edn). Cambridge, MA: Harvard University Press.

Raustiala, K. (1996) 'Non-State Actors', in D. Sprinz and U. Luterbacher (eds.), *International Relations and Global Climate Change* (PIK Report No. 21). Potsdam: Potsdam Institute.

(2002) 'The Architecture of International Cooperation: Transgovernmental Networks and the Future of International Law', *Virginia Journal of International Law*, vol. 43, no. 1, 1–92.

Reclaim the Commons (2006) 'Secret G8 "Nuclear" Communiqué Revealed', Infoshop News [reproducing the press release of Reclaim the Commons], 17 March, available at www.infoshop.org/inews/article.php?story=200603 17174531825&query=secret%2Bg8.

Reed, D. (ed.) (1996) *Structural Adjustment, the Environment and Sustainable Development*. London: Earthscan.

Reinicke, W. H. (1999–2000) 'The Other World Wide Web: Global Public Policy Networks', *Foreign Policy*, no. 117, 44–57.

Reiterer, M. (2009) 'Asia-Europe Meeting (ASEM): Fostering a Multipolar World Order through Inter-regional Cooperation', *Asia Europe Journal*, vol. 7, no. 1, 179–96.

Rietbergen-McCracken, J. and Narayan, D. (1998) *Participation and Social Assessment: Tools and Techniques*. Washington, DC: The World Bank, available at siteresources.worldbank.org/INTISPMA/Resources/toolkit.pdf.

Riker, J. V. and Sikkink, K. (eds.) (2002) *Restructuring World Politics*. Minneapolis: University of Minnesota Press.

Rittberger, V. and Zangl, B. (2006) *International Organization: Polity, Policy and Politics*. Basingstoke: Palgrave Macmillan.

Robertson, D. (2000) 'Civil Society and the WTO', *World Economy*, vol. 23, no. 9, pp. 1119–34.

Robertson, R. (1992), *Globalization*. London: Sage.

Robles, A. C. (2008) *The Asia-Europe Meeting: The Theory and Practice of Interregionalism*. London: Routledge.

Rodley, N. (1986) 'Le rôle d'une ONG comme Amnesty International au sein des organisations intergouvernementales', in M. Bettati and P.-M. Dupuy (eds.), *Les ONG et le droit international*. Paris: Economia, pp. 127–52.

Rodrik, D. (2001) *Global Governance of Trade as if Development Really Mattered*. New York: United Nations Development Programme.

Ronalds, P. D. (2010) *The Change Imperative: Creating the New Generation NGO*. Bloomfield, CT: Kumarian.

Rootserver (2009) See www.root-servers.org. Accessed 1 July.

Round, R. (2004) *Who's Minding the Store? Legislator Oversight of the Bretton Woods Institutions*. Ottawa: Halifax Initiative.

Rowden, R. and Ocaya Irama, J. (2004) *Rethinking Participation*. Washington, DC: ActionAid International, Uganda and USA.

Ruggiero, R. (1998) Opening Statement to the Geneva Ministerial Meeting, 18 May.

Rukuba-Ngaiza, N., Lubis, R., Cullen, M., Li, Z. and Mausolff, C. (2002) *Public Consultation in Environmental Assessments 1997–2000: Findings from the Third Environmental Assessment Review* (Environment Department Paper No. 87). Washington, DC: World Bank.

Rumford, C. (2003) 'European Civil Society or Transnational Social Space? Conceptions of Society in Discourses of EU Citizenship, Governance and the Democratic Deficit: an Emerging Agenda', *European Journal of Social Theory*, vol. 6, no. 25, 25–43.

Rutherford, A. (2007) Author Julie Gilson's interview with Andy Rutherford of One World Action, 10 September.

Saguier, M. I. (2004) 'Convergence in the Making: Transnational Civil Society and the Free Trade Area of the Americas', CSGR Working Paper No. 137/04, June.

Said, Y. and Desai, M. (2001) 'The New Anti-Capitalist Movement: Money and Global Civil Society', in H. Anheier, M. Glasius and M. Kaldor (eds.), *Global Civil Society 2001*. Oxford University Press, pp. 51–78.

Salamon, L. M. *et al.* (1999) *Global Civil Society: Dimensions of the Nonprofit Sector*. Bloomfield, CN: Kumarian.

Salzman, J. and Terracino, J. B. (2006) 'Labor Rights, Globalization and Institutions: The Role and Influence of the Organisation for Economic Cooperation and Development', in V. A. Leary and D. Warner (eds.), *Social Issues, Globalisation and International Institutions: Labour Rights and the EU, ILO, OECD and WTO*. Leiden: Martinus Nijhoff, pp. 318–409.

Sampson, G. P. (2000) *Trade, Environment and the WTO: The Post-Seattle Agenda*. Washington, DC: Overseas Development Council.

Sanders, R. (1988) *Inseparable Humanity: An Anthology of Reflections of Shridath Ramphal*. London: Hansib.

Sanger, C. (2007) 'A Clear and Steady Voice: the CHRI at 20', *Round Table*, vol. 96, no. 391, 477–88.

Saul, G. (2003) *Transparency and Accountability in International Financial Institutions*. Washington, DC: Bank Information Center.

Schedler, A. (1999) 'Conceptualizing Accountability', in A. Schedler, L. Diamond and M. F. Plattner, *The Self-Restraining State: Power and Accountability in New Democracies*. Boulder: Lynne Rienner, pp. 13–28.

Schedler, A., Diamond L. and Plattner, M. (1999) *The Self-Restraining State: Power and Accountability in New Democracies*. Boulder: Lynne Rienner.

Schmidt, H. (2007) 'Observations on the Present State of the World: Keynote Speech to the 25th Plenary Session of the InterAction Council', 21 May, available at http://interactioncouncil.org/speeches/paper/pschmidt07.pdf.

Scholte, J. A. (2001a) *Civil Society and Democracy in Global Governance*, Warwick University/ESRC Centre for the Study of Globalisation and Regionalisation Working Papers, No. 65/01, January.

(2001b) 'The IMF and Civil Society: An Interim Progress Report', in M. Edwards and J. Gaventa (eds.), *Global Citizen Action: Perspectives and Challenges*. Boulder: Lynne Rienner, pp. 87–103.

(2002) *Civil Society Voices and the International Monetary Fund*. Ottawa: North-South Institute.

(2004a) 'Civil Society and Democratically Accountable Global Governance', *Government and Opposition*, vol. 39, no. 2, 211–33.

(2004b) 'The WTO and Civil Society', in B. Hocking and S. McGuire (eds.), *Trade Politics*. London: Routledge, pp. 146–61.

(2005a) 'Civil Society and Democratically Accountable Global Governance', in D. Held and M. Koenig-Archibugi (eds.), *Global Governance and Public Accountability*. Oxford: Blackwell, pp. 87–110.

(2005b) *Globalization: A Critical Introduction*, 2nd edn. Basingstoke: Palgrave Macmillan.

(2007) 'Civil Society and the Legitimation of Global Governance', *Journal of Civil Society*, vol. 3, no. 3, 305–26.

(2008a) 'From Government to Governance: Transition to a New Diplomacy', in A. F. Cooper, B. Hocking and W. Maley (eds.), *Worlds Apart? Diplomacy and Governance*. Basingstoke: Palgrave Macmillan, pp. 39–60.

(2008b) 'Looking to the Future: A Global Civil Society Forum?' in J. W. St. G. Walker and A. S. Thompson (eds.), *Critical Mass: The Emergence of Global Civil Society*. Waterloo: Wilfrid Laurier University Press, pp. 231–50.

(2009) *IMF Interactions with Member Countries: The Civil Society Dimension*. Washington, DC: Independent Evaluation Office of the International Monetary Fund, Background Paper BP/09/08, available at www.ieo-imf.org/eval/complete/pdf/01202010/Background_Paper_III_IMF_Interactions_with_Member_Countries_The_Civil_Society...pdf.

Scholte, J. A. and Schnabel, A. (eds.) (2002) *Civil Society and Global Finance*. London: Routledge.

Scholte, J. A., O'Brien, R. and Williams, M. (1999) 'The World Trade Organization and Civil Society', *Journal of World Trade*, vol. 33, no. 1, 107–24.

Seary, B. (1996) 'The Early History: From the Congress of Vienna to the San Francisco Conference', in P. Willetts (ed.), *'The Conscience of the World': The Influence of Non-Governmental Organisations in the UN System*. London: Hurst, pp. 15–30.

Shabecoff, P. (1976) 'Ford Issues Call for a Worldwide Economic Report', *New York Times*, 28 June, pp. 1, 6.

Shaw, T. M. (2004) 'The Commonwealth(s) and Global Governance', *Global Governance*, vol. 10, no. 4, 499–516.

(2005) 'Four Decades of Commonwealth Secretariat and Foundation: Continuing Contributions to Global Governance?' *Round Table*, vol. 94, no. 380, 359–65.

(2007) 'Commonwealth', in R. Robertson and J. A. Scholte (eds.), *Encyclopedia of Globalization*. New York: Routledge.

(2008) *Commonwealth: Inter- and Nonstate Contributions to Global Governance*. London: Routledge, Global Institutions Series.

(2009) 'Commonwealth', in D. Forsythe (ed.), *Encyclopedia of Human Rights*. Oxford University Press.

(2010) 'Commonwealth(s) and Poverty/Inequality: Contributions to Global Governance/Development', in J. Clapp and R. Wilkinson (eds.), *Global Governance, Poverty and Inequality*. London: Routledge.

Shaw, T. and Jobbins, D. (2009) 'Review Article: Learning Abroad: a History of the CSFP', *Round Table*, vol. 98, no. 404.

Shell, G. R. (1995) 'Trade Legalism and International Relations Theory: An Analysis of the World Trade Organization', *Duke Law Journal*, vol. 44, no. 5, 829–1995.

(1996) 'The Trade Stakeholders Model and Participation by NonState Parties in the World Trade Organization', *University of Pennsylvania Journal of International Economic Law*, vol. 17, no. 1, 359–81.

Sherman, M. (2001) *Skills Enhancement and Team Building: Forest Policy Implementation Review and Strategy Consultation Process*. Social Development Department, World Bank.

Sikkink, K. (2002) 'Restructuring World Politics: The Limits and Asymmetries of Soft Power', in S. Khagram, J. V. Riker and K. Sikkink (eds.), *Restructuring World Politics*. Minneapolis: University of Minnesota Press, pp. 301–18.

Sinclair, T. J. (ed.) (2004) *Global Governance: Critical Concepts in Political Science* (4 vols). London: Routledge.

Singh, P. J. (2007) '.xxx, igc and igf', email to Internet Governance Caucus mailing list, 11 April, available at www.igcaucus.org.

Sivaraksa, S. (1999) *Global Healing: Essays and Interviews on Structural Violence, Social Development and Spiritual Transformation*. Bangkok: Sathirakoses-Nagapradipa Foundation.

Slaughter, A.-M. (2004) *A New World Order*. Princeton University Press.

Smythe, E. (2003–2004) 'Just Say No! The Negotiation of Investment Rules at the WTO', *International Journal of Political Economy*, vol. 33, no. 4, 60–83.

Smythe, E. and Smith, P. J. (2006) 'Legitimacy, Transparency, and Information Technology: The World Trade Organization in an Era of Contentious Trade Politics', *Global Governance*, vol. 12, no. 1, 31–53.

Soederberg, S. (2006) *Global Governance in Question: Empire, Class, and the New Common Sense in Managing North-South Relations*. London: Pluto.

Sommet de Pauvres (2008) 'Au Mali, le "Sommet de Pauvres" exhorte le G8 à tenir ses promesses', 7 July, available at www.maliweb.net/category. php?NID=33253&intr=.

Sørensen, G. (2004) *The Transformation of the State: Beyond the Myth of Retreat*. Basingstoke: Palgrave Macmillan.

Steffek, J. *et al.* (eds.) (2008) *Civil Society Participation in European and Global Governance: A Cure for the Democratic Deficit?* Basingstoke: Palgrave Macmillan.

Steger, D. P. (2007) 'The Culture of the WTO: Why It Needs to Change', *Journal of International Economic Law*, vol. 10, no. 3, 483–95.

Stiglitz, J. E. (1998) *More Instruments and Broader Goals: Moving toward the Post-Washington Consensus*. Helsinki: United Nations World Institute for Development Economics Research.

(2003) 'Democratizing the International Monetary Fund and the World Bank: Governance and Accountability', *Governance*, vol. 16, no. 1, 111–39.

Stiglitz, J. E. and Griffith-Jones, S. (2007) 'Growth with Responsibility in a Globalized World – Findings of the Shadow G8', *Dialogue on*

*Globalization*, no. 31, New York, available at http://library.fes.de/pdf-files/iez/global/04472.pdf.

Stokhof, W. and Van de Velde, P. (eds.) (1999) *ASEM: The Asia-Europe Meeting: A Window of Opportunity*. London: Kegan Paul.

Structural Adjustment Participatory Review International Network (SAPRIN) (2002) *The Policy Roots of Economic Crisis and Poverty: A Multi-Country Participatory Assessment of Structural Adjustment*. Washington, DC.

Sullivan, S. (1997) *From War to Wealth. Fifty Years of Innovation*. Paris: OECD.

Taskheeri, A. (2004) *Structural Adjustment: The SAPRI Report. The Policy Roots of Economic Crisis, Poverty and Inequality*. London: Zed Books.

(2007) Interview with author Saied Ameli.

Thirkell-White, B. (2004) 'The International Monetary Fund and Civil Society', *New Political Economy*, vol. 9, no. 2, 251–70.

Thomas, C. (2002) 'Trade Policy and the Politics of Access to Drugs', *Third World Quarterly*, vol. 23, no. 2, 251–64.

TNI (1998) 'Asia Europe People's Forum II', available at www.tni.org/detail_page. phtml?&page=asem-london_aepf1998&menu=11a. Accessed 15 September 2009.

(2000) 'ASEM 2000 Peoples Forum III', available at www.tni.org/detail_ page.phtml?page=asem-seoul_aepf2000. Accessed 15 September 2009.

(2002) 'Asem4people', available at www.tni.org/detail_page.phtml?page= asem-copenhagen_pr200902. Accessed 15 September 2009.

(2005) 'Charter of the Asia-Europe People's Forum', available at www.tni.org/ detail_page.phtml?page=asem-docs_charter. Accessed 30 August 2009.

(2008) 'Final Declaration – Asia-Europe People's Forum', 17 October, available at www.tni.org/detail_page.phtml?&act_id=18836. Accessed 15 September 2009.

(2009) 'Asia Europe People's Forum 7', available at www.tni.org/detail_page. phtml?&&text10=aepf7beijing&menu=05at. Accessed 18 August 2009.

Tocqueville, A. de (1835) *Democracy in America*. New York: Dearborn, 1838.

Transparency International (2007a) 'G8 Progress Report', Berlin, 5 June, available at www.transparency.org/publications/publications/g8_progress_ report.

(2007b) 'Statement on 2007 G8 Communiqué by Cobus de Swardt, Transparency International Managing Director: The Commitments Look Promising but We Need to See Action', Kühlungsborn, 8 June, available at www.transparency.org/news_room/latest_news/press_releases/2007/2007_ 06_08_g8_now_act_statement.

TUAC (2006) 'TUAC Internal Analysis of Treatment of Cases Raised with National Contact Points February 2001–September 2006'.

(2007) 'The OECD Guidelines for Multinational Enterprises. TUAC Internal Analysis of Treatment of Cases Raised with National Contact Points February 2002–April 2007'.

Turek, E. (2003) 'The Role of NGOs in International Governance. NGOs and Developing Country WTO Members: Is there Potential for an Alliance', in S. Griller (ed.), *International Economic Governance and Non-Economic*

*Concerns: New Challenges for the International Legal Order.* Vienna: Springer, pp. 169–210.

Turner, B. S. (1994) *Orientalism, Postmodernism & Globalism.* London: Routledge.

(1999) *Classical Sociology.* London: Sage.

Ullrich, H. K. (2007) 'Toward Accountability? The G8, the World Trade Organization and Global Governance', in M. Fratianni, P. Savona and J. J. Kirton (eds.), *Corporate, Public and Global Governance: The G8 Contribution.* Aldershot: Ashgate, pp. 99–125.

UNAIDS (2007) *AIDS Epidemic Update.* Geneva: UNAIDS, December.

United Kingdom, Prime Minister's Office (2005a) 'British Prime Minister Tony Blair Reflects on "Significant Progress" of G8 Summit', Press Conference at the Conclusion of the Gleneagles Summit, 8 July, previously available at www.g8.gov.uk/servlet/Front?pagename=OpenMarket/Xcelerate/ShowPage&c=Page&cid=1078995903270&a=KArticle&aid=1119520262754.

(2005b) 'Special Address by Tony Blair, Prime Minister of the United Kingdom at the World Economic Forum in Davos', 27 January, previously available at www.g8.gov.uk/servlet/Front?pagename=OpenMarket/Xcelerate/ShowPage&c=Page&cid=1078995903270&aid=1106749656900.

UN (1992a) *Agenda 21.* New York: United Nations, available at www.un.org/esa/sustdev/documents/agenda21/english/agenda21toc.htm. Accessed 10 May 2005.

(1992b) *Rio Declaration on Environment and Development.* New York: United Nations, available at www.un.org/documents/ga/conf151/aconf15126-annex1.htm. Accessed 10 May 2005.

(1996) 'Consultative Relationship between the United Nations and Non-governmental Organizations', Resolution 1996/31, 25 July.

(1997) *Renewing the United Nations: A Programme for Reform* (Doc. A/51/950), 14 July.

(1998a) *Arrangement and Practices for the Interaction of Non-Governmental Organizations in All Activities of the United Nations System* (Doc. A/53/170), 10 July.

(1998b) *Work of the Non-Governmental Organizations Section of the Secretariat* (Doc. E/1998/43), 8 May.

(2001a) *Report of the Committee on Non-Governmental Organizations on Its Resumed 2000 Regular Session* (Doc. E/2001/8), 22 February.

(2001b) *Report of the Committee on Non-Governmental Organizations on Its Resumed 2000 Session* (Doc. E/2000/88, Part II), 13 July.

(2004) *We the People: Civil Society, the United Nations and Global Governance. Report of the Panel of Eminent Persons on United Nations-Civil Society Relations* (Doc. A/58/817), 11 June [Cardoso Report].

(2005) *World Economic Situation and Prospects 2005.* New York: United Nations.

(2009a) *Composition of the Secretariat* (Doc. A/64/352), available at daccess-dds-ny.un.org/doc/UNDOC/GEN/N09/515/01/PDF/N0951501.pdf?OpenElement.

(2009b) *General Assembly* (GA10909), 23 December, available at www. un.org/News/Press/docs/2009/ga10909.doc.htm.

(2009c) *List of Non-Governmental Organizations in Consultative Status with the Economic and Social Council as of 1 September 2009* (Doc. E/2008/INF/5), available at esango.un.org/paperless/content/E2009INF4.pdf.

(2010) *United Nations Peace Operations 2009 Year in Review*. New York: United Nations Department of Public Information.

UNDPI (2010) Department of Public Information: Non-Governmental Organizations, 'About NGO Association with the UN', available at www. un.org/dpi/ngosection/about-ngo-assoc.asp#. Accessed 15 April.

United Nations Development Program (UNDP) (2002) *Human Development Report 2002: Deepening Democracy in a Fragmented World*. New York: Oxford University Press.

(2007–2008) *Fighting Climate Change: Human Solidarity in a Divided World* (Human Development Report). New York: UNDP.

UNOG (2010) 'NGO Database', available at www.unog.ch/80256EE60057 E07D/(httpPages)/3101491B86487F6D80256EFC0061DFD9?Open Document. Accessed 15 April.

US Department of Commerce (1998) 'Management of Internet Names and Addresses', Docket No. 980212036–8146–02, 10 June 1998, available at www.ntia.doc.gov/ntiahome/domainname/6_5_98dns.htm.

Van den Bossche, P. (2008) 'NGO Involvement in the WTO: A Comparative Perspective', *Journal of International Economic Law*, vol. 11, no. 4, 717–49.

Van Dyke, L. B. and Weiner, J. B. (1996) *An Introduction to the WTO Decision on Document Restriction*. Geneva: International Centre for Trade and Sustainable Development/Center for International Environmental Law.

Van Rooy, A. (2004) *The Global Legitimacy Game: Civil Society, Globalization and Protest*. Basingstoke: Palgrave Macmillan.

VCS (2008) 'Voluntary Carbon Standard Program Guidelines', 18 November, available at www.vcs.org/docs/Voluntary%20Carbon%20Standard%20 Program%20Guidelines%202007_1.pdf.

Waddell, S. (2002) 'Fair Trade and the International Federation of Alternative Trade: Focusing upon Implementation'. Draft paper prepared for GPPN Conference Delegates.

Wagner, M. (2007) 'Presentation by Martin Wagner at the International Council on Human Rights Policy', Geneva, 12–13 October.

Walker, J. W. St. G. and Thompson, A. S. (eds.) (2008) *Critical Mass: The Emergence of Global Civil Society*. Waterloo: Wilfred Laurier University Press.

Wallis, W. (2007) 'China to Eclipse Donors with $20bn for Africa', *Financial Times*, 17 May.

Wapner, P. (1995) 'Politics Beyond the State: Environmental Activism and World Civic Politics', *World Politics*, vol. 47, 311–40.

Watson, M. (2006) 'Towards a Polanyian Perspective on Fair Trade: Market-based Relationships and the Act of Ethical Consumption', *Global Society*, vol. 20, no. 4, 435–51.

(2007) 'Trade Justice and Individual Consumption Choices: Adam Smith's Spectator Theory and the Moral Constitution of the Fair Trade Consumer', *European Journal of International Relations*, vol. 13, no. 2, 263–88.

WDM (2007) *Building Scrutiny of the World Bank and International Monetary Fund: A Toolkit for Legislators and Those Who Work with Them.* London: World Development Movement.

Weiner, J. B. and Van Dyke, L. B. (1996) *A Handbook for Obtaining Documents from the World Trade Organization.* Geneva: International Centre for Trade and Sustainable Development/Center for International Environmental Law.

Weiss, L. (1998) *The Myth of the Powerless State: Governing the Economy in a Global Era.* Cambridge: Polity.

Weiss, T. G. (2000) 'Governance, Good Governance and Global Governance: Conceptual and Actual Challenges', *Third World Quarterly*, vol. 21, no. 5, 795–814.

Weiss, T. G. and Gordenker, L. (eds.) (1996) *NGOs, the UN and Global Governance.* Boulder: Lynne Rienner.

Weschler, J. (1998) 'Non-Governmental Human Rights Organizations', *Polish Quarterly of International Affairs*, vol. 7, no. 3, 137–54.

WFTO (2009a) '10 Principles of Fair Trade', 9 February, available at www.wfto.com/index.php?option=com_content&task=view&id=2&Itemid=12. Accessed 19 April 2009.

(2009b) 'The World Fair Trade Organization', 9 February, available at www.wfto.com/index.php?option=com_content&task=view&id=890&Itemid=292. Accessed 19 April 2009.

(2009c) 'Fair Trade Organizations and Fair Trade Labelling', available at www.wfto.com/index.php?option=com_content&task=view&id=10&Itemid=17&limit=1&limitstart=5. Accessed 8 May 2009.

(2009d) 'Event: "G8 Summit"' (2009), available at www.wfto.com/index.php?option=com_jcalpro&Itemid=105&extmode=view&extid=68. Accessed 9 May 2009.

(2009e) 'The WFTO Board of Directors', available at www.wfto.com/index.php?option=com_content&task=view&id=30&Itemid=4. Accessed 19 April 2009.

(2009f) 'The WFTO Office', available at www.wfto.com/index.php?option=com_content&task=view&id=36&Itemid=4. Accessed 26 July 2009.

(2009g) 'WFTO Global Conference', available at www.fairtradegroupnepal.org/?page_id=43. Accessed 10 May 2009.

(2009h) 'WFTO Meets in Nepal', available at www.wfto.com/index.php?option=com_content&task=view&id=957&Itemid=305. Accessed 17 May 2009.

(2009i) 'Monitoring', available at www.wfto.com/index.php?option=com_content&task=view&id=21&Itemid=302. Accessed: 19 April 2009.

(2009j) 'Draft Two SFTMS Standard', available at www.wfto.com/index.php?option=com_content&task=view&id=915&Itemid=285. Accessed: 19 April 2009.

(2009k) 'Who Is 100% Fair Trade', available at www.wfto.com/index.php?option=com_content&task=view&id=896&Itemid=300. Accessed 19 April 2009.

(2009l) 'WFTOMarket.com: One Stop Fair Trade Shop', available at www.wfto.com/index.php?option=com_content&task=view&id=970&Itemid=305. Accessed 25 July 2009.

(2009m) *Constitution of the World Fair Trade Organization*, Culemborg, Netherlands (as adopted at the WFTO AGM, 21 May).

WFTO and FLO (2009) 'A Charter of Fair Trade Principles', January.

WGIG (2005) 'Report of the Working Group on Internet Governance', June, available at www.wgig.org/docs/WGIGREPORT.pdf.

Whaites, A. (ed.) (2002) *Masters of Their Own Development? PRSPs and Prospects for the Poor*. Monrovia, CA: World Vision.

Wilkinson, R. (2002) 'The Contours of Courtship: The WTO and Civil Society', in R. Wilkinson and S. Hughes (eds.), *Global Governance: Critical Perspectives*. London: Routledge, pp. 193–212.

Willetts, P. (ed.) (1996) *'The Conscience of the World': The Influence of Non-Governmental Organisations in the UN System*. London: Hurst.

(2000) 'From "Consultative Arrangements" to "Partnership": The Changing Status of NGOs in Diplomacy at the UN', *Global Governance*, vol. 6, no. 2, 191–212.

(2006) 'The Cardoso Report on the UN and Civil Society: Functionalism, Global Corporatism or Global Democracy?', *Global Governance*, vol. 12, no. 3, 305–24.

Williams, M. (1999) 'The WTO and "Democracy"', in A. Taylor and C. Thomas (eds.), *Global Trade Issues*. London: Routledge, pp. 151–69.

(2004) 'Contesting Global Trade Rules: Social Movements and the World Trade Organization', in L. Beneria and S. Bisnath (eds.), *Global Tensions: Challenges and Opportunities in the World Economy*. London: Routledge, pp. 193–206.

(2005) 'Civil Society and the World Trading System', in D. Kelly and W. Grant (eds.), *The Politics of International Trade: Actors, Issues, and Regional Dynamics*. London: Palgrave Macmillan, pp. 30–46.

Williams, M. and Ford, L. (1999) 'The WTO, the Environmental Social Movement and Global Environmental Management', *Environmental Politics*, vol. 8, no. 1, 268–89.

Williamson, J. (ed.) (1983) *IMF Conditionality*. Washington, DC: Institute for International Economics.

Willis, O. (2009) 'Civil or Religious Paths to Respect and Understanding? Two Commonwealth Reports', *Round Table*, vol. 98, no. 400, 3–15.

Wills, C. (2007) *Comparison Between the Current IFAT Position, the Agenda for Change and the New Strategic Plan*. Kolkata: EKTA Trust.

Wolfe, R. (2005) 'See You in Geneva? Legal (Mis)Representations of the Trading System', *European Journal of International Relations*, vol. 11, no. 3, 339–65.

Wood, A. and Welch, C. (1998) *Policing the Policemen: The Case for an Independent Evaluation Mechanism for the IMF*. London and Washington, DC: Bretton Woods Project/Friends of the Earth.

Woods, K. (2003) 'Transboundary Environmental Governance in the Mekong River Basin: Civil Society Spaces for Transboundary Participation'. Presented at 'Politics of the Commons: Articulating Development and Strengthening Local Practices', Chiang Mai, 11–14 July. Available at dlc. dlib.indiana.edu/archive/00001110/00/Kevin_Woods.pdf. Accessed 28 September 2007.

Woods, N. (2000) 'The Challenge of Good Governance for the IMF and the World Bank Themselves', *World Development*, vol. 28, no. 5, 823–41.

Woods, N. and Narlikar, A. (2001) 'Governance and the Limits of Accountability: The WTO, the IMF, and the World Bank', *International Social Science Journal*, vol. 53, no. 170, 569–83.

Woodward, R. (2008) 'Towards Complex Multilateralism? Civil Society and the OECD', in R. Mahon and S. McBride (eds.), *The OECD and Transnational Governance*. Vancouver: University of British Columbia Press, pp. 77–95.

World Bank (1992) *Effective Implementation: Key to Development Impact. Report of the World Bank's Portfolio Management Task Force* (Wapenhans Report). Washington, DC: World Bank.

(1993) *Annual Review of Environmental Assessment 1992*. Washington, DC: Environment Department, World Bank.

(1996) *The World Bank Participation Sourcebook*, available at www.worldbank.org/wbi/sourcebook/sb0100.htm. Washington, DC: World Bank.

(1997) *The Impact of Environmental Assessment: A Review of World Bank Experience* (Technical Paper 363). Washington, DC: World Bank.

(2000a) *Consultations with Civil Society Organizations: General Guidelines for World Bank Staff*. Washington, DC: World Bank.

(2000b) 'Good Practices 14.70: Involving Nongovernmental Organizations in Bank-Supported Activities', in *World Bank Operational Manual*. Washington, DC: World Bank.

(2000c) *Participation Process Review* (unpublished report). Washington, DC: Operations Evaluation Department (OED), World Bank.

(2000d) *Quality at Entry in CY99 – QAG Assessment*. Washington, DC: Quality Assessment Group (QAG), World Bank.

(2001a) *The Cost of Doing Business: Fiduciary and Safeguard Policies and Compliance*. Washington, DC: World Bank.

(2001b) *The World Bank Position on the Report of the World Commission on Dams*. Washington, DC: World Bank.

(2002a) *Annual Review of Development Effectiveness*. Washington, DC: Operations Evaluation Department, World Bank.

(2002b) *Empowerment and Poverty Reduction: A Sourcebook* (Draft). Washington, DC: Poverty Reduction and Economic Management, World Bank.

(2002c) *Non-Governmental Organizations and Civil Society Engagement in World Bank Supported Projects: Lessons from OED Evaluations: Lessons and Practices No. 18*. Washington, DC: Operations Evaluation Department, World Bank.

(2002d) *Revised Forest Strategy for the World Bank Group: Management Response to Executive Directors' Comments and Suggestions*. Washington, DC: World Bank.

(2002e) *The World Bank Policy on Disclosure of Information*. Washington, DC: World Bank, available at http://www1.worldbank.org/operations/disclosure.

(2004a) *Operational Policy 8.60: Development Policy Lending*. Washington, DC: World Bank.

(2004b) *World Development Report 2004: Making Services Work for Poor People.* Washington, DC: World Bank.

(2005a) *Enhancing World Bank Support to Middle Income Countries: Second Progress Memorandum.* Washington, DC: World Bank.

(2005b) *Issues and Options for Improving Engagement between the World Bank and Civil Society Organizations.* Washington, DC: External Affairs, Communications and United Nations Affairs, Environmentally and Socially Sustainable Development Network, Operations Policy and Country Services Network, World Bank.

(2005c) *The Effectiveness of World Bank Support for Community-Based and -Driven Development.* Washington, DC: Operations Evaluation Department (OED), World Bank.

(2005d) *World Bank-Civil Society Engagement: Review of Fiscal Years 2002–2004.* Washington, DC: World Bank.

(2006a) 'International Launch of the G8+5 Legislators, Business Leaders, and Civil Society'. Previously available at http://go.worldbank.org/NXFETP9EN0.

(2006b) *Environment Matters: 2006 Annual Review.* Washington, DC: World Bank.

(2006c) *Feedback from Initial Consultations on Strengthening Bank Group Engagement on Governance and Anticorruption.* Washington, DC: World Bank.

(2006d) *World Bank Group: Working for a World Free of Poverty.* Washington, DC: World Bank.

(2006e) *World Bank-Civil Society Engagement: Review of Fiscal Years 2005 and 2006.* Washington, DC: Civil Society Team, World Bank.

(2007a) *The World Bank Annual Report 2006: Financial Statements.* Washington, DC: World Bank, available at go.worldbank.org/YCNJFU0GX0.

(2007b) *Quality of Supervison in FY 05-06 (QSA7): A QAG Assessment.* Washington, DC: Quality Assurance Group (QAG), World Bank. Available at siteresources.worldbank.org/QAG/Resources/QSA7SynthesisReportJune-07.pdf. Accessed 20 July 2009.

(2009a) *About Us,* available at go.worldbank.org/DM4A38OWJ0. World Bank. Accessed 20 July 2009.

(2009b) *Independent Evaluation Group (IEG)*; see www.worldbank.org/oed/about.html. World Bank. Accessed 20 July 2009.

(2009c) *Quality Assurance Group (QAG)*; see go.worldbank.org/J4OO0PFYM0. World Bank. Accessed 20 July 2009.

(2009d) *Safeguard Policies*; see go.worldbank.org/WTA1ODE7T0. World Bank. Accessed 20 July 2009.

(2009e) World Bank Policy on Disclosure of Information, *Disclosure Policy Review and Global Consultations,* available at go.worldbank.org/TRCDVYJ440. World Bank. Accessed 20 July 2009.

(2009f) Development Committee October 2008 Communiqué.

(2010) *Toward Greater Transparency through Access to Information: The World Bank's Disclosure Policy (December 10, 2009).* Washington, DC: Operations Policy and Country Services, World Bank.

World Bank Group (2003) *Poverty and Climate Change: Reducing the Vulnerability of the Poor through Adaptation.* Washington, DC: World Bank Group.

World Commission on Dams (2000) *Dams and Development: a New Framework for Decision-Making*. London and Sterling, VA: Earthscan.

(2002) 'Letter from Former Commissioners of World Commission on Dams to President James Wolfensohn, dated July 12, 2002', available at www.irn.org/wcd/021008.wbletter.pdf. Accessed January 2008.

World Economic Forum (2007) 'Opening Address by Angela Merkel, Chancellor of the Federal Republic of Germany, at the World Economic Forum on 24 January 2007 in Davos', available at www.weforum.org/pdf/AM_2007/merkel.pdf.

(2008) [Special address by Japanese Prime Minister] Yasuo Fukuda, 26 January, available at www.weforum.org/en/knowledge/KN_SESS_SUMM_23955?url=/en/knowledge/KN_SESS_SUMM_23955.

WRI (undated) 'Written Submission on Consultations on Strengthening World Bank Engagement on Governance and Anticorruption'. Washington, DC: World Resources Institute.

WSIS (2003) Official Documents of the World Summit on the Information Society, Intersessional Meeting in Paris, 15–18 July 2003, available at: www.itu.int/wsis/documents/listing-all.asp?lang=en&c_event=pci|1&c_type=all.

WTO (1996a) *Guidelines for the Circulation and De-Restriction of WTO Documents* (WT/L/160/Rev.1), 22 July.

(1996b) *Guidelines for Arrangements on Relations with Non-Governmental Organizations* (WT/L/162 ), 23 July.

(2002) *Procedures for the Circulation and Derestriction of WTO Documents – Decision of 14 May 2002* (WT/L/452), 16 May.

(2004) *The Future of the WTO: Assessing Institutional Challenges in the New Millennium*, a Report by the Consultative Board to the Director-General, Supachai Panitchpakdi, pp. 41–8.

(2005) 'The WTO after 10 Years: the Lessons Learned and the Challenges Ahead, 11 March, available at www.wto.org/english/news_e/spsp_e/spsp35_e.htm.

(2008) 'Registration Begins for Public Observation of the Appellate Body Oral Hearing in the Appeals in US/Canada – Continued Suspension of Obligations in the EC – Hormones Dispute (complainant EC) on 28–29 July 2008 in Geneva', available at www.wto.org/english/tratop_e/dispu_e/public_hearing_july08_e.htm.

(2009a) 'For NGOs', available at www.wto.org/english/forums_e/ngo_e/ngo_e.htm. Accessed 28 August.

(2009b) 'Overview of the WTO Secretariat', available at www.wto.org/english/thewto_e/secre_e/intro_e.htm. Accessed 14 August.

(2009c) *WTO Analytical Index: Dispute Settlement Understanding*, available at www.wto.org/english/res_e/booksp_e/analytic_index_e/dsu_06_e.htm#article13.

WWF (1999) *Sustainable Trade for a Living Planet* (Gland: WWF International).

Yamamoto, T. and Yeo, L. H. (eds.) (2006) *ASEM in its Tenth Year: Looking Back, Looking Forward*. Tokyo: Japan Center for International Exchange.

Yamin, F. (2001) 'NGOs and International Environmental Law: A Critical Evaluation of their Roles and Responsibilities', *RECIEL* [*Review of*

*European Community and International Environmental Law*], vol. 10, no. 2, 149–62.

INTERVIEWS

Long and Duvvury (Chapter 12 – GFATM)

(2007a) Confidential discussion between the co-author and a CSO respondent, Washington, DC, 21 February.

(2007b) Confidential discussion between the co-author and a CSO respondent, Washington, DC, 23 February.

(2007c) Confidential discussion between the co-author and a GFATM Secretariat respondent, Washington, DC, 23 February.

(2007d) Confidential discussion between the co-author and a CSO respondent, Washington, DC, 23 February.

(2007e) Confidential discussion between the co-author and a CSO respondent, Washington, DC, 20 March.

Ougaard (Chapter 8 – OECD)

(2007a) Confidential discussions between the author and three senior OECD officials, Paris, 19 March.

(2007b) Confidential discussion between the author and senior OECD official, Paris, 21 March.

(2007c) Confidential discussion between the author and senior OECD official, Paris, 19 March.

(2007d) Confidential discussion between the author and senior OECD official, Paris, 20 March.

Scholte (Chapter 4 – IMF)

(2007a) Confidential discussion between the author and a veteran NGO campaigner, Washington, DC, 14 April.

(2007b) Confidential discussion between the author and a senior IMF official, Washington, DC, 17 April.

(2007c) Confidential discussion between the author and an IMF official, Washington, DC, 18 April.

(2007d) Confidential discussion between the author and a veteran NGO campaigner, Washington, DC, 18 April.

(2007e) Confidential discussion between the author and a veteran NGO campaigner, Washington, DC, 19 April.

# Index